Lee

Lee

A Memoir

Pamela Marvin

faber and faber
LONDON · BOSTON

For my mother and father

First published in 1997
by Faber and Faber Limited
3 Queen Square London WC1N 3AU

Photoset by Parker Typesetting Service, Leicester
Printed in England by Clays Ltd, St Ives plc

Photographs courtesy of Lee and Pamela Marvin's family, the St Leo Abbey Archives, Robert Filkosky & Lester Juergenson, the Woodstock Historical Society, Jean Bellows Boothe, Herb Ball of NBC, Hamilton's Gallery Photography Limited, John Mondora, the University of Texas Health Science Center, Scope Features, Graham MacCarter, Mahoney Communications and Magnum Photos

Copyright in the photographs in this book is held by the following: the Marvin family, Robert Filkosky & Lester Juergenson, NBC (*The American*, Marvin and Wynn racing), MCA (*M Squad*), MGM (*Point Blank, The Dirty Dozen*), Paramount Pictures (*Donovan's Reef, Paint Your Wagon*), Orlando Suero (*Hell in the Pacific*, fishing photographs), John Mondora (fishing photographs), Jerry Seely (fishing photograph), Cinema Center Films (*Monte Walsh*), Terry O'Neill (photo from *Pocket Money*), the University of Texas Health Science Center, Michael Dobo (trial photograph), Scope Features (photograph of marlin on wall), Graham MacCarter (family portraits), Mahoney Communications (wedding photo), and Magnum Photos

Pamela Marvin is hereby identified as author of this work in accordance with Section 77 of the Copyright, Designs and Patents Act 1988

A CIP record for this book
is available from the British Library

ISBN 0-571-19028-6

2 4 6 8 10 9 7 5 3 1

Contents

Acknowledgements

Shortly after Lee's death John Boorman suggested to me that I write Lee's biography. 'You're the one to do it,' he said. And so I did.

In writing this book, I found that there was so much I wanted to say about Lee's personality, his life and mine with him, that it was next to impossible to limit it to a four- or five-hundred-page book. I looked up from my typewriter one day (the IBM Selectric II Lee had given me years before), to find that the manuscript was over twelve hundred pages. Without the editing suggestions of John Boorman during this time, along with his constant encouragement, care and help throughout, I cannot now imagine that this book would have been written. I am immensely indebted to him and deeply grateful. And to Dr Harry A. Wilmer for also giving unconditionally of himself, his vast knowledge and his unflagging support.

I thank my family, who gave me up for these past years of writing and for their enthusiasm; my mother and my father whose memory stirred me on; Kim Cox who transcribed every word and kept me straight; Lee's friends, fans and film collectors who sent me recollections and impossibly hard-to-find copies of his early TV performances and movies; Matthew Evans, publisher of Faber and Faber and, last but not least by a long shot, editor Walter Donohue who skilfully (and nearly painlessly) incised one half of the original, dauntingly long manuscript and suggested a later book.

Introduction

We made two movies together: *Point Blank* was an exhilarating but exhausting collaboration. We were constantly pushing the limits, improvising, daring each other to go closer to the edge. Towards the end of the picture we were shooting on Alcatraz. I had been up late rewriting a scene and in the morning I was too tired to think straight. A hundred MGM technicians were waiting for me to tell them what we were going to shoot. Lee was suddenly at my shoulder: 'Are you in trouble?' My denial was unconvincing. He went back to Wardrobe. He started roaring and singing. I looked up as he staggered and crashed on to that harsh concrete floor. The Production Manager ran over to me, 'You can't shoot on him in that state.' With the pressure off, it took me only ten minutes to work out the set-ups. I gave Lee the nod and he amazed everyone by sobering up in an instant.

Making a movie with Lee was combat. You went to war. He was on your side, but you could get killed by friendly fire, for he was the kindest, cruellest man. If he detected anything fake or shallow in your work, he became a ruthless critic or got drunk on disappointment. He was interested in limits – emotional, physical – exploring them, extending them, breaking them. War left him fascinated and horrified by violence. In fact, his time in the Pacific as a young Marine defined his life. He was in many hand-to-hand battles with the Japanese and was finally wounded in an ambush that wiped out his platoon. The guilt of surviving haunted his life. His comrades attest in the book to his bravery, yet he thought of himself as a coward. Because of this, he always felt the need to test his courage and so he lived on the edge; he inhabited dangerous emotional territory, which is what made his acting so compelling. In his work he was on a constant quest to discover the truth in every moment, to stare it in the face and to find the perfect gesture, the metaphor that would reveal it for us.

It is hard to think of him as gone when he has left so many indelible moments on the screen. Who can forget him bursting into that home for the blind in Don Siegel's *The Killers*, the bumbling gun fighter in *Cat Ballou*, that fight with John Wayne in *Donovan's Reef*, his clash with Brando in *The Wild One*, striding down the corridor and shooting out the empty bed of his faithless wife in *Point Blank*.

He taught me much about acting and making flicks (as he called them) and, indeed, about life. He became a dear, life-long friend yet I never fathomed him or got to the bottom of him and I thank Pam for so wonderfully capturing this elusive, complex, outrageous, loveable man.

John Boorman, 1997

Prologue: Arlington

It was 7 October 1987. We were gathered. We were going to Arlington National Cemetery. Lee was going to Arlington National Cemetery. It was final and it was fitting.

I looked out of the window of the Hilton Hotel in Washington just before dawn. I had spent a fitful night after flying from Tucson the day before with my son and daughters, our son-in-law, our nine-year-old granddaughter and our neighbours Howard and Marlies Terpning. Jim Mahoney, Lee's publicity agent for more than thirty years, was already there, arranging everything for Lee as he had done so many times before: the hotel, the cars, talking to the Marines and the officials at Arlington, mapping the route. Dawn had not yet broken, and I was afraid that the day would be as bleak and rain-drenched as the night before. It wasn't. My mother and sisters had come from Woodstock, and Lee's eldest daughter Courtenay from California. My brother and his wife were there. John and Christel Boorman were arriving from London. John and Nancy Bryson were only just back from Israel.

The suggestion of burying Lee at Arlington National Cemetery had come from his close friend John Boorman. When the decision was made, another friend (photojournalist, *Life* photographer and editor John Bryson) took it in hand and called the commandant of the Marine Corps. Help and arrangements were immediate, and when the plan became known, the people who knew Lee best felt the rightness of it. Another still photographer friend called. He had not only been on many movies with Lee but, also as a Marine, had met him during the war in a hospital in New Caledonia. In a voice choked with tears, he agreed emphatically, 'You bury Lee in Arlington!'

Forrest Gist – friend, artist, blacksmith and potter – made the urn for Lee's ashes. He drove to a small town in Texas for a certain deep red-colored clay, and when the urn was formed, pressed two wild thistles into the vase for design. It was strong and earthy, the colors of the south-west where we lived and which Lee loved so much. I see Lee now as I write, patiently trimming dead cactus branches, his great fishing hat shading him from the merciless sun. It was such a familiar sight that it just blended into his personality. I never thought about it at the time.

The lid of the urn was loose. Howard Terpning, an artist, lovingly took it and placed a piece of rawhide leather inside the top. He had painted an eagle's feather underneath, a symbol of great importance to the American Indian – a symbol of courage and strength. Howard did not know at the time that Lee had kept an eagle's feather by his hospital bedside before he died.

I had not yet seen Christel and John Boorman; I had not seen my mother since Lee died. I felt that if I could survive seeing them without breaking down, I might be able to keep my composure. You think of such things. Are my sunglasses dark enough? My skirt straight? Does my lovely borrowed blouse have a loose button? Oh God, where is my handkerchief? I can't use a Kleenex. Of course mothers and close friends, grieving themselves, suppress their own feelings to support you in yours.

The black limousines filed through the gates of that most poignant of all cemeteries and took us to the chapel of Fort Myer. We were taken to a small anteroom and waited to be ushered into the chapel itself. The chaplain came in and asked that I pick, row by row, where each member of the family would sit. I wasn't prepared. Children, stepchildren, sisters, Mother. Whose feelings should I think of first. Theirs? Mine? Together we worked it out. In the meantime our friends and Lee's fellow Marines had all been seated, and we were led in, I shaking on the arm of a young Marine. We sat listening to the music and the chaplain intoning, 'I am the Resurrection and the Life.'

Suddenly I was aware that two Marines, in absolute cadence, had marched slowly up the aisle and were carrying the folded flag and Lee's ashes under a purple cloth. I had not expected it. It was suddenly true. Lee really was dead and his ashes were being carried by two young men in the uniform he once wore. They stood in front of us and unfolded the flag, then folded it once more, with such precision that they could have been just one in a mirror.

When their ritual was done, the two Marines looked at each other with a gaze that I had seen once before. It was at Camp Pendleton. Lee had been invited as an honored guest to an officers and staff NCO traditional Mess Night. At the end of the dinner, for the very last toast – a toast to the United States Marines – all chairs scraped back in unison. Each man stood toasting the man opposite him, and each face took on a look of such deep respect and absolute devotion that I suddenly witnessed a glimpse of genuine *esprit de corps*. Those men had it; these boys had it.

Mercifully the chaplain spoke on, reading the twenty-third Psalm, the favourite of so many: 'Yea, though I walk through the valley of the shadow of death, I will fear no evil for thou art with me. Thy rod and thy staff they comfort me . . .' The length of the service eventually served as a respite from the overwhelming waves of emotion. At the end of the sermon, the chaplain asked if anyone would like to speak. John Boorman rose and stood at the lectern. He spoke of meeting Lee, of their friendship and of the movies they had made together. He spoke of Lee's drinking and why he felt that Lee so often wanted to blot out things that he perceived in the world – he saw so much and felt so keenly. John spoke of Lee as the Warrior Spirit, the Spirit Warrior. The way he talked about Lee was so personal and so heartbreaking that our composure melted as we listened, and John had to struggle to keep his own.

When the service was over, we filed out of the doors and into the waiting sunshine to the honor guards who would escort us to the graveside. There we sat in chairs facing the podium on which stood the urn holding Lee's ashes. The wind picked up and the branches of the surrounding trees began to rustle. With us were several men from Lee's division. Two, Robert Filkosky and Bill Weaver, were with him in combat, and had been with him the day he was wounded. I was thinking about that day forty-three years before. The flag was unfurled and held over the ashes by six Marines of the honor guard while the service was conducted. The flag was then folded for the last time, and as it was presented to me by one of the men I steeled myself: I had dreaded this presentation – it was so symbolic, so final. He came with measured step, bent down, and quietly said, 'Ma'am, this flag is given you by a grateful nation for the services of your husband.'

Taps were played, the echo coming from behind the hill.

> Day is done, gone the sun,
> From the lake, from the hill,
> from the sky,
> All is well, safely rest,
> God is nigh.

The ceremony, carried out with such tradition, was timeless, ageless. It could have been for any time – the Civil War, the First World War. When I stood up, I went over to the two wreaths of flowers and read the inscriptions. One was from the United States Marine Corps. The other was from 'the Peoples of the Northern Mariana Islands' – Saipan, where Lee was wounded, shot by a Japanese bullet during the Second World War.

1 Woodstock

I met Lee in the summer of 1945. I remember the first time I saw him: it was at the Big Deep, a swimming hole in the Sawkill Creek. I know it was 1945 because he was at my sixteenth birthday party the following February. He was standing in the water with a group of our local boys, wearing a pair of green khaki shorts. A ray of sunshine suddenly broke through the overcast sky and beamed down on him as I stood transfixed. Seeing him like that, with his loud, resonant voice – atotal stranger in our insulated midst – struck me like a body blow. He was not only tall, six feet two, and lean, but also a war hero *and* wounded. It was like an awakening, the importance of which I didn't understand until shortly after.

The only other real awakening I can remember previously was when I was a small child. Out of the mist of nothingness came a thought, 'Here I am, just three years old, and I am crossing the street alone.' No matter that it was only a country road in the 1930s, in Woodstock, New York.

The Second World War was the war of my generation growing up . We were eleven or so years old when it broke out, and nearly sixteen when it ended. Our teenage years were spent under its influence. I remember asking my grandmother, 'What *is* war, anyway?' and having visions of tanks grinding over us. We listened nightly to President Roosevelt's soulful voice over thxe static-filled airwaves. We were filled with the spirit of joining in, combined with a vague feeling of anxiety for the future. We collected pieces of tinfoil from discarded cigarette packets and made them into large balls for the war effort. We gathered rubber and scrap metal and turned them in at collection points – our local garage or a fenced-in spot on the village green; we collected clothes for Bundles for Britain; we also rolled Red Cross bandages. We worked in our family's victory gardens planting pole beans, snap peas, tomatoes and other things, I'm sure. We had a few chickens. One, a pet of mine, ran out and was run over by a passing car. My mother was horrified when, after crying bitterly at first, I asked if we could have it for dinner. You did not come by chickens so easily then. Rabbit, squirrel, deer, trout, yes – but chickens were a treat.

As the war went on, we listened to the news on the radio and saw the newsreels on the movie screen before every feature film, which were usually glorified versions of combat. We were kept right up to date, and became familiar with names such as El Alamein, Tunis, Bizerte, Anzio, Monte Cassino. We followed the gradual, tortuous progression of our troops in the Pacific – Guadalcanal, Tarawa, Kwajalein, Peleliu and Iwo Jima – cheering in the movie theaters or the town hall. Little did I know that Lee was among them and that I would soon meet him.

Of course, in the movies the bad guys were all 'Japs' (inhumanely diabolical and grinning) or 'Krauts' (impeccably uniformed and coldly brutal). The good guys were John Wayne and our own wonderfully handsome, boyish and blond Richard Jaeckle. When I met Richard Jaeckle many years later, I felt an immediate rush of warmth, familiarity, and love for him and the time we had 'gone through' together: me as a teenager sitting on a stiff wooden chair, eyes glued to the screen watching him crawl through the mud on Guadalcanal.

We knew every war song by heart ('The White Cliffs of Dover', 'My Buddy', Vera Lynn's 'We'll Meet Again') as well as every aeroplane, both ours and the enemy's. We joined the 'spotters' (the Aircraft Warning Service) and sat for hours atop the lookout tower on the side of the mountain. We went to classes to learn to identify the planes. The classes, taught by a fine local artist named Eugene Ludins, were held in the Town Hall; everything was held in the Town Hall. The movies were played noisily on a grinding reel, run by a rather intimidating man who was also the dog catcher. We played our basketball games there, graduated from school on its stage, had our vaccination shots there, and put on plays for the Red Cross benefits.

The aeroplane spotters' observation post was built by the people of the town. It had a little pot-bellied stove fed with the wood everyone had helped to chop. It was manned twenty-four hours a day in heat and cold. The temperature was well below zero in the winter months, so we drank hot bouillon and felt very patriotic. I even called in a Red Alert once, my heart racing, having spotted an enemy aircraft; I believe it was a German Heinkel or Junkers Ju88. Unfortunately, I was the only one in the country with such sharp eyes and it flew safely on, otherwise undetected.

Gasoline was rationed, along with meat, butter, cigarettes and more. My closest friend Joanie Yager and I would wait for her father to fall asleep after having too much to drink, then we would take a few of his gas ration coupons and parlay them into driving lessons in the truck of a boy we knew, Harley Park.

We learned to live without older brothers, fathers, cousins and the town's young men, who were away at the war. My own father, badly wounded in the First World War, was turned down by the Army because of his wounds. He joined the Merchant Marines instead, and was on high-octane gas tankers for the duration. He was on the Murmansk run, and had three narrow escapes when ships from which he had just been transferred blew up. Another ship he was on went aground on shoals in heavy seas, but he and the others were rescued. We later saw it all on a newsreel. Some men – twelve altogether, and we knew them all – never came back. My friend Caleb Milne, who lived across the road from us, did not return; it was Caleb, his mother and two brothers that I was going across the street to visit when I had my awakening at three years old. He was an ambulance driver attached to the British Eighth Army and was killed in North Africa. He sent me an African doll and a beaded bracelet and letters. One of my letters to him came back to me after he was killed.

Many of the men and women who were unable to serve worked in the munitions plants that sprang up in nearby cities. I remember my aunt Dorothy, her hair safely tucked up under her turbanned scarf, going off for her midnight shift at the Hercules Powder plant. We had Red Cross first aid classes taught by our town doctor, Hans Cohen, before he went off to the Army as a paratrooper. My mother took the course and I was often used as the victim. I seemed to be constantly on the floor, face down, with the town's elders straddling my back to resuscitate me. I was poked, albeit gently, for pressure points and wrapped with bandages. I was most chagrined by the hole in my shoe that was exposed as I lay there. But we all had holes in our one pair of shoes then. When it got too large, we would cut out cardboard in the shape of the sole and push that down the shoe.

Shoes really were a bother. Years later, Charles Bronson and I had a conversation about them. We compared stories about how when you had a flapping sole, you had to fling your foot up and quickly slam it down so that you didn't trip over it; you would fix it by gluing it with rubber cement from your bicycle tire patch kit or trying to sew it down with the biggest needle you could find. Actually, Mother's first aid course came in handy not long after: she saved my life when my leg was very badly cut after a fall and an artery severed. On the way to Dr Cohen's, with my leg in a tourniquet, we came across a man having an epileptic seizure, lying across the road in the snow. Mother stopped and treated him before going on.

Like every small town with a central green square and a white church with spire, we had parades and a band: the Woodstock Fife and Drum Corps. I was a drum majorette; my sister Gale, the head majorette, was my merciless teacher. I had a white, short-skirted, shark-skin uniform with gold braid and buttons, white boots with tassels, swollen black and blue elbows and a crush on the bugle player with red hair and freckles. Everyone from school paraded. There were perhaps twenty of us altogether, our numbers swollen by several children who had escaped the war in Europe. The Red Cross ladies rode in open convertibles with their flowing white headscarves, the Red Cross emblazoned over the forehead. My grandmother was one of them, having been the wife of Wood-stock's original 'horse and buggy' doctor. She also sold many war bonds at the little American Legion booth in the center of town. Amazingly for such a small hamlet, more than $175,000 of these bonds were sold.

Mr Peacock paraded in his kilts throughout his eighties and into his nineties. Born in Scotland, he had served in the Boer War with the British. His grandson Jackie, a ball-turret gunner in the Air Force, was killed in 'our' war. Most of those parading were Legionnaires. We marched to the cemetery for the memorial service, where a hearty-voiced woman in flowing blue Legion-naire's cape would read 'In Flanders Fields'.

When he wasn't away at the war, my father, as Sergeant of Arms, led the frighteningly loud gun salute. Taps was played solemnly, with the haunting echo coming from behind the mapled hills. After the war in 1945, Lee marched in his Marine uniform with the local detachment; I, deeply in love, marched behind.

Though seemingly ordinary, Woodstock did more for the war effort than most small towns in the country at that time, perhaps because of its diversity of people, comprising many different lifestyles, nationalities, philosophies, religions and professions. It was an artists' colony as well as a farm community. It had three theaters, a music hall and several schools of art. Communists and America First groups, Free French movements, bohemians, isolationists, anarchists, pacifists, Roosevelt's New Deal WPA (Work Projects Administration), the CCC (Civilian Conservation Corps) and the DAR (Daughters of the American Revolution) were all to be found in this small New England town with a population of around two thousand.

It had a rich history of 'happenings': every movement in the land seemed to start there. It was no accident that it became known as the site of the famous music festival of 1969 (although that was actually held fifty miles away). 'Woodstock' became synonymous with the awakening of the generation of love and peace. Bought from the Esopus Indians, a tribal offshoot of the Mohicans, for sixty English pounds, Woodstock became a cluster of farms spread out beneath the gentle slopes of the Overlook Mountain (growing up under the mountain's majestic contours, we called it 'The Sleeping Giant' or 'The Minister's Face'). Here Indians once hunted and roamed on their way to the meetings of the five nations of the Iroquois. The Indian myths held that no one should lie down to rest there: it was so pleasant a place, it would sap your strength and you would sleep for ever.

Woodstock was secure and healthy: in summer we were outdoors all day swimming in fresh mountain streams; and in winter we sledded and skied. We played football and baseball equally with the boys, and square-danced in the winter to the Cheats and Swings, a group of fiddlers at the Artists' Association's meeting hall, walking home by moonlight in the snow. We walked everywhere. The houses – ours at least – had only one fireplace in

5

the living room for heat and a wood stove in the kitchen. Snow regularly appeared under my bedroom door sill and edged the panes of my windows, which faced the deep woods behind. It was the 'perfect place' to grow up, said my mother, Gladys Downer Feeley, of her own childhood. Born there in 1900, she had a large and loving family who lived in gracious and peaceful surroundings. She was a strikingly beautiful woman, extremely kind, totally non-judgmental: throughout her lifetime no one ever heard her say an unkind word about another. She wasn't placid, however, and was well-known for an independence of thought, a keen sense of observation, and a quick and often amusing assessment of a person or situation. She was also known for her marvelous cooking, baking, candy-making and generosity. Her own mother was a very devout member of the Dutch Reformed Church and her father was a physician. Mother was an adamant atheist and only married my father, a Catholic, on condition that we were not to be raised in that or any other religion. My father, however, said of her, 'She was the most religious person I have ever known. She had her own.' I recall many trips down our country road carrying steaming plates of complete dinners to people who were sick or very poor. This was, after all, the Depression and shortly after. She was also very independent. She still lived alone and drove a car in her ninety-fifth year.

My father, Jack [John Joseph] Feeley, an artist, was born in 1896, in Brooklyn, New York – and a pretty tough part of Brooklyn as well. He left Brooklyn in 1915 to serve under General 'Black Jack' Pershing in the cavalry on the Texas border during the punitive expedition against Pancho Villa. He had volunteered; 'I couldn't wait for adventure,' he said. Again under General Pershing, in the American Expeditionary Forces during the First World War, he received not only the Croix de Guerre, Belgium's highest award, but many other medals. Badly wounded, he came to Woodstock in 1918 to my grandfather's small hospital, where he met my mother. Given three months to live in 1918, he fooled them and died in 1982. He was a large man, rugged and strong, a 'fighting Irishman'. As a member of the Polar Bear Club he swam ten miles in the East River of New York in winter, but he was also an artist, actor, sought-after bridge player and prize-winning dancer.

We had very little money when I was growing up, but no one else did either and we were better off than most. My father was a fisherman too, so we were brought up on stream trout, pike, pickerel and all the other fish in those renowned streams. He was also an expert rifleman and hunter, so we had game. It all sounds quite idyllic to me today, and it really was. There was enormous warmth from both parents – although my father had what is now called post-traumatic stress disorder. Then it was known as shell shock, or just rages. When they came on, we children and my mother would sleep outside on blankets under the trees while he raged inside the house. He never came out or touched us, but we could see him pass the windows with his rifle clutched ominously in his hands.

My parents lived for several years in Santa Fe, New Mexico, in the early 1920s, where my mother developed her lifelong love of the American Indian culture and people. Maria Martin, a famous potter from the San Ildefonso pueblo, was a good friend, as were Mabel Dodge Luhan (the matchless salon entertainer and writer who had married an American Indian), D. H. Lawrence and his wife Frieda, Andrew Dasburg and all the Cinco Pintores – the artists who were credited with establishing Santa Fe and Taos as art centers. I grew up with Navaho rugs and pottery and with my mother wearing her lovely silver and turquoise jewellery in this very eastern town.

My grandfather, Dr Mortimer Byron Downer, was revered in the whole township and had delivered most of its inhabitants. The feeling of goodwill that I always experienced while growing up could have been due in part to that, along with the great popularity of both of my parents.

In the 1940s Woodstock was a bustling summer resort with many boarding houses and art schools. It was only one hundred miles from New York City. But when school started, the day after Labor Day, the town shrank back to just the locals again, where everyone knew everyone else, their parents, their grandparents, their histories, the skeletons in their closets. No street had a name: there was just 'sled hill', the Meade's Mountain road (which we all trudged up every spring on our way to the top of Overlook Mountain) or 'turn right after Sully's bridge'. On a warm, Indian summer's day in September, you could stand in the middle of the village and see little more than a fallen autumn leaf playing hopscotch along the empty, newly-paved state road. It was into this setting that Lee, along with his mother, father and his slightly older brother Robert, arrived in the spring of 1945.

Lee's father, Lamont Waltman Marvin, was descended from a long line of Puritans. The first to arrive in this country was Matthew Marvin, who sailed into Boston Harbour from England on the ship *Increase* in July 1635, along with his wife, five children and two servants. A wealthy landowner, he also had a high position in government. He and his family had left Great Bentley in Essex (the family home still stands and people live in it to this day) as followers of the Reverend Thomas Hooker, who had fled certain imprisonment under Charles I and Bishop Laud for his revisionist religious teachings. Matthew Marvin came for religious freedom, perhaps also to escape the royal tax collectors, or maybe just because of an overwhelming desire for hard work and adventure – who knows?

In the late 1600s a Marvin married a Seymour. Lady Jane Seymour was the fourth wife of Henry VIII, and the only one to give him a male heir. Unfortunately the boy, Edward VI, lived only into his teens, and the Seymours lost favour at court. They emigrated to the colonies and one of them there married a Marvin.[1]

Matthew Marvin and his family and Richard Seymour and his lived in Hartford, Connecticut, in the 1640s, and then in 1651 almost across the road from each other in Norwalk, Connecticut, the small hamlet they founded. It was not surprising that they intermarried.[2]

My mother's family, the Downers, came at the same time, also from England, and also settled in Norwalk, Connecticut, after arriving at Newbury, Massachusetts. They included deacons, doctors and one John Downer who, my uncle always claimed joyfully, was jailed for gathering clams on a Sunday. During the revolutionary war Eliphalet Downer was called 'the fighting surgeon', serving as both a medical man and a soldier at the battle

---

1 Virginia Marvin Wing.
2 Information from *The Puritan Migration to Connecticut, the Saga of the Seymour Family 1129–1746* by Malcolm Seymour.

of Bunker Hill. The Marvins and the Downers very probably knew each other, and may even have intermarried.

The religion of these immigrants was rigid: Puritan, anti-papal and devoid of the trappings of the Church of England. It was religion down to the bare bones, with hours upon hours of sermons extolling virtue and damning sin, especially 'bawdiness and drunkenness'.

In the early years of this century Lee's great-uncle Ross Marvin went to the Arctic with Admiral Robert E. Peary on his last two attempts to reach the North Pole, both the 1905–1906 expedition and Peary's last in 1908–1909. Ross was twenty-five years old, a graduate of Cornell University and a professor of mathematics at the School of Civil Engineering. He was six feet tall and weighed one hundred and sixty pounds.

In December 1905 his mother, Mary J. Marvin, wrote a poem to him. The last stanza's pleas for his safe return were sadly unfulfilled:

ROSS GILMORE MARVIN, A Mother's Meditations

May you turn your face homeward
With joy and delight,
Thanking God you have lived
Through the long Arctic night.

Oh, our hearts will be filled
With thanksgiving and joy,
To greet you once more,
My darling, brave boy.

Marvin boarded the *Roosevelt* for the second expedition in July 1908. On 25 March 1909 Peary left Marvin's supporting party for his final dash to the Pole. They were to meet up at Cape Columbia, but Ross Marvin never made it back to the ship. He died there. In his book *The North Pole*, Peary devoted a chapter to him entitled 'Good By to Marvin':

No shadow of apprehension for the future hung over the parting. It was a clear crisp morning, the sunlight glittered on the ice and snow, the dogs were alert and active after their long sleep, the air blew cold and fresh from the polar void, and Marvin himself, though reluctant to turn back, was filled with exultation that he had carried the Cornell colors to a point beyond the farthest north of Nansen and Abruzzi, and that, with the exception of Bartlett and myself, he alone of all white men had entered that exclusive region which stretches beyond 86° 34′ latitude.

I shall always be glad that Marvin marched with me during those last few days. As we tramped along together we had discussed the plans for his trip to Cape Jesup, and his line of soundings from there northward; and as he turned back to the land, his mind was glowing with hope for the future; the future which he was destined never to know. My last words to him were, 'Be careful of the leads, my boy!'

So we shook hands and parted in that desolate white waste, and Marvin set his face southward toward his death, and I turned again northward toward the pole.

Leading the party of Eskimos, Marvin fell through treacherous thin ice over a streak of open water, too far ahead to be rescued.

The bones of Ross G. Marvin lie farther north than those of any other human being. On the northern shore of Grant Land we erected a cairn or stones, and upon its summit we placed a rude tablet inscribed:

In Memory of Ross G. Marvin, of Cornell University, Aged 34. Drowned April 10, 1909, forty five miles north of C. Columbia, returning from 86° 38′ Lat.

One can only imagine the sadness Mrs Mary Marvin must have felt upon receiving this telegram from Admiral Peary:
In the late 1930s Lee's father went to visit Matt Henson, the black explorer who accompanied Peary, at his home in Harlem. Henson told him of the rumor that Ross had actually been murdered by two Eskimos.

Lee's father Lamont shortened his name to Monty when he returned from Europe after World War One. Family rumor had it that a lovely French mademoiselle was responsible for the nickname

POSTAL TELEGRAPH COMMERCIAL CABLES

CLARENCE H. MACKAY, PRESIDENT.

CABLEGRAM

REGISTERED TRADE-MARK. DESIGN PATENT No. 36369.

The Postal Telegraph-Cable Company (Incorporated) transmits and delivers this message subject to the terms and conditions printed on the back of this blank.

NUMBER	SENT BY	REC'D BY	CHECK	220 East	Water St., Elmira, N. Y.
BNy.83.	Bz.	Mo.	57.Paid.		*Received at*

(WHERE ANY REPLY SHOULD BE SENT.)

From

Battle Harbor, Via Marconi Wireless Cape Race, N.F. September 11.1909. *190*

Mrs.M.J.Marvin. #409 Dewitt Ave, Elmira, N.Y.

Every member, of expedition joins me in deep sympathy for you in your great affliction,Marvin was a favorite with every one on board,   his services to the expedition were invaluable,his loss,a personal blow to me from which I have not yet recovered,a lasting momment to him stands at Cape Sheridan. God keep you.

                              Peary.

and for the sweetly-scented lavender handkerchief that occupied space in a revered, and much whispered-about, small wooden box.

Monty was a tall, slim, handsome man. He wore a trim mustache and very much resembled the actor Melvin Douglas. A pistol enthusiast and marksman, he won many exhibition bouts including the United States Smallbore Championship in 1936. His gun, a Colt .45 with the serial number C 98688, was bought in the 1920s from Abercrombie and Fitch; it was said to be a 'Government Model.'

When Lee was leaving for combat in World War Two, his father gave him this gun with the admonition not to lose it. Lee did lose it, but not before it had saved his life in a foxhole during the Pacific war. He also lost it in a good cause. He lent it to a buddy – 'my best friend', Lee called him – who lost it, along with all his kit, after winning a Silver Star and getting wounded. Lee felt guilty about the gun all his life (as did the Marine, who has searched for it in vain). Lee's father never let him forget it. In an interview for a British magazine, Lee said of the incident, 'Even to the end my father used to say, "You lost my pistol," and I would say, "It wasn't a pistol, it was an automatic," but he knew that!' Lee also said that it was a civilian model, not a government one, and hence somewhat better finished. In the same article, Lee said of his father:

> He was working for Kodak at the time and he made a 16 mm film of himself. He stripped to the waist firing that gun. It was to improve general shooting technique, but it also helped me to shoot that gun properly because it's a big weapon and hard to handle. To watch it in slow motion: the ripple from the gun going off travels up and down the arm three times before the hand moves with the recoil . . . and then the hand moves up and to the left [because of the cartridge ejecting to the right] and it goes bob, bob, bob. No one can fire it straight, but my father taught me how.[3]

In *Point Blank* Lee imitates this action when he shoots the empty bed of the wife who has betrayed him.

Lee's father, an advertising executive for the Florida Citrus Commission and for the New York and New England Apple Institute, had weathered the Depression well. During the Second World War, with Lee in the Marines and Robert in the Army, he too enlisted in the Army as a volunteer, after first asking both Lee and Robert for their opinions. He joined as a private, declining the commission offered him (he had been an officer in World War One), and became a 1st sergeant in an anti-aircraft gun battalion in England and Belgium. He was once saved from death by a premonition when about to go into a cinema in London. As he stood outside the cinema looking at the playbill, the premonition turned into a vision: a telegram saying that he had been killed in action. He turned and fled, and at that moment a bomb landed on the cinema, killing everyone inside.

At roughly the same time in history as the Marvins were landing in Newton, Massachusetts, Lee's mother's ancestors were arriving in Virginia. Courtenay Washington Davidge Marvin was a direct descendant of the original Washington – John the Immigrant –

3 Chris Peachment, *Time Out*. 1 April 1968.

coming down the line from Augustine, George Washington's brother.

John Washington was about twenty-five years old when he came to the colonies on the ketch *Seahorse of London* early in 1657. He was the son of an English clergyman, a Royalist ousted from his parish by the Puritans in 1643. The reason was rumored to be 'frequenting ale houses . . . not only by himself sitting tippling there, but encouraging others in that beastly vice'.

John the Immigrant was returning to England on that same ketch with a full load of tobacco. As luck would have it for the future of this country, the ship went aground before it reached the open sea. He stayed and married Anne Pope, the daughter of a wealthy Virginia landowner. They started off their married life with some seven hundred acres of land on a plantation between the Rappahannock and Potomac Rivers, giving the name of Washington to that parish. By the time of his death in 1677 he had acquired many thousands of acres of land, 2,500 of them awarded for services rendered to the colonies. The name of the last tract was Little Hunting Creek.

When John died, he willed Little Hunting Creek to his son Lawrence. Lawrence in turn married, prospered and had three children: Lawrence, Augustine and Mildred. At his death, he willed the land to Mildred. She then sold it to Augustine, who named it Mount Vernon. Augustine was the father of George Washington, another Lawrence and another Augustine, from whose line Courtenay was descended.

Others of the family distinguished themselves: Colonel William Washington of the Cowpens was notable in the War of Independence. Other distinguished colonial families were the Baylors, Popes and Davidges, with the Washingtons marrying the Davidges. Lee's grandmother, Estelle Washington, married William Davidge, who also shared a lineage with George Washington. Most families settled entirely in Arlington, Fredricksburg, or Virginia as a whole.

Lee's mother was a gracious gentlewoman. She was tall, elegant and always beautifully dressed. She had silvery blonde hair worn in a page-boy and usually covered with a fashionable hat. A fashion editor for many years, she wrote for *Silver Screen* magazine, *Photoplay*, and for Helena Rubenstein. Although she was very softly spoken, you felt an undercurrent of strength. She was always polite – almost formally so – and I recall how pleasantly she always greeted me when I was only a young girl. She would smile in surprised recognition, lifting her head to see from under her wide-brimmed hat, 'Why, it's you, Pam, dear.'

The coming together of these two bloodlines culminated in Lee's birth on 19 February 1924. He was born in New York City, seventeen months after his brother Robert. They lived in an apartment in the east seventies of Manhattan and had an African-American housekeeper to care for them. They dressed in wool gabardine shorts and long stockings, and sailed toy boats in the lake in Central Park. Part of the year they lived in Florida, where their father's work took him. Courtenay and Lamont lived the gay social life of the day, drinking bootleg alcohol. Lee's mother wore the latest flapper outfits, lovely beaded dresses and cloche hats hugging her head.

The early Puritan ancestry of the Marvins conjures up a picture of shaking fists, the faithful crying out against sinners: whomsoever fell – and especially to the evils of drink – must have felt the hounds of hell biting at his heels to his dying day. So there might have been a nervous stirring beneath the ground at the old cemetery in Norwalk, Connecticut, on the day Lee was born. Along with his genetic makeup and generations of family pride and accomplishment (coupled with his own upbringing), Lee was imbued with a strong dash of irreverence which ranged from being extremely funny to devilish and, at times, shocking. His mother had this in mind one afternoon in the late 1950s after a day of family drinking and sparring at home. After some remark by one of the family, Lee's eyes turned with more than just an impish gleam toward an antique crystal bowl perched on the mantelpiece. The bowl, which had belonged to George Washington at Mount Vernon, was a continuing source of comfort and reassurance to his mother. In an instant, her thin, wavering, Virginia-accented voice stopped him in mid-thought with a measured, 'Don't you dare!!'

Another time many years later, at my father's funeral, Lee's irreverence really peaked. Lee was unreservedly close to my parents, in many aspects far closer than to his own. They were able to like each other without any bad memories or emotional complications. My mother was a very warm and straightforward person, whom Lee unabashedly admired. He could be very open and amusing with her. Once, on seeing a photograph of her as a beautiful young woman, he exclaimed, 'My God, I've married the wrong one.' Lee and my father were alike in many ways. Both were men's men, so to speak, popular with their own gender as well as with women. They were both avid fishermen and hunters, very familiar with weapons, and both had fought in wars. My father was also an artist. He had been a movie actor and, in the past, a hearty drinker.

When my father was sick, Lee retained nurses for him for almost two years so that he could be at home and die in his own bed. My father's death pained Lee greatly. It seemed to bother him far more than his own father's death. When we went home to Woodstock for the funeral, Lee drank 'before, during and after' in enormous quantities. The night before the burial Lee kept me awake until three in the morning, talking, taunting, arguing. I was terribly angry with him, as I was trying to keep myself together and rested for the next day's service. Of course, he was wonderful the next day and greatly supportive. He sat quietly next to me as the priest gave the eulogy. He walked up to give the casket his three-knock tribute. At the graveside, he was one of the pallbearers and a very dignified part of the military ceremony.

When we got back to my mother's house for the gathering, though, it was another story. He was everywhere – talking, drinking, roaring. At one point I looked over and saw him squatting down talking to a cousin of my father's. She was a sedate Catholic lady in her seventies from Brooklyn. I became aware of Lee's sonorous voice coming to a crescendo with a most incongruous question about her sex life that put her right off the chair on to the floor: 'Did you ever get your cock sucked?'

By the time we reached her side to pick her up, Lee was already across the room with an arm slung chummily around the priest's shoulders, saying, 'Father, now tell me honestly, are you really gay?' And then, after a moment, 'But, but, do you ever GET any?' Although slightly flushed, the priest did not seem unduly horrified, just laughing and tut-tutting a bit. Later I saw them toasting something with their drinks held high.

I suppose this was Lee's way of shaking his fist in his deep rage and frustration at God, or whatever power it is that controls destinies. Somehow, the victims of Lee's irreverent wit usually forgave him as soon as the shock had worn off, perhaps intuiting that, outrageous as his behaviour might be, there was an underlying feeling of care for the person and it really was without malice. More often than not, his roving eye struck right at the core of someone's being, exposed it to the light for all to see, then buried it again under his own outrageousness as though to show it was all right with him. I'm not sure this would give comfort to my father's cousin, but I know she forgave him completely and, I hope, had a private chuckle later.

Which is something that did happen on another occasion when Lee shockingly questioned an older woman on an intimate subject, this time a titled dowager – and this time he was outdone. We were visiting John and Christel Boorman at their home in Ireland. A number of their close friends and neighbours had been invited for dinner to meet Lee. One was a duchess, an elderly widow with her two sons and a daughter-in-law. We were on our way to or from a movie location in Europe, and Lee was either anticipating the film and drinking or celebrating its end and drinking. He was in high form by the end of the evening. The wealthy, respected duchess had been intrigued by meeting an American movie star. They were chatting – if one could call Lee's conversations when he had been drinking 'chatting'. It was again one of those moments when someone says something and it falls at a time of sudden silence. Lee, looking decidedly like *The Caine Mutiny*'s Captain Queeg, was peering at her, his bushy gray eyebrows rising up and down. He closed one eye in a conspiratorial wink, cupped his hand to the side of his mouth, and asked her in a well-heard stage whisper, 'Did anyone ever kiss your cunt?' Lee wanted, I'm sure, to shock by using that word, though he was somehow able to use it in a way that wasn't quite as bad as if someone else had. No one could get away with it like he could. This lovely woman was silent for a moment, then drew herself up and in her very proper manner replied quite haughtily, 'As a matter of fact they have.'

I of course was mortified and just closed my eyes, hoping I would disappear entirely. The person most shocked was undoubtedly her son, not just with the question but perhaps with the reply – particularly the word 'they'. Apparently the whole episode was taken in great good humor by the duchess, because she told it against herself with pride for years thereafter.

Lee and his brother, father and mother bought a house in Woodstock in the spring of 1945. They had moved briefly to Chicago, and then came to Woodstock after a failed suicide attempt by Lee's father. Lee was just getting out of the Marine Corps. His father and brother had also just returned from the war.

The beautiful house they bought was built by local craftsmen, descendants of the earliest Dutch settlers of the Hudson Valley. It overlooks a pastoral scene of grazing sheep from a nearby farm in the valley. It is hidden from the road by a thick stand of lilac trees, which bloom in deep purple, pale lavender and white. There are majestic maple trees and pine, and a lawn sloping to the pastures below.

All Lee's life he was an avid fisherman, starting as a young child. Although he was born in New York City, the family summered at Woodstock and here he began his love of fishing. His mind was obviously more on trout streams, lakes and swamps than it was on school – to which the number of schools he attended will attest. One of the many private boarding schools in which he was deposited by his parents was Oakwood School, just outside Poughkeepsie, New York. He took his fishing rod there and used it on all the surrounding streams.

Lee had a problem with schools: rules seemed to get in his way. He was brought home more than once before the term was out by his dejected parents. He did quite well at Oakwood for a time. It was a Quaker school whose teachers left in droves to join the Republican cause during the Spanish Civil War. He remembered Oakwood fondly, but eventually his time there was cut short too. Lee always had a strict sense of justice – so when his room-mate sprinkled dirt all over his neatly-swept floor, he threw him out of the second-storey window.

'It didn't hurt him. But the building faced the ball field where the classes were lining up. It was like assassinating the President at inauguration. I wasn't really a bad kid. I was naughty. I didn't like

17

school. I wanted to be out with the cowboys having adventures.'4

He couldn't have been completely incorrigible: witness the following letter he received from one of his teachers:

I still remember a freckled-faced, pug-nosed, reddish-blond, tousled-haired lad named Lee Marvin (shades of Huck Finn he was) a pupil in my 4th or 5th grade class at PS 166 on W. 89 St. in NYC.

He'd just come from Florida where, he told me, his father did advertising for citrus growers. He also taught me facts I did not know about citrus processing.

A toy gun *always* in his pocket or hand. Shooting cowboy performances were a daily feature & realistic – He was a thespian then –

How a détente with my new, young friend was established is a comic episode all its own too lengthy for this note. You were a lamb.

I first saw you next, watching a bedtime TV shooting movie about 15 years ago. The youngster I knew was there in the flesh. 'I taught that fellow when he was about ten. I'm sure he's Lee Marvin,' I said to my husband.

There's much fun material from your little boyhood . . . I remember as if it were yesterday.

Take care of yourself

Lillian Stiefel

October 17, 1973

In the end Lee arrived at his last school: St Leo College Preparatory School, Benedictine Monastery and Benedictine Priory in Pasco County, Central Florida. The Order of St Benedict of Florida founded the college and the monastery in 1889. It was way, way back in the pinewoods, though on the shores of a lake. Lee's parents were not fooling around. Since Lee had been sent there after a short stint at St Petersburg's stern Admiral Farragut Military Academy at mid-term, his parents must have thought the monks were their last hope. They did not underestimate the powers of the Benedictine discipline. After all, the monks had had

4 Tom Seligson in *Parade Magazine*, 27 April 1986, 750 Third Avenue, New York City, New York 10017.

centuries to train for their encounter with Lee. He stayed. The monks won.

He was there from the winter of 1940 until he joined the Marine Corps early in 1943. He starred in track events and javelin throwing, and wanted very much to pitch in the baseball games. The *St. Leo Chronicle* of 24 April 1942 quotes him as promising, 'If Father Ed lets me pitch for his team, I'll guarantee that we will take at least second place in every game I pitch.'[5]

Although he isn't listed anywhere as a baseball player, 'in track he was high point man in the annual inter-class tournament, and he took three firsts in the 1942 state-wide meet in Jacksonville, as St Leo again took the all-Catholic title.' His specialities were high and low hurdles and the javelin. Father Marion Bowman remembers 'his hunting for wild pigs in the heavy underbrush on the lake shore across from the college with a knife strapped to a bamboo pole, just like a Greek javelin user of old.'[6]

The Fathers must have made an impression on Lee. He had an uneven record, but he failed no subjects; he excelled in German (with 91.7 average) and history (92). He definitely made an impression on them as well. He was described as a 'scene stealer' in two productions of the Dramatic Club; a student reviewer said one play was 'A riot of a comedy as played by Lee Marvin.' Father Marion said, 'He was never an actor here. He was just playing himself.' He was a 'high profile character' at St Leo's, and was frequently quoted in the school *Chronicle*, usually saying something sarcastic. On the outcome of the 1940 presidential race, Lee observed, 'The biggest bait hooks the most suckers.' And to the question of what puzzles you most about girls, he said, 'How they look without the paint and whitewash.'

Father James Hoge remembers him as an indifferent student who was 'constantly on the carpet'. It was also noted that he had created such recurring problems in one class that the faculty member granted him amnesty out of frustration.

Lee visited his old school in 1958. He and Father Marion, who

5 *Pioneer College: The Centennial History of St Leo College, St Leo Abbey, and Holy Name Priory* by James Horgan, St Leo College Press, St Leo, Florida copyright 1989 James J. Horgan.
6 *Pioneer*, etc. interview of Fr. Marion.

was by then the abbot, had developed a strong friendship. Lee had also befriended Father Bernard, whom he was helping with a story he had written; they corresponded regularly. In 1969 Lee was given an honorary doctorate of fine arts from St Leo's, and a new dormitory was named in his honor. In the introductory remarks Lee's old mathematics teacher Father Hoge said, 'Lee Marvin was not the best student St Leo ever had, nor was he the worst. But he was the damnedest.' While the old guard at St Leo's seemed to take Lee in their stride, the new hierarchy (according to *The Monarch* of 3 March 1980) saw him with different eyes. Even though he was listed under 'Notable Students'– 'Of them all, by far the most well known was Lee Marvin' – by 1980 his name had been removed from the dormitory. This demotion was for two reasons: 'he fell into scandal through a sensational "palimony" suit in 1979,'[7] and 'he made no financial contribution to the college' (having been told not to by the Fathers).

Lee told the school reporter during his visit in 1958, 'I liked everything about St Leo, but what I like most is that it does not try to set a boy into a mold. It helps him develop his own personality.' To me he had nothing but good to say: 'Those monks were tough, but it was good for *me*!'

Like so many other people, Lee was at a loose end after the war. He was taking a few courses at school and trying to decide what career to follow. At Woodstock in 1945, however, he had his fishing. The streams around the town are famous for trout. The Catskill Mountains have some of the finest rivers in the country, and he fished them all. I was 'allowed' to come along and watch, walking quietly along the bank while he waded in the stream, or sitting on a rock while he fished a 'hole'. Other times he would go with his friends David Ballantine, Don MacShane, Bobby Early or other young men of the town just home from the war.

One day when he was fishing the Esopus near Phoenicia, Lee saw a man in trouble in the middle of the stream – his rubber hip waders were filling with water in the swift current. Lee went out and helped the man to shore. He insisted upon taking Lee's name and address, and one day a fine fishing rod arrived in the post. It

7 *The Monarch.*

was an Orvis Battenkill, nine and a half feet long, and the thank you note was signed Charles F. Orvis, founder of the famous Orvis Company. Lee treasured that rod all his life.

I was still in high school when Lee decided to go back to school for more credits. He was very good at mathematics, as his great-uncle Ross Marvin had been, and thought of a career in economics at that time. He would drive me to school in Kingston, New York, some eleven miles away, in his father's hazy blue 1938 Plymouth. We spent a great deal of time in that car: going to school, movies and parties, and also parked on deserted country roads on cold winter nights in the snow, with the heater running and making love under his Marine Corps blanket. We would lie there in the back seat for hours twined together while he made up marvelously imaginative stories. I still recall that feeling of deep love and total security. Lee embodied so much to me: tenderness, masculinity and strength, a knowledge of so many things combined with his great sense of humor. I didn't, I'm sure, think specifically about these attributes at the time: I just felt my heart pounding whenever I thought of him, when I saw him coming up the road in his car to pick me up, or when he put his arms around me.

We used to find a field at night, shine the headlights on the grazing deer and just sit there for hours watching them. After we were married, we joked that we ought to find a car just like that and install it on a pedestal in our Malibu bedroom.

In fact, he had to buy the car from his father after we turned it over in an accident. The whole side was smashed in and the top dented. It was a New Year's Day. He had just taken me to the doctor to get a large splinter of wood taken out of my foot that I had picked up dancing the night before. We were driving along in two deep grooves in the icy road, and in front of us a man was riding his bicycle in one of the grooves. As we got closer, Lee kept honking his horn more and more desperately as we couldn't stop on the ice. The man, a friend of ours named David Fairbanks, kept looking over his shoulder at us and pedalling for all he was worth, but staying in the groove. Finally Lee had to swerve out of the rut to avoid hitting him, and we turned over in the process, passing Fairbanks upside down. Lee – always one for the dramatic – swears that he shook his fist at him while sliding by. We wound up in a clump of pine trees on the edge of the golf course. I clambered out through the door by now at the top of the car, stepping on Lee underneath me. Many weeks and $300 later, the car was his.

This of course was 1945–46–47, and we girls had to learn quickly how to resist the advances of the returning soldiers. The young men had lost their youth to the war. Now they had come back in triumph – and with some pretty lustful thoughts. We heard many a pitiful plea: 'I haven't seen a woman [wow, to be called a woman!] in four years!' 'You are the only girl I ever felt this way about.' 'You are the only one in the world who can help me forget the war.' And so on. 'Nice' girls didn't have sex before they were married. 'Petting' was really on the cutting edge, and bad enough that you wouldn't even tell your best girlfriend. You seemed to be protecting yourself constantly, and an evening out would have you fending off wandering hands from the clavicle down. 'Soul kissing', or any attempt at it, was so risqué that it was cause for great giggles *and* told to your best friend. We even wore the tight girdles which for some reason were so popular – maybe for the look, however redundantly, or maybe as self-imposed chastity belts. They were awfully hard to get out of.

For me, Lee was different. There was no questioning, no hesitation and I believed everything he said. (*And* I didn't tell my best friend.) I was a goner from the moment I first saw him at the Big Deep. He remembered our first kiss as being under the bridge – Sully's Bridge, over the stream by my parent's house – but I didn't even recall this. He was very handsome and outgoing, and was one of the heroes we back home had been rooting for during the past quarter of my young life. He was also very popular, particularly with the young Woodstock men who had been away in the war – men I had known when I was growing up as my older sister's and cousins' friends and boyfriends. Among them Lee was not only quickly accepted, but was admired as something of a leader.

With me, although I was six years younger than he, he seemed almost shy, but he was very warm and loving. If I was sick with tonsillitis he would bring me ice-cream and sit with me on the couch while we ate it together. He would pick me up at the school bus and bring me home with my books. He braved my parents for nearly three years, which was quite an accomplishment. Neither was happy about me having a boyfriend so much older; my father, big Jack Feeley, was not only very strong, but Irish and tough. Lee was hard to dislike, however. He was respectful, well spoken and had many things in common with my father. His parents too, although 'newcomers' to the town, were well regarded by the 'natives', as we original Woodstock families were called. They lived in one of Woodstock's loveliest houses, they had come from 'the city' and they were comfortably wealthy. This was not the case with many people after nearly four years of a world war. I can't say that any of this mattered, however, because even before I knew all about him, it was love at first sight.

We went to many great parties in the 1940s, often at the home of one of Lee's friends, David Ballantine. His father, E. J. Ballantine, was a retired Shakespearean actor turned sculptor. Stella Ballantine, David's mother, was a niece and protégé of the feminist and radical anarchist Emma Goldman. Stella had a deep, raspy voice and smoked heavily while she talked. She had a magic way of smoking and talking while at the same time growing the longest cigarette ash I have ever seen. It seemed finally to fall off, as if in defeat, when there was barely a thread of paper left to cling to.

Teddy and Stella were both intellectuals, so the dark, wood-paneled living room was crammed with books. There was a large record collection of folk songs in the house, as well as blues, New Orleans jazz and classical music. David's brother Ian was a publisher of paperback books, and along with his wife Betty brought Penguin Books to America from England. They later had their own Ballantine Books, and now Bantam Books. It all made for lively nights of wine, beer, music and talk.

The country was in a happy, exhilarated mood now that the war was over. We all discovered Bessie Smith, Leadbelly and the wonderful Negro blues and wails of the 1920s and 1930s. There was the 'new music' of Artie Shaw and Benny Goodman; and there was Peggy Lee, whose singing we both loved. She was our favourite vocalist, with songs like 'Why Don't You Do Right?' Lee was absolutely thrilled when only a few years later she was in a movie with him, *Pete Kelly's Blues*. And who could predict that she would say in her autobiography how thrilled *she* was to be with Lee, calling him 'a real actor'?

We sang 'Goodnight, Irene' and 'In the pines, in the pines, where the sun never shines'. Lee, with his deep voice, would sing, 'In tha pine, in tha pine, wherah the sun nevah shine, and you shivoa! when the cold wi-ind blow'. We danced the jitterbug and whatever dance it was where you get thrown over your partner's back and slung between his akimbo legs. At the end, you were lifted to the ceiling by your elbows held stiffly at your side.

We had the best bar to gather in, the SS Seahorse. Originally built in 1875 as a house, it became stables in the early 1900s. Dick Stillwell bought it in 1937 and made it into a bar. During the war, when he was serving in the Navy, it was turned into a youth club for us teenagers, where we played records and drank cider from our local apple trees. The old wooden cider mill was an integral part of the town then. It was owned and run by Dave Mossetti, a much-loved man with a heavy Italian accent who chain-smoked and wore dark, baggy sweaters and heavy work pants all year round. The mill clanked away all fall, and when the snows came some secret process known to a few of the locals turned the remaining cider into applejack, the American version of the French apple brandy Calvados. The reason for Dave's great popularity was not hard to imagine. The cider at the youth club sometimes turned a bit 'hard' – fermented – giving a bit of a buzz, which we loved, of course.

Dick Stillwell came back from the war and restored the place to its original function. It's probably as famous as Harry Hope's bar in *The Iceman Cometh*, although not for its air of hopelessness. It was a neighbourhood bar par excellence. It had portholes for windows, was decorated with Naval signal flags, along with fine art on the walls, and had the darkest, oiliest plank floors, walked on (and often fallen on) by some of the most interesting people in the world.

It was a place where artists, musicians and actors gathered, each usually on his or her own favourite bar stool – everybody had one. Adolf Heckeroth, the plumber for whom Lee worked at the time, sat and sipped his martinis after work. He was a remarkable man with a heavy German accent and a droll sense of humor. Also sipping martinis – often ten or more at a sitting – was a woman in her seventies or eighties with flaming red hair and lipstick, great gaunt cheeks, a long cigarette holder (never empty), a slightly bulging stomach, and very thin legs ending in shoes that always looked too wide for her feet. I never saw her eyes more than half open. Louise Hellstrom had been a madame during Prohibition days, but was now a generous patron of the arts. She bought up many of the young local artists' works before they had recognition, thereby allowing them to continue to work *and* eat. Her ability to consume prodigious amounts of gin filled us with wonder. I can still see her clambering off her stool and wandering off into the night.

There was another couple, a retired New York City policeman and his wife, who both sang opera. She was a large Swedish woman with an erect stance, huge voice and heavy chest; we called her the Swedish Nightingale. One night after a number of drinks she rose from her stool with her arms outstretched, singing some aria and backing away slowly for effect. Unfortunately, someone had just gone into the cellar and left the trap door open. She fell into it backwards and went down the steps, thudding as she hit each one. There was a brief moment of silence, then the aria continued as lustily as before, though sounding rather hollow as it came from beneath our feet.

Eugene O'Neill Jr was a big, burly man, bearded and kindly, who sat there and expounded to us all. He was very erudite and tremendously knowledgeable about the Greek classics (or so it seemed to me at the time, at any rate). He also talked about suicide, and it was rumored that he was in a club – perhaps the Hemlock Club – whose members were pledged to perform that act when life seemed hopeless.

Gene did indeed carry this through. He had been living with a woman who fell in love with another man, an older man, a businessman – an untenable thought for an artistic soul. She was moving out of Gene's house and her suitcases were by the door. His body was found draped over these suitcases. He had slashed his wrists and ankles, and then sat in a warm bath until he weakened. He had cut the telephone wires, I suppose to insure that he would not weaken in his resolve and ask for last-minute help. We were shocked, since we all liked both of them very much. Who could know that some years later José Quintero, another friend and habitué of the Seahorse, would become a famous director of Gene's father's plays? Or that Lee himself would give one of his finest performances as Hickey in *The Iceman Cometh*?

Another unforgettable person was a beautiful girl who was said to have an illness: nymphomania. There were rumors about her illness breaking out on entire dormitories and football teams. I was there myself the night she came into the Seahorse quite naked under her raincoat. She opened it to prove that someone had stolen her clothes as she swam in the night stream. She was stunning with long, curly dark hair; sensual – zaftig. There was nothing obviously aggressive or predatory about her. She just seemed to drift dreamily through the world, silently exuding an aura. She usually sat alone (as many of us noted uneasily), but when she left, someone was sure to step quietly out after her.

It was enough to keep you on your toes. Perhaps it was her name: Joy. I once arrived late at a party at the Ballantines' – just in the nick of time. Lee was walking down the wooded path close on Joy's heels. He stopped dead in his tracks when I called his name and turned, I thought a trifle reluctantly, back to the party. Later he would jokingly growl, 'See what you saved me from?' and sigh heavily.

Dick Stillwell was the guiding spirit of the establishment. He had neatly trimmed graying hair, firm eyebrows and eyeglasses; he was self-assured and organized, with a surprisingly paternalistic attitude toward most of us younger ones. Of course, a good deal of that might be attributed to a justified concern over whether we were sneaking an under-age beer.

It wasn't the only bar Lee and I spent time in, of course. There was the Wheel Inn, where the owner didn't mind opening up on a Sunday morning or late in the evening if you banged on the door. You had to watch him when he poured a beer, though, as he had a habit of pouring everyone's unfinished beer into a great pitcher he kept beneath the counter to serve to the unwary. Another bar, directly across from the cemetery, was the Brass Rail. One night we crowded into the doorway on hearing the mournful sounds of a trumpet: one of our group was in a maudlin mood and was sitting on a gravestone playing in a downpour of rain. This particular bar was a favourite of the backwoodsmen living in the mountains outside town. There were still family feuds going on, and the warring factions always seemed to know when the other side was coming to town. It resulted in wild fights which were the topic of conversation for days after. These weren't our places, though; the Seahorse was where we were. It was where everything started and everything ended. You went there before going anywhere else, and you came back after.

Lee, just home from a terrible war, was really finished with violence. I didn't think about it, it was just part of his personality. The closest I ever saw him come to a physical show of anger was one evening outside the Seahorse when his friend David Ballantine had been struck by some man. I came out and saw Lee gripping the man's shirt, pressing him down on the hood of a car. Lee was telling him in no uncertain terms to stop; he was very controlled and very quiet.

Lee did go hunting occasionally, however. Guns were second nature to him and the other boys home from the war. He also met some of the local 'country' men when out hunting. One – 'Old Hickory' as he was affectionately called – was well known to people like my father who fed their families with game, in and out of season. They enjoyed the challenge of outwitting and outrunning the game wardens. Jacking deer was an art. Every kid in the school knew enough not to mention to the teacher that they had a deer hanging in their back yard, and if they did say anything the kids in the know would give them a sharp elbow in the ribs as a reminder (as happened to me once from my girlfriend Joanie Yager). Old Hickory had palsy, or perhaps an habitual alcoholic shake, until his hunting rifle had a bead on something. In a second, steady was not the word. His aim was dead and true.

We were invited to a pig-slaughtering one day by a backwoodsman Lee had met hunting. He had a little run-down farm in a paper-thin valley between two mountains. We piled into Lee's car about dawn one morning and made our way over the rutted dirt road to Keefe Hollow – or 'Holler'. With us were Billy Pierpoint, a few others who had been in the services and my cousin, Faith, an Army nurse. When we kids heard about a farm family ready to slaughter, we would go to watch in fascination. I suppose it's a stage kids go through, drawn to the most violent and frightening things. It was mixed too with the joyous feeling among the family: a great get-together where everyone pitched in and helped.

The huge porker was hauled up by its hind legs after the

slaughter, lowered now and then into an enormous bin of boiling water, then singed over coals and its stiff bristles roughly scraped off. All this was accompanied by strange smells and the farmer's children running around laughing and poking and having a hand in the whole business. Probably a great meal was shared by all afterwards.

I remember that I was not squeamish about this, and actually felt excited about the adventure. The men, of course, were laughing and studiously casual. We climbed upon the pig-pen's crooked, weathered old fence while the farmer went in with his big knife (an ice-pick really comes to my mind). He stuck the pig, but the wrong way. The animal rushed around like greased lightning, bleeding, squealing, thrashing and running between the legs of the rest of the family who had jumped in. I was sickened, and Lee's clinical interest and sense of 'fun' quickly turned to angry dismay. He demanded a rifle that someone had ready and dispatched the poor pig with a single shot. He grabbed my hand and we rushed away.

The war was not something Lee talked about much, but he proudly showed me the wallet that had been hit by the bullet before it hit him. The plastic around the pictures in it still bore the reddish-brown stains of dried blood. The bullet had sliced through the heads of all the people in the photographs: a pretty girl (he never mentioned who she was); his brother in Army uniform; a miniature self-portrait by his brother; his father and mother with himself in Marine Corps uniform; Lee with two of his Marine buddies. He sent the wallet home to his mother along with his Purple Heart medal. His letter to her is on American Red Cross paper, now yellowed. The lettering and cross at the top are a faded red:

> Dear Mother,
> Here is the P.H. medal and also my wallet that you gave to me before I came in the Marine Corps. Please save this wallet and you will notice that a bullet that hit me also went through it first – well, for now be good. I will write soon.
> Your loving son, Lee

Lee's was a personality filled with exuberance and exhilaration – an urgent lust for life. He was the life of any party, full of energy and enthusiasm for everything. He wouldn't just arrive somewhere: he would explode through the door, either in mid-sentence or playfully falling in with a box full of beers that would roll everywhere. He was always doing something, going somewhere, and pulling me with him. When we went swimming – which we seemingly did every summer's day – he would leap down the forest path to the stream, running ahead over the slippery pine needles, roots and fallen logs with agility. The stream, the Sawkill Creek, was three or four miles from the village and about a mile through the woods from the road where you parked your car or bicycle. The Tannery Brook, named after a tanning mill in the 1880s, runs through the village and meets up with it just above the country club.

Together they both roll eventually into the Hudson River, but first comes the Big Deep. It is both wide and deep, with rock ledges and a great overhanging pine tree from which to jump and dive. The opposite bank is a pebbled sandy beach. The path down from the road through the woods skirts the edge of steep cliffs for part of the way. We knew it so well we could walk it blindfolded – and did, actually. We went there at night for picnics of stolen cow corn roasted in their husks. Handily enough, a farmer's cornfield was just near by.

Lee drove his car the same way as he did everything else – with a good deal of panache. After the accident the car was highly recognizable because of its bashed-in side; in summer a drying bathing suit was tied to its antenna. It was a familiar sight whizzing through town. He was even undeterred one night when, on the way to a party some miles out of town, the headlights suddenly went out. I was nervous but he drove confidently on, the brilliant moonlight guiding our way there and back. I recall it being one of those magic nights when the snow had a frozen crust that sparkled with a million little lights. Occasionally two of the lights glistened slightly larger and wider apart, and you knew it was some small winter rodent caught for a brief second staring up in surprise.

The atmosphere in which Lee lived with his parents and brother in those years was also very cold. This bothered him, and affected him all his life. Dinners were silent, broken only by jibes and terse criticisms. There was always an undercurrent of hostility: compliments and approval one minute and cold, scathing, cutting remarks the next. It was a silent house of lovely antique furniture, Persian rugs, silver and crystal, and a clock ticking. Lee's mother delicately sipped from a gold-rimmed coffee cup with her little finger in the air. It wasn't until after her death that they discovered it wasn't coffee in the cup. They found a number of carefully-hidden bottles of Southern Comfort. 'Oh, *that's* what it was,' Lee said, commenting on her rather puzzling silence at the end of the day.

As a child, Lee remembers being taken to tea by his mother in his Buster Brown haircut, shorts and knee-socks and watching the ladies chatting. As an adult, when Lee drank coffee or tea, his fingers would automatically take the same position. When he drank alcohol, you could almost measure how much he had consumed by how far out the little finger extended. He used the gesture in an exaggerated way in his films.

Lee's father – 'Chief' to Lee and Robert – increasingly drank bourbon through the years until he reached oblivion. Lee's brother, an artist also trying to find himself after the war, was caught up more and more in the family quadrangle. He would egg his father on in almost gleeful exercises of sibling rivalry. Once, when a forty-year-old adult, he urged his father to hit Lee with a heavy stick. Years later, when watching a ten-minute film clip of *The Home-coming* with Lee, I suddenly burst into tears. The clip had evoked such memories of those days for me – but what must it have done for Lee? I had bitter memories of that interwoven family, so involved with each other. It was all done with such a veneer of gentility too. My own family was so different: warm, straightforward – you knew where you stood.

Things weren't always that way, certainly. As children, Lee and his brother were inseparable. As young adults, they shared an apartment on Third Avenue by the El. Lee's concern for his brother went on until Lee's death. His affection for his mother and father was also obvious. He was very close to his mother: during the war, on the day he was wounded in the central Pacific, she awoke with a terrible pain in her head and thought he had been hurt or killed. And just before Lee was shipped out from San Diego for combat in the Marshall Islands, his father – forty-seven years old and in the Army himself – hitchhiked to Lee's camp. The Marines put him up for the night. Lee was deeply affected by that visit, which was when his father gave him the prized .45 that saved his life. Unfortunately for Lee, this affection was a painful and unrequited one.

Lee was twenty-one when we met and I was fifteen. He turned twenty-two three days before my sixteenth birthday, for which he gave me a lovely crystal perfume atomizer. He had got it from his mother – with or without her permission, I never knew. I knitted him a scarf, the first of three I have knitted in my lifetime; the third was a replacement made some thirty years later for the first one. It was decidedly simple, just 'knit one, purl two'. My mother gave me a small party at our house with just four people: Lee, Billy Pierpoint, my cousin Faith and myself. At home in Tucson in 1986, forty years later, Lee sent me a 'sweet sixteen' birthday card.

Some time during the first year we met Lee was asked to perform in a play as a benefit for the Red Cross. It was (perhaps prophetically) entitled *Ten Nights In a Barroom*, and he loved doing it. It had grown men in baby carriages and bonnets, and someone hidden behind the couch to give cues for the many forgotten lines. It was Lee's first acting role in public. The person who 'produced' it was Ted Mann, who later went on to be a professional producer. This was his first production.

José Quintero was pressed into service as director. This was his first directing effort. He later set up the acclaimed Circle In The Square theater company and became a well-known director of actors such as Geraldine Page, Sylvia Miles, Jason Robards Jr and many others. This funny little benefit play was the start of all three careers.

After the 'show' a cast party was given by the parents of the baby in the carriage, Billy Pierpoint. All the men home from the war tended to gravitate together. Bill and his twin brother Charles (Buddy) had been in the Navy, Billy on a submarine. Buddy was killed in 1942 when his ship, the *Meredith*, was sunk in battle near Guadalcanal. Billy and Lee had become close friends right away.

I went to the party with Lee and joined in the revelry. It was winter, and I was sitting next to a red-hot pot-bellied stove for most of the evening, drinking beer along with the rest and talking to Mrs Pierpoint. At the end of the evening I rose to leave. Everything swirled around me and I nearly fell. Lee had to carry me to his car to drive me home. When we arrived, helped by several others, Lee opened the door of the living room very quietly so that my less-than-pleased mother would not hear. However often she got angry with him, she was never quite able to catch him. Lee told me later, with some glee, that he stood me on my feet, gave me a gentle push with his fingertips and fled out of the door. It sounds right. I recall other occasions when we came home later than my parents allowed. He would cut the engine of his car and turn the headlights off. Since I lived on a downward slope, he would slow down with his brakes and I would leap out at a run. My father was – or tried to be – quite protective of his three daughters.

Besides going to school, Lee got a job with Adolf Heckeroth, the local plumber. When I got off the school bus I would sit in the news shop and wait for him to quit work and come in for coffee with the guys from work. I started to drink coffee and smoke, so that I could sit with them and look older. Or I would be sitting there when Lee came in, trying to look so casual while choking down coffee, something I'd never drunk before.

Plumbing was a job Lee always said he enjoyed. 'First,' he said, 'you can see what you have accomplished. You dig and dig and dig, and there it is – a hole. Most importantly, when you are digging, cleaning out or fixing, it's at someone's house. They come out or in to watch and talk to you.' Many of the customers were brilliant and creative people; there were sculptors, philosophers, scientists, writers and actors. Lee never forgot a conversation nor anything he saw. People would note his keen interest and take him in to show him their life's work. He had that effect on people.

In 1947 he was repairing some plumbing at the Maverick Playhouse. The small summer stock company was about to put on its first play, *Roadside* by Lynn Riggs, when disaster struck: the leading man fell sick and left. The part called for a tall, larger than life, wild-eyed Texan. They were desperate. Lee had already endeared himself to members of the company during his days there, and they knew he was anything but introverted. Also, in searching for a replacement they had spoken to Teddy Ballantine, himself an ex-Shakespearean actor who had once played Laertes to John Barrymore's Hamlet. Teddy had been deeply involved with the Maverick for some years and enthusiastically recommended Lee for the role.

That was the end of Lee's life as a plumber. He was wonderful. He *was* the part. It's a real Americana comedy, written in 1930 about a young girl (hard as nails but naïvely and hot-bloodedly searching for love) traveling with her pa who loves to wander the country in his covered wagon. Texas, Lee's character, levels a town in drunken hilarity. Sobered and fleeing the law, he falls in love with the girl. She is hard to get and he is trying to impress her. I can still see him delivering this colorfully booming speech:

> I wasn't borned in the ordinary way . . . one night Liza lay in her pappy's cabin. Wild hosses come anickerin' and trompin' around. Great big b'ars as high as hills begin to growl sump'n fierce. All of the sudden there was a crash and a bang and a clatter! Thunder and hail and lightnin', hell f'ar and brimstone! The cabin whur Liza lay cracked itself wide open from stem to stern, beam-end to beam-end, hind-end to gullet. And when the smoke cleared away, out *I* stepped, full-sized, dressed to kill, in a ten-gallon hat, boots and chaps, a gun in ary hand, and both guns a-poppin'! And that's how I got started!

What could have been better? There were so many wonderful lines. Thirty years later he would suddenly come out with one or another; he particularly liked to say to me, on appropriate occasions, 'D'you reckon you'd not say another word fer a minute er two, like a good girl, nen we'd appreciate hearin' yore voice again, a-soundin' like a gold trumpet the way it does?' (He also later ad-libbed the line in his movie with John Wayne, *The Comancheros*.)

He needed a wide-brimmed cowboy hat for the role but did not have one. Lee had encountered a Woodstock writer, Walter O'Meara, a large handsome man, part Native American, who wrote stories of mountain men. He had just such a hat, a black Stetson with the words N. PORTER, SADDLE AND HARNESS CO., TUCSON, ARIZONA in faded gold lettering on the leather band inside, along with 'John Stetson Company'. He loaned it to Lee.

Twenty-four years later Lee, I and our daughter Kerry went to visit O'Meara in Nogales, Arizona, where he had moved. Lee was making *Pocket Money* in Arizona at the time. When we talked about that play, Walter rose and went to his hall closet. He took out this old, weathered hat and gave it to Lee. He said he remembered being surprised when Lee returned it so beautifully cleaned and blocked after he had borrowed it. He himself had later cut off some of the wide brim, but he told Lee, 'You are welcome to have it.' It occupied an honored spot in our house from then on.

In the summer of 1947 I was studying at the Art Students' League summer school in Woodstock (mostly painting Lee's jaw and profile). The League was full of young men on the GI Bill of Rights. Lee would drop into class once in a while to check on me. He needn't have worried; on the other hand, *he* was surrounded by budding actresses. Lee had continued acting as well as working behind the scenes at the Maverick Theater.

The history of the Maverick, situated a few miles out of Woodstock, is entwined with the beginnings of the town as an artists' colony. The theater was built deep in the woods in 1924 by a man named Hervey White. Hervey – poet, novelist, musician, socialist and social reformer – and a wealthy Englishman, Ralph Radcliffe Whitehead, had arrived in Woodstock in spring 1902 with the express intention of developing a colony for artists and craftsmen. They had searched the country over for the proper setting: a certain altitude and a place of esthetic beauty. Standing on the top of Overlook Mountain, looking over the treetops to the valley below, they felt they had found the place.

With Whitehead footing the bill, they bought up a number of farms on the south slope of Overlook Mountain that overlook the town. They built their houses, raised sheds for the artists and craftsmen who were to follow, and constructed boarding houses for the expected students. This area was, and still is, called the Byrdcliffe, and almost all the structures are still standing and in use; wisteria and grapevines still twine around the arbors and fences. Years later, after the project had risen and faded, one of these buildings, the Villetta, became a summer stock theater. It was here that José Quintero, Eddie Mann and a small group of actors came and later formed the Loft Players, which eventually became The Circle In The Square. In 1989 our own grandson Jess King was striking sets for the River Arts Repertory in that same old creaky-floored wooden theater.

Hervey White and Ralph Whitehead had a falling-out in 1904. Hervey left the Byrdcliffe group and bought a large farm and wooded property a few miles out of town. With very little money he somehow managed to build one decidedly rustic cabin after another; many friends and visitors came – Clarence Darrow among them – along with various other intellectuals in the labor movement. Classical music was also one of Hervey's interests, and he quickly attracted noted musicians to the place. He named the colony the Maverick after the free-spirited wild horse. After the First World War more musicians came, and townspeople began coming to the private outdoor concerts held under the trees. Hervey opened these to the public and eventually concocted the idea of having a fund-raising festival, a pageant in the woods. With the enthusiastic help of a handful of people, he laboriously carved out an open amphitheater in a bluestone quarry in the forest. Members of the Metropolitan Opera Orchestra under the direction of Leon Barsin Sr played there during the afternoon and evening of the festival, and later into the night. Hundreds of townspeople came in wildly original costumes. It was a great success, so much so that Hervey White, dressed as Pan with a vineleaf wreath on his head (and little else), promised that he would hold this festival yearly and that he would build a proper concert hall in the woods on the same spot – which in 1916 he did. It still stands and concerts are performed every Sunday during summer.

Hervey built a new open-air theater in 1921. He sometimes wrote his own plays. The Metropolitan Opera Orchestra musicians appeared there; sometimes two hundred or more performers were on stage at one time. But the last play on this stage outdid them all. A ship eighty feet long and sixty feet wide was built by the local commercial artists. At the end of the play, to the delight of the audience, it was burned to the ground. At ninety-four my mother still remembered it.

Actor Dudley Diggs, one of the founders of the Irish National Theatre, was with the Provincetown Players at the time and proposed combining efforts to build a theater. Hervey White immediately agreed and once more hired local carpenters to construct the building in his woods. Alf Evers, in his account of the history of Woodstock, describes it: 'The theater was from timber cut in the Maverick woods. Bark covered timbers, earthen floors sloping toward the stage which was equipped with a row of kerosene lamps by way of footlights.'[8]

There were wooden benches for about six hundred people, and the acoustics were wonderful, as everyone who ever performed there noticed. The boards were not always tightly fitting and the sound of thunder and the scents and sounds of the forest were all a part of any production – as was the occasional rivulet of rain, often heavy, which found you no matter where you sat.

The Maverick Theater opened on 4 July 1924 (the year Lee was born) with *The Dragon* by Lady Gregory, featuring Helen Hayes as the *ingénue* along with Edward G. Robinson and E. J. Ballantine, who twenty-three years later would urge Lee to join this theater. My father Jack Feeley acted with the Dudley Diggs Players in the Maverick that year too. He was also a movie actor for Pathe Studios in New Jersey and Florida in the 1920s.

Hervey White, though an eccentric, lived very simply, practising what he preached with a deep commitment to humanity. He admired my grandfather, Dr Mortimer Byron Downer, and often volunteered his services as a nurse in difficult cases. During the great influenza epidemic of 1918, which 'hit Woodstock hard, Hervey White took time from the Maverick to serve with great devotion and energy as Dr. Downer's assistant . . . where most people hesitated for fear of contagion, Dr. Downer asked Hervey how he felt "about taking a chance at death," Hervey replied, "Life is not so sweet that I can't do my duty."'[9]

The Maverick Theater was closed during the war years because of gas rationing, and in 1944 Hervey White died in his sleep. The news buzzed through town, and even we teenagers felt a sense of him passing from our history. In 1989 stone pilings were all that remained of the beautiful old theater. The woods have grown completely over it, and Aileen Cramer, who had acted there herself, had to show me where it stood as we walked the land behind the concert hall. A pine tree grows in what used to be one of the two front entrances.

8 *Woodstock, History of an American Town*, Overlook Press, Lewis Hollow Rd, Woodstock, NY 12498, 1987.
9 *Woodstock, History of an American Town*, Alf Evers.

In 1947, however, Lee trod the boards as 'Texas' and received an enthusiastic response from the local newspaper: 'I get the biggest kick out of that Marvin. When he kisses the girl he rocks back and forth! Later, after the play, when we came down the road behind the theater, we heard a lot of noise coming from the platform on the back of the theater where they made the sets. We could hear shouts, real "whoopee" and shots going off! There was Lee Marvin striding up and down and just shooting it up, having the most wonderful time. He had found what he wanted to do.'[10]

There was another review in the Kingston Freeman's *Sunday News*: 'As for Lee Marvin, who made his first appearance on the legitimate stage, he is a "natural" for the part of Texas, slow but sure, and with an excellent drawl. He could hardly have been better. One hopes to see him in a sophisticated part during the season, which would test the acting ability he certainly shows in Roadside.'[11]

After his success Lee became completely absorbed with the Maverick Theater. He was an Actor. The entire summer of 1947 was spent constructing sets, striking sets, lighting, stage managing, acting. They put on ten plays. In *The Affairs of Anatole*, Lee did construction; in Thornton Wilder's classic *Our Town*, he played Constable Warren; he was Nonny in *Thunder Rock* and Mingo in *Home of the Brave*. He was totally caught up with the excitement of the theater, the all-importance of it and the bonding with your fellow actors and actresses, all working feverishly toward one goal: the Play. These were heady days. Much to my anguish, he even went out with his leading lady one night after the closing of *Roadside*. I found out, and when I asked him about it he tried to cover up, hemmed and hawed, and finally explained that it was completely altruistic on his part; he had felt compelled to try to save her from herself. She was pondering, it seems, her romantic future. Would men or women be her destiny? Lee was simply trying to help tip the scales, so he said. Perhaps it was an initial case of being happily immersed in a theatrical role – a budding Method actor. Or perhaps it was because she was also very pretty.

10 Dick Thibaut in the *Kingston Daily Freeman* from an as yet untitled book by Jean Gaede and Fritzi Striebel, *Woodstock – Festivals, Mavericks and Hervey White*.

11 Marion Bullard; Kingston Freeman's *Sunday News*, 29 June 1947.

The pay scale for the Players was commensurate with the price of tickets. Since that ranged from eighty cents for the wooden benches at the back to one dollar eighty cents for the wooden benches in front, it meant the actors were paid seven dollars a week. This had no adverse effect on their enthusiasm, however, and everyone pitched in with great energy and love. I saw each production and even tried to join them, or so I am told by my dear friend Dulcy Peters, who kept a diary. She claimed that I was always trying to drag her to tryouts. I proudly applauded Lee's work, and at the end of each play I went to the wrap parties. They always seemed to be in someone's draughty, woody rooms with candles stuck in wine bottles, perhaps to enhance the mood, perhaps to save electricity bills. That year the Art Students' League held its summer's end costume ball in the Maverick woods. The band played from a small gazebo-like structure there, and the two groups combined their celebrations. Even Joy was there, in a red eyelet dress of such scant material – more eyes than cloth – that it is still remembered some forty years later. On 13 August 1947 Lee joined Actor's Equity, stating that his pay for the summer had been $46 and worth every penny. The Maverick Players disbanded: the locals went back to school or their jobs, and the 'professionals' went back to where they had come from – trying to get work in New York City.

Lee's parents still had their apartment in New York. Lee and I had friends with apartments in the city, and my older sister Gale lived there. We both went back to school in the fall, but drove to New York at weekends and continued seeing all the old members of the Players: Kenny Paine, Jeanne Jerrems, Lynne Charney and others. Long hours were spent recalling the plays, discussing books and philosophies, arguing for or against very important things. Homosexuality was a big subject: trying to change those of that inclination by logical argument, but fiercely defending them against criticism or taunts from anyone outside our group. We had cheap and wonderful dinners in tiny basement Italian restaurants in Greenwich Village: the San Remo, Minetta's Tavern, the Old Colony, all around MacDougal Street, Washington Square or thereabouts. There were parties, play readings, happenings. You never had a problem finding somewhere to sleep; everyone piled into someone's apartment – usually Kiki and Paul Godwin's – sleeping on couches, chairs, cushions or the floor. One night we hadn't got the key to their apartment (which was on the fifth floor, of course), but there happened to be a window in the main hallway. A window across the courtyard below belonged to the apartment's kitchen. Lee judged the distance, and while I worried about the five-storey drop, he opened the hall window and stepped out on the ledge. Admittedly he was very strong and had been well trained in the Marine Corps, but it was harrowing to watch. He managed to have one foot on one ledge and the other under the kitchen window, which was mercifully unlocked. He seemed to accomplish it without missing a heartbeat.

Inevitably, around this time – and I can't imagine why it hadn't happened sooner – I became pregnant. Sex was not spoken of in my family, it was hidden from one's closest friends, and so I was totally unsophisticated in such matters. I suppose time and youth had lulled both of us into a false sense of security. I was not quite eighteen, too young – as they said in the romance magazines of the day – to get married (although I would have), and Lee was on a mission. He was focused on his acting career, a passion that would not be denied. Someone in our group found a doctor in Spanish Harlem. It was illegal to have an abortion, and it was all done with great secrecy. A young girl, daughter of the wealthy owner of a well-known baking company, had just died in New York from an abortion and her body had been cut up in little pieces by the doctor to hide the fact. It was in all the news, and the entire matter was a dangerous, painful and frightening experience. I had to be alone in the apartment with the 'doctor'. It was performed literally on the kitchen table, and in the end I nearly died with a high fever. My sister had a friend who was a real doctor, and he gave me a new drug, penicillin, with the admonition that if I didn't get better quickly, he would call an ambulance and we would all probably be arrested. Luckily, I did get better, with no lasting effect other than years of guilt, but it left Lee and me so shaken we vowed never again to go through anything like it. He and my sister came in as soon as the doctor left, and it was one of the few times in my life I saw Lee cry. I know it affected both of us for life. I hope we never go back to such a Dark Age that something like this cannot be performed in safety and dignity. On reflection, I was glad that we didn't get married at that time, because I doubt we would have stayed together. As it was, we each had our own sons later, and life worked it out for us to be together after all.

2 New York

Some months later, Lee decided he had had enough of high school. He had been in many schools, public and private, he had fought in a world war, been wounded, had lived in Florida, Chicago, New York. He found it difficult to sit in a classroom being taught by those who had far less experience of life than he did. He was taking me to high school dances. I was in bobby sox, plaid skirts and – as he always remembered later – fuzzy angora sweaters. He was also driving me to high school plays that I was 'stage managing' while he was *really* acting. He no longer wanted a career in business, and decided to pursue acting full bore. Using his GI Bill[1], he joined an acting school, the American Theater Wing in New York, commuting back and forth to Woodstock – or I would go to the city on weekends to see him.

For whatever reason – either dissatisfaction with life in school without Lee's presence, or the busy weekends taking their toll – I soon followed suit and quit high school several months before graduation. I recall the supposed reason, an argument with the particularly authoritative teacher Lee too had disliked. I lived to regret it, though. It took me six months of night school some years later to make it up. By then I was a mother of two small children; I found I needed, and wanted, a graduating diploma.

One day in the spring of 1948 Lee and I stood in the driveway of my parents' house. He had just brought me home from somewhere. The maple trees were just beginning to sprout new yellow-green leaves; it was warm, the sun was shining. It must have been early June. Lee told me he was 'going away'. He was going to a summer stock company in North Carolina – 'Flat Rocks,' he said – and he

1 It was right after the war and hundreds of thousands of young men had come back from the service. The GI Bill was wonderful, affording training that they could otherwise not have had.

would write. 'How do you spell your last name?' he joked. I recall an emptiness, an overwhelming sense of sadness and loss as the car drove down the road and disappeared around the bend. I knew by the clutching feeling in my stomach that it wasn't just for the summer.

Many years later my sister told me that she had bumped into Lee a few months after this in New York, and he had said to her, 'Some day I am going to come back and marry your sister.'

He did go to North Carolina and join the Vagabond Players for their summer season in Hendersonville (Flat Rocks or Tuxedo – they're all close together) at the Lake Summit Playhouse. They performed ten plays here, and he had a really good season once more. They did *Whistler's Mother*, in which Lee played two roles; *The Male Animal*, *John Loves Mary*, *Three's a Family*, *So's Your Uncle Dudley*, *Thunder Rock*, *Years Ago* and *The Vinegar Tree*.

Jean Bellows, who posed for the famous painting *Lady Jean* by her father George Bellows and was an actress with both the Maverick and the Vagabond Players, wrote to me: 'The whole playhouse operation was run on a shoestring – as you can tell by those gorgeous sets!' Lee was the leading man, her husband Earl Booth was the juvenile, and Jean the leading lady.

At the end of the season Lee returned to the American Theater Wing and began studying in earnest and pounding the pavements looking for roles. He did get work with a national road company in *A Streetcar Named Desire* and *The Hasty Heart*, touring through the winter on a circle throughout the country and parts of Canada and coming back through the southern route, Texas. He remembered the stiff, cold linoleum of the cheap hotels on his bare feet and 'twenty-five thousand miles of one-night stands at $75 a week – wow!' All expenses had to be paid by the actors themselves. He had the car, so he could at least get help with petrol money from the others riding with him.

Lee's rise to stardom was a fairly steady progression. He never really struggled for long in making a career, but went from his first small roles to bigger and better ones quite rapidly. Other than during the first light-hearted days in New York, when he was more often broke than not, he was never in the category of the starving actor who has to work as a waiter or sell Christmas trees – which many did – while waiting for a role. Also, his GI Bill paid for acting lessons at the American Theater Wing. Lee began supporting himself as an actor right after the Theater Wing, in off-Broadway shows, summer stock and touring in the National Companies. Eating was not a problem, and if it was, he could always go to his parents' apartment just off Fifth Avenue. He was charismatic and popular, and was invited to many parties and dinners in those New York days: to Martha Graham's (with whom he had studied dance) and other theatrical parties; to weekly gatherings with publishers and Ian and Betty Ballantine; and to dinners with a few already-successful actresses who were attracted to him – and he them.

He recalled one of the theater bashes he'd been invited to. Out-of-work or striving young actors and actresses mingled with the stars of Broadway plays and movies. 'Boy,' he chortled, 'talk about high-powered repartee . . .' He shook his head, remembering with a kind of lingering awe. 'Marlon Brando was IT in New York. He was having something of a go-round with Tallulah Bankhead. She said something to him, and he retorted in his most irreverent, "Oh, fuck you." Without missing a beat, she looked over her shoulder as she walked away, saying huskily, "And you will, dahling, you will."' This impressed Lee no end.

Lee was full of enthusiasm and energy, with a speed and sureness about him. He was tall, agile and well built, and had a deep voice: all great attributes for a young actor, along with his unshakeable determination. He went from the play *Billy Budd* on Broadway directly to Hollywood, where he rose from small parts to featured roles in no time. In his sixth movie, *Eight Iron Men*, he had a leading role. Stanley Kramer had convinced Harry Cohn of Columbia Pictures to take a chance on starring him in this Edward Dymtryk film. After they had worked together, directors tended to ask for Lee again. Stanley Kramer produced *The Wild One* and later directed Lee in two films, *Not As A Stranger* and *Ship of Fools*. The three with Edward Dymtryk were *Eight Iron Men*, *Raintree County* with Elizabeth Taylor and Montgomery Clift, and *The Caine Mutiny* with Humphrey Bogart.

So early in his career he worked with the great stars of the era. He never forgot the lessons he learned watching them in both their acting and their dealings with studio executives or producers. Lee was a stickler about wardrobe. It was very important to him and he paid a lot of attention to it. He appreciated seeing Bogart once ask, just before a scene, to have his shirt replaced. He, in turn, was asked to make do with the one he was wearing. At that, Bogart took the shirt off, dropped it on the dusty floor, stepped on it, and walked off. 'You got two of them, don't you?' he asked, and went to his dressing room while they hastily got another; he knew very well they had doubles. After all, *he* was the one the audience saw. Lee also liked to quote Bogart's advice on acting – 'Just hit the marks and say the lines' – even though he did not do it himself.

It was during the early 1960s, when Lee was already attracting great interest as a movie and television actor, that he filmed a television psychodrama he later described as a 'breakthrough' for him, one that deeply affected his acting. It was one of the most significant roles of his career and of his life. Entitled *People Need People*, it depicted a segment of the life of Dr Harry A. Wilmer, Jungian psychiatrist and author, when he was a captain in the Navy during the Korean War.

The hour-long production for Alcoa Premier Theater, aired in 1961 on ABC, was narrated by Fred Astaire. Lee played the lead role of a homicidal, suicidal war veteran in Dr Wilmer's psychiatric ward at the Oakland Naval Hospital and Arthur Kennedy portrayed Dr Wilmer. *People Need People* was so successful that it earned five Emmy nominations, one of them for Lee for his extraordinary performance.

Lee's character, a Marine sergeant, was the most difficult and violent of the patients. In the first scene Lee is alone in the 'Quiet Room', lying on the floor by a toilet with restraints strapping his arms to his sides. For the rest of his life Lee remembered the feeling of powerlessness it gave him. He talked about it during a dialogue between himself and Harry Wilmer at an international film festival at the University of Texas Health Center in San Antonio:

'I remember a funny little thing that happened to me when they brought me in. They put this restraining belt on me . . . I never had one on before. And this is an old used restraining belt . . . it was well worn. On the inside, burned in like a brand, it said "San Pedro Receiving", and all those holes had been pulled. They put that thing on me, and I didn't like it. And they put me down on the stretcher and they tied me in it. And suddenly panic hit me because I was looking at the ceiling of the studio. If this place caught on fire now I couldn't get out. And I was really this close to panic. And so finally when they released me I told Harry about it. He asked me how I was feeling, and I said, "I felt awful." And he said, "Good." And I said, "Oh, that's where we are going."'

The film was deeply moving and Lee's performance was powerful: frighteningly violent, but also showing vulnerability. In one scene he flings himself repeatedly against the heavy mesh over a solid door until he finally falls in exhaustion. Harry asked of this scene, 'Did you hurt yourself?' Lee said, 'You can't fake that. And that is part of the commitment of acting: there are certain things that you have to do. And so I just did it until I literally couldn't do it any more, and that's the scene. That's the obligation of the actor to the scene and that's how far you must go.'[2]

Although Lee felt that way about physical actions, he did not approve of an actor physically altering his looks for a role, such as gaining or losing weight to get the character across. He felt that you should be able to give the impression of fat, thin, energetic or frail in your acting performance. (He once said that of Robert de Niro in *Raging Bull*, though he thought the performance and the direction of Martin Scorsese were terrific and very demanding. He also said afterwards, 'Jesus! If I ever get a call from Scorsese I'm hiding until he is off the phone!')

He discussed the making of *People Need People* and what it meant to him. 'I don't know what the other actors did at home or how they survived – or their wives or their girlfriends or their mothers – but we did take it home. We lived it for the ten-day cycle in the film of what the ward was like. We were actually patients, even though we hadn't been committed officially. And that became very interesting. I was in the Marine Corps, and I did have all those dreams and stuff. The film gave me a chance to break through that wall of acting because, oh yeah, I had all that kind of stuff, I was scared but I couldn't tell anybody about it. And so here was a chance to act out my fright, my cowardice, my very weaknesses – not necessarily the mother theme, as in the last scene, or in

2 Taped discussion at San Antonio.

45

reference to *my* mother – but I could at last fill in what I had never felt before. So after this presentation I think I became a different actor. Directors or writers say, "Here's what you do," and you say, "Well, it's not that simple." So I became a layman, which is worse than being a professional, right? Because you know they "know it all". And I think I have been a troublemaker ever since in my performances. But I did have a lot of fears doing it because I thought I might show something in myself that I didn't want to see. I'm not proud of my performance in this; I'm proud of the guy up there, not me. I still have that rationale on my mind. It is an interesting thought. I was one of the few guys in the Marine Corps that really had a chance to act it out for profit. And ever since then I have been free because I can do anything I want to do now. Because I know that I am acting out me.'

Lee was asked by a doctor in the audience, 'After a shoot [of a movie] how do you let go of the role once it is past?' Lee's answer was one that not too many actors are willing to admit, or perhaps for them it is not the case: 'You don't. You live with it. And what happens is that it eventually goes away because other things supersede it. Fortunately, there is another job coming on. It wears out. You don't cut it off. It opened up perspectives in myself that I still haven't figured out because it is an ongoing process. Now, how far an actor should go . . . there is a danger point, but then of course, if you reach that danger point, let them go because maybe you can get them out of it if it gets too bad. But they must reach in all the way, which is the fateful process of acting. What you do is make sure that you don't get hurt physically when you're doing it, and just hope that mentally you can handle it when the scene is over. It is a dangerous business in that area.'

When asked if he had to psych himself up for a scene – in particular, the one about contemplating suicide – he said, 'Yes, you can't get out of it. If you get out of it, you might lose it – because it is so difficult to find, once you find it, you've got to keep it. That relates to an earlier question, "Do you take it home and does it affect your family?" Well, you can imagine now. Actors' families have very difficult times because they are living with whatever the role is.'

Lee also spoke of violence and his feeling about it. 'All I can say is that, in Europe, American pictures are the most popular, which amazes me. They do love the violent pictures. And, of course, they have seen violence. So maybe an acting-out on the screen alleviates the pressure on them. I know when I was a kid and would see John Wayne punch some guy and knock him through the wall, I'd say, "Boy, I'm glad I wasn't that guy." Or I didn't want to be involved in that relationship. So maybe there is a good value to it. Now in acting, when craziness is shown in a sick manner or, in other words, "to no value", I look down on it. Because real violence is a thing that must not be tolerated, and in order not to tolerate it you must be educated in knowing what it is. Violent films come out with value . . . When I play these roles of vicious men I do things you shouldn't do and I make you see that you shouldn't do them. I played a lot of what I hate, now I like to play parts which I love. I can play bigots etc, parts no one else will. I am not fascinated by death any more: there is lots of anti-violence in my heart, and after committing murder it was hard to find peace. Acting is a search for communication – that is what I am trying to do, get my message across. Marines are all volunteers: when it gets rough, you say to yourself, "Well, you asked for it." *Cat Ballou* was about an aging ex-gunfighter who took the easy way out; to me, he became the Marine I once was, or had wanted to be.'

This appearance at the University of Texas was eleven years after the making of *People Need People*. During the filming of the movie in 1961, Lee formed a close friendship with Dr Wilmer and his wife Jane that lasted for more than twenty-seven years, a relationship that had an enormous impact on Lee's life. In 1972 Harry Wilmer asked Lee to become a member of the board of directors for a series of film festivals, the International Festival of Culture and Psychiatry, of which he was both founder and director. These were under the sponsorship of the University of Texas Department of Psychiatry in San Antonio, Texas. Lee accepted with alacrity, and became deeply involved not only on the board but also as a member of the discussion panels during the seminars. Lee's down-to-earth delivery struck a chord, but at the same time he really had a fierce intellect. He was also a good speaker, a good listener and a sought-after member of these panels.

Lee had previously felt disregard for some aspects of psychiatry.

When his marriage to his first wife was unravelling, she asked him to see her doctor, a Freudian analyst. Lee didn't like him at all, and felt he was getting absolutely nothing out of his fifty minutes. He would lie on the couch while the doctor sat silently nearby, his eyes closed, occasionally scratching his pencil on a pad whether Lee was saying anything or not. Lee began to suspect that he was writing a grocery list, napping, or doing something that had nothing to do with him. One day Lee was determined to get the doctor to do something more than just grunt noncommittally. He stared at the doctor's tightly-shut eyes and said in a threatening voice, 'How do you know I'm not going to get off this couch and throw you out the fucking window?' When he saw the doctor's eyelids quiver, he jumped up from the couch in disgust, saying, 'Oh, for Christ's sake!' and went out, slamming the door behind him, never to return. His years with Harry in these various endeavours changed all that; during the first festival, where the theme was Switzerland and the contributions of Carl Gustav Jung, Lee became inspired to read many of Jung's writings.

Harry Wilmer, himself a Jungian psychiatrist, was a member of staff at the Mayo Clinic in Rochester, Minnesota, after the Korean War. Later he was professor of psychiatry at Stanford University, the University of California at San Francisco and afterwards at the University of Texas Health Center. As director of the Audie Murphy Memorial VA Special Treatment for schizophrenic patients, he began a study of their dreams, which no one had paid attention to before. His study, *The Healing Nightmare*, made long before the subject of Vietnam war veterans became popular, became the basis for one of his many books. Lee and Harry talked a great deal about this manuscript; in fact, Lee wrote the preface for the book. During the 1960s Harry had donated much time to treating 'flower children' in clinics at Haight Ashbury, San Francisco. He also treated prisoners at San Quentin prison, and just after *People Need People* was aired in 1961, Lee was asked to go with him to the prison. The prisoners had written a play of the production, and Harry asked Lee to be technical advisor. Lee agreed, and later said of them, 'They were good, but that wasn't the point: they got a chance to act out in a disciplined form. It was an exciting thing to watch these guys work in a structured form

48

together, because they are not a together group – they are individuals in the joint, so to speak.'

'They all knew who Lee was,' Harry said, 'and when he walked the "yard", the men would all chant loudly, "*M Squad! M Squad!*" The prisoners were in awe of Lee.'

The film festivals ended after eight years, but Harry had already founded the Institute for the Humanities at Salado, Texas. Lee immediately became a member of the board of trustees as well as a speaker. It quickly became the internationally-respected institute it continues to be, with guest speakers including many Nobel laureates, philosophers, physicians, authors, playwrights, poets and generals; Linus Pauling, M. Scott Peck, Maya Angelou, Edward Albee, John Kenneth Galbraith, Sir Laurens van der Post, Karl Menninger and John Boorman, to mention a very few.

Late in October 1987 Lee was to have spoken at the symposium 'Understanding Evil', which was televised by Bill Moyers to open his public television series 'The World of Ideas'. Less than three weeks before, Lee had been buried in Arlington National Cemetery, so I spoke briefly in his place.

Instead of Lee being there to speak, the symposium was dedicated to his memory. As Rod and I were about to board our plane from Tucson airport to the symposium, we met Oliver Stone. He said to me with almost angry vehemence, 'But I have a script for Lee. I wanted to work with him!' Lee thought he was a good director, and applauded his success. I know he would have wanted to work with him, too.

Even in the early days of his career, Lee had refused to be typecast. Although he made a great villain – who could outdo him in viciousness? – in his own TV series *M Squad* he starred as a good police detective, and of course he won the Academy Award for his comedy role in *Cat Ballou*, which he said he played as 'a tragedy'. He refused to be signed by any studio, and so had far more freedom than most actors of the time.

While Lee was 'on the road' in the late 1940s and early 1950s or working in off-Broadway productions, I spent part of the summer at the Art Students' League and part working at a restaurant across the street from the other theater in town, the Woodstock Playhouse. It wasn't exactly a restaurant but a diner: all shiny and silver with a rounded, Art Deco-looking structure. It had been brought in on a flatbed truck and plonked down at the foot of the village, a pretty unwelcome sight in an artists' colony. The owner's father knew and admired my mother, so I got the coveted position as one of the two waitresses. I wasn't much used to working ways; the opening night of the diner was to be a private party, so I came nicely dressed and in my one pair of high heels. The owner, Herb Rubin, asked in surprise, 'Where is your uniform?' I replied that I thought it was a party. He looked at me incredulously. I had to hurry home and put on the white dress with the white apron. He and his wife were really wonderful people to work for. They came from a Hudson Valley industrial town not far away, but had learned to adjust to, and even appreciate, the eccentricities of our small town.

It was a great job for me, as the actors and actresses, the managing director and the owner of the Playhouse came into the diner all the time, and we became friends. I was given season passes and saw all the plays. It was a 'star system' that year, which really means that most of the money was paid to the one or two top stars and the rest of the actors received little or sometimes nothing – just the privilege of painting sets, acting in small parts and being part of the magic of theater. The actors were asked to form a baseball team and play against the locals at a benefit for the Red Cross. Some of us were asked to be runners for the older actors or townspeople, and I ran for Arthur Treacher. Another actor that season was a handsome stage performer and Conover model who was in the play *Sailor Beware* with the stripper turned actress Anne Corio. His name was Murdo 'Mac' McLeod; he was from Scotland, but had dropped the A from MacLeod for Equity reasons. Eventually he changed his first name to Duncan. We became good friends.

When the summer ended I went to New York to live with my sister Gale and find work. Even though we lived in the most wonderful of places while growing up, we felt we *had* to get out of this small town and head for the city lights. Gale and I lived in a dark basement apartment (though it had a yard!) with a locked grille for an entrance. Before my sister, who was very beautiful, became a model, we had almost no money. We pooled our meagre finances and each took out barely enough money for the subway (a nickel) and for coffee. We made our own lunches, often onion sandwiches. Gale worked at what she described as a 'greasy spoon', a Greek diner, until she made enough money for photographs, and I had a boring, poorly-paid job way downtown. I went to New York with dreams of working on a newspaper, but I must have been living in the wrong era, because after repeatedly trudging from one to the other it soon became apparent that, with no college education, delivering the newspapers was about all that was open to me. A newspaper clipping office was the closest I came to the printed word. It was a large room where a loudspeaker would drone out the names of businesses or movie stars. (I daydreamed about how funny it would be if some day I'd be cutting out Lee's name.) You would quickly find the name, underline it with red pencil, cut it out and race to file it before another name was droned. The boss was very nice, however, patient and kindly. After reading about my schooling and lack of it, my art classes and interests, he asked if I would not be bored by the job and might wish to leave. I hurriedly assured him I would not: 'No, no, I swear it.' He was quite right, of course.

I sometimes wondered later how our lives might have worked out had I accepted Lee's invitation to dinner one night during that time. I declined – mostly because my sister was nudging me urgently in the back, reminding me that I had a date with the handsome and busily working Mac McLeod – but with some misgivings, I recall. The next time Lee called me, we met in *the* drugstore on Times Square where all the actors hung out. We had coffee together and I told him I was getting married.

To the surprise of my family and friends – even myself, I think – Mac and I were married in December 1948. I had always thought I was adventurous and somewhat rebellious, planning tramp-steamer trips to Africa or Arabia: the last – not the first – person my friends thought would get married. After meeting Mac, my father said, 'He's very nice, he's very good-looking, but don't ever marry an actor.' He had been an actor himself. I was puzzled – and, of course, in the end I married two.

Mac too had been in the Second World War. Anticipating war, he had enlisted just before Pearl Harbor, while he was on Broadway in the play *Best Foot Forward*. He was in the Horse Cavalry at Fort Riley, Kansas (where my father had trained before joining General

Pershing's outfit). Later, Mac's unit was mechanized under Patton's 3rd Armored Division. He fought in Sicily, England, France and on the Normandy beach-head. His was one of the first tanks into Paris on Liberation Day; his division then went on to the Battle of the Bulge. When they were making their way toward Berlin, Mac was suddenly ordered to Eisenhower's SHAEF headquarters, where he served under the British – he thought the request came from a Scottish officer who picked out his name. His physical injuries were caused by shrapnel from a buzz-bomb, and his mother told me that the war had upset him and changed his personality. One of the many by-products of war, I came to find, is that it seems to spawn rage and good actors.

Forty years later, when Lee was filming *Canicule* in Orléans, France, Lee took a picture for Mac of the monument the French erected commemorating Patton's army. Shoulder height, it reads very simply:

> Le 16 Août 1944
> La ville d'Orléans
> A été libérée
> Par l'armée du Général Patton
> (3rd Armée USA)

Mac's friends and companions were mostly the people he worked with: handsome models and their wives, beautiful models and their husbands, actors and actresses. I was eighteen years old and they were ten or so years older, so they all took me in hand. I recall walking down the streets of New York with the world's best-looking and most photographed models of the time; heads turned as they passed. In those days modelling was a profession which many serious actors relied on for steady incomes. We went to all the Broadway plays; as actors in Equity, we only had to pay the tax. Mac was in Broadway plays, off-Broadway at the Equity Library Theater, Six O'Clock Theater and the Henry Street Settlement House, as well as in summer stock shows. We lived in an apartment on East 25th Street with a 'studio' living room, meaning it doubled as a bedroom. It had a fireplace, a very small dining room through an archway, a tiny kitchen so small that all four walls could be touched at once by standing in the middle of the room, and a bathroom with a tub out of whose drain a mouse once struggled as I ran the water. Our friends all had different, often innovative, methods of dealing with New York apartment mice, not to mention cockroaches. One swore that if one mouse had a violent demise, all the others would hear about it and depart. We paid $75 a month rent, but first, as was common practice, we had to give the supervisor of the building $150 for the privilege. Mac was once at the Henry Street Settlement House in a Sean O'Casey play *The Plough and the Stars* with another actor, John MacLiam. One evening Mac was very late coming home after the play, so I, worried, called Johnny. He told me that he had last seen Mac walking his leading lady home. Recalling Lee and the Maverick, I wondered if this was another case of 'Method acting'.

Many New York actors we knew went on to be very successful in movies: Eva Marie Saint (with whom Mac had acted in a play at the Six O'Clock Theater), Marty Balsam, Gregory Peck. Many others gave it up to do other things. We played poker, canasta or whatever card game was popular. We had small dinner parties or ate in the little French restaurants all along Lexington or Third Avenues. My son Roderick and my daughter Wendy were born (only eleven months apart) while we lived there, and Stephen Elliott, whom Mac had met in 1946 when he was in *Paths of Glory*, was Rod's godfather. His wife, the actress Nancy Chase, was also from Woodstock, and we walked our carriages together in the neighbouring park, she with a toddler and pregnant, and I with one baby in the carriage and another on a seat at the foot of it. Her nephew Chevy Chase became a celebrated actor himself. We had to pay rent for carriage space in the basement of the adjoining building, and wash off the sooty grime and tiny animal footprints before putting the babies in.

Mac worked a lot in early live television. He was a more experienced and better-known actor than Lee at that time. He would come home occasionally and say – particularly in the early days of our marriage when he still resented him – 'I saw your old boyfriend Lee Marvin standing in line looking for work at CBS' or some theatrical call somewhere.

Lee did have some small roles in television during these years, but then landed a role in a movie being partially shot in the East,

USS Teakettle, a Gary Cooper film directed by Henry Hathaway. It was to be Lee's film début, along with another unknown actor, Charles Bronson. The film, later retitled *You're In the Navy Now*, served not only as Lee's start in movies but also earned him the respect of Hathaway, one of Hollywood's great directors. Lee tells the story of getting the part. He had stood in line for some three days waiting for the interview when someone came out and told them all to go home. 'That's it . . . calls over.' Lee was not a timid soul and said, 'Listen, pal, I'm going through that door or someone's going through that fucking wall!' He got in, needless to say, and Hathaway said, 'Well, what can you do?'

'I caught a twenty-inch rainbow trout' was Lee's way of starting the conversation. Finally, Hathaway asked him if he could act. Lee countered with 'Can you direct?'

'How much do you get?'

'$100 a day.'

'I'll give you $175 a week.'

'I'll take it.'

I guess a marriage was made: Hathaway added lines for him and kept him for three weeks instead of one. When the role ended, torn between 'selling out to Hollywood', as New York actors called it, or pursuing his first interest the stage, Lee packed up his car and raced back to New York and a part on Broadway in Herman Melville's *Billy Budd*. He chafed at the bit, wanting to play the lead part of Claggart, feeling that the actor who was cast in the role did not understand Melville and was doing a bad job of it. Many years later he remembered the lines, quoting them with appropriate squints and fire: 'The sea is deceitful. While all the surface dazzles, storms wait for a wind. Who knows what ribs, bones and decay are fathomed at her base and move when the long tide gestures? Do you like me?'

It is a chilling speech, especially if you are miles out at sea and the surface is dazzling but you know that a sudden quirk of fate or change of heart of the 'weather gods' may indeed send your own ribs and bones down to the bottom. Lee was not above teasing me with this quote, adding to my unease on occasions, usually when we were a hundred miles from shore in the Coral Sea on a small fishing boat awaiting an approaching storm.

In July 1951 Lee was playing Mitch in *A Streetcar Named Desire* at the Clinton Playhouse, Clinton, Connecticut, when Henry Hathaway's words came ringing back to him: 'Kid, don't waste your time. You belong in the movies.' At Hathaway's urging he packed up once more and left Broadway, Woodstock, the stage and the east for ever. He began his rapid climb to becoming one of the top performers in his profession. He left New York 'on the come', he would say, full of enthusiasm, hungry; but later he was fond of saying to all who would listen, 'I went out to the great Golden Hollywood . . . Got there just when the lights went out . . . and they've been trying to turn them on ever since.'

By 1954, having been featured actor in many roles, he co-starred with Marlon Brando in *The Wild One*. He had married and had had his own television series, *M Squad*; in one episode he looked exactly like my father – the way he wore his hat, walked and talked. He must have been drawing from him, even before he became an actor.

3 Life Without Lee

While Lee was finding fame and fortune, I was busy with my life and children. Mac and I moved to New Jersey. It was cheaper there; bigger apartments cost less and it was just a quick bus ride to the city. We spent the summers in Woodstock, where Mac was in summer stock at the Woodstock Playhouse once more if he wasn't off on tour. Others in the company that year were Heywood (Woody) Hale Broun, his wife Jane Lloyd-Jones and the director Joe Leon, and it was the beginning of long and fond friendships with them all. Woody's father was the famed newsman Heywood Broun and his mother was Ruth Hale, feminist and America's first war correspondent. Each was a part of the Algonquin Round Table, the group of wits, writers and pundits. Edward G. Robinson Jr was there at the same time. He was not too accomplished an actor, but he was young and very sweet, though intense and troubled. We sat with him and his wife Frances – a beautiful red-haired model from Georgia with a china plate complexion – in their little attic rooms above a farmhouse in Woodstock. He talked about his famous father and how frustrated he felt having to live 'under his shadow'. He would work himself up and finally storm, 'Why, I wouldn't take the – the *crumbs* from his table!!'

I pointed out that we were at that moment eating crackers, bread and salami from a big basket his father had just sent to him from California. Poor Eddie died only a few years later, leaving Franny to meander aimlessly in and out of the misty worlds of alcoholism and mental illness, leaving behind a little dark-eyed daughter.

I left Mac after five years of marriage and took my two small children back to Woodstock. It's difficult now to recall the exact reasons: we are such good friends now, and we had children together. Perhaps it was the difference in our ages; I was not yet nineteen and he was thirty when we married. The children and I seemed to form a closer unit. It might also have been the results of the residual anger and impatience caused by Mac's war experiences. For whatever reason, I found solace in another relationship and we parted amid a good deal of acrimony, which, happily, faded in time. My children and I lived at home with my mother and father until I opened a small nursery school in the bottom half of a rambling old house on Lower Byrdcliffe Road. It was of weathered brown wood and resembled the Whitehead houses, its doors all rimmed with sweet honeysuckle vines growing up the sides of the house.

My 'work' started out as a nursery, but ended up with a lot of children spending nights, sometimes weeks. I did all my laundry on an ancient wringer-type washing machine and drove several neighbouring children to school for petrol money. The car came as a gift from a friend, John Henning Brown, whom I loved dearly and nearly married two or three times, but somehow didn't. He had won the car at the Woodstock Library Fair. Now his children are all my nieces and nephews – actually, cousins somewhat removed – since he later married my first cousin.

I did get married again – I tended to marry all my boyfriends – to someone I felt I 'knew' because his family lived in Woodstock as I was growing up. He was born in the Philippines to a career army officer father from Virginia, whose stern-looking, rigid figure was a familiar sight striding through the village. I always remember a leather quirt smacking against a twill legging. His grandfather was General McCaw, a Surgeon General of the United States, and his mother was a softly-spoken Virginian who had been a schoolteacher in her youth. William Patteson Moncure (nicknamed 'Bim' by his Filipino amah) had just left his own army career, retiring in a huff after the war. He had been in the Counter Intelligence Service during and after the war in Austria. He spoke Russian, French and German, and taught skiing to troops in Austria, but he hadn't been in combat.

We had a daughter Maury, named after a relative of Bim's, Matthew Fontaine Maury, who charted the Gulf of Mexico. We bought what had once been a farmhouse, built in 1835 across the road from my parents.

For a time we moved to Nashville, Tennessee, the lovely old

Southern city in whose schools my older children learned penman-
ship and manners and I learned about the Civil War; both past and
present. We went to the Nashville Sunday symphonies – one dollar
per family – outdoor concerts at the Parthenon, to the Observatory
and the Steeplechase to watch the horse racing. We also learned
about chiggers and tornadoes: one struck a block away, tearing up
enormous trees by their roots and flinging them across the street
along which we had just walked home from school.

We returned to the Woodstock farmhouse and a nervous
breakdown that immobilized Bim. I went to work for a year –
thinking week by week that it was merely a stopgap – as a waitress;
a *real* waitress this time, seven days a week. One restaurant was
twelve miles away, where I worked during the week, and the other
was on top of the Ohayo Mountain (facing the Overlook
Mountain), where I worked at the weekends with a newspaperwoman friend of mine, Tobie Geertsema. She also had three
children and worked at night while her husband was laid off. We
were both in our late twenties and politically astute – or so we
thought – and we startled many a customer by interjecting our own
particular viewpoint into their overheard conversations. Standing
there, plates Choyn hand, we were more like guests at their table
than what we were supposed to be. Hard work though it was, this
was a great education in human nature. Everyone should work in a
restaurant at some point in their lives, not for a week but a good
year.

I tried unsuccessfully to get Bim help. He alternated between
dark swirls of Southern aristocratic depression and bouts of
grandiose highs. One psychiatrist said that if I left him, his suicide
would be on my head. I left after an episode in the middle of the
night, drove to Connecticut with the three children, the cats and the
birds swaying in the cage, and settled in a weather-beaten house at
Milford on Long Island Sound, eventually getting a divorce. Bim
lived for many years, remarried and became quite rich, thus
achieving everything he craved: an estate (a whole mountainside
really), Irish wolfhounds patrolling the fences, and Scottish High-
land cattle (which unfortunately froze to death, from facing the
wrong way to the wind, I believe).

I married the Irish Catholic owner of the company for which I was working, which made prefabricated houses; they were all the rage after Levittown, Long Island. It was the kind of business that left lots of room for those with enterprising minds and few ethics. I was the secretary, did the advertising, and even laid out a septic leach field. Since I believed that everything I was told was the truth, I was made treasurer of the company, dealt with the lawyers and banks, and was sent out into the field to talk the workmen into signing the hard-to-get waivers of lien.

After years of (1) death-defying vacations in the form of aeroplane trips in his small, single-engined Luscombe without radio, lights or heater; landing on a farmer's field in the middle of woods having run out of sunlight; flying through restricted areas and nearly being shot down; flipping over on landing, causing gasoline to pour into the cockpit and fumes to swirl around the recently extinguished pipe clenched between his teeth (2) trips in small boats that ended with my children being run aground in storms in Long Island Sound, and (3) drinking and other problems, the marriage was over. With my new daughter Kerry, I once more moved back to Woodstock. Having won a legal separation, I then faced years of court trials, always winning but exhausting my whole family and our finances.

Lee's mother died suddenly at about this time, and I saw him briefly in a restaurant where my mother and I were having lunch. He was sitting with his wife Betty, and he came to our table and asked me, in so many words, to forgive him. 'Some people,' he said, 'can sometimes be very stupid, and can think about it all the time.' I had seen Lee only once before in the past eleven years. I had been walking in Woodstock with my four-year-old son Rod and three-year-old daughter Wendy in a stroller and he was suddenly in front of me. He was tanned, wearing a bright shirt, long yellow madras shorts, sandals and knee socks, and looked very much the Californian. He always did dress handsomely. I proudly showed him my son and daughter and he tried to find his wife and son and daughter, but she was nowhere to be found. I did not see him again until 1962 – except, of course, on the screen.

Between Lee's first film, *You're In the Navy Now*, in 1951 and 1962 he was in thirty-one movies! I felt such pride when I saw him: he was so very good at whatever he did. In *Eight Iron Men, The*

Glory Brigade, Attack and other war films he played soldiers in combat – which he knew a good deal about – and when he was villainous or diabolical, in movies like *The Big Heat*, *The Comancheros* or *The Man Who Shot Liberty Valance*, it made me laugh so much. During that same time he was also constantly on television in an incredibly wide range of roles. In one *Twilight Zone* episode he was an ex-boxer struggling to make a living as manager/promoter of a boxing robot, 'Battling Maxo'. When it breaks down before a fight with a rival robot, Lee takes its place, only to be beaten to a pulp. He was very believable as the fighter, just as he was as the other characters he portrayed: 'Mr Death' with Eva Marie Saint in *A Rider On A Pale Horse* for General Electric Theater; a clown of a pitcher for the New York Giants as 'Charlie Faust' for TV Reader's Digest; Pima Indian Ira Hayes in John Frankenheimer's *The American*. He was in other television movies, in *Bonanza*, in *Dr Kildare*, in Kraft Suspense Theater productions and, of course, his own series *M Squad*: 'My name is Detective Lieutenant Frank Ballinger, M Squad, a special detail of the Chicago Police.' He was everywhere.

Once more I went back to Woodstock with my four children – and now a horse, dog, puppies, cat and kittens – and started working in radio. First with taped programs, interviewing artists, craftsmen, local characters and later performers in New York; then with a children's story hour called *Kerry's Magic Castle*. I was the fairy godmother coming to the castle tower bedroom to read to my daughter Kerry every night, with appropriate sound effects of horse-drawn carriage, drawbridges clanging and gentle, whispery music. I wish I still had some of those tapes, but they were destroyed when my house burned down. I also worked as an announcer from four until midnight, 'running the board' as DJ, newsreader, engineer, often running the whole station. On Sunday I ran both AM and FM, which in the beginning led to a fair degree of havoc: church services were broadcast where they were never expected to be. It was very exciting, though being newly-hired *and* a woman guaranteed me all the worst possible shifts. I loved it however – and I was the one who announced that a man had stepped on to the moon.

One day a shiny black car drove into my driveway and Lee

stepped out. I was painting my living room, and paint had dripped on my hair and down my arm. I had jeans on and an old shirt. It must have been in the summer of 1966 or 1967. He had come to visit his father. I hadn't seen him for years. By then he had won the Academy Award as best actor. Whenever I saw him in a movie, on television or read about him, I always had the unreasonable feeling that he was 'mine': my other half gone away. There was a formless sense of future promise that I felt in my being, though not in my head – something like knowing that a storm is approaching when the sun is brilliantly shining.

I was very excited about just having seen *The Seven Samurai*, and I said to Lee that he must some day make a movie with Toshiro Mifune: 'You both have such force and such speed on film . . . you get from one side of the room to the other so fast.' Lee smiled and lowered his head, saying nothing.

He took me to a small party at his father's neighbour's house. The man in the wheelchair unable to speak because of a stroke was the son or nephew of George Innis, a member of the 1890s Hudson River school of painting. Lee was convinced that the man's wife Ruth and his father were having an affair, and that Innis knew it but was helpless. He and Lee looked at each other with under-standing. Soon after he died, Ruth married Lee's father and kept up the tradition of drinking and stirring up family battles. This afternoon they were all drinking, and so was Lee. We drove around to places we had driven to years before, and then, in a restaurant, at the bar, he said to me, 'Will you come with me *now*?' He was very drunk; I had never seen him like that. I didn't know what to say to him.

A year or so passed. There was a knock on my door and it was Lee again. I was in the middle of tiling my bathroom floor and once again was in an absolute mess, very bedraggled. It was quite discouraging. He looked great, but was appallingly thin. He said, 'Well, I did it!' and I said, 'Did what?' 'Made the movie with Toshiro Mifune!'

He told me that when I had mentioned Mifune the year before, he and the Japanese actor had already decided to do *Hell in the Pacific* together, and had just signed the agreement. Lee made the film with John Boorman on the Palau Islands in Micronesia. He lost forty pounds during the shooting, which involved five months of great physical exertion and little substantial food.

Lee pulled out the script of *Paint Your Wagon* and we went over it with cups of coffee in my kitchen. He asked who I thought would be good as the female lead. I thought briefly, visualized a blonde and suggested Faye Dunaway. His reply was, 'Oh, that's OK, never mind.' (My opinion was not sought again.) Jean Seberg was, of course, chosen for the role.

Whenever Lee came to visit his ailing father he stopped by for coffee and to catch up on the years – this happened perhaps five or six times after our chance meeting when his mother died. On one visit he took me to see *Point Blank*, the movie he had filmed with John Boorman just before *Hell in the Pacific*. It was playing at a drive-in! He put his arm around my shoulders *and* bought me an ice-cream cone.

With Lee, nothing was ever trivial. He only asked important questions and he only told me the highs and the lows. He wanted to know if my son was OK as far as the draft was concerned. The Vietnam War was then at its height and he was totally against it. He thought he had fought *the* war: for his son, my son, everybody's sons. My son was OK, his son was OK – but if my son were not, I was to call him.

I knew from our mutual friends and the newspapers that Lee was long separated from his wife, a fact he mentioned to me as well. He also told me about a 'girlfriend', Michelle Triola. He described her briefly and not ungallantly, but I thought something was not right. Thereafter, she called me several times looking for him, and wouldn't believe me when I said I didn't know where he was. In fact, she surprised me with her insistence.

By now we had added a goat to our menagerie, and Lee thought it most amusing when my daughter Wendy sneaked it in through her window and had it prancing around her bedroom. Always interested in nature and animals – in fact, in everything – and somewhat medically inclined (his long fingers could work with great precision), he once 'operated' on a kitten of Kerry's, removing a grub from a hole in its side with sterilized tweezers. Children loved Lee for his voice, his straightforward approach, and his refusal to talk down to them. At four or five years old Kerry would sit on his lap contentedly, though she hardly knew him. Later on, our grandchildren would giggle happily when he roared at them in mock anger: the booming voice and menacing gestures seemed to delight all children.

I was fired from the radio station by the manager after about five years of working there. He told me when I was hired by the owner that he would be actively trying to replace me as he personally did not like women on radio. This was my first experience – I've since had a few others – of that kind of attitude. The other DJs and engineers were a great help to me, though, not only in learning the 'board' but in getting my engineer's license too. I said to the station manager, 'You know I can sue you for discrimination.' He replied that he knew I could. He also knew that I wouldn't. He had found his male replacement: a small, skinny young man with a deep voice. I did enjoy the last word because years later, after Lee and I were married, he asked to interview me on the radio. 'Uh uh,' I replied, 'you don't like women on radio.'

I was disappointed about leaving radio as I was beginning to feel quite accomplished at the whole business: such as *not* breaking up when I was reading the news and another DJ was making funny faces at me through the control-room window; making my own commercials and selling them to the advertisers; and doing taped interviews with interesting people on my program. The station was in the small Hudson Valley city of Kingston, but I did these interviews in New York City, Maine or wherever I could. I had a very old portable Apex tape recorder (almost too heavy to carry), which I lugged to Sol Hurok's productions of D'Oyly Carte operettas, to ballets, to meet actors (Anthony Quayle and others), comedians (Henny Youngman) and radio personalities (Soupy Sales), Bob and Ray, who took me into their own recording studio and used their engineer. People like Ann Corio (who told me about her stripteasing days), José Quintero (now a famous director), Merv Griffin and Shel Silverstein (writer-musician) were all gracious and giving of their time. I talked to engineers on old steam railways, lobster fishermen, back-country farmers playing the fiddle and to folk singers such as Sam Eskin, who also lived in Woodstock and would often help me with dubbing or retaping on the professional Ampex in his recording studio. And I talked to Lee after he won the Oscar for *Cat Ballou*.

Lee told me it was a very difficult movie to make because of the pressure of the twenty-eight-day shooting schedule and the fact that the director, Elliot Silverstein, was at odds with the producer. Lee shared Silverstein's vision of the film, and appreciated his courage in holding out for what he wanted. Lee had accepted the role after many actors – including Kirk Douglas, who didn't think it was much of a part – turned it down. Lee had also wanted the silver nose of Kid Sheleen's twin brother to look very sharp and be pointed downwards like a can-opener, but the studio didn't like the idea. It was only a minor disappointment.

Radio was something I could do in my own time, working mostly at home splicing the tapes, editing, laying in music and so on. I did have to work, of course; I had four children and little money to support them. Although I felt that the children's fathers should be financially responsible for them, I thought it was my responsibility as well, and perhaps more so. In each case I was the one who had insisted upon leaving the marriage; I also had the joy of raising the children and having them with me every day. I did not ask for alimony nor accept any; after all, I was not helpless. I didn't believe in it – and still don't, in most cases. My feeling about child support was that if a man did not have his own sense of right and wrong, or care about his child's welfare, he would have to live with that on his conscience. And it worked out, up to a point. This is not to say that I am a martyr or that I disapprove of the law going after parents who don't support their children; I did, after all, go to court on one occasion to win a legal separation as well as support for one of my children. I won, but after that I was repeatedly drawn into court for more than five years, not fighting for alimony or child support but for a child's total welfare. In the end I traded child support for a divorce.

When a barn of mine burned down, Lee heard about it and told a friend of mine, Tobie Geertsema, that he was disappointed I hadn't asked him for help. I had never mentioned it to him. But when I had to hire a new and very expensive attorney, I did call Lee and he lent me the money, which I paid back!

At this period I came to realize that judges are not always what one imagines: black-robed dispensers of perfect justice, all-knowing, scrupulously honest, absolutely fair and above all *interested*. I found that they are human beings with all the frailties of the rest of us: as a favourite expression of one of my attorneys goes, 'he puts his legs in his pants one at a time just like the rest of us'. I learned about the politics of law, and how people can manipulate the law. In America anyone can keep you in court if they have a mind to until you are mentally, physically and financially exhausted. It is truly a wonder that so many correct judgments come down. This legal action robbed me and my four children of years of mutual attention, as we had to focus on defending these suits. I sold my engagement and wedding rings and anything of value to pay costs, and had it not been for my lawyer Frank Gavin, who fought for me constantly and who accepted whatever the court awarded as payment, we would have not persevered. The case was not even brought to a definitive end until Lee and I were married and a local judge found it interesting enough to get outraged himself.

4 Marrying Lee

In the summer of 1970 my mother and I decided we would take a trip. My son was twenty-one years old and almost out of college, my oldest daughter was twenty. I didn't even have a bar of sweet-smelling soap! My life had to change. My parents had lived in Santa Fe, New Mexico, in the 1920s, and my mother had not been back for a long time. We decided to go there and then on to California: we had been invited to stay with my first husband Mac and his mother in West Hollywood. I rented my small house for the month of August to a man, his wife and their big white dog for $400, a fortune at the time.

My sister Gale lent us her car, which being eastern had no air conditioning, and my brother Jimmy gave us his Texaco credit card. Just before we left I saw Lee's brother and sister-in-law, who told me that Lee was away in Palau where he had a fishing boat. We also took along my youngest daughter Kerry, who was eight years old, my daughter Maury, thirteen, and my niece Pixie, ten. We had a glorious time crossing America. We learned that every 'reason-able' motel was next to the railroad tracks; that, yes, truck drivers know the best restaurants on the road, and that the further west one got, the bigger the stack of pancakes and the more free coffee was poured into an empty cup. We circled Chicago, then on through the corn and wheat fields to Colorado Springs, Santa Fe, New Mexico and Taos. Here we brought artist Andrew Dasburg taped messages from his old friends in Woodstock. Andrew's voice was used many years later at the beginning of the movie *Reds*. The reason he doesn't appear on screen in the movie is because, after all the time it took the movie crew to set up the lights and equipment, cameras etc, he was tired (he was over eighty years old) and took a nap. The company was so incensed at his being unavailable that they struck it all and taped only his voice when he awoke.

66

Andrew and my parents had been great friends both in Woodstock and in Santa Fe and Taos, in the early days when the artists from the two towns went back and forth.

We planned to drive through the hot desert from Flagstaff, Arizona, to Barstow, California, at night, but managed instead to reach Needles, California, the hottest spot in the country, at high noon. The temperature at the tiny gas station was 120°. My mother rode the rest of the day with an icepack on her head, the children with wet towels around their heads, their long straight hair drenched and whipping around their faces in the wind from the open windows. People in passing cars looked at us in horror. For some reason I – who drink hot tea on the hottest days – thought it all terribly funny and laughed all the way until we screeched to a halt outside the Howard Johnson's restaurant at the edge of the desert. We straggled out of the car, faces beet-red. Johnny Weissmuller was just leaving and opened the door for us. He burst out laughing at our entrance to California. I later learned from Lee that he had bought Weissmuller's house in Santa Monica and lived there with his wife and four children until their divorce.

We stayed a week. One day, thinking that Lee was away, I called his business manager to leave a message that I had been there. 'Oh, but he *is* in town,' was the reply. Lee came that evening in his enormous white car. He and Mac shook hands with a somewhat forced heartiness, I thought. He took me to dine on my first clawless lobster at a restaurant in Venice. Lee did not have a drink. Afterwards he took me to his handsome house on the beach at Malibu, where he proudly showed me his many awards: his Gold Disc for 'Wand'rin' Star' from *Paint Your Wagon*; the horse and rider statue, the Western Heritage Award from the National Cowboy Hall of Fame for *The Man Who Shot Liberty Valance* ('Gosh,' Lee said, 'John Ford had John Wayne, everybody's hero, shoot me in the back!'); the British Academy Award for Best Foreign Actor; Spain's Silver Nugget Award; Best Costumer's Award; Best Actor from the Hollywood Foreign Press; the shoe Vivien Leigh beat him over the head with in *Ship of Fools*; the Berlin Bear Award for *Cat Ballou* – and the Oscar for his performance in the same film. It's much heavier than one suspects, I found, when he handed the statuette to me. It was a lovely, reflective moment, sitting on the floor together, his Oscar in my lap, he so quietly joyous. He talked about his friendships on *Paint Your Wagon* with Clint Eastwood, Jean Seberg and Josh Logan, the director, and his wife Nedda. I could see he really loved the movie and the filming, laughing and shaking his head as he recounted it. 'Alan J. Lerner, who was the producer, had a nervous habit of chewing his nails when watching a scene or getting "into it" with Josh Logan, so he wore these white gloves. By the end of the day they were in shreds and had to be replaced.' Lee's descriptions were vivid, and when he talked of the location it came alive for me. The last time we had talked about *Paint Your Wagon* was with the script in my kitchen two years before. He enjoyed telling me what had happened in the meantime. We listened to records of musical scores from his films, particularly *The Professionals*, one of my favourite movies. 'Maurice Jarre – great!' Lee said. He played 'Wand'rin' Star' and hummed along in that deep voice of his. He showed me his shell collection from Palau and from his beach in Malibu. We walked out on to the beach, we did not even hold hands; stars were shining in the wide sky, the waves rolled peacefully back and forth. He went over to what was probably the end of 'his' beach and urinated. 'My God!' I thought, 'he still loves me.'

Driving back that evening, he told me he had just had a call from his father, who was sick again. Lee said he would be flying back and would arrive in Woodstock at around the same time as I would driving . . . *also* that he would be in New York with Jeanne Moreau promoting his movie *Monte Walsh*. My heart sank. I had heard of their affair during the filming, and felt deflated; she had been quoted as saying, 'Lee Marvin is more male than anyone I ever acted with. He is the greatest man's man I have ever met, and that includes all the European actors that I have worked with.'[1] She was very beautiful, a French film star, and had moreover asked him to come and live with her in the south of France. I couldn't see Lee living in the south of France; in the end, I guess, he couldn't either.

Lee did come back to Woodstock. We had dinner together with friends, Connie and Corrado Goeffredi. The next day he picked me

1 *The Great Movie Stars – The International Years* by David Shipman, St Martin's Press, 175 5th Avenue, New York, New York, 10010.

up and we went to his father's house, where they talked about Jeanne Moreau. They had heard that Lee was seeing her, and asked if he was going to marry her. He didn't answer. Then he was off to New York for a week of promotion with Jeanne Moreau. I watched all the shows. On *Johnny Carson* they played a game of questions – one of those where you try to find out someone's true likes and dislikes. I watched with mounting apprehension. As it turned out, amid great excitement and applause, Jeanne Moreau's first love was work and Lee's was hearth and home!

He called one day and asked if I would be home on a certain night and that I not go anywhere. I baked an apple pie and sent the children to my mother's. It was nine or ten o'clock when a huge black limousine drew up and Lee and his driver Tony stepped out. Lee flung open my kitchen door and with one push slid his suitcase all the way into the living room. He stood in the doorway and said, 'You know I've come to get you, don't you?'

Tony came in, we all had pie, then Tony clambered back into the limo and drove away.

We spent a week together, talking, reminiscing, filling in. We walked for hours in the soft rain, the autumn leaves underfoot, and at long last we made love again. Lee bought a tape of the Beatles, 'The Long and Winding Road', for me and played it over and over. We talked of our children: his son and three daughters, my son and three daughters, all about the same ages. We talked of what we could do for them together. We talked of our doubts. Our lives were vastly different, but also very similar. We had both separated in the same year, divorced some six years later, and had both just finished turbulent and very uncomfortable relationships. We even found that the doctor in New York City who had delivered all my children was a close friend of the doctor in California who had delivered all Lee's children. There were so many amazing coincidences that it was as if some other hand were bringing order to our separate lives, drawing them unerringly together. Although we had only seen each other on six or seven brief occasions in twenty-three years – and without one intimate moment – it seemed as though no time at all had gone by. He was the same, I was the same. The closing of a circle.

At the end of the week we went to my parents' house and Lee

said to my father, 'Jack, I want to marry your daughter.' My father was sitting in his usual spot, just close enough to the front door to be annoyed when it opened. It was a wonderful moment: Lee asking for my hand. I was forty years old and he forty-six. My father looked at him over the rim of his glasses: 'You're crazy.' Then his eyes turned to me: 'You're both crazy.' And he went back to his book. A moment later, he lowered the book and said, 'Well, maybe you're not.'

California in October was brilliantly sunny and warm – we had left Woodstock immediately. Lee's housekeeper Mae Osborne was excited and welcoming. I had one dress. Lee insisted I leave everything else behind, like some shedded outer skin. The dress was rayon blend, machine washable, patterned in muted colors with castles, flowers, leaves. I arrived in it, went to the Malibu market in it, and went to a huge press conference in it, where I sat listening while Lee told the Foreign Press Club that no, no, he was quite done with marriage, he would never marry again.

The following day Jim Mahoney, Lee's publicist, and his wife Pat met us at Santa Monica airport. He ushered us aboard Frank Sinatra's De Havilland jet *Christina*, kindly lent for the occasion. We soared up and down and were soon in Las Vegas, secretly and unpublicized. Lee wanted no snags, no hold-ups, no attempts at sabotage. He also had a great and sometimes impish sense of theatrical timing. We were swept along, filling out licenses that had already been arranged. Up we went in the elevator to the penthouse of the International Hotel with its lush, pale-colored carpets, the evening breeze fluttering the filmy yellow drapes as it blew in from the balcony overlooking the city's lights. The room was enormous and filled with bouquets of red roses; a gigantic, many-tiered wedding cake was waiting. Pat and Jim were our best man and matron of honor, as warm and loving as though I had always known them. They witnessed our vows, presided over by a funny little man who gave the stamp of approval for our life together. I was shaking, Lee was absolutely not. He slid the ring on to my finger calmly, confidently. It fitted. It still fits. It had not been measured: Jim had bought it from Tiffany's for me, sight unseen, the day before. After the ceremony the minister asked me my name. I said, 'Pamela Feeley.' He laughed – a set-up. 'No, it's Pamela Marvin. Don't worry,

you'll remember it soon enough when you start writing the checks.'
A cynicism borne of too many Las Vegas marriages, perhaps.

On cue, the maître d' flourished the cake knife, but Lee stopped him with a joke about not spoiling it for the next wedding party waiting to use the room. We did have our own cake, actually, made by our friend Connie Goeffredi. We ate it with champagne, sitting on soft leather couches in the aircraft 25,000 feet up in the air. We sat with the pilots in the cockpit and watched the evening lights of Los Angeles come into view. As we landed, Jim took his black leather book and pen from his jacket pocket and said to me, 'Tell me something about yourself. By tonight you will have become a household word.'

We were home and propped up in bed in time for the eight o'clock news on television. It was like an explosion all over the country. The telephone started ringing. I saw what Lee had meant. His agent called; Michelle Triola called. Lee answered wearily, 'No, Michelle, it's not a joke' – the first of hundreds of telephone calls from her by day, by night, in the middle of the night. Friends, detractors, the press called. Most were happy. Lee's son Chris came bounding in with a compliment – 'Gee, Dad, I'm happy for you. I'm glad to see it wasn't some ding-a-ling!' – and sat on our bed eating wedding cake.

Earlier, having heard rumors that Lee might marry and becoming convinced it would be to Jeanne Moreau, his father kept shaking his head and saying, 'I wasn't aware Moreau had children.' Lee called him the following morning and said, 'Chief, I got married.'

'I heard.'

'Well, what do you think?'

'No comment.'

Which, instead of upsetting Lee, seemed to amuse him, and he chuckled when he told me.

We went back to pick up my younger children. I hadn't been aware of the effect of the marriage on Woodstock. Impromptu, joyous parties had broken out among our friends, we had telephone calls and letters. White-haired ladies on canes said to Lee and me, 'Oh, I'm so glad you two children finally got married.' I had no idea anyone had noticed at the time. Thomas Wolfe, you're wrong – you *can* go home again.

5 Malibu

Lee's small house in Malibu was on the beach called LaCosta. It was directly across the street from the old sheriff's station, which was sometimes rather unlucky for Lee in his old rambunctious days. The Los Angeles Sheriff's Department and the Pacific Coast Highway Patrol kept a wary eye out for any weaving car. There were times when he had only to back out of his driveway to be surrounded by a cordon of waiting police cars. He bought the house after his separation from his first wife, and had one of the two bedrooms ingeniously remodelled into a children's room for all four of his young children, Christopher, Courtenay, Cynthia and Claudia. (All of them also had L as their middle initial, as did Lee's mother Courtenay.) It was an otherwise very masculine house of dark wood, deep red carpeting and handsome, strong-looking furniture. The sliding glass door led to the outside wooden porch. There were five steps down to the sand – except when a storm had recently beaten away the beach, leaving them suspended in the air. In rough seas the surf could be felt pounding under the porch and the house, like most on the beach at Malibu, was built on pilings and logs banged together underneath. It was unsettling to me, but exhilarating to Lee.

We didn't leave the house for several weeks after we were married, except to go to the Malibu Market and shop together for food. We sat on the patio in the brilliant sunshine, having the breakfast that Mae cooked and served. She adored Lee and obviously enjoyed working for him. She was wonderful, taking over the care of Kerry when we went away, as well as everything else.

One day we were invited to a party at the home of Jennifer Jones, who lived just down the beach. José Quintero was sitting on the porch as we walked up, and when he saw me coming he joyously reached down and lifted me up over the railing. We had not seen each other for many years, nor had he seen Lee since the late 1940s. It was a sweet reunion. Jennifer Jones was charming, having obviously forgiven Lee for once joking to the press about life on the beach in Malibu, 'You never know when you are going to come out your door and see a nude Jennifer Jones surfing in on a wave' – alluding to her well-publicized suicide attempt when she *was* found floating in on a wave. Stewart Granger was at the party, wearing a safari suit and a tiger-skin band around his khaki hat, looking as though he had just stepped out of his role in *King Solomon's Mines*. It was a very pleasant introduction to Hollywood.

There are few more delightful places than Malibu for your morning coffee when the sun is sparkling on the sea and the breeze is warm. Pounding waves break rhythmically on the shore, receding gently to the swishing sound of small shells and pebbles. Lee knew every species of bird: the sandpipers, the marbled godwits, the different terns. We threw pieces of toast for the gulls, which appeared from nowhere to snap them out of the air before they hit the sand. He pointed out the gray whales swimming, feeding, rolling and whacking their tails on the surface on their way to the warm waters of Mexico. At night we cooked steak on the hibachi on the porch and watched the sun set over Point Dume. Lee, usually a trim one hundred and eighty pounds, for the first time in his life now weighed two hundred and fifteen pounds! Bliss, as described by Joseph Campbell, is 'The deep sense of being where your body and soul wants you to be.' I felt now that I finally understood the term.

We were married on 18 October 1970, and about three weeks later Lee took me into Beverly Hills to meet his business manager Ed Silver and go over his accounts, sign checks and so on. When that was finished, Lee looked over at me expectantly and said, 'OK, now tell me. What do you owe and where do you owe it?'

He was quite prepared to bail me out of all my debts, expecting plenty of them. Luckily I had few, but he clearly would not have criticized me if I had; pen in hand, he was going to fix it all for me.

The first person Lee brought into our quiet was John Boorman. He called in on his way from London bringing the script of *Deliverance*, the movie he eventually made with Jon Voight and

Burt Reynolds. John and Lee were close friends with a deep respect for each other, gained initially by making two movies together, *Point Blank* and *Hell in the Pacific*. Of their first meeting Lee said, 'I was filming *The Dirty Dozen* in London when I met John Boorman for the first time. A young producer, Judd Bernard, wanted me for one of his projects, the adaptation of a thriller that was to become *Point Blank*. Boorman came to my home several times and we immediately got on the same wavelength. We'd talk about emotions, about mythologies . . . It was one of those chance meetings that evolve into a friendship. Later I suggested we make a movie together. We had a good relationship on both a personal and an intellectual level. We swapped ideas on Zen Buddhism, on war, on the movie's visuals. Boorman's very good at speaking with actors; for some of them he can even be too intellectual. Working with him isn't easy; but for me that's a compliment, because he forces you to think. When you begin a day's shooting under his direction you know that by the evening you're going to be worn out by the demands he makes on you. And that's his right. I've worked with other directors – Ford, Lang, Hathaway – but they belonged to the old school and they never addressed a word to you. Boorman knows everything there is to know about movies, from the editing down to the choice of a color scheme. He's also got a terrific sense of humor.'[1] It was a wonderful meeting for me, and then later to get to know him and his wife Christel.

Lee was fascinated by John's script of the James Dickey novel, and was very interested in making the film. He and John sat and talked about the story and about moonshine, which Lee knew a lot about – how it's made, what the old stills looked like. He played John some hillbilly music from his collection. Marlon Brando also wanted to be in this movie. Each said he did not care which of the two major roles he played. Both characters were powerfully written; one rising to great strength, the other falling to the depths of weakness. In the end Lee did not do the film, for two reasons. Firstly, he felt that if he and Marlon, being older men, were to play the roles, they would not have got into the quandary or suffered the guilt required to make sense of their reactions to the plot.

---

1 *John Boorman* by Michel Climent, Faber and Faber Ltd.

Given the decisions the characters in the movie would have to make, he felt they should be played by younger men. After seeing the finished film, he felt that not only had he made the right decision, but that the performances of Jon Voight and Burt Reynolds could not have been improved upon. It was also nice to see, after the movie was screened before release, all the actors coming one by one up to Lee for his reactions and comments: Jon, Ned Beatty and Ron Cox. Lee was generous and thorough in his critique.

The second reason was because Lee's theatrical agent Meyer Mishkin wanted him to make another film, *Prime Cut*. Meyer's argument was that he, Meyer, needed the money, and whereas *Deliverance* was only at the initial stages – not all the financial backing had been found – the other movie was ready to go, money in hand. Meyer said that his 'nut', as Lee would put it, for the rent on his office on Sunset Boulevard was not being covered at that time, as few of 'his' actors were bringing in much commission. Lee felt a supreme sense of loyalty to Meyer, who had been his agent since the early 1950s, ever since Henry Hathaway had asked him to represent Lee. Lee also had something of a son–father feeling toward Meyer, perhaps seeing him as an authority figure because of his expertise in 'the business'. At this point in his career Lee did what movies he wanted to do and declined those he did not (although I think that may always have been true): for example, he turned down *Jaws*, flinging the script into the fireplace saying, 'What a piece of shit!' much to the extreme and everlasting chagrin of Meyer. As his agent, Meyer would have received 10 per cent not only of Lee's $1 million salary but also of the approximately $10 million more Lee would have earned from his 10 per cent share of the profits. At the time, however, Lee said he didn't want to 'scare old ladies and kids from swimming in the ocean,' and furthermore, he wouldn't 'cop out' on all his fishing buddies and make such nonsense. 'Besides, fish don't kill me – I kill fish!' I know Lee's heart lay in *Deliverance*, but he opted to make *Prime Cut*.

During the first few weeks after we were married, we hid out a great deal in the protected environment of Malibu. I slowly got used to the publicity, the press and the public. Then, early on, Lee introduced me to two of his closest friends, Betty and Norman

Lessing; Norman, a television writer and playwright, had written some of the stories for *M Squad.* They had long been neighbours of Lee's when he lived in the lush green Rustic Canyon in Santa Monica, at 2 Latimer Lane, the house he bought from Johnny Weissmuller. 'And can you believe,' Lee said, 'it didn't even have a swimming pool!'

Lee was always interested in architecture, and remodelled the Latimer Lane house, adding a den and a bar – where he occasionally shot the whisky bottles off in exuberance or anger. After he left his first wife Betty, he put in the swimming pool for his kids.

There were two popular neighbourhood bars in Malibu at the time. One that Lee had had much to do with building, and then with supporting, was the Raft. Another hang-out for the Malibu old guard was the Cottage, a thin little place backed on the ocean by Malibu Pier. Having heard stories about it – the camaraderie, the characters, the loyalty of the regulars toward the different stars who might come there (they knew their secrets would not be told) – I was prepared for a really fascinating place. I was disappointed. If it had been great once – like some old pub in Dublin, perhaps, or the Seahorse in Woodstock – it certainly wasn't great any more. It was a dingy place where people only remembered, where hangers-on sat and drank and smoked and pretended that movie stars meant nothing to them. Lee, having his own DWI (Driving While Intoxicated) citation at that time, would occasionally ride his new bicycle there of an afternoon (I'm sure he bought it for just this purpose), wobbling home with victorious salutes to the inquisitive police cars as they cruised slowly by.

We moved from the small house on the Pacific Coast Highway to the Malibu Colony when more and more of our collective children came to live with us. We moved twice in the Colony, from a sprawling four-bedroomed house with a lanai – a long sun-room facing the ocean – to a huge house with ten bedrooms, five bathrooms and three living rooms that Julie Christie called a 'bloody 'otel'. The Colony was a wonderful place for us to be at the time. It was safe and well away from the heavy traffic of the Pacific Coast Highway. There were lots of other kids, berms in the one street to slow down the cars, and everything that was needed was close by: the fire station, the police, and the markets. It is a long thin line of opulent houses ('Yeah, but they're all built on sand,' said Lee) on one of the finest stretches of beach in the country. There was a guarded gate at the entrance and fences cut off the area at either end. The people who lived there were almost entirely from the movie industry in one form or another and, at least at the time, there was a community spirit. We had great neighbours: Larry and Maj Hagman lived just a few doors away, Burgess Meredith just next to them, director John Frankenheimer and his wife Evans lived down one way, Rod Steiger up the other. Everyone, kids and all, were often at the Hagmans', where we'd sit in our bathing suits in the living-room jacuzzi sipping wine . . . or just visiting. Maj designed and built the jacuzzi herself. She also sewed costumes, not just for their children but for Larry too, who would march up and down the beach in them on holidays or Sundays: one day he might be a fireman, another day in karate garb.

Cary Grant, who lived nearby, would come out on Easter Sunday with his camera, smiling and taking pictures of the kids with their baskets. One morning, Lee and I were sitting on our patio having breakfast when I noticed a man walking down the beach in a very handsome yellow shirt. I pointed him out to Lee, who immediately retorted, 'You know perfectly well that is Cary Grant. Why don't you go over there and wiggle your varicose veins at him!' Wonderful, spirited Shirley MacLaine occasionally poked her head in at the door from the beach. Shirley was so full of light and color that my oldest daughter Wendy adored her. She also adored Cloris Leachman for her love of animals and her humor. Wendy worked for a time at the LA County Animal Hospital, and often brought home animals that were sick or going to be destroyed. She filled the neighbours' houses with them, especially that of producer John Foreman and his wife Linda.

Clint Eastwood and his wife Maggie also stopped by. For me Maggie personified the Californian 'golden girl': healthy-looking, blonde, tanned and very attractive. The first time I met her she was wearing a pair of suede gaucho pants she had bought in Spain, where Clint had just been filming. He was one of the handsomest men I had ever seen, tall, straightforward and warm.

Throughout the years, from early on in his career, Lee's closest friend had been Keenan Wynn. They met when Lee was filming *The Wild One* with Marlon Brando – the 1954 Stanley Kramer movie which pitted Lee and Brando against each other as rival motorcycle gang leaders. The movie was inspired by the account of a group of bikers who supposedly took over and terrorized the small town of Hollister, California, in the late 1940s.

Lee was a novice at riding motorcycles when he started the film, but not for long. He was a natural born athlete, tall, lean and graceful, and riding these powerful bikes was just up his alley. He quickly learned to love biking and threw himself into every aspect of it for years. As with almost anything else he attempted, he mastered it easily and with style.

Keenan Wynn was already an expert rider. He raced in competitions and was known in motorcycling circles and in the world of the movie stunt men as the all-time best of the many movie people who gravitated toward the sport. It was Keenan who taught Lee to ride, and he very quickly became not only his riding buddy but one of his closest friends.

Sharley Wynn, Keenan's wife, says, 'Keenan desperately wanted to be in the movie *The Wild One*, but he was under contract at the time and the studio would not release him. He was heartbroken, but he offered his services anyway. He took Lee riding through the desert, taught him, helped him with his equipment, and advised him on bikes. They rode with Cary Loftin [stunt man and co-ordinator on the film, also responsible for helping Lee] and a bunch of other men. Later, Bud Eakins and Clyde Earl and one guy who seemed to fascinate Lee, "Wino Willie". Lee kept watching him when they were riding, and then fashioned Chino, his character in *The Wild One*, after this Wino Willie. He was a real person.'

After the movie was finished, Lee really got into motorcycles and then into competitions with Keenan. 'Keenan,' Sharley said, 'took him to Ted Evans, who had the motorcycle shop where everybody bought their bikes and where Lee bought his . . . then into the shops in Culver City for all those custom made leathers Lee wore: the jackets, pants, special boots and helmets. Lee bought a truck to haul the bikes up to the mountain trails or out to the desert. The truck was kept in our garage. Betty didn't want it in theirs. We had a cabin up in Wrightwood and Lee bought a ski lodge there where they would all ride.'

When they went in for the races – the Hare and Hounds or the Big Bear runs – Sharley went along. 'I *loved* it! I loved going out there and watching them start off . . . or I'd wait at a checkpoint or at the finish. Packed the picnics. *Loved* it . . . and the first motorcycle race Lee was ever in was the Big Bear Race . . . and he *won* it! . . . he beat Keenan!'

Hundreds of riders lined up for several miles across the Mojave desert at the start of the gruelling ride to the top of Big Bear Mountain. Rider after rider was disqualified or wrecked or fell out during the four hundred miles of track. As we have seen, Lee not only finished the first time he entered, he won it. The race happened to be sponsored by *TV Guide* and the Motorcycle TV Actor's Annual Award of 1958 went to Lee.

'They never drank before riding or a race,' said Sharley, 'but afterwards – oh, oh! Later on too, much later in the game, Steve McQueen also took it up, and would ride with them. Keenan and Lee also covered for each other in the drinking: one on, the other off – such as the time Lee was filming *Donovan's Reef* in Hawaii. He and Duke Wayne got drinking one night during the filming, and Lee must have forgotten what he was doing in Hawaii. He went to the airport shoeless, they made him buy a pair of thongs – he was wearing his blue flowered Hawaiian jams and a T-shirt that said "Suck 'em up". We were in bed in our house in Brentwood about eight o'clock in the morning and a loud knock came on the door. Our maid answered it and we heard Lee's booming voice ask, "Where's the King?" She answered that we were still in bed. We heard a thundering up the steps, the door was flung open and Lee threw himself on our bed saying, "Hiya, sweethearts!" We took him downstairs and tried to get some coffee into him and breakfast, but he'd only have coffee – and only if bourbon were in it. Keenan asked him, "Aren't you still working in Hawaii?" and Lee said, "Yeah, yeah." He'd borrowed some money from the unit manager, it turned out, and jumped on a plane. Keenan knew they would be looking all over for him, so he called his agent, who said, "Don't let him go!" About a half hour later his agent showed up in a limo and took him back. Went right with him to Hawaii. But one of the sweetest, funniest things that ever happened with them was when Lee won the Academy Award for *Cat Ballou* and was leaving the very next morning to go back to London where he was filming *The Dirty Dozen*. Keenan knew what time his flight was leaving and drove down to the airport on his motorcycle . . . the side hack. He pulled up just as Lee was getting out of the limo in front of the airport. Keenan had a *nosegay* in his hand, which he presented to him. The newspaper photographers went wild, and there was a picture in the LA papers, front page, Keenan Wynn giving Lee Marvin a little nosegay.' Sharley shook her head, smiling and remembering.

The Catalina Island race was another that Lee and Keenan competed in. Only three of them, actually, as the race had to be closed down because rowdy motorcycle gangs came to watch and kibitz – they got wild and drank and left the small town full of garbage. One day Lee and Keenan (Keeno as Lee called him) were on the boat that ferried everyone over to the island for these races, about a two-hour trip. Sharley's brother, a member of the pit crew (as was actor Everette Sloan), was with them. On the same boat were members of the Hell's Angels. They weren't in the race, of course, but were going over to watch and party. At that time, the late 1950s and early 1960s, Lee's television series *M Squad* was very popular. When they were out an hour or so offshore, one of the boat's security officers came up to them, nodded at Keenan and addressed Lee. 'Mr Marvin,' he said, 'we are having a problem here. The Hell's Angels are aboard and they are giving us some trouble. Would you mind coming and giving us a hand?' Lee put on his most serious detective mien and followed the officer over. Whether these tough-looking bikers identified Lee with his role in *M Squad* too, or respected him as a fellow-biker, or perhaps thought of him as 'Chino', no one will ever know, but with a few non-combative words – something like 'How's it going, guys? Think maybe you could keep it down a bit? Thanks, gentlemen' – and maybe a handshake or two, Lee dissipated the threat. He went back to Keenan and they quietly collapsed in laughter.

The first movie they made together was *Shack Out on 101* (the old name for the Pacific Coast Highway). Lee played a Russian agent posing as a short-order cook in a diner. (Once, just after Lee and I were married, I got up at three in the morning to see the film because of all his stories about it.) Terry Moore, to her everlasting delight, was in it with them. Keenan was also with Lee in *Point Blank* and, of course, a lot of television. I asked Sharley how she would describe Keenan's feelings for Lee, and without a pause she exclaimed, 'A brother!' As for her own feelings: 'Lee was fantastic. He was generous and he was just, just . . . *fantastic.*'

Very early on New Year's Day 1971 Lee came upstairs to wake me. He told me to hurry into a robe and come downstairs. I put on Lee's big bright-red bath robe and went down, not knowing what to expect. The kids were all downstairs, Chris, Rod, a friend of Rod's from Woodstock who had spent a lot of time living at our house there, Donovan Martin (Donovan's father was the artist Fletcher Martin with whom I had studied at the Art Students' League in 1947), Kerry, of course, Wendy, her son Jess and husband Lon. Keenan Wynn was there, and immediately ushered me outside to his motorcycle. It had a sidecar which I was invited to sit in to take a spin. Somehow I felt I didn't have a choice. Lee was also standing there, nodding his head. I thought to myself that it could do no harm to ride down the little Malibu Colony street, quiet on that New Year's morning, and I certainly felt an obligation to rise to the occasion. I got in and Keenan roared down the street, out of the main gate past the guard, on to the Pacific Coast Highway and north up and over the long hill, then sped back. I said not a word. It must have been a peculiar sight – I'm just lucky I didn't have curlers in my hair. When we got back, Keenan smiled at me and gave me a pat on the back. Lee looked pleased. I must have passed some sort of rite, mostly because I was able to hide my consummate fright. Sharley told me later that Keenan came home that day and reported to her that the house was so full of kids it was like the Brady Bunch – which is what he called us from then on.

The people most often at our house in Malibu at that time were those who had been with Lee in the movie *Monte Walsh*. They included Mitchell Ryan, a New York stage actor (also a member of the Actors' Studio), who had played Lee's adversary Shorty in the movie. Mitch often brought his wife Linda and their small son Timmy. Timmy reminded me of Peck's Bad Boy with his wind-tousled, blondish hair, runny nose, little tanned chest braced out in front of him, and his perennial shorts or bathing suit. He had a husky voice for a four-year-old and would say to his parents, 'Let's go visit Mabbabaloo,' his name for Lee. Other good friends were Matt and Carol Clark, who brought their new baby in a bassinet. Matt, an actor and director, had been in several movies with Lee, including *Monte Walsh* and *Pocket Money*. We had lunches, dinners and picnics together at our house or at theirs. Mitch and Linda lived on a horse ranch at Agoura on the other side of the Malibu Mountains, and Matt and Carol had a house they had built themselves on the top of a mountain above Malibu. They had goats, chickens, a donkey and a large vegetable garden. Carol, besides being a great and sweet mother, was also an artist.

A young man who came to see us a lot as well as the kids was Richard Doughty. Dick had been in the Peace Corps on Palau in Micronesia when Lee was there building his boat after the movie *Hell in the Pacific*. After meeting Lee, Dick decided he would like to try his hand at acting, so Lee got him a job as a dialogue coach on *Monte Walsh* to start him off. He would later have a very rough time in the trial brought against Lee by Michelle Triola. It always saddened us and it cost him dearly.

What I recall most about that time was the laughter. We laughed all the time. We had so much fun together, and so much fun with the kids. Lee had an enormous presence: he was a positive force in all our lives, and wonderful to live with. He was sometimes exasperating and complicated, at times even cruel, but never dull. At home between movie-making (he called these times of hibernation 'riding the low') we read, we swam, we entertained (Lee proudly introducing me with the claim 'the home-grown tomato is the best, you know') and – mostly – we talked. And sometimes Lee would drink. When we were young we all drank, of course, but not really a lot. Lee's drinking had now turned into a problem. He did not drink all the time, but at intervals: but when he *did*, he would drink until he was drunk, and he would stay that way for two or three days. At times, admittedly, the drinking was fun – even in its excess. It took you to places and people and situations you wouldn't be in if all your senses were intact. I joined in. Lee's high energy from alcohol took us to all-night bars in New York or around the world – long evenings of affectionate, jousting exchanges with Richard Burton, Oliver Reed, Robert Shaw, Robert Mitchum. Talk, talk, talk: his mind was always exploding with thoughts and we never lacked an audience, whether we were at home, at a restaurant or a party (the few we went to), or on a movie location. Lee was always searching with his quick mind, and when he drank the dams opened and every thought would bring him one more. He was a magnet, and not just because he was a very recognizable star: he seemed to open other people's floodgates as well.

When Lee and I were young, he was not an alcoholic; it grew on him later in Hollywood. The five or six times I saw him between when he left and when we were married, he drank about half the time. When sober, he was a gentleman. When he drank, he could be courtly as well, but he was just as likely to fling off the most exotic swearwords, or some not so exotic – such as when he referred to someone, either with affection or not, as a 'cunt'. After one such evening at a restaurant filled with people, Charles and Jill Bronson among them, Lee was in high ill-humor. He was noisily calling me, my mother and others at the table all sorts of unpleasantries. When we got home, he made some slurred remark and I, having taken all I could in public, picked up a plate in our kitchen and threw it at him. It crashed against the wall near his head, and then I slapped him. I simply lost it. My son-in-law remarked, 'It's about time.' Lee ambled off to bed, I think almost happy to be chastised, and the next day he was as usual so thoroughly apologetic and remorseful that I could only love him more. When he was drunk, it was as if some schizophrenic side erupted out of a dark recess. It wasn't the major part of him.

It was violence, but a violence of the mind expressed in words. He was not physical. His actions appalled him so much that it was almost as if he was standing to one side watching someone else. I once taped his conversation when he was drinking, but he was so frantic to have me stop I erased it immediately. On the first Christmas we had together after we were married Lee began to drink late in the morning. 'Just one wassail,' he declared. This had always been an important holiday for me and my family. My sisters, my brother and I descended upon my mother's house in

Woodstock from wherever we were living at the time, bringing our spouses and our children. My mother made an enormous fuss about Christmas. She baked for weeks beforehand, making cookies and all kinds of candies which she stored in big crocks in the attic. When we were kids we raided them as fast as she could make them. She had stockings on the mantelpiece for everyone in the family, young and old, and presents were piled high under the tree.

This was the first Christmas of my life I hadn't gone 'home'. We put a tree up in Malibu, and I had my decorations sent from Woodstock. Lee helped, but he wasn't really into it. He seemed to resent it, in fact – all that attention lavished on the tree! I also think he was somewhat taken aback by the fervour of this family tradition; it wasn't *his* tradition. Maybe it reminded him of other times perhaps not so happy. He had several 'wassails' and then, hurrying down the tiled hall floor, slipped and fell, hurting his elbow. We went over to the Malibu Medical Clinic and found that he had a broken bone. That pretty well took care of Christmas Day – *and* he hadn't given me a present. I had visions of a car, a Jaguar at the very least, or a big jewel of some sort on this first Christmas, but there was nothing! I was shocked after such high expectations. *Later* he bought me lovely gold necklaces, but as a surprise. I think he was so afraid of getting hooked into doing the normal thing, or of being forced to give a present because of a calendar date, that it went against the grain. On the other hand, on the following Christmas and every one thereafter he did a complete about-face and seemed to enjoy it as much, if not more, than anyone else. He insisted upon picking the tree, and would sit in a chair directing where each bulb or decoration would go, or doing it himself with us helping: 'More tinsel,' 'No, no, not there. Over here!' He inspected each present I bought for people, happily giving his approval or reminding me not to forget so-and-so, and himself going to great pains to surprise me with something meaningful. Lee was not someone who fitted into a mold.

The big house in the Colony was full of kids all the time. Kerry was nine and came with us almost everywhere we went, whether it was on movie locations around the world or to Hawaii fishing. Lee's son Chris came to live with us almost immediately, as his prep school at Lake Tahoe had folded. Lee's eldest daughter Courtenay –

My mother Gladys Downer, as a young woman of twenty-one, circa 1921.

Left to right: me, aged eight, my sister Ellen, my father John 'Jack' Feeley, my brother James, my mother Gladys D. 'Pid' Feeley. (My sister Gale is missing.)

Top right: Lee's mother, Courtenay Davidge Marvin, aged about nineteen.

Above: Lee's javelin days at St Leo College Preparatory School 1940–41. (Courtesy St Leo Abbey Archives.)

Left to right: Lee's older brother Robert and Lee at summer camp.

In the Marine corps at camp Maui, Hawaii, just before the invasion of the Marianna Islands: Lee (later wounded in action), Raymond Motter (W.I.A.), Harry Osborne Jr (W.I.A.), Leonard F. Trudo (K.I.A. on Iwo Jima), Wade A. Rayburn (W.I.A.) (Courtesy of Marines Robert Filkosky and Lester Juergenson.)

Left to right: Sergeant Macauly, Lee's father Lamont W. Marvin and Lee at Club Babalu in Los Angeles, Christmas 1943.

Lee's father 'Monty' and Lee in front of the Woodstock, New York, house in the 1960s.

Left: The young actor emoting.   Me, aged fifteen or sixteen.

Lee, as 'Texas' in *Roadside*, his first professional play at The Maverick Theater in 1947. (Courtesy of the Woodstock Historical Society.)

Lee in *Streetcar Named Desire* in summerstock with the Vagabond Players in 1948. (Courtesy of Jean Bellows Boothe.)

1950s portrait.

As 'Chino', in *The Wild One*, 1953.

lovely, tall and looking so like Lee – came soon after our marriage, having abruptly left her school in Switzerland. Shortly after that, Lee's ex-wife Betty returned from Italy, where she and Lee's youngest daughters, Cynthia and Claudia, had been living. We picked Cynthia and Claudia up at the airport hotel on their arrival and they lived with us while Betty looked for a house. My eldest daughter Wendy, with her husband and three-year-old son Jess, moved in with us to help care for everyone when Lee and I went off on movie locations. My son Rod, just out of college, stayed only a short time; he went almost immediately to Texas, where he worked for Lee's friend Dr Harry Wilmer, then the head of psychiatry at the Scott and White Clinic in Temple. Having majored in psychology at college, Rod went back for post-graduate premeds at the University of Texas in Austin while he was working at the clinic.

Chris and a group of his friends organized a band. They practiced in the living room; Chris played the drums. Lee and I would cook hot dogs and hamburgers, seemingly hundreds of them, for the steady stream of kids coming in and out. Our normal number for dinner each night was ten, often enhanced by one or two of the kids' schoolfriends. Lee and I shopped together for food; I cooked and he chopped up the vegetables and salads. Lee took care of everybody's problems, not to mention their expenses and their cars. He bought a little white Mustang coupé for whoever grew into it at the time, and when each of his children turned sixteen, he bought them a new car. Lee and Kerry immediately became very close, and he became her protector. Living with Lee was to know that you were safe and well cared-for. We were both very enthusiastic about having all the kids together: a total of eight, plus one three-year-old grandchild. We had a house, money for them all, and high hopes.

Of course, not everything was perfect. My fifteen-year-old daughter Maury had adamantly declined to leave Woodstock. Lee felt sure she would change her mind when we left for California without her. Since she had never lived without me, she would, Lee thought, miss her family. He was wrong. Despite many trips back to try to get her to change her mind, and her few brief stays in California, we failed to win at the time. The lure of the 1960s generation in Woodstock, an indulgent father and a boyfriend proved too much to beat.

Lee's ex-wife rented a house just a mile away from us in Malibu. Betty was an angry, bitter woman who, it seemed, had never accepted the separation (a full seven years before) or the divorce. There always seemed to be swirling fury in her personality, and much of the time she was at odds with one, if not all, of her children as well. Although Cynthia and Claudia went to live with her, they came to us at weekends, holidays or whenever Betty went away on vacations. Although we had never met before and I was taking care of her children, Betty was very unpleasant to me – noticeably cold and dismissive – and spoke with an angry tone of authority. Having settled in a house, she immediately took Lee to court to increase her child support, but the judge rejected this and admonished her for bringing it up. Lee was clearly taking care of everyone. He very much loved his children and felt responsible for them. He was also an absolute gentleman with women: he had anguished about leaving the marriage when he did, and felt he was shirking his duty, but 'there was absolutely no communication on any level'.

He left Betty in 1964 during the filming of *Cat Ballou*. Returning from location in Colorado, he had walked up the brick path to the house on Latimer Road and, getting to the door, 'backed up. I could not go in there,' he said, 'I simply could not.' He left for a motel, with only the clothes he had with him. Leaving had not been easy, and it set off some heavy drinking along with what he called 'carousing'. This was a sad and bitter time in his life, which he paid for dearly on many levels and over a long time, culminating in what later became known as the 'palimony trial'.

This, however, was 1971, seven years after he had left. Betty had four wonderful children and was now a wealthy woman, but she could not seem to move on in her life, complaining bitterly to mutual friends and to her children that Lee had left her penniless. Although this was as far from the truth as one could possibly get, it had an effect. Lee always seemed to be held accountable for some past, unpayable debt; he had deserted his family and was replacing it with a new one. 'Give them until they're thirty,' Lee said, 'they'll come around.'

Chris is very good-natured and appealing. Tall like his father, he was always smiling and appeared to take life in an easy-going, laughing way. Lee did not treat Chris how his own father had treated him. He was easy with him: open and honest, not competitive or belittling. But I'm sure it was difficult for him to be overshadowed by a father of such great fame and powerful personality.

Courtenay was, and is, very artistic: she painted, drew and welded. She reminded me physically of Lee's mother: tall and striking, with a soft voice that cracked with emotion or when she raised it. Cynthia, too, is creative in sewing and design, and now has a career in wardrobe on television shows. Claudia – our little chronicler, I used to call her – would recap all our actions or conversations. She is sweet-natured, very enthusiastic and full of energy.

Of course, we had wonderful times together afterwards, but this was essentially the beginning of the end of our 'one big happy family' idea. After less than two years Chris went to live with his mother, and Courtenay went away to college in Iowa. 'Right in the middle of the country,' she announced with a wry smile, 'equally away from everybody.'

Eventually Wendy, Lon and Jess moved to San Francisco and Cynthia went to San Francisco to study at the School of Design. With no one left but Kerry, Lee and me to fill the ten bedrooms, Lee decided we should move back to the house on LaCosta beach a few miles down the road. We were home so seldom, and he loved the little house anyway. (I wondered if its small size didn't have something to do with the decision – perhaps an added guarantee that no one could change their mind and move back!)

I enjoyed living in the Malibu Colony, not only because of the beach and the wonderful weather, but because we had so much company. Whenever Lee made a movie, people who had been with him on the film and lived in LA or nearby would come for dinner or just drop in. A comfortable aspect about life there is that you can have complete privacy and quiet when you want it, or you can walk up and down the beach to other people's houses, or you can just visit outside by the ocean.

Clothes meant nothing to Lee any more. 'I've *done* that,' he said. Not long after we were married, he piled high three couches in our living room and gave everything to his housekeeper Mae Osborne, for her to distribute to people in her neighbourhood. I looked on with some regret. The indication was clearly that social life and elegant occasions were being cut back, and I rather enjoyed parties. I was also trying to save a few things for Rod or Chris, including the beautifully hand-sewn leather jackets, vests and bags from *Paint Your Wagon*. The wardrobe of that movie was extraordinary. Director Josh Logan not only wanted the authentic look of the era but insisted that the wardrobe – even that not visible – should be perfect, right down to the elegant silk underwear worn by the actresses playing the French prostitutes. The studio was not happy about the expense, but they got even. Although the salaries were of course paid, no one who had profit percentages (Lee had 10 per cent) ever got any money. Logan told us, however, that producer Alan J. Lerner sued the studio and did win his percentage. They were all told that Paramount did not make enough money from the movie to warrant profit participation, as it is called. This is rather hard to believe, as Lee received many awards world-wide for his role as Ben Rumson, plus a Gold Record for singing 'Wandr'in' Star'. Clearly, people all over the world saw the film. As far as the Gold Record is concerned, he received only a bill from the studio for the recording! 'Ah, come on, fellas,' is what he said, 'this is going too far,' and they hastily withdrew the claim. 'Somehow, many studios had two sets of books,' Lee told me. 'One you could look at, and then there was the real one!'

6 The War

A few months after we were married, Lee took me to Hawaii for a 'honeymoon,' he said. I discovered it was really a fishing trip. (It turned out to be the start of my own obsession with big game fishing.) Big game fishing was the only type of contest Lee engaged in between movie-making. In 1969 he had built a fishing boat on Palau, in the Western Caroline Islands of Micronesia. He built the boat for two reasons: for himself, and because he thought it might help the economy of the poor people on the island. He felt that as he had taken part in the destruction of the area during World War Two, he should now take part in its repair. In the end, the gesture was a failure. He didn't realize that the Palauians don't like to go 'beyond the reef' – which is where the big marlin are – and that they were not as worried about their circumstances as he was. Also, the sharks outside the reef were creatures the islanders would rather not run into.

Ray Accord, the captain of Lee's boat, eventually took it up to Guam, and there died of a heart attack on board. After Ray was buried at sea from the boat, it fell into disrepair from dry rot, toritas and disuse. This was some two years after Lee and I were married, and by then we had our own boat in Hawaii. He had his fine fighting chair – a Rybovich given to him by Jim Kimberly, a fellow fisherman from Palm Beach – sent to us for the fishing boat in Hawaii. The engine was shipped up to a gold mine Lee owned in the Sierra Nevada mountains of California. The name of the boat in Palau was *Ngerengchol* ('where the heart is'), and the idea for the boat came to Lee while he was filming *Hell in the Pacific*.

Lee did his wartime fighting in that area. He was on all those islands and the neighbouring Marshalls: Kwajalein Atoll, the islands around Roi-Namur, Eniwetok Atoll, islands named Teiteir-ipucci, Bogan, Bogairick, Elugelab, Ruehi, Bogalla, Rigili Islands,

Grihem, Libiron, Mui, Igurin, Parry Island – twenty-one in all – and then on to the Marianas, where he was finally wounded. He almost died there – many of his friends did die there.

On our honeymoon in Hawaii, Lee chartered a boat from a captain he had fished with some years previously, after filming John Ford's *Donovan's Reef*. The boat was a simple one: island style with a sampan hull. One quiet afternoon, while trolling off the coast of Kailua Kona on the Big Island, Lee started to talk about something he had not really mentioned to me before: his part in the war. We sat sipping home-made Kahlua – a wedding gift from Betty Fay, a local newspaperwoman friend – and for the first time since I had known him, he told me about the day he was shot by Japanese machine guns. When he finished describing it, I was crying. He put his arm around me and said, almost as if he hadn't known before, 'You *do* love me, don't you?'

Lee enlisted in the United States Marine Corps on 12 August 1942 'to serve for the duration of the national emergency,' swearing to give his mother 90 per cent of his basic pay. He was '73 inches tall [he was actually 74 inches], brown eyes [not true: they were hazel to green], dark brown hair . . . ruddy complexion.'

In October 1942 Lee, already familiar with weapons, qualified as Rifle NCO, Rifle Sharpshooter, and was disappointed to miss an expert rating by one point. He *was* expert in bayonet. Lee was in the 4th Marine Division (The Fighting Fourth), and his last outfit was I Company, 3rd Battalion 24th Marines. Wounded in action on 18 June 1944, he was given an Honorable Discharge as Private First Class on 24 July 1945 and received $136 mustering out pay from the Naval Yard in Philadelphia. It was one month before the war ended. He had been awarded the Purple Heart 'for wounds received in action against the enemy on Saipan Island, Mariana Islands, on 18th June, 1944'. Somewhat ironically, the order of the Purple Heart was established by his distant relative George Washington in 1782. Lee received a Letter of Commendation (which later became The Navy Commendation), Presidential Unit Citation With Star, American Defense Service Medal, Asiatic-Pacific Campaign Medal with Star and the World War Two Victory Medal. The Good Conduct Medal was not awarded, but only because of his early discharge. He spent thirteen months in hospitals throughout the Pacific and Stateside; the last of these was the Chelsea Naval Hospital in Massachusetts. When he was coming home to New York by bus, an irate woman whacked him over the head with her umbrella, loudly accusing him of shirking his duty. He should be out there, she railed, fighting with our boys!

Boot camp for Lee was Parris Island, South Carolina. He was in top physical shape already from his sports and track at St Leo's College and the earlier years of track at Oakwood School. He went on to Quartermaster school in Camp LeJeune, North Carolina, where he was rated 'a very good student' and promoted to corporal. Here the Marines' rigorous training turned him into fighting shape. 'We got up at 3:45 a.m. and hit the sack at ten, but we needed every minute of that time.' By September 1942, however, he scoffed to his brother Robert, who was in the Army: 'We're treated like gentlemen and it's really swell. We get up at five or five thirty and work until four, then get off. It's a darn good life and I like it!' But even before going into combat he was becoming well aware of what he was training for. As he wrote his brother: 'You were saying you always wanted to be a soldier. Well, I'm glad you aren't here because all the dirty tactics that they taught us proves it's a dangerous outfit.'

At Camp Eliott, California, he was demoted to private for various reasons. One, he said, was for 'putting my hand in the quartermaster till and handing out shirts to my buddies'. Another was disobeying a lawful order by a superior officer: 'Quitting post before being properly relieved.' Jack Shiff, his commanding officer at the time, said that he personally put him in jail twice for going 'over the hill' in San Diego to get fried egg sandwiches and once for being drunk. But he said he left the door open that time so that Lee could just sleep it off. Lee repeatedly annoyed another officer with a rhythmic answer at muster, all in rhyme:

MARVIN, LEE
PFC
FOUR THREE NINE SIX SEVUUUUN THUREE

He was jailed again once for five days in Maui, as his best combat buddy Robert Filkosky recounts: 'It was during R and R between combat campaigns after Kwajalein, during a forced training march of seventeen miles. The men were in full uniform in the muggy heat, very thirsty and with blistered feet. (Many of the men went to sick bay after this march.) Lee saw a water fountain by the road in the pineapple fields, and broke out of line to fill his canteen with water – and his casual answer, "Just getting water, Lieutenant," when asked, "What the hell do you think you're doing, Marvin?" by Lieutenant Ed MacDonald was taken poorly. "Water!" said MacDonald, not too happy about the march himself, "I'll give you water!" and put him in the brig on bread and water for five days.' Bob Filkosky enjoyed going by the brig and teasing Lee: 'Do you have enough water?'

At Camp Pendleton he was in Company B, 20th Marines (engineers); in H and S Company D, Scouts and Snipers in the 4th Tank Battalion, and there trained for the invasion of the Marshall Islands, where he was reconnaissance and rifleman. Lee's Fourth Marine Division was the only division to go directly into combat from the USA, traveling to the Marshall Islands on the USS *Schley*. 'The Division, in some sixty days of actual combat, saw more action than any other division in six hundred.' They had the highest casualty rate of any Marine division and were the first to capture a mandated territory, in Japanese hands since 1914.[1]

The Marshalls were thirty-two coral atolls, islets of coral, sand and rock built by the action of surf, tide and wind. Kwajalein was the largest atoll in the world, with 867 reefs in eight hundred square miles of ocean. They lie in a double chain entitled Ratak ('sunrise') and Ralik ('sunset').[2] Going among the offshore islands around Roi-Namur the night before the invasion of that island in small rubber boats made Lee one of the first Americans to invade Japanese territory during the war. They had to 'neutralize' the island and gather intelligence before the main landing. Capturing these islands was strategically very important: Saipan, the next in line, would put our B-29s within range of the home islands of Japan itself – 'Unsinkable Aircraft Carriers', the islands were called. The plan was to capture them in three phases: first, the four offshore islands; second, the two islands of Roi-Namur; third,

1 Robert Sherrod. Fourth Marine Division in WW II.
2 *The Marshalls, Increasing The Tempo*, by Lt. Col. Heinl, Jr. USMC and Lt. Col. John A. Crown, USMC, pub. 1954 by Historical Branch G 3 Division HQ USMC.

eleven more in the Kwajalein atoll. The Roi-Namur islands controlled the northern entrance to the atoll: Roi had the airfield that was the center of Japanese aviation in the Marshalls; Namur was a heavily-defended bastion with fire trenches, pillboxes and blockhouses full of explosives. As the men in Lee's outfit remember, one blockhouse did blow up, killing many troops on both sides. Fighting was so fierce that in twenty-four hours of battle four Medals of Honor were awarded as well as numerous Silver and Bronze Stars – many posthumously. Lee's outfit went right down the chain of islands until the Marshalls were secured. After a brief rest and recuperation on Maui, Lee – now in I Company, 3rd Battalion, 24th Marines – sailed to Saipan in the Marianas on the USS *Fuller*: 3,715 miles from Hawaii, but only 1,400 miles from Tokyo.

Armed to the teeth, Saipan was the headquarters of the Japanese Pacific Fleet. Also waiting for the Marines were the Japanese of the 31st Army and the Northern Marianas Defense Force, which included the crack troops of the Imperial Japanese Marines. The island was thirteen miles long by five and a half miles wide with rugged terrain: sharp ridges, fissure-like valleys and numerous caves, in which the Japanese were strongly entrenched. Held by Japan since 1919, Saipan was the most bitterly defended of the three islands of Saipan, Guam and Tinian. Here, in thirty days of bitter fighting, the Fourth Marine Division sustained nearly six thousand casualties killed, wounded or missing. The victorious American troops had the added horror of watching Japanese soldiers and civilians flinging themselves and their babies over the cliffs to their deaths; no amount of pleading could stop the suicides. The Japanese also vowed that for every one Japanese killed there would be 'seven lives to repay our country'. General Saito ordered banzai attacks under the Bushido code: 'I will calmly offer up the courage of my soul. I will never in the end suffer the disgrace of being taken alive.' Vice Admiral Chuchi Nagumo, commander of the aircraft carriers in the attack on Pearl Harbor, now killed himself before the advancing Marines. The wounded, some carrying only sharpened bamboo sticks, followed his orders, and all else having failed, he committed hara-kiri himself.

The jail compound where many of our downed flyers were so

harshly imprisoned is on Saipan (where many think Amelia Earhart and Fred Noonan were also kept and then executed by the Japanese before the war). On D-Day, 15 June 1944, Lee with his 24th Regiment under Major General Holland M. Smith ('Howlin' Mad Smith') and Colonel Franklyn A. Hart went ashore on Yellow Beach Two. The legendary war planner Major E.H. 'Pete' Ellis had many years before predicted that the Japanese would attack the United States and that they would have to fight in the Pacific. Having wandered surreptitiously through these islands charting the waters and harbours, Major Ellis died under unexplained circumstances in Japanese-held Palau in 1923, trying to prove his point. He choreographed this 1944 invasion with his plan of 1921 entitled 'Advance Base Operations in Micronesia'. The United States Marine Corps, he wrote, 'were to be prepared to accompany the fleet and reduce resistance in the Marshalls; to hold there a temporary base for our fleet and to deny the use of the remaining available islands or atolls as suitable bases to the enemy'. This blandly-stated manifesto turned into the bloody Operation Flintlock.

As we sat there on the peaceful boat in 1971, this is more or less what Lee told me. I will also quote the men who were with him and wrote down his words. Malcomb Smith writes:

> I was Lee's platoon leader for some two years. After training at Jacques Farm and later at sniper school, we sailed off to the Marianas.
>
> We landed on a small island as A Company the night before the main invasion. Our job was to try and catch a prisoner who could tell us about the situation and also to take the island so that artillery could be set up to support the invasion of Roi and Namur the next day. (The artillery had to be far enough away to operate.)
>
> We did well, got our prisoner which led to moving up the invasion of Eniwetok.
>
> Lee was in his element at Parry Island on Eniwetok. There was a landing made after we had taken all the islands on the eastern rim of the atoll . . . some 18 in all. We started these landings in rubber boats the night before the main attack on the airfield and worked our way down the islands . . . sometimes at

night and more often in broad daylight. We discovered that a regiment of Japanese Marines was ashore on the last untaken island . . . Parry.

The first afternoon on Parry Island we were given the job of mopping up after the attack and later took over as front line and assault troops. We had some night. Lee was in a hole next to mine with Corporal Ott and my runner, named Sutherland. We had to hold the line that night and the next day attack along the seaward side of the island which was heavily dug in by the Japanese. You may not have known this, but in the Scouts, we all went by nicknames, Lee's was 'Boom Happy'. He loved to blow things up and was an expert with dynamite and Composition C (a plastic explosive). He blew up everything in sight and lots of things out of sight as we progressed. He was a great help.

The first night on Parry Island was a bad one. The Japanese hung land mines on themselves and kept walking into us and blowing themselves up with a hand grenade. They also threw grenades at us all night, but fortunately we were able to throw most of them back before they exploded.

At any rate, we came through and won a Regimental Commendation from the commanding officer of the 22nd Marines for our efforts.

The next invasion came after our rest on Maui. Our original assignment was to land on Saipan five days ahead of the main invasion. We were to scout the airfield and then proceed to the top of Mount Taipacho and keep our people informed until they caught up with us. Fortunately Col. Carlson changed this after reading a report from a destroyer which encountered 11 knot currents where we were supposed to paddle our rubber boats.

We landed the morning of D Day and held over a mile of beach extending up the northern tip of the island. We had our problems but did hold for, I believe, three days after which the army landed and took over our positions with a regiment.

We then conducted various scouting jobs. Captain Katzenbach (whose brother later became Kennedy's Attorney General) was wounded and lying in a shell hole. Lee was among those who gave me covering fire when I went a couple of hundred yards in front of our lines to get him. The Captain got a Legion of Merit for his efforts in uncovering a bothersome group of Japanese before he got shot, and I was given a Silver Star for my part in the episode.

We were a small platoon . . . 21 men . . . so I got to know your husband well. He was a spirited man to say the least. In action he was courageous and very effective in a key assignment. He was a natural born leader. I was indeed fortunate having him as a member of my platoon.

This is the first time I have written about our actions. But I thought you would like to have a word from Marvin's platoon leader about some of his exploits from one who had the greatest respect for him.

With kind regards,
Malcomb N. Smith (Beartracks)

Colonel Albert Arsenault, retired, said:

There aren't many combat Marine veterans who have won Academy Awards. Most of his fans probably never knew what a great Marine he was in real life . . . and what many in the Corps may not realize is that the battle-tested fighter he often portrayed on the screen was in large measure a reflection of himself, a tough combat Marine. Lee joined my unit, 3–1–24, in April 1944 when we were on Maui, training for Saipan.

Even in those days a fair description of Lee Marvin was 'irrepressible'. Within a few days after joining us he picked up the nickname 'Captain Marvel', after a noted comic strip character of the day, a doer of great deeds. One day he was walking down our company street when an approaching Marine saluted. Thinking this was recognition of his 'Captain Marvel' status, Lee returned the salute. A voice behind him boomed out, 'Marvin, there's only one captain in this company and his name isn't Marvel, it's Arsenault.'

On D Day that June, Lee Marvin landed with us on Saipan. About the sixth day he was badly wounded, had to be evacuated, and was never able to return to active duty. From his wartime friends the best compliment we can pass on is that he was a fine Marine and a brave one. The Corps can be proud of Lee Marvin as truly one of our own.[3]

Robert Filkosky was a fellow-Marine from Lee's outfit and a friend for more than forty-three years, until Lee's death. Bob was the youngest Marine ever to enlist: he was fourteen when he joined and then served in combat! He had forged his mother's signature giving permission and his age as well. He was written up in *Ripley's Believe It or Not!* and was wounded in action three times. On Saipan he was hit twice by 'friendly' artillery fire when he was sixteen years old. After serving through the entire war he was out on the streets, barely seventeen years old and with three Purple Hearts. I asked him about the flag-raising on Iwo Jima. He laughed and said:

> Do I remember it? I sure do. I was shot in the head and was lying on the beach waiting to be evacuated. It was February 23, 1945. By some act of fate I had just turned my head and was hit in the top of my helmet by two bullets from a Japanese machine gun. The two bullets came out of the same hole in my helmet, but the lining, separated by about eight threads, shows two distinct holes. Lying there I heard some commotion and asked for a Lieutenant's field glasses. There was the flag being raised on Mount Surabachi.

Bob says of Lee: 'Marine, actor, friend, blood brother and a hell of a man, Lee Marvin. Any man who's been under fire well knows the meaning of blood brother; one Marine who would, without hesitation, give his life to save another.'

Bob seems to have total recall and was with Lee when he was wounded. He remembers where everyone was at the time and what they were doing. Even then, Bob recalls, Lee's humor was legendary: 'We were fighting for our lives down in "Death Valley" on Saipan. Bill Weaver was with us, as was Charles Zickafoose, when Lee was shot right across both buttocks. You could have put your hands down in the meat. It later took fifty-six stitches. Lee looks over at Zickafoose and says, "Hey, Zeek, if you get home before me, tell Maw to sell the outhouse cause I'm not going to be able to sit down."'

3 *Fighting Fourth of WW II.* Newsletter, December 1987.

Bob visited Lee in 1955 during the filming of *The Caine Mutiny*, the movie Lee made with Humphrey Bogart:

When the movie was over, a party was given at the Royal Hawaiian in Honolulu. The director, Stanley Kramer, told Lee that Admiral Radford would be there, and cautioned him not to be telling him how to run the Navy as he was at that time Commander of the Pacific Fleet. Well, when Kramer came in with the Admiral, he brought him over to where Lee was talking to a Marine General and much to Kramer's surprise, he was an old friend of Lee's, Franklyn A. Hart, Regimental Commander of the 24th. Lee made the colonel's grandson a water-cooled machine gun out of wood at Pendleton. Colonel Hart said to Admiral Radford, 'I want you to meet Lee Marvin, he and I won the war in the Pacific together.' That's the way it was with Lee – you couldn't get ahead of him. He would always end up on top.

Marine buddy Harry Osborne writes of being in hospital with Lee after they were both wounded. Harry had been hit on the back by a Japanese hand grenade. With six seconds to go before it exploded, he ran – setting a world record, he figured. In trying to escape the blast, he ran round a tank, startling a fellow Marine who bayoneted him in the stomach. On the stretcher being carried away, he was hit by Japanese machine gun fire as well, but survived to write of Lee:

We were all pretty close in those days and I loved him like a brother. When Lee and I were wounded in Saipan I didn't know he was on the hospital ship *Solace* until we got to Fleet Hospital 108 on Guadalcanal in the Solomon Islands. The end of the world. No dancing girls there. Then we were in the same ward side by side for 57 days. He was still there when I left. I never saw him again. I remember how he had an awfully large cast and his right arm was held away from his body. His morale was great and he kept everyone laughing all the time. I had gunshot wounds in my legs and a bayonet wound in my stomach and it hurt to laugh. Sometimes I wanted to wring his neck. Only kidding. I loved the big guy.

Lee had his own Phase I, II and III. They probably also had something to do with conquering, but the enemy was not so clear-cut as the wartime opponent one is trained to recognize. These are his own words about what Operation Flintlock came to mean to him:

Phase I
Saipan, Mariana Islands
June, 1944
Fourth Day – Called up to replace K Company of 3rd Battalion, 24th Marines as they had received heavy fire and casualties and had fallen back, fifteen feet, to their original cover. The assault platoon, 1st Plt, and Fourth Plt of I Co, 3rd Bt, 24th Marines would jump off from the same position, only in flanking positions, 1st to the left, 4th to the right. All positions are looking North. Meanwhile the 2nd and 3rd platoons would push straight forward. At the signal we moved out. Mike Cairns and I were the 'point' of the assault platoon. Moving at a slow walk, we bore to the left and forward. There was nothing to be seen, the ground cover was thin and high, high brush with an occasional tree. The terrain was flat and slightly dish-shaped. All was quiet. We had just passed an abandoned thatched hut approaching a slight mound with three palm trees on it about thirty yards in front of us when suddenly a shot and a loud slap to the immediate left of me. It was Mike and he was down. He said a quiet 'Oh,' and then 'Corpsman' just as quietly. There was blood on his dungaree blouse. I went down to him and tore open his jacket, and there, just one inch below his left nipple, was a small dark hole. The blood was pink and bubbly, a lung shot. I tried to put my finger in the hole but it would not fit. His eyes were closed and he said 'Corpsman' twice more in a whisper and was dead.

The high-sounding Jap machine gun and rifle fire, then I heard Mac's voice, our platoon leader (Lt Edward McDonald), shouting for all BAR men to stand and fire magazines. Mike's BAR was next to me. I picked it up and put 20 rounds into the brush at the base of the three palms but didn't see any thing. Mac was shouting for me to pull over to the right and join the rest of the platoon. There was no way that I could get Mike's ammunition belt off him as it had shoulder straps, so I pulled the trigger group off his BAR and threw it away and grabbing my M1 rifle, headed off low and fast where I thought the rest of the platoon were. All was chaotic, shouting voices, the heavy sound of our weapons and the high, shrill fast sound of theirs. I still could not see the Japs! They were close for I could feel the blast of their weapons. Then I could see the 1st Platoon: they were all down, some firing forward, some on their backs and sides, 'Oh my God! They got us.' As I was running the twigs and small branches were flying through the air as their machine guns were cutting everything down. I figured I had better get down too. And just in time. All the brush around me knee high just disappeared. I looked forward and my leg flew to one side, I couldn't feel anything. 'This is getting bad.' Looking down my side, I saw that the heel had been shot off. Looking up again to see where it had come from, there was another crack and my face was numb and eyes full of dirt. It had a set-up of rhythm I knew. Burying my face in the ground and gritting my teeth in anticipation, SLAPPP!! The impact caused a reflex that lifted me off the ground. I lay still for a long time. I knew that I was hit. I shouted, 'I'm hit,' and a voice nearby said, very calmly, 'Shut up, we're all hit.' I was slowly tensing my various muscles. By a process of elimination I figured it was somewhere below the chest. By then Scheidt and Pedagrew crawled up and told me that I was hit in the ass and proceeded to dump some sulfa in the wound and said they would try to get me out of there and to follow them. I disassembled my M1, and my cartridge belt had already been cut off, so we began to crawl to the right. I could not believe the number of dead Marines. I would recognize certain personal touches of equipment my friends had and there they were, lifeless. We got over to the 2nd Platoon area and they were as bad off as us. We started back toward our line. Now most of the fire was Jap. Where were our mortars and tanks? When all at once we were stopped by an opening, completely with no cover, a fire lane about 20 feet wide. There was no way to get through there crawling. Scheidt said, 'If we could get you up, could you run?' They did get me up and shoved me out into the cover on the other side, then crawled to a large trunked tree, about four feet thick. Rose was sitting there with his back to the fire. He asked me if I wanted a cigarette and gave me one, also he offered me water. On returning the canteen to him, he leaned out a bit to put it away in its cover on his cartridge belt. He was hit immediately and fell over on me and died without a word. I could not get him off me. Then somebody stepped on my wound, I shouted, fortunately they were stretcher bearers. Then Callelo was brought in, he had been hit in the head and screaming he could not see. They loaded him on the stretcher and at the same time got hit again, killing one of the bearers. He was out of his head now. They got him out of there fast. I shouted, 'What about me?' They said I was next. What frightened me now was that I would be lying face down on the stretcher about one and a half feet above the ground. Just the height their machine guns usually were set at. There was nothing I could do. I had to get out. The bearers were running as fast as they could, the fire was all around, then one of the front bearers went down, only a stumble, they got me back on and over a little ridge, loaded three of us on a recon truck and back to Battalion aid, still under heavy fire. At Battalion a guy, stripped to the waist with two nambu pistols stuck in his belt, asked me if I needed plasma but I didn't know; he gave me a surrette of morphine and had me put behind a long stack of 81 mm mortar HE shells. They were still in their clover leaves and I could hear the strays hitting them. All at once I noticed Scheidt squatting by me and he was asking me for my .45 automatic that I had in my shoulder holster. I had to give it to him, he had gotten me out of there. I told him it was my father's pistol and not to lose it. He thanked me and took off. Just then somebody in the distance started shouting, 'Counter attack, counter attack,' and the panic of trying to get the wounded out of there began. I didn't even have my .45 anymore. And by now my leg was totally useless. Things had gone from bad to worse. Then a terrific explosion, a big ammo dump about 100 yards away had gone up and I could see people floating through the air. A lot of confusion and I found myself in a stretcher jeep, two of us and two ambulatory, but we were going the wrong way, back to the fire fight. I shouted at the driver a number of times and finally he swung around and headed for the beach. I don't remember too much of the trip, we were about three or four miles in on the fourth day. When the haze cleared, a corpsman was filling out a tag and attaching it to me with its wire. Then he took a red crayon and made a mark on my forehead saying that he had given me morphine. There was a lot of heavy stuff going off around us. I was under a torn canvas fly on the beach. Equipment was stacked everywhere and it was getting dark. I asked him if there was any chance to get off tonight and he said NO! My heart sank. The Japs had the beach zeroed in and were pounding it. We would never make it through the night. Above all the noise a voice from the water shouted, 'Anybody going out?' The corpsman hollered, 'How much room you got?' The next time I awoke I was listening to the diesel engine throb, I knew we were passing ships but didn't much care. I was face down on the stretcher and was aware of much light, then a pair of shiny black shoes with white pants. A lot of shouting and then I was in a bright companionway painted yellow with Glenn Miller's 'Moonlight Serenade' playing from somewhere. A nurse in white was reading my tag and asking if I wanted some ice water or ice cream. I didn't know what to say. Some man's voice said, 'GU,' and they took me away. Still on the stretcher I was next to a low bunk with a thick mattress and white sheets on it. A voice asked if I could climb onto the bed. I said I'd get the sheets dirty, and the voice said, 'That's OK, we got more.' They cut the dog tag off my shoe and put it in my hand. I asked them not to take my helmet, and please turn off the lights. 'Don't worry.' In and out of focus for awhile, then I heard it. From the island, the fire fight was still going on. My company, what was left of it, was still there, and I was safe on a hospital ship. Ice cream, water, clean sheets, Glenn Miller, nurses. I was a coward! and cried.

Reading the first few words of the official telegram must have been a terrible shock for his mother, as it was for all families who received them:

> We deeply regret to inform you that your son, Private First Class Lee Marvin, has been wounded in action in the performance of his duty and service of his country. I realize your great anxiety but nature of wounds not reported and delay in receipt of details must be expected. You will be promptly furnished any additional information received. To prevent possible aid to our enemies do not divulge the name of his ship or station.

The long delay in getting information must have been excruciating. Her anxiety was surely shown by the repeated requests, polite and stoic, that the Marine Corps received from her asking about his condition and whereabouts. It wasn't until 6 December that she knew the exact extent of his wounds, nearly *six months* after the telegram.

Of the 244 men in I Company to land on Saipan, only thirty-eight remained when the island was secured. The others had either been killed in action or wounded badly enough to require hospitalization. Out of six lieutenants, only one, Edward MacDonald, was not killed. Ed – 'Mac' to Lee, and as he said, 'one hell of a man' – was the Old Man, twenty-four years old to their seventeen or eighteen. Ed, wounded twice on Saipan ('got messed up,' he says, 'but we all got messed up'), went on, like all the men in Lee's company, to Iwo Jima – the worst of them all, most say. Ed received three Purple Hearts, a Silver Star for bravery on Saipan, and a Bronze Star for Iwo Jima (after he was promoted to captain). He went back to Saipan after the war to visit the cemetery full of the white crosses of his Marines. He saw a name on one cross and then a row later saw it again: same name, same serial number. He went to the cemetery headquarters and told them about it: 'For God's sake, no parent would want to see that!' He was still caring for the men and their families forty-five years later. I asked him if it were common to bring back the bodies and he said a few: 'But I think – no, I *know* for a fact – that any bones under those crosses are not the same as the headstone says. They are all just shovelled together.

The crosses are just to make the families feel better, that they're grieving at the right spot.'

He had started to tell me the usual story – and then adamantly, bitterly, told me the truth. The men are all deeply and for ever hurt. Ed remembered the awful discomfort on Iwo Jima: his body black and scaly from dirt and no baths, and the smell of the warm, sulphuric draughts of air seeping up when a shell hit or you dug a foxhole. He once had to hit the dirt saving a green lieutenant in a machine-gun attack, and splashed down into a Japanese latrine. He had to live with that smell and dirt for days until he got a wash. His men meant everything to him, however, and once, in a fury about a mistake which cost some of his men's lives, he decked an officer and held a .45 under his chin threatening to kill him. Lee used Ed and his war experiences in his movies; this incident was used in *Attack* (Jack Palance played the man).

Ed tells with pride how, on only the second day of terrible fighting on Iwo Jima, they were able to secure enough of the airfield to allow disabled B-29 bombers to land, saving many a crew and plane. The Marines watched with satisfaction as crippled planes unable to make it to Saipan (also held by our troops because of them) were now able to land in safety because of the Marines' sacrifice.

The Gunnery Sergeant, Lawrence 'Gunny' Hart, had to take charge when the other officers were killed or wounded in battle. Even though flattened by dysentery, he refused to leave his men, and fought the last days in dungarees so stiff he could hardly move. Paregoric kept him going. He laughed, 'The last days of fighting on Saipan I was high as a kite!' He went on to be wounded on Tinian and then to Iwo Jima. The men never forget and, as Gunny Hart said, '"dream the faces" of the young men who never had a chance to grow up'. Joe Krawczyk, who was in Lee's outfit, remembers bitter feelings after the war: 'I know that Lee was bitter. Seemed like we were the enemy when we came home and it took a long time for me to change. I always keep in touch with my old Marine buddies that lived through it. It seems that all we did was wasted anyway.'

Joe felt that Saipan was worse even than Iwo Jima. He recalls not changing his socks, shoes or clothes for thirty-four days, and when he did get out of his things after the engagement, his grimy, discolored skin peeled off with them. One night he was sitting in a foxhole with a buddy, pinned down by Japanese fire. When things had quietened a little, his buddy offered him something to eat from his tin. As he bent over to get it, he heard the zing of a bullet and felt it pass by his ear. He said something to the other Marine, but there was no answer. He looked at him and saw a bullet in his chest meant for *him.* He had to stay in the foxhole all night with his dead buddy, and spent the night praying for him. He, too, was later wounded, in his arm, but was sent on to Iwo Jima anyway. Joe earned two Purple Hearts.

Walter Furman, also from Lee's outfit, took his first steps in combat on the beaches of Roi-Namur. As he went ashore, the two men on either side of him were killed. He went through all the Marshalls unscathed, but on Saipan he was shot, badly wounded as he was going up the side of Mount Taipacho. He felt a searing pain in his shoulder and saw blood shooting. He weakened and fell unconscious, but was given plasma just in time before he bled to death.

The chaplain, Charles Goe, was wounded by shrapnel on Tinian; the man praying next to him was killed instantly. Richard Scheidt, who had been wounded on Roi-Namur and awarded a Silver Star for bravery, was back with his outfit on Saipan. After he had borrowed Lee's gun, he was badly wounded once more, and to his sorrow, the gun and all his other gear was taken from him on the hospital ship and disappeared for ever.

The men who fought on Roi-Namur went right on from Saipan to Tinian and the slaughter of Iwo Jima. At a recent Marine Corps reunion of the Fourth Division, I met and talked to many of those men who fought, ate, and slept with Lee: Bob Filkosky, Captain Ed MacDonald, Joseph Krawczyk, Bill Weaver, Colonel Albert Arsenault, Gunny Hart, Walter Furman, Al Lesiak, Al Carrington, Jack Paugh, Charles Eaton, Henry Deskiewicz – men who were familiar names from Lee's descriptions but now materialized.

I was deeply struck by the intense bond between these men. I suppose it has always been so in war. They sleep together as foxhole buddies, paired off in a bond stronger than any lovers: they save each other's lives, they kill for each other, they die for each other. No relationship could be more potent. When they get together later, forty-five years is a flick of Time's eyelash. Everyone is freeze-framed; age melts away. These are the close-ups of the figures we all saw whenever we watched the newsreels of the day, which preceded every movie. Tiny men on the screen jumping off boats, sloughing through the surf with their M1s over their heads, lobbing grenades in battle. The real men who John Wayne and the other movie stars were portraying in films. Now as you look, no one is fat or gray-haired or limping or mute from strokes; you see them crouching, running, dropping to the ground and firing, huddled together under the worst of it all, the artillery barrages. You look at them with awe, admiration, love. It could be today.

But what about them? They go to reunions more and more as the business of life winds down and the memories crowd back. The only people who can understand are their comrades. You hear the loneliness; they remember, they cry. When they talk about each man killed, they talk as if he is still part of their lives: it could have happened just the day before. The names of the dead, memorized by a Marine blinded in World War II, are called out at annual memorial services.

I stood with lighted candle with the other widows while taps were played at a reunion in a huge Las Vegas hotel ballroom. I faced a Medal Of Honor winner as he stood saluting on the podium, and wondered what he was thinking. With overwhelming emotion, a thousand Marines behind me rose and sang the Marine Corps hymn. Some are too depressed to come at all; some write books and poems about it. Carl Dearborn writes to me: 'I find it impossible to discuss World War Two battles with other men I was with. I can put it in poetry.'

Dearborn says that the reunions bring back memories of our deceased. 'Our big problem as combat Marines – we saw too many die and never had the time or means to render proper feelings of loss or burial. To see them wrapped in ponchos and blankets and laid in quicklime was only a prophecy of our own fate waiting.' He writes many poems. One, entitled 'In Memorial', begins:

> The assault begins, and men go down,
> they draw their final breath

And Widows weep as warriors sleep,
the endless sleep of death.[4]

Many of the men return to the battlefields, as Lee did to Saipan's 'Death Valley' in 1967. He found the spot where he was shot, but so well had he come to terms with it that he said:

I never missed a heartbeat. I was waiting for it to hit but it didn't. You see a jawbone or a skull and you say, 'Yeah, but that was a long time ago.' The urgency was in that man's living, not his death ... Now it's a garbage dump. The aftermath of war is nothing and we proved it on those islands. They left everything. All the trophies of the last war. They didn't clean it up at all. The armor is still there ... and the bones. Tanks are still lying all over the joint ... fallen Zeros stuck right in the earth. The second largest source of income in Micronesia is still scrap metal. Twenty-five years later I'm walking around Saipan again. Who can threaten me? Nobody. I had already thought out the memories of the nights and the sounds and the killing before I went back.[5]

Lee went back to those islands not only to make a movie very much against war, but with a Japanese actor (himself seven years in the Japanese Army) who was doing the same thing. When Lee and Toshiro Mifune were filming *Hell in the Pacific*, they went together to lay a wreath at a cemetery on the island of Peleliu – 'Bloody Peleliu' as it was called after the battle. It claimed the lives of an estimated ten thousand Japanese troops and more than two thousand of the 1st Division Marines and soldiers; many thousands more were wounded. Bones were lying exposed everywhere. In a perverse gesture, Lee kicked a whitened skull to Mifune, startling him out of his reverie with bowed head. The film's still photographer Orlando Suero, an ex-Marine who had fought in the Pacific himself, was with them. Suero was extremely nervous and couldn't wait to get off the island. He kept prodding Lee and whispering hoarsely, 'My God, I can just see it. I made it once, and now I'm going to get killed twenty-five years later stepping on some

4 *Marine Verse from WW II*, Carl Dearborn.
5 *Playboy Magazine*, January 1969.

old mine or something! . . . and we're outnumbered here. We're
with ten Japs and just the two of us!'

John Boorman, who directed *Hell in the Pacific*, recalls the
incident well:

> Lee and Toshiro went down there with the photographer and
> laid a wreath. There were no bones down there, actually. It
> was really a horrific story, the kind of thing that only Lee
> would have done, and I think that when they came back, Lee
> in a sense got talked into it. He didn't feel it was somehow
> right for him, this act of remembrance and forgiveness, and he
> was angry with himself. He came back very drunk on the ship
> [where everyone was living during the filming] and he came
> roaring into the dining saloon and went over to the Japanese
> crew and Mifune, and said in this roaring voice, 'Which one
> of you jokers put that Jap skull in my bed?' knowing how
> tender they felt about this. It was the kind of joke in the worst
> possible taste that only Lee could get away with. And with all
> the frictions in making the film, Lee was loved and adored by
> Mifune and the Japanese crew.

Shortly afterwards Lee narrated *Our Time In Hell*, an hour-long
documentary on the war in the Pacific. Using Marine Corps color
footage (the only footage of its kind), it traced the major battles,
including Saipan where Lee had been wounded. After the
documentary was shown on ABC in 1968, the critics called it the
greatest of all American war films, and men who had been in
combat said it was the best they had ever seen. Much of its
authenticity came from Lee's own experiences and his insistence on
'getting it right'. He brought the same qualities to his war movies,
such as *The Dirty Dozen* and *The Big Red One*.

Bob Filkosky has heartbreaking memories of battle-weary men
hearing their dying comrades calling, ever weaker, 'Tell my mother
good-bye,' or calling out for a corpsman when no one could get to
them under fire. You feel it will always come back to haunt them,
and they will never again find peace.

Lee said: 'One of my most poignant memories: we were high on a
ridge and we heard it coming, a gull-winged Corsair. He was about
fifty feet off the ground and his canopy was back and he laughed at

us. Then he went into a slow roll, a victory roll. He went out to sea and we watched. About two miles out, still in the roll, he went in . . .'

Lee had many dreams about his war years. Two of them in particular were like still photographs, appearing to him over and over again. He mentioned this to Dr Harry Wilmer, who said, 'Why don't you paint them?' And so Lee did. One is a large painting, four feet by three, which he entitled 'Country Roads'. It depicts five brown masses on a blue background; the fifth has a large red splotch on it. I didn't see it until he hung it on the wall for me. I immediately blurted out, 'Oh, that's where you were wounded in the war' – I was never one for subtlety. 'Well, did you have to *say* it?' Lee said, annoyed at my jumping the gun. He told me the painting showed fire lanes during the war.

The next painting is even larger and three-dimensional. Expertly constructed from plywood, it is pale green on one half and pale yellow on the other, and the surface bears a series of concave rectangles. Lee felt that it was an abstract memory of the hospital ship *Solace* with its maze of hallways. Both paintings hang in our living room where he placed them.

Lee was thinking more and more about his old friends and having more contact with them. He would search them out and call or write. As his wife, I often became impatient with the stories, the long drawn out conversations and the memories repeatedly rehashed. I thought he should dwell less on the past and more on the present, and try to forget all the pain. But I was wrong: the catharsis isn't in the forgetting, it's in the remembering. I learned that during the reunions.

Lee had his own way of dealing with it, by continuing to describe his life phases. The second phase he put into these words:

Phase II
Oahu
Hawaiian Territory
November, 1944
Out on the south-west beaches of this beautiful island they had it all set up for us. Plenty of beer, good chow and even things like inner tubes so that we could play in the surf if the

fancy caught us. There was no schedule except for eating and
lights out. A real rest camp. We were told that we would
probably be here for two or three weeks so enjoy it. After this
the doctors would examine us again and it would be back to
duty or stateside. There was a general uneasiness among all
the men.

I had a lot of time to think about things starting with the
hospital ship *Solace*, then three months at Fleet 108 on
Guadalcanal, Espirito Santo, New Caledonia, and finally
Navy #10 at Aheia Heights. I had long ago arrived at the
decision that I could not go back.

The days drifted by. But I was starting to have a recurring
half dream and half fantasy. As taps would sound each night
we would climb into our bunks and pull the mosquito netting
down. There were eight of us to a paramedical tent with the
sides rolled up as the nights were so balmy. Each evening as I
was drifting off to sleep, I would see figures slipping from one
palm tree to the next. Very quietly and with caution, coming
toward me. They were Japs! I would sit bolt up and stare at
them and they would disappear. I would look around in the
tent and peer under my bunk and all seemed secure, my M1
was there but we had no ammo. We were in a rest camp in a
rear area. It was 3,000 miles to the action, but we had slipped
in on them at night. Why couldn't they do the same thing? By
now I was fully awake and realized how foolish I had been so
I would change the subject of my thinking and fall off to sleep.
I got very comfortable with this fantasy, even anticipating it as
I would go to bed. After all, how secure can a guy be? 'I will
wake up and they will all disappear.' Then one night as I sat
up to look at them, the loudest siren I have ever heard turned
on. What! Then the 90 mms started up. It sounded as if the air
raid siren and the anti-aircraft guns were right in my tent. I
leapt out of bed grabbing my rifle at the same time landing on
my knees on the plywood floor. There was a lot of shouting
and screaming, lights were flashing and the 90s kept blasting
away. I had my rifle clutched in my hands but no ammunition!
Caught again: I tried to stand but my legs would not respond.
Just immobile panic. I stayed like this for I don't know how

long and then things began to slow down. The guns ceased firing and the siren wound down. I could see and hear men running around and shouting, 'It's all right, it's all right – just a test, just a test.' The lights went on in the camp and in our tent. We were all in strange positions and just looked at each other. I don't think much was said. Slowly we all crawled back into our cots and lights went out again. I don't know, I don't know.

In later years, he likened the experience to his own birth: the noise, the lights, pandemonium:

The explosion of the birth into the light. The sounds of your own crying is the siren – must be the original fear. From security, being blown out to a cold world.

For me, Hawaii was wonderful the first time we went there and every time thereafter. The feel of the warm, moist air on my skin as I stepped off the plane, the sea breeze bringing the sweet smell of tropical flowers, and the pleasant, warm attitude of the people never seem to change. In the airport Lee looked for a drink stand to get a glass of milk, but couldn't find one any more: 'Coming back here during the war between invasions, the first thing we looked for were these stands with the huge glass bottle of ice cold, pure white milk, all frothy coming out of the spigots. We dreamed of it. We were always thirsty in combat.' (This was so universal a condition that it was dubbed 'battle thirst' in the First World War.)

Lee immediately took me to a little restaurant bar in the airport for my first Mai Tai. On the way to the Big Island, Hawaii, we stopped briefly on the wind-whipped windward side of Maui, where Lee rested, recuperated and trained before going on to the Marianas and Saipan. He pointed, 'Right up there on that slope,' and stood a moment reflecting. After he was wounded in that battle he eventually returned to Hawaii, to the US Naval Hospital at Aheia Heights on Oahu (now Marine Camps H. S. Smith).

We stayed at Kona on the Big Island, then a small village. Lee was a popular person there, as he had spent some time fishing off the coast after filming John Ford's *Donovan's Reef* on the nearby island of Kauai. He and John Boorman also came to the island in

1967 when scouting locations for *Hell in the Pacific.* John tells a story about a near-fatal experience they had while descending into a volcano in a small aircraft:

> I sat next to the pilot, Lee sat behind with Lloyd Anderson, the production manager, and as we went into this volcano we circled inside it – it's about a mile wide, the crater. Terrifying really, a steep bank turn inside the crater of a volcano. I was terrified but exhilarated, and Lee adored it. Lloyd Anderson suffered terribly from air sickness and was utterly miserable. When we came up out of the volcano, the plane suddenly spluttered, the engine packed up and we started to lose height, of course. We came down toward these vicious lava beds, with this black, spiky lava jutting up toward us. As we came down, I was pressing hard on the floor of the plane trying to keep it up. The pilot didn't give much room for confidence because he started screaming at the plane, 'Fly, you bastard, fly!' Which I didn't think was a particularly scientific approach to the problem at all. As the lava was rushing up toward us, I looked around to see first of all Lloyd Anderson, who had looked so grim but was now smiling because his ordeal was thankfully coming to an end. I looked around at Lee, and there was this slight smile on his face of absolute serenity that here at last it was. Somehow it seemed for Lee an appropriate way to go, crashing into a volcano. Whatever he was feeling inside, I had this absolute conviction that he was completely serene in that moment. Finally, the engine spluttered into life and we just skimmed the surface and climbed up again. It was a case of a lot of Mai Tais that night.

Lee and I stayed at the old Kona Inn, which was owned by his good friends Dudley and Marylou Child. (Marylou was born in Hawaii, a descendant of early settlers who had owned sugar cane plantations there.) Their company, Inter-Island Resorts, owned several hotels in the island chain, but this one, the oldest and the most 'island style', was Lee's favorite.

The lobby, with its huge trophy marlin on the wall, spoke of the hotel's history as a stopping-off place for fishermen from all over the world. In earlier days, prize catches were brought up to the beach below the hotel while a big iron bell tolled from the grounds to call the weighmaster. Interested townspeople and tourists came flocking to see what might be a world record or just good catches of fish, as they do now at the village pier.

Sport fishing is a major and much-loved industry in Hawaii. The Japanese inhabitants, for example, must have their fresh tuna at Christmas, and marlin is often served along with the Kailua pig at *luaus* for births, weddings and other feasts. We often sent marlin to these *luaus* after catching them on our fishing trips.

The lobby, dining room and bar of the Kona Inn were all open to the sea. There was a ship's figurehead hanging on the wall of the bar which I remember for the expression on the carved wooden face of the woman, her long hair streaming behind in the imaginary wind. It had such a feeling of eagerness about it: you could imagine it bursting up out of a heavy wave on the ship's prow with its expression of awed rapture combined with open-mouthed fright – rather like my own approach to big game fishing.

One morning on that trip a water spout struck shore right in the open dining room, much to Lee's delight. He had been having an early coffee while waiting for me, and watched it approach. He loved nature's violence as well as its beauty. He once drove several hundred miles from a film location in Oregon to a bluff in northern California to see a predicted tidal wave. It petered out before he got there, much to his disappointment, I'm sure. On another occasion, he was returning home wounded on the troopship *Annie Arundle* in December 1944 when the whole fleet encountered a typhoon, which capsized three destroyers. Against orders, Lee and another man ran out on deck. The huge ship was pounding down many feet in the enormous waves and rising up in a near-vertical slant. The waves came over like an immense wall of opaque blue, he said, and crashed down yards ahead of him, but leaving him in a giant bubble of air. He had to wrap his arms around a stanchion to avoid being swept overboard, but the experience was thrilling.

After the water spout struck the hotel, Lee hurried about reassuring old ladies and helping up people who had fallen. Then he went out to follow the path of destruction through the town. The spout had flattened the ugly new concrete post office that the residents hated, but had spared the little wooden schoolhouse next to it. The Hawaiian population nodded knowingly: living on a small island underneath volcanoes that often erupt gives one a certain respect for the gods as well as the elements.

The waitresses, waiters and bellmen, all the hotel employees, welcomed Lee with great fondness. We woke up each morning to the news on the radio, the Coconut Wireless, and one day heard that a major earthquake had hit Los Angeles: highway overpasses had collapsed, streets were buckled, and there was a lot of damage. This was February 1971, and all our children were there at the beach in Malibu. The telephone lines were so jammed that I could not get through. Lee called the operator and explained the situation: 'This is Lee Marvin. Can you help me get through? My children are all in California.' He was through in no time and we were relieved to find that everyone was fine. People liked to help Lee.

We fished nearly every day after breakfast, looking out over the sparkling blue-green sea. In Kona, it's a rare day when the ocean isn't calm. Many times the hotel boxed us up lunches of cold, delicately-battered *mahi mahi* we had caught the day before. I began to learn deep sea fishing myself, expertly taught by Lee.

On this trip we were fishing from the little boat owned by 'Rope' Nelson, who would later be the captain of our boat *The Blue Hawaii* in what was loosely described as a 'partnership' – well-meaning on Lee's part, at least. The arrangement came to a sorry end, but before it did, we came here year after year with our children, my parents and friends. They were idyllic times. We rented the Spalding House, a lovely two-storeyed dwelling on a point of land; some years before, John Wayne and Pilar had been married there. The open sea was at the front of the house and lagoons filled with colorful fish were on either side. Stone steps led down to the water, where we swam and snorkelled. Across the bay was the Kona Surf Hotel, and every evening we could hear the drums beating out the rhythm for the hula dancers. There were tall palm trees at the edge of the lawn, and one evening a coconut fell to the ground with a loud thud. Lee immediately sprang down into a startled crouch; twenty-seven years after the war he was still on the alert.

There was a very large banyan tree down the road from the Kona

Inn, and Lee told me that he felt very uneasy whenever we passed it, particularly in the evenings. The great roots of banyans and the crevices in their trunks were favourite hiding spots for both sides during the war, and he never lost that wary feeling when he saw one.

We fished from our boat, swam in Captain Cook's Bay, and cooked our catches over the volcanic lava coals at night: fresh *ahi*, tuna, *ono*, *mahi mahi*, or ate the tuna raw, *sashimi*-style. We went to Huggo's Restaurant where we sat on the porch open to the water and watched the sting rays gliding in the shallow surf and the Hawaiians out on the rocks with their sacks picking up prickly sea urchins or prying the tiny *opees* off the dripping stones.

These were the happiest days of my life, until the Hawaiian captain of our boat fell victim to the promptings of his new 'howlie' wife and stole our vessel, justifying his action with a claim we were to hear on another and highly-publicized occasion. 'Lee promised,' he said, 'by *oral agreement* to give me the boat.' It was a bitter disappointment for us both, and the end of our time in Hawaii.

7 Pocket Money

Soon after our honeymoon Lee's father went into a coma. Toward the end of 1970, after a spell in a Florida hospital brought on by a terrible bout of alcoholism, Lee's father had asked Lee what he could do to help Lee's tormented brother Robert. 'Die before spring,' was Lee's sad reply.

And in March 1971, after sixty-nine days in a coma, he did die. After visiting his unconscious father in hospital, Lee knew it was the end. Before leaving him, he bent over and kissed his forehead, saying, 'That's it, Chief. I'll see you down the line.'

He sat on the aircraft and ordered a martini from the stewardess. The movie being shown was *I Never Sang For My Father* starring Melvyn Douglas, who physically very much resembled Lee's father. Lee was stunned. The martini remained untouched.

'It was my life right on the screen before my eyes,' he said when he got home to Malibu. He wrote a letter to Melvyn Douglas telling how it affected him, but never sent it:

Dear Mr Melvyn Douglas
Actor to actor if that is possible – from Garbo to this time. I have seen your performances not all but most. I am a FAN – but what you did at one point in your film career lifted or dropped me to my knees. One which is not important, the other is, if I might explain.

It is seldom that I have seen utter control of self and not indulgence or vice versa. So – on flight No 000 of Delta Airlines LAX from Miami in 1971 AD, First Class – I first saw on a small screen *I Never Sang For My Father*. I was absolutely enthralled having a martini (not six to one), then the cloud lifted and I turned to my fellow passengers and said, 'Dead on'. They were either asleep or bored, I was absolutely enthralled.

My career – then twenty some odd years into the wind – major actors, stars etc – suddenly became real. There was not a moment that I did not anticipate, not a move, a pause, a glint and I was CHEERING! I think I was forty-five years old. There is no need to compare, *it was over* and they did not know it.

I returned to my family much relieved.

There is no need to compare: it is all there, and to force you to relive would be sinful, I know!!!

What a joy it must have been to play – I must get slight at this point, your actors, sets, design etc were impeccable. Much less or more the selection of direction.

I could have played any of the roles.

I commend you for your performance, your time, envelope, and your

WILLINGNESS

LOVE

LEE

PS I had a professor in high school who said under the whip of the cane 'You think I'm fooling around with you?'

The funeral of Lee's father was in Woodstock, with services at St Gregory's Episcopal Church, where he had been an elder for many years. We were to stay at the family house on Wittenburg Road, where Lee's brother Robert and sister-in-law Joan were living at weekends. During the week they lived in New York, where Robert taught art history at a school in the South Bronx: quite an accomplishment considering the poverty and violence of that area. It was April 1971 and still quite cold, with left-over patches of snow here and there. Robert, so deeply involved with his father and still caught up in the tableau of the past, was surprisingly composed. Lee seemed to have worked through his relationship with 'the Chief', and though sad and reflective, was also calm (save for one moment when, having a drink, he suddenly tensed his shoulders so much that the seam ripped out of one arm). Later, Lee and I went out to dinner, arriving home in the crisp moonlight; the car tires crunched on the still-frozen driveway. We went to the mailbox on the porch where the key to the back door had always been kept, even in the 1940s. No key. We went round to the front door. All was dark and quiet, and the door locked. Every door locked. We got back into the car, crunched out of the drive and drove to my parents' house. We went back to the Marvin house the next day, and eventually Lee enquired, 'What happened to the key last night, Robert?' 'Well, brother,' Robert replied, 'you were out after midnight, and in this house we take the key in after that!'

Lee just shook his head. It was discouraging to see the old ghosts back, this time with his brother immediately taking on the role of father.

Paul Newman was on the plane when we flew back to California at the Easter weekend. It was a coincidence, as he and Lee had just signed to co-star in *Pocket Money*. The movie was to be produced by Paul's company, First Artists, which he owned jointly with Steve McQueen, Barbara Streisand and Sidney Poitier. Lee liked the script, and welcomed the opportunity to keep busy so soon after his father's death. Paul said, 'If you agree to do this one with me, I'll do any film of your choice next with you.'

The band Chicago was also on the plane, a 747 with an upstairs lounge. We all went up there to listen to tapes of their music. There was a lot of strange-smelling smoke in the air and we wondered if it would affect the pilots, who had opened the cockpit door to listen to Lee's banter with the group. Paul came upstairs and Lee introduced me to him. When Lee turned away, Paul immediately pinched my bottom. I was startled, of course, but secretly flattered. But then I did not know much about actors starting a film together – yet.

We had pretty much been hiding out at home, and I had never been on a movie location. There had been a few interviews, a few photographers, perhaps a television special or two: *The David Frost Show* and others. Fans, of course, were everywhere Lee went. This was a new part of our life for me. The location for *Pocket Money* was in Arizona, just north of the Mexican border. Since it was only five hundred miles away we took our own car, Lee's great white Chrysler Imperial. Lee flew there with the rest of the cast and crew while I drove the car with Kerry. I later came to know that Lee always liked time alone with the company and cast at the beginning of each film. It was a time of mental sparring and feinting, of feeling each other out in the roles they were to play. He wanted to be free of outsiders, especially such a close outsider as a wife. His outward calm and absolute control of himself as an actor always lulled me into forgetting how charged and intimate an atmosphere surrounds every day of a film or play. Every sense is electrically alive, apprehensive; it's almost like preparing for combat. Particularly at the beginning.

As a matter of fact, Lee said that being in the Marine Corps had taught him how to act in the first place. Even in simply representing the Corps, you had a heavy responsibility for how you carried yourself, your stature. He said in an interview with Second Lieutenant Robert Johnson, Jr USMC, in July 1986, 'The discipline learned in training allowed you to perform in combat, no matter how you felt inside; even when terrified, you had *esprit de corps*. You learned to work together in harmony – which by the way is the real meaning of the often-misinterpreted expression "gung ho". This all works in acting too.' The closest thing to the Marines for Lee right after the war was the camaraderie of summer stock theater at the Maverick, and he took to it immediately. As he said, 'After being in combat I didn't intimidate easily.' He used all this in acting, and had an absolute loyalty to each project he was involved in. The play was the thing for Lee, and few people were more protective of his fellow actors, more helpful to them and more involved.

About acting Lee once said, 'You know, there is no such thing as talent. Either you know or you don't. But once you know, there is no going back. I must add, it's nice to have a buck in your pocket.'

Kerry and I arrived at the Rio Rico, the motel where the company was staying, at about 11 o'clock at night. Lee was waiting for us in the dining room with Paul Newman, the producer John Foreman, the director Stuart Rosenberg and the cinematographer Laszlo Kovaks. We were about ten miles away from Nogales, the twin town that straddles the Mexican border. Having felt out everyone connected with the filming, Lee said to me that night, 'Baby,' (which is what he called me when he was enthused and trying to emphasize a point) 'you will never be on a better film in your whole life!'

John Foreman was a humorous, gently-spoken 'gentleman producer', who not only had class personally but believed in doing everything in a movie in a first-class manner. He was very protective of his actors and cared as much for the artistic objective as for the financial – not a usual thing for movie producers. Producers often have a real disregard for actors, feeling that they are an annoying but necessary part of their money-making projects. If they could figure out a way to have movies animated instead of using real people, many producers would be ecstatic. Most of the time producers are juggling to keep everything *under* budget, *within* schedule: trying to give the appearance of being concerned and forthcoming with expenses and salaries, but underneath trying to wring the most work possible out of cast and crew. Often this is carried to the point of overwork, illness and even death. Some actors do have petty demands and ego problems that require constant approval, but this is not usually the case with the truly professional actor. John Foreman cared about his actors – he was a 'fan'.

Pocket Money is a light-hearted western about two bumblers 'of a rather low class' (Lee's description) trying to make a killing buying cattle in Mexico. They are trying to swindle the natives but get conned themselves. The script was written by a 'brilliant guy', as Lee described Terry Malik, based on the novel *Jim Kane* by western author J. P. S. Brown. The billing on the movie's credits was resolved by the various agents, with Paul's name first, but lower and to the left, while Lee's appears to the right but higher. Lee described Paul's wardrobe as 'the Levis, the tight ass and the sombrero'. Lee wore a rumpled pin-stripe business suit, snap-brim fedora and dusty, black, down-at-heel shoes. While filming, Paul hated wearing the hat, but Lee kept telling him how great it looked and finally got him comfortable about it. One day Joanne Woodward, Paul's wife, came to visit. He was ready for the scene, and came up to her as she sat on a camp chair tatting: 'What do you think?' She looked at Paul and remarked that he looked just like an Easter egg in that hat! Paul sagged, 'Augh,' he moaned. Lee described his role and Paul's as 'obsolete losers, two hustlers – but like the kind of hustlers kids are'. As for his character, he said, 'His name is Leonard, so figure it out. He's a jerk, yes, a meanie, no.'[1]

1 Mary Daniels, *Chicago Tribune*, 13 February 1972.

The last time Lee and Paul had worked together was many years before on a film titled *The Rack*; it was released in 1956 before either one of them was well established. Lee was excited about the real 'two star' aspect of this film, something that hadn't happened for a long time. He hoped it would work out. 'Sort of like *Boomtown* with Gable and Tracey, but with no girl.' It started out, as with most films, with a positive and happy atmosphere. Happily too, our good friends Matt Clark and Strother Martin were in the movie with Lee.

Most of the early sets were exteriors in the beautiful spring weather of the southern Arizona desert. There were cattle drives and cattle pens, Mexican hacienda courtyard banquets, a rodeo and camp-fire scenes at night alongside streams surrounded by enormous cottonwood trees. Paul and Lee had twin trailers on the set in which to rest between shots, change wardrobe or have make-up applied. These were large motor homes with beds or couches, a bathroom, a kitchen with stocked refrigerator, and a booth-style table. They would be driven to each site every day (or left with guards) and brought back after each day's shooting. The size of the trailer is always dictated by the rank of the star and, for those who care about that sort of thing, it is often a bone of contention when actors are jockeying for position or stature. This was for me the first of many more trailers, of countless hours of sitting in ones similar to this, all over the country and all over the world. It was at this location that I first learned about the enormously hard work and the repetition and the tedium of film-making. Sometimes there is one take, and sometimes ten or more, each involving extra time to reset the camera, or cameras, the lighting, and whatever else is required for that particular set-up. I saw Lee's attention to detail; how important his wardrobe was to him – its authenticity – as were the props. He knew history and the historical aspect of everything. He knew guns, modern and old, knives, saddlery, ropes, knots. He usually watched every scene whether he was in it or not, even on the days when he was not filming at all. I asked him why, seeing that other actors didn't. He said he didn't want to be 'surprised'; he wanted to know the continuity of each scene for his own reactions. Everyone respected him greatly for his professionalism and knowl-edge of every aspect of movie-making: directing, sound, cameras;

he knew lenses, angles, what the camera maximizes or minimalizes. When I first watched a close-up I thought he wasn't doing a thing, there was no reaction at all. Later at the dailies, I saw a different story altogether in his expressions, movements, or his eyes reflecting emotions. As they say, he knew his craft.

Lee identified with all people and he spent many hours on a set talking to the stuntmen (most of them old friends from many other films), the cowboys and wranglers, as well as the other actors and bit players. The trailer drivers always appreciated Lee's neatness – important when a trailer is used daily for months at a time – and his interest in their job. He knew everyone wanted to do a good job and had pride in their work. Lee never took the frustrations of work out on the crew, the wardrobe people or the make-up artists who are often the target of an actor's misdirected ire. In his mind, they were all together in this project and however long it took, two months, six months, *this* was the family. Paul, too, was not aloof. He joked and mingled with the crew and called himself the 'grey fox'.

Lee usually left for the day's shooting at five-thirty in the morning, having coffee and breakfast at the outdoor tables or in the big tent the caterers had set up. The caterer was wonderful on this location, which makes a huge difference on a film. If the food is bad, it is very demoralizing; you are usually out in some far-flung place with just one hour for lunch in a long working day. You get very hungry and are stuck with what is served.

My daughter Kerry and I would either go early in the morning with Lee to watch the day's filming or go later, after her tutor left and after horseback riding with our Mexican-Indian guide, José. He spoke no English at all, but managed to tell us all kinds of things as we rode through the desert – or mountains or stream beds. We saw Indian petroglyphs on cave walls, old mine entrances, railroad tracks with nails from 1830, Indian pottery shards, small scrub brush deer and running herds of javelina (wild boar with tusks). Lee bought me a pen-knife for my pocket, saying I should always carry one when riding. He also took me to Paul Bonds in Nogales and had hand-made ostrich riding boots made for me. We always went to the set for lunch, lining up with Lee, the cast and crew, presenting our trays in turn at the catering truck window. We usually sat at the 'A' table reserved for the 'principals'. The protocol for dining on a movie location is very well defined with the producers, director, leading actors and cinematographer at the first table, graduating 'down' to the other actors, crew (electricians, carpenters, crane operators, and the rest); the drivers of the army of cars and trailers needed on locations usually had their own table. As often as not, however, Lee would sit with other actor friends, the stuntmen, or with anyone he wanted to talk with. On rare occasions we would sit in his trailer if he felt like being quiet. At that particular location I recall the cinematographer, Lazlo Kovaks, a lovely Hungarian – his straight black hair falling to one side and always with a long black cigarette holder – good-humoredly talking and sipping his daily glasses of wine at lunch. When the film was released, high compliments were paid to his photography, his brilliant whites and the beautiful luminous quality of the film. He was delighted to hear that my middle name was Csinos, the Hungarian name of my mother's best friend. We all became best friends, as you always do on a film.

The rest of the day Kerry and I would watch the filming. Often the director, gentle-speaking Stuart Rosenberg, would offer me his director's chair to watch a scene, as would John Foreman. I was completely spoiled by these lovely men. I didn't know at the time how unusual it was, even for the star's wife, to be treated so deferentially. At the end of the day, after a drink and before dinner, we would all troop to a basement room and watch the dailies (the previous day's uncut filming), applauding the acting and laughing at the flubs, asides, retakes, disasters. We often had dinner in our room, and then fell into an exhausted sleep.

One night, at dinner in the hotel dining-room, Paul, Lee, Lazlo and several other men at the table all began talking about their relationships with their fathers. I knew Lee's quite well, but I was not prepared for so many similar stories. Although different, each seemed to have unresolved feelings and deep frustrations – they seemed to be striving for an approval that would always be denied, and an unhappiness that didn't end with the death of their father. It seemed such a waste and I wondered why it was so. I had no such problem with my mother; in fact, quite the opposite.

One day, like an elegant circus troupe, the entire company moved to Tucson; the long trucks, horse trailers, catering vans, and the producer, director and leading actors driving their limousines. We were ensconced in the old Tucson House, one of the few high buildings in Tucson at the time. It was on its way to being turned into a geriatric residence and the bottom half had already been converted. We were in the penthouse 'suites', such as they were, and the elevators and the small dining-room in the basement were full of wheelchairs and walkers. We weren't sure whether the inhabitants were overly delighted to share their Formica tables with this rather boisterous crowd – which was usually the case with the cast and crew after the day's wrap. As a consequence, most of the company went next door to the Hilton, a favourite place at the time for movie companies.

If Lee was not too tired, we went to neighboring restaurants. It never took Lee too long to tire of eating dinner out, no matter how good or elegant the food or restaurant. He rarely enjoyed it after working and more often than not fans would interrupt just as he was putting his fork into his mouth, almost always opening with, 'I hate to bother you at dinner . . .' He usually finished the sentence for them, saying, 'But . . . you will.' This was one of the few times when he was bothered by fans asking for an autograph.

Usually, Lee said, it is nervousness and ignorance of an actor's life that makes people seem rude with their requests. But he appreciated fans. 'Where would we be without them?' he'd say. Paul Newman absolutely refused to sign autographs. However, while Lee, typically smiling, complied and went on his way, Paul was left talking and having to explain that he didn't, wouldn't, and why not.

Lee's opening scene (where he is waking up and rising out of a cot) was filmed in the barrio section of Tucson in a lovely old hacienda-style house. Balconies overlooked the interior fountained courtyard. During one scene Lee was sitting at a table laden with beer bottles and tortillas when two dogs unexpectedly ran into the shot, fighting and yelping. Lee continued, immediately using the interruptions, flinging a tortilla at one and shouting at both. It happened so quickly that I thought the scene had been ruined and would have to be reshot, and I laughed out loud. Of course, the camera was still rolling because the director liked the candid reaction. Luckily my voice was in a spot on the tape that could be cut out, and I quickly learned a lesson about both 'quiet on set' and Lee's quickness at improvising. (The sequence, the way it was later edited, was a good example of how some of Lee's scenes were so pared away that they lost some of their great humor – pauses were shortened, changing reaction beats, for example.) This was my first experience, too, with the habitual use of Beesmoke on a movie. This is acrid smoke wafted in front of the cameras in tin pots or with bellows to simulate smoky interiors, mist rising, railroad steam, or to create an atmosphere or mood.

The telephone in our room rang one night and it was Dr Max Jacobs calling for Lee. He was known in the business as 'Dr Feelgood', and he had a 'whole bag of tricks', as Lee explained it. He was often called in to keep actors on their feet in emergencies, of one form or another, while working. This could include drug problems, alcohol excess, exhaustion or bad health from the weather. Lee was startled, hurrying out the door, wondering why he had been called. 'I'm not out of hand,' he assured himself. He came back about forty-five minutes later, relieved. Max had simply wanted to meet him and show him a new technique he had just discovered for turning black and white film into color. He also brushed some liquid on Lee's eyes which immediately made his eyesight crystal clear. His real purpose for being in Tucson was to calm down a young, out-of-control actor on another film being shot in Tucson, *Dirty Little Billy*. Lee recalled having routine vitamin shots in England while he was filming *The Dirty Dozen* when the weather was cold and rainy. A German doctor once gave him an injection of a new vitamin combination he was trying out. It made Lee extremely angry and gave him thoughts to violence. 'Ah, yes,' the doctor said later. 'A form of this was given to the Nazi SS troops at certain times of stress.' Unfortunately Lee had been visiting Vivien Leigh, whom he adored, at Tickerage Mill, her home in the country, and had ripped up a deck of cards that turned out to be a priceless set, hundreds of years old.

We had children coming and going all during the filming. Maury came for a time and after she left, Rod arrived. He came just as we moved from the relative city atmosphere of Tucson to the dusty town of Gila Bend in Arizona, which is named after the poisonous, beautifully beaded lizard of the area, the Gila Monster. We stayed at the best place in town, the Space Age Motel, which suffered many raucous remarks from us all for its décor. The actual filming was in another town, Ajo, where the central square doubled as the film's plaza in Mexico. There was a large bar-room in a building on the square and one afternoon Lee started drinking there with the local inhabitants. When I came in the door he pulled me over to introduce me to the men he was talking to, Hispanic men from the town. One stood up and kissed my cheek warmly as I enquired what line of work he was in. 'Graveyard,' he answered. As hastily as I could without seeming rude, I retired to the bathroom and washed the cheek and my hand – only to find out later, in my ignorance, that he was talking about the graveyard *shift*, not the cemetery. Most of the men worked in the copper mine there. Lee became very drunk and I had to hold him up and walk with him across the whole square to his trailer. The filming stopped and the whole town – or so it seemed from the numbers watching – was silent. When we got to Lee's trailer, John Foreman came in and asked me what I thought was wrong. I asked in turn where Lee's double was. Bud Stout, a cowboy and Lee's stunt double in the movie, had been left behind, fired to save expenses. We were going to Santa Fe, New Mexico, for the next location and it would have been cheaper to hire someone there. I knew this had bothered Lee at the time and I could only think that this was his protest. To John's credit, Bud Stout was there the following morning.

Lee certainly did not drink every day. He could not, of course, and work so efficiently or at all. If he drank, he would get drunk – very drunk – with great energy and speed. He was hard to keep up with as he would sail quickly from one place to another: his chest thrown out, shoulders back, elbows swinging to some inner military beat. We, Kerry, Rod, Wendy, Maury, or whoever, followed behind like a scene from a children's fairy tale . . . the whole family always stuck together wherever they touched. Lee would have one conversation with someone which would lead off to another. Most of the time he was extremely amusing and quick-witted and could stay awake for many hours. Sometimes he would fall briefly to sleep only to bounce up, still drunk even the next day.

He was then up and off again until he finally slowed, sagged and eventually gave up. It was hard to keep from being exhausted and we would have to take turns, my son, my daughters or his driver on the movie. The following day he would feel very remorseful, the next he would be rather grouchy, on the third he was back to normal for another week, two, three, sometimes for two months at a time. He was also very resourceful. Once when we were shooting far out in the countryside, Lee appeared to be drinking – but there was no bottle to be seen anywhere – he got drunker and drunker until John Foreman begged me to find the vodka. I couldn't – a few days later Lee laughed at my question. 'Don't you remember that I had an ice pack on my broken toe? Well, it wasn't water in there, sweetheart.'

He *never* missed a day going to the set and never overslept. He might be quite drunk, but he knew exactly what he was doing. Often, amazingly, he could work when drinking; very few times on a film would they have to shoot around him. He, like some of the other good actors who drank, might cost a film studio an occasional day of shooting, only to make it up in spades when sober – which was most of the time. Occasionally, when he didn't like a scene, he would use getting drunk as a way to 'walk' – not do the scene until it was right. Not a few directors have commented they 'would rather work with Lee Marvin drunk than most actors sober'.

In the next location for *Pocket Money*, Phoenix, we stayed at a fairly grand hotel, the Westward Ho. One morning Kerry and I had been riding and arrived for lunch which was held that day in the hotel dining-room. A dancer, Pupe' Bocar, who was to have a small scene with Lee later on when we got to Santa Fe, had arrived just that day. As I came into the courtyard I saw Lee talking to her and looking at her with an expression that looked decidedly intimate, sensual. I was taken aback and stopped in my tracks, staring. Lee noticed immediately and shot me a very angry look and motioned with his thumb for me to 'get into the dining-room!' I knew he didn't even know her, but it was disturbing, a puzzle which I was not to figure out for some years – if, indeed, I ever did accurately figure it out. I learned that one of the things that Lee did not do was explain himself, particularly on a film.

As luck would have it, Lee found a way to 'punish' me. That night we were invited to dinner with an old friend of his and her husband, both older people, at their club's penthouse restaurant in Phoenix. He was still angry with me and he began to drink an alarming amount of vodka martinis as soon as we sat down. The wife was a sturdy-looking, gray-haired woman in her sixties, perhaps, and had acted with Lee in a small summer-stock production in the early 1950s. It was a horrible evening with Lee talking almost entirely to her, with the exception of being down-right rude and angrily competitive with her husband. I was not even in the picture. The crowning blow at the end of the evening was when she put her hand to the side of her mouth, bent her head to me and in an aside whispered, 'Oh, how I remember that lovely scar on Lee's behind.' When we got back to the hotel, we went to the lounge where Paul Newman, John Foreman and the whole group were sitting at table. We sat with them for another drink and then someone urged Pupe' to get up and sing. As the band struck up and she began her number, Lee pulled me to my feet and yelled loudly, 'Get up on your feet and applaud . . . you'll *never* be as good as *she* is!' To add to my supreme embarrassment, not only had the buttons popped off my blouse and I was having to hold it together, but he grabbed some woman at the bar and started to dance with her and kiss her. It was the worst night of my life. A complete shambles, and completely out of character for Lee, even when he had had too much to drink. He had been so attentive during the movie, explaining everything, proudly introducing us to everyone and to the entirely different world of film-making. I wondered – is this all a punishment? It had to be, and all because of one doubting look from me, an instant reflex in my eyes, just a widening, perhaps. And to add to this, from then on, whenever Pupe' was on the set, she was very sweet to me and very attentive, as though she too thought I was jealous and wanted to reassure me. Everyone else began treating me very tenderly and I couldn't even try to dispel the notion for fear it would seem I 'protesteth too much'. So I was stuck with it. I couldn't very well say, 'Oh, hello . . . I'm not jealous.' There was nothing for me to be upset about, except for the way Lee had treated me.

From then on, in later movies, something similar of varying

degrees would happen. I always felt hurt and perplexed. I began to question myself. Was I indeed jealous, suspicious, right, wrong, nuts? Eventually Lee offered the explanation that actresses were very insecure, they needed to feel important and that they were of prime importance to him for a scene. 'At my expense?' I did protest! How better to elevate an ego than to squash the wife in front of them. I finally came to the conclusion that in order for Lee to play a scene with another woman, he had to 'get rid of me' emotionally, and that it was not only the many actresses who were in need of the 'pumping up' when it came to play-acting love, but *he* was the one who was insecure – at least that's what I thought sometimes.

The company moved, for the last two weeks of filming, to Santa Fe, where the skies were deep blue and dark green piñon trees colored the surrounding mountains. We stayed at the La Fonda Hotel, the old Harvey House Hotel, where railroad passengers of the 1920s would take their dinners (my mother and father included). Paul Newman, who always traveled with a portable sauna, plugged it in the socket the first night there and plunged the entire hotel into darkness. It is remembered to this day by the staff.

Lee and Pupe' Bocar's scene arrived. The script described it: 'As she passes back past him, he catches her arm and swings her out on to the deserted dance floor. They fall into a slick, practiced step. She is bored; he is businesslike.'

The night before this scene, Lee was about to try on the tight pointy-toed Mexican boots he was to wear for the dance. Walking across the room barefoot, he stubbed his toe on the couch leg in our suite. It immediately sprang out at right angles to his foot and he looked at me in horror. Off we went to the hospital in Santa Fe where the doctor explained there is no way to treat a broken toe. He then took a pencil off his desk as a lever and snapped the toe back in place. A *pencil*! Lee said, stunned. He did the scene in the morning. It was very, very funny with Lee in his shabby striped suit, stomping his heel and emulating the stiff elbowed postures and gestures of a grand flamenco dancer. Pupe' already was a good dancer. When it was finally over, the boot had to be cut off the throbbing and swollen foot by the wardrobe man. As so often happens, however, the whole episode was cut out of the movie entirely, and so ended the whole business – all for naught.

Our last setting was some twenty odd miles south of Santa Fe at the little, no longer in use, railway station of Rowe, New Mexico. In a sweeping valley, it was once the home of the prehistoric tribe of Pecos Indians. Lee was talking to an older man, a local Mexican-American policeman who remembered poignantly how grand a valley it had been in his youth; filled with thousands upon thousands of head of cattle waiting to be shipped all over the country from that little station. Now the trains hurtle past as though it had never existed.

We were about to go to lunch one day here, when two young children ran up to Lee. Pulling at his arm, they asked him to come to their house instead, to have lunch with their mother. The surrounding houses were a cluster of shacks, with pig pens, chickens running loose and muddy paths in between. I thought he would surely refuse, but he accepted with alacrity, urging me (quite against my will) to come along. They took his hand and we entered one of the houses to be met by attractive surroundings. The mother and another woman friend who shared the house were both ex-Peace Corps workers who had served in Micronesia in Palau and the neighboring islands. They knew many of the people Lee had known there, the Ibedule, the chief of the islands, and the local priest, Father Hoar.

We had a lovely lunch, a pleasant interlude. Lee was always open to such invitations to meet people. He was ever inquisitive and did not let opportunities pass him by.

The last scene, the wrap of the movie, was shot by the tiny yellow station with Leonard 'thinking about a big can of yellow cling peaches', and both musing about their future. Paul wanted to improvise some dialogue at this point, which caused Lee his only loss of cool in the entire movie, when he burst out, 'You want to improvise with me?!' The director yelled, 'That's a wrap!' and the movie was over.

Lee later said he was greatly disappointed in the project and in Paul Newman because he really loved the script: 'We had it – we got it all down on film and it just didn't get on the screen. When I saw the final edit, I thought, well, fuck, you'll never see two, let's say top ten stars work together again. I don't know why they can't do it, but it was Paul's company, and if he's got to win, well, that's up to him. It's his prerogative. He got the dough together, so if he wants to cut the finesse points out, he can do anything he wants.'²

When the movie was edited, the director, Stuart Rosenberg, called a meeting of protest and wanted Lee to know that the cutting was not his. Even so, it is still a good movie – just not what it might have been.

The feeling at the end of a film is bittersweet. Over two months of very hard work, six days or nights a week, emotions charge and change with roller-coaster ups and downs; you are close together with a whole group of people all day, every day, like a family, and then you have to say goodbye, knowing you won't meet again for quite some time, if ever. It's a far more exhausting job than one would think, so the sweet, of course, is that the work is done and you're on your way back home, back to the kids, back to seclusion and privacy.

Lee came down from the movie by driving me slowly home to California by way of a visit to Taos and the pueblos of the Navajo Indians, up to Aspen, Colorado, where we stopped the car and rushed out to wade in the freezing cold water of a snow-fed stream. We had just left the desert when we saw cattle bloated by the side of the road, having died of thirst from the terrible drought that year. It seemed so pathetic that there could be so much water so close by. Lee was an expert skier and, as with motorcycling, he skied not only for pleasure but competed in races, really throwing himself into it. He showed me all the different slopes, although now it was early summer and the aspen trees were quivering in the breeze. He took me through the breathtakingly beautiful Bryce Canyon and Zion National Park. We went on to Las Vegas, staying not at a grand glittery hotel but a small motel on the outskirts. Lee wanted to hide out after having just spent two to three months being totally in the public eye. As we dropped down over the mountains on the way to Los Angeles, the entire basin was covered by a sea of yellow smog. We looked at each other and said, 'My God, that's where we live and breathe.' That sight began our slow but inexorable move to the desert of Arizona.

2 To Grover Lewis, *Rolling Stone*, 21 December 1972.

8 Fishing

Fishing was such an important and integral part of Lee's life that it is difficult to know what it really represented to him. Even he likened it to a Jungian experience, a dream of some kind: 'The magic of Moby Dick. Big game fishing is a challenge on three levels, physical, intellectual, and emotional . . . acting is only a challenge intellectually.' It wasn't just the sport, and it didn't have to do with catching the biggest fish, or the challenge of the fight, or the 'winning'. Whatever it was, it went on unrequited throughout his lifetime.

Even Lee's earliest recollections have him rod in hand, exploring streams on summer vacations in the country. Once, before he was five years old, he wandered off from home to a lake for a whole night of fishing. He quit the lake in the morning, not because he was cold and shivering – though he was – but because he was out of bait. The police, called by his frantic parents, found him, and he says of himself, 'he wasn't as tall as the striped leg of the trooper who brought him in'. He wrote a poem in 1984 about the experience. The first lines state his feelings about fishing:

> Whether it's money or line
> Or patience or time
> The end comes all too soon.
> It's off to the lake with pins bent and straight
> And string from the butcher and kite
> Grasshoppers and worms, a cricket or two
> And possibly crawdads (whatever in nature will do)
> Now the sun has set and it feels like rain
> But a stout hearted angler feels no pain
> The mother wails and the father phones
> They've all been alerted, a boy on the roam.

The dawn comes breaking from a chilling night
A family filled with fright.
But the troopers have done one hell of a job
This time they don't miss, they have him in tow.
Twelve sunfish, two cats, a wall eyed pike
And a small mouth bass half ate.

They spotted the runt at a quarter to eight
Sitting on a log that floated in the lake.
His hook was in the water, his eyes wide awake
But the silly little bastard had run out of bait.

So it's homeward bound with lights all aglow
Flashing and turning (red and blue) you know.
Faces all happy and full of joy – drinks are
passed around as they talk of the boy.
But soon that's all over – the hero's on the way
Mothers still hugging . . . Dad doesn't have much to say.

So it's off to bed for mummsie . . . She had a hell of a night.
And me and Dad to the bathroom to set things right.

The fish are in the garbage, my pants are on the floor.
My father's hand is stinging and my bottom is all aglow.

Ahhh – and that was long ago.

As a ten-year-old away at boarding school he writes an exuberant
letter of birthday thanks to his father. At the top, in the humor of
the day, he writes in mock Chinese lettering 'Foo Too Yoo',
followed by:

!!Dear Pop!! [this swings into a map of New York State]
    Boy, the rod is a pip! I have been playing with the plug in the
tub (rimes nice). Yesterday the mailman brought two air mail
and a registered letter. Ann sent $5.00 and some more Mark
Twain books and Estelle sent me a (buck fifty) $1.50. Mother
bought me a Jiffie Kodak and 2 rolls of film. After that I went
to the Sportsman's show. I saw some wight trout (you know,
the color of this paper). They had two trout about 3 feet (fresh
water too) 3 times this [he draws a line]. I am going to buy a

pair of hip boots at Sears and Robuck in Carmel when I get back to school.

My school work is coming along swell. I have a report on Wendell Phillips and also on John Jacob Astor. I have made Estelle a wooden mapel leif at shop and also something for you and Mother.

There was this man. Boy could he cast. There was this chip about 100 feet from him and he landed right on top of it with a fly.

I can never thank you for the rod and reel. There swell.

Give my regards to cooke.

Your loving son

Lee Marvin

[more Chinese lettering]

PS Thanks for the rod. So long.

Lee could spell long and difficult words with no problem, but probably through indifference, the spelling of simple, everyday words eluded him all his life.

Lee's father had an office in Lakeland, Florida, and his parents kept an apartment in the Lakeland Terrace Hotel. Lee spent a great deal of his time fishing in the nearby lakes and in the mangrove inlets and bayous near Tampa Bay. He fished for tarpon both by day and night, poling along in flat-bottomed boats. He caught rays, striped bass and snapper, and also surf-cast all along the Florida coast again for tarpon and snook. When he was at St Leo's College in nearby San Antonio, Florida, he spent his free time casting from the heavily-underbrushed shores of the lake – in between hunting wild pig with a knife strapped to a bamboo pole, hunting deer, puma and wild turkey with shotguns in the everglades, or looking for alligators to wrestle.

When he lived in New York and acted in summer stock productions, he fished the shores of Long Island, surf-casting for bluefish, or he would hire boats for deep sea fishing off Montauk Point. Lee knew every kind of bait, from worms to flies and lures, and studied tackle avidly. It was a natural progression for him to add big game fishing as soon as he moved west, 'when I became successful enough as an actor to *afford* it!'

I'm sure he passed from being a 'fisherman' to an 'angler' very early in his life. His expertise put him in the same rank as western writer Zane Grey, who was a pioneer marlin angler in the early 1920s and fished from his own boat in the waters of New Zealand, Australia and Tahiti. Others well known in the fishing world were Kip Farrington Jr, Ernest Hemingway and Alfred Glassell Jr (although neither Lee nor anyone else has yet surpassed Glassell's world record catch of a 1560 pound black marlin in 1953). A fairly small group of anglers around the world managed to combine a lifelong love of fishing with the physical attributes it takes: the mental focus, the tenacity, being where the big fish are with a good captain and boat – along with the essential ingredient of luck. Although Hemingway was an avid angler, with catches in Bimini, Peru and Cuba, a thousand-pound marlin catch eluded him all his life.

The Pacific Ocean became the ultimate fishing ground for Lee, and then for me as well: California, Mexico, Hawaii, Palau and finally Australia. He caught marlin, the queen of fish – small, striped, blue and black – and also sailfish, tuna, dolphin fish (dorado, *mahi mahi*, they are all the same beautiful blue and green fighting fish). When he built his boat in Palau after filming *Hell in the Pacific*, he fished with the native fishermen and learned about tides and currents and winds.

Lee once asked a Palauian about to go out for just one day of fishing why he was taking along a whole case of evaporated milk. The man looked at him pointedly and asked, 'You ever been on a drift?' Since the next island was two thousand miles away, Lee understood. Flying over Palau once, he told me, 'The pilot asked us all to look out the windows and try to spot a fishing boat lost at sea. Oh boy, baby, you can't believe how wide that Pacific Ocean is until you fly over it!'

On one of his many Mexican fishing trips he chartered a fishing boat that ran out of fuel many miles out to sea in bad weather. He and the crew were eventually rescued, but he never again trusted anyone else's preparations without checking everything himself. 'God, those uninhabited shores and rocky coasts are wild!' he reflected.

Lee was so avid about fishing that not even gunfire could stop him. He was in Panama in June 1964, fishing from the Club de Pesca, when violence broke out in the streets. He went immediately to observe the fighting, which resulted in four US soldiers and twenty-one Panamanians being killed. He was finally ordered to leave by the US government, who flew him out – but not before he had caught a 224 pound marlin.

Over the years, Lee was a member not only of the International Game Fishing Association but also of fishing clubs all around the world. He was, for example, a charter member and president of the Los Angeles Billfish Club in 1963, a member of the Cairns Game Fishing Association in Queensland, Australia, and of the small Cooketown Sport and Game Fishing Club, also in Queensland, which was about as far north as one can get by land before the wild and remote Cape York. Nothing much is above *that* but the Torres Strait and the shores of New Guinea.

Lee was a natural leader in fishing as in so many other things. I was a complete novice when I started fishing in Hawaii, but he taught me well and patiently. He started off by talking about safety, telling stories instead of giving instructions. If I stepped near a coiled rope on the deck, he would say something like, 'Oh, yeah, I saw a guy once step in the middle of the rope, the boat jumped forward, and it unwound so fast it broke his ankle.'

Each day's conversation was laced with anecdotes and warnings. He showed me how to hold the rod, how best to get it from the rod holder when a fish had taken the bait; how to strike it, and how best to get to the chair and set the rod in the gimbal, the small metal holder at the bottom of the chair – not easy to do when a thousand-pound marlin is on the line. He always let you do something on your own first, and would then make suggestions so that you didn't feel like a complete idiot. Lee also had extraordinary mechanical gifts, not only for fixing things that were broken, but also for redesigning them to work better. He also knew many different knots, and could tie and untie anything, it seemed; he was often called on at home to untangle necklaces. He personally oiled and cared for the complicated Fin Nor reels we had on our Tycoon rods. The captains of the other fishing boats would come over and ask Lee to fix their reels if they had a problem. He would sit on the deck and take the reels apart, all the tiny parts carefully set out on a towel, repair the reel and meticulously put it back together.

Lee taught me everything, supplied me with the best possible equipment, and placed me on a great series of boats in water where the big fish were. On top of that, I was lucky. I caught the first fish from our own boat *The Blue Hawaii*, a *mahi mahi* just outside Maui. We were bringing the boat from Honolulu to Kona, and Lee gave me the first strike. It was a good thing I caught it, for as I was told later, the first fish tells the story of whether the boat will be lucky or not. We were lucky.

In November 1971 we had flown to Fort Lauderdale, Florida, where Lee had bought the fifty-six-foot fishing boat with an eighteen-foot beam. Built in North Carolina, she had a LeMay hull, twin diesel engines and a soaring tuna tower. Lee hired two young English sailors to sail the boat down the coast, across the Gulf of Mexico, through the Panama Canal, and then north past central America and up the coast of Mexico to San Diego Harbour, where we met her – no small trip! We then brought the boat up to the San Pedro Boat Works in San Pedro, California, for a complete overhaul, new screw, new paint and the lettering of *The Blue Hawaii*. Lee would spend the entire day down at the harbour watching the boat being worked on. I picked out pale blue coverings for the interior and exterior seat cushions, upon which we were to spend many an hour sitting or dozing, waiting for strikes. When the fourteen-ton boat was ready, a huge crane lifted her aboard a Dillingham Lines barge and she made the long trip to Hawaii to Honolulu harbour for more refurbishing. Ray Accord, Lee's captain from the *Ngerengchol*, brought Lee's fighting chair from the boat in Guam and it was bolted to the deck.

After *The Blue Hawaii*'s arrival in Honolulu, we boarded her for the two-day trip to the Big Island of Hawaii. The boat was adorned with *ti* leaves for good luck, and no bananas were allowed on board as they are considered to be very bad luck. We had a Japanese deckhand with us, and Hawaiians Rope Nelson (the captain) and his wife Lori. Lee was as happy as I have ever seen him, and the day, like almost every day there, was sunny, warm, slightly breezy and clear as we made our way out of the harbour past Diamondhead. Passing between Molokai and the island of

Lanai in the Kalohi Channel, we put our baits out and I caught the *mahi mahi*. We put in at Lahaina on Maui that evening and stayed at the old Pioneer Inn, where the chef cooked the fish for us. That night Lee and I were in a second-storey bedroom overlooking an enormous banyan tree in the courtyard. The ceiling fan with its big white blades whirred softly as Lee reminisced about his Marine camp on the other side of the island during the war.

'God, it was funny,' he recalled. 'You'd go into town and get a shave and a haircut from these Japanese women with straight razors in their hands. You'd sit there with your neck exposed, your hands in your lap. A month before I'd been shooting at their relatives. You thought ummmmm.'

The next day the sea was calm as we headed out of Maui. Leaning on the bow rail of the boat as we sailed by the tiny island of Kahoolawe, Lee told me that the entire island was a US Naval bombing range and was covered with live explosives. As we passed the island, Rope Nelson came down from the bridge and told us that we would soon be crossing the Alenuihaha Channel, a passage of wildly-merging currents that could sometimes create very rough seas. There was no way of knowing in advance whether it would be rough or not, and there would be no way of turning around. Very shortly after, we began to meet heavy seas, until eventually we were bobbing and wrenching through twelve- and fifteen-foot waves. The boat was groaning and shaking, pounding down and rising up in shuddering leaps. The Japanese deckhand was lying on the deck with a wet towel over his face, waves were breaking over the bridge as the captain clung to the wheel, Rope's wife – a Hawaiian who had spent most of her life on the sea – was below decks, violently ill. I kept going down to her with pails and basins and wet cloths. The rest of the time Lee and I spent wedged between the table and the wall to avoid being thrown about in the open cabin. At one particularly thudding descent, he put his hand over mine and squeezed in reassurance, but when I looked at him I noticed that his eyes were absolutely green, the color they became when he was under stress. Often it meant he was about to have a martini, perhaps a double martini, straight up. Seeing this, I was even more scared, but I summoned my best stiff upper lip and asked him – knowing nothing about ocean survival – if he thought I should get out the lifejackets. He just shook his head, chuckled wryly and said, 'No, no, that wouldn't do.' What a shakedown cruise! We made it through the channel, whose name means 'the laughing waters' – and they were certainly laughing that day. We pulled into our slip into Honokohau Harbor, battered but proud of our boat.

The next summer we rented the Spalding house. Lee, Kerry and I came there directly from Spain and the movie *The Spike's Gang*. We had come to fish and that is exactly what we did, every day for thirty-three days without exception.

One day Rope suggested that I had fished enough to be able to do it entirely on my own, and we agreed that I would take the next fish that struck on the eighty-pound test line reel. Lee's 130 was out on the other side. When the reel did whirr alive, I jumped up in front of Lee, put my hand up, surprising myself as much as him with my ferocity, and commanded, 'Don't touch that rod!'

He drew back with a laugh, saying, 'OK, OKayyyyy,' and I grabbed the rod and ran to the chair. There was a good tuna on the line, but the reel was an aged Penn International that kept slipping. As I put pressure on the reel, one screw popped out and then another until there were screws and springs all over the deck. I would bring the fish in and it would circle for a while and then be off, taking all the line I had worked so hard for. By the International Game Fishing Association (IGFA) rules, no one but the angler can touch the reel or rod, so Lee ran below and came back with a screwdriver which he handed me to stop the reel from slipping back. Hours went by and dusk came. Lee was guiding the chair – which had to be facing the line and the fish – wiping my brow and giving me sips of water. I had been on this fish for two hours, then three. The captain kept calling the hours out like marking twain. I felt every emotion from exhilaration to sadness, from anger to hope. Lee said at one point that if I wanted to give up, it was OK with him, he understood. 'I don't want to,' I told him in no uncertain terms. I had no idea I had such determination: I felt that I could sit in that chair until I died or the line broke. In the end I was hand-lining the fish in, and after four hours I finally got it to the boat for the deckhand to gaff. It weighed just under two hundred pounds, only a few pounds below a world record. I was exhausted, but the fish looked as if it did not even know it was hooked. When it was brought on board I felt an overwhelming feeling of love for this fish, a powerful feeling of togetherness with it – difficult emotions to imagine when I had in fact killed it. But it gave me a clue as to what makes people do this time after time and started me fishing in earnest. Lee's reaction was to send immediately to Kerr's in Beverly Hills, one of the top sporting goods stores in the world, for two Tycoon rods and two Fin Nor reels for me to accommodate eighty-pound test line, and one 130 Tycoon rod and Fin Nor reel for himself. He had brought with him a case of his favourite Garcia line and we all began to have very fine catches.

We had by now begun to take turns, although Lee preferred the 130 tackle. Occasionally we would get a double strike and each would take one.

A marlin is the most magnificent of fish: it often leaps out of the water repeatedly, thrilling everyone who is watching and keeping the angler very busy making sure no slack is in the line when it takes off again at breakneck speed. The person guiding the chair has to keep the angler facing it. Lee always held the chair for me and Kerry, and I guided the chair for him. Kerry, who was eleven at the time, caught a 196-pound marlin one day. That evening at home, Kerry thought that Lee would probably celebrate with a few martinis, so she scotch-taped the vodka bottle closed (and any other bottle she could find). She put a note on the vodka, and when Lee reached for the bottle, he was met by a firm message, 'FORGET IT!' It amused him no end, as it did my father, who was visiting us – but it didn't do much to discourage him.

Although these marlin we were catching were small, they did not go to waste. We always gave them to Hawaiian families who were having *luaus* for weddings, new babies or birthdays, and they were much appreciated. Occasionally we brought home marlin steaks for dinner. We began to have such success with big tuna after such short fighting time that we felt guilty about catching them so fast. They were sold at the market, of course, by the captain for extra money for himself; but we were *really* fishing for marlin.

On 12 September Lee and I were dozing on the cushion over the bait box, waiting for a strike. I dreamed that the huge head of a marlin rose up out of the water and looked at me. I was staring at it, in awe at its size, when I was startled awake by the sound of a reel spinning and the screaming whine of line being pulled out. I leapt to my feet, and as it was my 80 rod, grabbed it and went to the chair. The fish never jumped, and was not seen until nearly an hour later. When it appeared, rising up as I brought it in, it so mirrored my dream that I said, 'Oh God, no!' It turned out to be the women's world record. It was caught on eighty-pound test (Garcia Line No. 35156–66) with a yellow Kona Head lure and on the Tycoon rod and Fin Nor reel from Kerr's.

Lee wrote the following account for the IGFA to record the catch:

Kailua, Kona, Hawaii
September 12, 1973
by Lee Marvin
On that day, the 35th of a forty day fishing trip, the following events took place. Leaving Honokohau harbour at the usual time, 7:30, we proceeded north to the ground. We had six rigs out: three 130s and three 80s. Pam was fishing the 80s, I had the 130s. Our daughter Kerry, 11, said she was along just for the ride, having the week previously landed a 196 lb. Blue 'with a little help'. Also on board was Rusty Unger, acting as deckhand, and, of course, Rope Nelson. The lures were in their right positions and working well. At about 11:30 we had a strike on one of the 130s, a bill wrap which I did not get to the chair. We kept trolling north and by 3 o'clock we were alone as the day charters had already started for home for their 4:30 docking. At about 3:10, there appeared a wall of solid white water about 15 feet long where one of our lures should have been and an 80 was screaming, so were we. Pam was right on the reel and Rope was shouting to 'back off', which she was doing. The fish was on the surface and plowing sheets of water so solid that none of us could see the fish itself. A fast, steady and solid run. Pam had backed off enough to move to the chair and be snapped into her kidney belt. The run was still heavy and steady, but below the surface. I was watching the reel and the first slowdown came at about 550 yards and at 600 he had turned. There were two more short runs, but less than 150 yards, and the fish settled to the work

of the angler. Forty minutes later the line was well down, the water was calm and clear so we started to look for color. At last, way down, he showed on his side, but still too deep to be accurate as to weight. Pam was steady on the fish. Then the line started up and we lost sight of him. Pam was gaining line on every pump and I suddenly realized that she had only 50 yards to go. Both gaffs had been set out, the meat hook ready and the persuader laid handy, so we all stood quietly and looked and waited. The arch in Pam's Tycoon rod was perfect, she cranked and we waited. Then suddenly, 50 feet straight back of the boat, a big dorsal rose, then the bill and finally the open mouth. They were big and Pam said, 'Oh God, no!' and we all muttered, 'Oh God, yes.' Then it turned to port and we saw it for the first time clearly. By that time the double line was on the reel and kept coming, and suddenly, there was the swivel and Rusty's gloved hand reaching for the leader and his other hand starting to lift. Pam slacked off the drag in anticipation of another run, but the leader came up steadily and Rusty was calling for Rope to come gaff. Rope leaned over and placed the big gaff between the pectoral fins and everybody began to shout. The second gaff was in and Pam left the chair. The rest was standard as it should be. It was a classic fight. The fish had struck hard, worked hard on the surface, and tried to sound. The crew had been perfect, as the boat and the day, no mistakes. A steady, cool angler who listened to her captain, and good equipment. Pam, who but a few weeks before had spent 3 hours and 55 minutes on a big Yellowfin, with a broken reel handle, a spongy drag and a soft tip, to miss the women's record by 3 lbs 14 oz, which prompted the author to order three new riggs of proper construction.

We were towing the fish into Kailua where the weighmaster had been alerted. The trip home took about two hours as we did not want to damage the fish. We could not get a tape on him as he was behind the boat and we did not want to stop. It was dark when we pulled into Kailua and the pier was crowded with tourists and locals and the marvelous captains and crews of the Kona fleet. As we pulled alongside, the crowd saw the fish for the first time and a cheer went up. Pam was sitting well forward and I said to her, 'They are cheering the fish. You caught the fish, take a bow.' She stepped aft into the light and another cheer went up. Two captains jumped on board to aid in tailing the fish and anticipation was high. When the fish was lifted there was a roar from the crowd and for the first time we saw the majesty of the fish. All our doubts and fears left us as fast as a short strike. Everybody was congratulating Pam and the captains were hugging and the crewmen were kissing her with pure joy. I was at the scale with Phil Parker. The existing record had stood for nine years at 555 lbs (previously held by Haku Baldwin of the Hawaiian Islands). He had the scale set and locked at 600 lbs before the fish was steadied and the handlers stepped back. Phil asked me if I were ready. I nodded and he released the lock. The arm shot up. Yow! As knowing eyes snapped and grins broadened, the scale leveled at 607. Flash bulbs popped. A magnificent fish. A magnificent lady and angler. The rest is madness.

The day after I caught the marlin I was besieged for my autograph. It was definitely an odd feeling, since I was sitting with *Lee* and he was in the back seat. I rubbed it in for as long as it lasted, which was only a brief few days.

Lee was a consummate angler, with many fine catches through-out the years. He was a far more accomplished fisherman than I was – but he never had a confirmed world record. Nor had John Wayne, another fisherman who was full of praise when Lee told him about my achievement when we were together on a TV show. Lee was extraordinarily proud of my catch, but I know it must have been both good and bad news for him. Nobody is *that* selfless when it comes to fishing.

About five years later we were at home in Tucson when he came up to me with an expression that promised something of import. He said to me, 'Guess what?'

Of course I asked, 'What?'

'You've lost your world record.'

I couldn't decide whether it was an expostulation of sorrow or triumph.

'You didn't have to tell me so suddenly,' I simpered.

'Oh, but I – I didn't want you to hear it from some stranger!'

I glowered back at him and he chuckled guiltily.

One night we were out to dinner in Kailua and ran into Sally and Fred Rice, friends of Lee's who lived in Hawaii and had a cattle ranch outside Kona. They were both fine fishermen and had their own fishing boat there. With them at dinner was an Australian fishing charter captain in his late twenties named Dennis Wallace, blue-eyed, stocky and bearded, with a hearty handshake. Suddenly he said to Lee, 'Why don't you come to Australia and really fish? Stop ginning around with this little stuff. If you've got the guts to, give me a call. I'm booked for the season but I'll give *you* my first cancellation.'

When we came back to Hawaii the next season, Rope Nelson had divorced Lori and married a howlie (white) woman, and the owner-captain relationship began to fall apart almost immediately. From the time we bought the boat, we had had an arrangement with Rope that was so generous it was a charter fishing boat captain's dream; in most people's estimation, the boat was the pride of the fleet. Lee also decided that he would give the captain ten per cent ownership in the boat each year until it reached fifty per cent; 'pardners' at fifty-fifty. I didn't think it was a good idea, especially since the boat was supposed to be a birthday present to me, but Lee said, 'Look, he loves the boat. You have to give a man some pride. He used to own his own boat; simple as it was, it was *his*. It's just a matter of pride of ownership.'

I shared his feelings, and decided that it didn't really matter anyway. Unfortunately, it did matter, as we were to find out about two years later when Rope stole the boat and sued *us*.

Soon after Rope's remarriage the situation became untenable: he refused to take the boat out – claiming that the seas were rough, or making one excuse after another – and eventually fishing was at a standstill. Lee felt it was no longer a pleasure, so he decided to sell the boat. I was heartbroken, but there was nothing else we could do.

Lee had given the captain thirty per cent of the boat over two years. He had made this a part of the legal agreement, and in two more years Rope would have owned fifty per cent of the boat, for which he had never contributed a cent. Lee called his attorney Louis Goldman to come over and terminate the agreement. His wife Judy came with him; both had fished with us, and they were also saddened by this turn of events.

Rope came to the meeting and begged Lee to allow *him* to try and buy the boat. Lee, never one to harbour ill feelings, agreed: 'The guy has to make a living. Let him have a shot at it.' Lee and Lou agreed to let him try, but Judy and I totally disagreed, asking why he should be rewarded when he had behaved so badly and cost us our lovely and very expensive boat. But for Lee the entire thing was a great disappointment – the loss of the boat he had loved, as well as what he had thought of as a trusted comrade – and he felt it was not worth exacting retribution. He not only agreed to let Rope try to buy the boat, giving him generous amounts of time to do so, but he also left some of our fishing rods, reels and equipment on the boat to help him make a success of it.

As we were preparing to leave the island, we were abruptly served with a summons accusing us of theft and fraud. It was claimed that Lee had given the boat to Rope in an oral agreement, that we had stolen *his* fishing rods and reels (our own that we were taking home), and that we should be arrested. The suit was for $570,000 for fraud, punitive damages, mental anguish, unpaid services and theft of fishing equipment. It was a total surprise and Lee was stunned; I was outraged.

It seemed to me that Lee's largeness of spirit set him up for some enormous disappointments when he gave too much to people who didn't deserve his trust. In a way, he brought these things upon himself. He felt that all people were basically good, and that, given the opportunity, all wanted to do the right thing. He was always reluctant not to believe in what he called 'the glory of man', a line from the director Jean Renoir. Lee had been introduced to Renoir by Jeanne Moreau when the great director invited them both to lunch. Lee always recalled his remark about films: 'If it doesn't show the glory of man, don't do it.' My feeling was that you should stop something before it got out of hand.

The trial, with Lee as defendant, was held in April 1976, nearly two years later, at Hilo, the small sugar cane processing city on the other side of the island. It lasted seven days and Lee was found not guilty; the jury was polled and the verdict was unanimous. In fact, Rope was found to be culpable, but because Lee had given him thirty per cent of the boat, it had to be sold at federal auction.

We were in our hotel room after the verdict when Rope's son and daughter-in-law came in. They were stunned and crying, and said to Lee, with what seemed an almost childlike lack of guile, 'For a long time there we thought that we would win and we were happy. Now what will I do?'

Lee put his arm around his shoulders and said, 'Take care of your father.'

The boat was put under federal guard, and we boarded her to look around. She was in bad repair, having been without Lee's care for almost two years.

The auction was held in the grounds of the federal courthouse in Honolulu. It was planned that Lee should buy back *The Blue Hawaii*, but he did not. Rope bid $80,000. Lee later explained to me: 'Look, I saw the boat and it's in rotten shape. It needs two new diesel engines – they haven't been cared for in two years. It needs paint and a lot of work. It will cost at least fifty to seventy thousand to get it in any kind of shape. They were obviously going to bid it up as high as possible, no matter what I bid, to get Rope's share as big as possible. For me fishing is ruined there anyway. We're not going back.'

He was right: we only went back once. We were on our way back home from a trip and decided to stop over in Kona to see old friends. We reached Honokohau just in time to see men with big chainsaws about to cut into *The Blue Hawaii*. She looked like some enormous apparition, listing to one side in the black volcanic gravel. We had no idea she was still there. The men stopped when they saw us, and said they were having a terrible time trying to cut her apart because she was so well made. We sat there as they told us what had happened.

Rope had apparently borrowed money from a bank to buy the boat. After some years he found he couldn't keep up the payments and sold her to someone else. This man couldn't keep them up either, so he took out a large insurance policy on the boat and tried to sink her in the ocean. She wouldn't sink. He then decided to blow her up in the harbour by feigning an accident. The explosion damaged the two boats on either side, but the flames went out by themselves.

Now the hulk of this once-proud boat, from which we had fished for a total of only seventy-three days, had been dredged up from the water and would be demolished piece by piece until she was no more. Rope, on the other hand, surfaced again some years later, taking the opportunity to testify – falsely, as it was quickly proved – against Lee in another court case: the one brought by Michelle Triola.

Fishing in Hawaii was indeed over – but in the meantime, Lee had discovered Australia.

9 God, Australia!

Australia – the people, the land and the fishing – evoked deep emotions in Lee and inspired him to concentrate on the next 'beats', or important years of his life. In his words, this was 'Phase III'.

Brazakka, the name given to Captain Dennis Wallace in his childhood by the aboriginals who he steadfastly claims raised him (in the face of all known facts), *did* have a cancellation of one of his charters. We immediately packed our bags and rods and took the next available flight to Australia. This trip in November 1973 began a yearly odyssey not only to the fishing grounds of the Great Barrier Reef but to the country itself and its people.

We fell in love with the country, both for what it was and because it made us alive to qualities that might have been those of America fifty or so years ago: straightforwardness and independence. People took responsibility for their own welfare, something we seemed to have lost. Australia is nearly as large as the United States but has a population less than that of the state of California, and, except for a few large cities, settlement is thinly spread around the periphery. The desert is so hot that in the Coober Pedy region, where they dig for opals, people live underground. In the south the cold winds come unhindered from the Antarctic, and in the north there are wildfires in the bush, droughts, flooding wets, cyclones. Something is always happening on land or sea. More of Australia's snakes are poisonous than those in Africa, the funnel web spider is far more feared than the Black Widow, and poisonous sea snakes swim in the ocean.

For the next ten years we trekked half-way around the world to Cairns in Queensland, the Gateway to the GBR (Great Barrier Reef), as the town is known. Year after year the journey became shorter as more routes and airports opened up. Even so, it meant at least thirty-five hours of travel. At times we stopped off, at times we went straight through. The season for marlin in these waters is only three months long, and for many years Lee refused any movie offers for the month of November. This made his agent very unhappy. Lee responded, 'I take care of a lot of people all the time, including him, and this is one time I'm going to do something for myself.'

Lee rarely spent money on himself, and then never frivolously. But he spared nothing when it came to what he felt was his responsibility: his family, me, the children, the grandchildren, his brother, the house, my parents' needs of any kind. Although it was a standing joke that he wouldn't let me have anything I could 'get away on' – a car, or even a bicycle – the only limitations imposed on me were my own, which I must admit grew fewer as the years went by. Lee once barked, in answer to a quip from a television host about the large amounts he was paid for his movies: 'I've probably put more kids through school with taxes on that salary in one year than a lot of people have in their lifetimes.' He was always somewhat defensive about the money he earned, as he didn't really believe actors should be paid as much as they were. His father once admonished him, 'My God, Lee, do you realize you earn twice as much as the President of the United States!'

Whenever he was asked by a journalist why he would turn down a movie role – paying around a million dollars – just to go to Australia, he would jokingly reply, 'Ah, I only make movies to finance my fishing.' But perhaps he wasn't joking.

On our first trip to Australia in November 1973, Lee – never one to waste time sleeping during an interesting experience – and a young Australian couple struck up a conversation that lasted from 2 a.m. when we left Hawaii until we got off the plane at Fiji. Artist Gus Cohn and his wife Jennie were returning from a year-long trip of sketching and painting around the world. When we left the plane for a few days in Fiji, we were presented with a series of sketches of Kew Gardens and an invitation to meet a group of their friends for lunch in Sydney, both of which we readily accepted.

A group of Fijian workmen recognized Lee outside the airport and hailed him over to share some of their home-made *pulka* – a palm toddy, Lee explained. We were offered a sip from the communal tin cup, and Lee appeared to take a drink. I took a taste, not wanting to offend. He might have tasted or he might not have: he was a good actor, and could seem to do things that he hadn't really done. After his times in Micronesia, he was also fond of the peoples of the South Seas.

We were met in Sydney by Gus and Jenny, and went directly to an extraordinary lunch at Doyle's Restaurant on Watson's Bay with a group of their friends: photographer Graham MacCarter (who became a lifelong friend), Fred Madderom, also a photographer and graphic designer, artist Tim Storier (one of Australia's best-known painters) and his wife Sharryn, art director for *Vogue* Australia. We didn't know it then, but this began an annual tradition, with more and more people added to the group. While the waves lapped gently on the sand and the water sparkled in the bright sunlight, we dined at a long table laden with Australian lager, splendid wines, John Dory, oysters, lobster mornay, heaps of mussels Portuguese in a milky broth with French bread, king prawns, and Queensland mud crab (which is more like a delicate lobster than crab).

Later, in Cairns, a cook from the Tradewinds Motel took us through the mangroves in his little skiff to pick up his mud crab traps. The Trinity inlet, in which crocodiles had prowled not long before (and do again), was wide and winding, with many tributaries and islands. The banks were choked with mangrove tree roots, making it impenetrable. We were bitten by the numerous sand flies that swarmed over us as we pottered slowly through the silty brown water. The mud was alive with scuttling crabs of many different colors. You could hear the loud cracking of their claws, which sounded like thick branches snapping in two. These crabs are so large and strong, weighing three or four pounds, that they can instantly break a person's wrist or snap off a finger or toe. I wondered how such an environment could produce so delicate and pure a creature. I had never been in this kind of tropical estuary before, and enjoyed it – though I was rather apprehensive about the possibility of tipping over into the dark water, not knowing what might be swimming below. Lee found the whole experience 'very spooky. It reminds me of wading through these swamps during the war at night. We had to paddle through all this on the Jap-held islands.' It also reminded him of an incident when he was filming

Hell in the Pacific on Palau: 'Once I was lying in the muddy swamp with bugs crawling all over me. I almost lost it . . . I had to silently talk to myself, "Hold on Lee, hold on," to finish the take.'

Big game fishing in Australia often brought back memories of Lee's fighting days, adding another dimension to something that was already exciting and dangerous enough.

The sight that greeted us on our first evening in Cairns was a two-thousand-pound Great White shark being hauled out of the water. We had sauntered down to the harbour to look at the fishing boat we would be going out on the following morning, and saw a knot of people working on the wharf. 'Wow!' Lee silently mouthed as we quickened our pace going toward it. A spotlight was trained on the fifteen-foot-long man-eating shark as the men tried to winch it up on the gantry. They were having great difficulty getting it up to the scales for the weighmaster, Daphne Neilsen, to get a proper weight. It was so heavy it could not be hoisted on the scales ordinarily used for thousand-pound marlin. The young American captain who had caught the shark, Peter Wright – whom we knew from Hawaii –was working feverishly to get a correct reading as it looked as if it might be a world record. In the end it wasn't, but as the creature was being hauled up, unborn baby sharks poured from it on to the dock. A cry of dismay rose up from the crowd of onlookers.

This was our introduction to what was swimming around in those waters, and what we saw underneath and around our boats in the years to come – and also to another dimension of the local people's enthusiasm for the sport. Although fishing is a well-respected industry that employs many people, there is also great empathy with a gallant fish and an abhorrence of wanton killing, even of the feared White, Tiger, Mako, Hammerhead or any other of the species of shark so prevalent in those waters.

Next morning we sailed out of Cairns Harbor on the thirty-four-foot fishing boat *Sea Strike*, going at full throttle out of Trinity Bay, through the Trinity Channel and past Cape Grafton on our way to the fishing grounds where the big marlin are. We traveled for more than three hours through the coastal waters, threading our way through the shallows and reefs that in 1770 kept Captain Cook away from the open sea. The best area for marlin is at least thirty-five miles out to the ribbon reefs, where the water is one hundred fathoms deep. Only a little further on it drops away to at least two thousand fathoms. The boat slowed for us to catch bait; Lee and I stood with light tackle rods in belly harnesses and caught the small scad or twenty to twenty-five-pound tunas that are the only bait for the big marlin. We went out to Linden Bank and north to reefs up the coast in the Coral Sea: Opal Reef, St Crispin, Agincourt, Escape. On future trips we went further north, past Cooktown and Cape Bedford, Cape Flattery, Lookout Point, on the way to tiny Lizard Island.

Along with our captain, Dennis 'Brazakka' Wallace, there were two deckhands, Brian Reeves and Peter Fairburn. We were also fortunate to have with us Emmet 'Mutt' Cobel, an American photographer and retired deckhand introduced to us by Dennis. Mutt was well known in the world of big game fishing and was very helpful with his advice. He also filmed our trip, which gave us a record of our incredibly successful fishing. He and Lee discussed tackle at great length; Lee was anxious to get the best gear for our own boat in Hawaii, and Mutt showed me several invaluable methods of reeling.

The *Sea Strike* was small, we were to stay out at sea for ten days and there was no sleeping accommodation. So a 'mother ship', the sixty-foot yacht *Sea Fox*, was hired for us – an apt name, as she became just that, a place of comfort and rest sixty miles out in the ocean and our home at night after long days of strenuous fishing in the humid heat. It was a great relief after reeling in enormous marlin, watching fish sewn up for bait: the days were all hooks, metal, gears and diesel smoke. But at night we had comfortable cabins with hot showers and were served gourmet dinners, good wines – anything we required from the well-stocked liquor cabinet plus, of course, the Australian national drink, beer. In the evenings we anchored just behind a reef, where at times there were other fishing boats some distance away. After you have showered and changed into clean, cool clothes, your skin tingles from the salt and sunlight, and you are deeply relaxed and tired – tired but not weary. The sunsets are glorious: gold and pink. The engines are silent, and in quiet weather the waves rock the boat with a gentle rhythm. An occasional sound drifts over from another vessel. The boat's decks are washed, equipment is put away in order and all is extremely peaceful.

Sometimes we would invite people from other boats over for hors d'oeuvres and drinks. We would all sit on the after deck watching the sun set over the majestic Australian highlands on the darkening horizon. Occasionally we visited other boats in the 'rubber ducky', as the rubber dinghy was called. I was very aware that we were sailing over deep waters filled with man-eating sharks as we humped over the waves between the boats in the dark, often after we had had several cocktails.

Our host on the *Sea Fox*, yachtsman George Fox, was from Melbourne and had been a pilot in the RAAF during the Second World War. Also on board were two friends of his, John and Mary Marion, who came along to cook and care for us, and a young mate, Peter Fairburn. There is sometimes rivalry between Australia's 'semi-aristocracy', as it might be called, and the more ebullient general population. We had some fairly spirited conversations: there was some muttering about 'dickheads' – a great Australian put-down – and general sorting things out in the first few days, with Dennis alternating between sticking up for his men's point of view and keeping them in line. Lee and I were impressed about how up-front both sides were: real democracy at work. We became a close-knit group in the end, and our daily success or failures were very much enhanced by our reception at 'home' each night.

John Marion was a softly-spoken yachtsman who had also been an RAAF pilot during the war. He and Mary lived on their sailing boat and spent their time racing or traveling out of Mooloolaba, the Whitsunday Islands and MacKay, with trips around the continent and the world. Mary was a gentle and sweet-natured person. She seemed so tiny and frail that I asked her how she liked her life at sea. She admitted to us that though she loved sailing, it often terrified her. At times, she said, her fear was so great she would lose all hope. But eventually the fear and constant panic would give away to passivity: the sea was so enormous and overwhelming that 'you give yourself up to it and a calmness takes over'. As she told us this, I was reminded of seeing the small tuna fish when they were caught for bait, flopping and fluttering about on the deck; but when they are loosely wrapped in a wet towel, they become quiet, with a trance-like stillness.

From the outset, fishing in Australia differed drastically from fishing in Hawaii. To begin with, it's a rare day in Australian waters when you put your baits out – live, dead or lures – and don't get a lot of action. We once fished ten days on our boat off Kona without a strike of any kind. In Hawaii, the coastal shelf drops off immediately to deep water, and the fishing grounds are very spread out. There are big marlin in the waters off Hawaii too, but mostly the more ladylike big blues; here in Australia they are predominantly black marlin.

Lee began catching small marlin the first day out. They were brought up to the boat, tagged for research and released. They were in the three-, four- and five-hundred-pound class. These are called 'rats'; a fish over one thousand pounds is a 'horse'; anything over 1560 pounds – Alfred C. Glassell Jr's record – is an 'animal'; and the biggest marlin anyone could hope for (two thousand pounds plus) is the 'big Julie'.

We had put to sea on 3 November, and the next day we started off early in the morning by snorkelling over a nearby reef. Lee was diving, coming up and pointing out the gorgeous coral formations to me, or just lying on his back in the clear, pale-green sea. I swam off and looked down to see two small (three or four foot) gray reef sharks about thirty feet below me, so I swam swiftly back to the boat.

Peter Fairburn came back too, but swimming very slowly, without a ripple. When he came up on deck and was taking off his flippers, he quietly admonished me: 'When you're swimming out here, you are supposed to sneak in and out of the water. I was below you in the water and you looked like a fish in trouble, slapping your fins and fluttering your hands – just what a shark is looking for.' Then he reassured me, 'Never mind, they never bite before eleven-fifteen in the morning.'

I had scuba dived before, but in the poor visibility of the Connecticut Sound. Lee was an avid scuba diver, but eventually gave it up: 'I felt like an interloper. It's not my world, I didn't want to be spying on them ... What interested me more was the unknown. You drop the line just below the surface, see and just a few feet below there is something strange that will bite it – like dropping into a dream.'[1] When you are on a reef, of course, the water is shallow, twenty to thirty feet deep and a lovely green; only at the edge does it swiftly become dark (thousands of fathoms in depth) – a blue you do not want to invade.

Early in the afternoon Lee had a powerful strike. Dennis, perched high in the tuna tower, yelled over the bullhorn, 'On the right! Coming in on the bait. Looks like a horse!'

We jumped up from our seat on the bait box and watched as the marlin came out of the waves on to the bait, whacking it with its bill to stun it. We saw a flash of blue-green as the marlin lit up, which it does when it gets excited; a 'Christmas tree', Lee called it. It took the bait in a swirl of foam and started to run with it. Lee grabbed the rod from the holder, struck twice, and went smoothly to the chair, putting the rod straight in the gimbal. Sticking the butt end of the rod in this when you have an enormous fish on the other end, jumping and pulling every which way, can be somewhat difficult. When the marlin leapt up, several hundred yards behind the boat, it danced on its tail and fell back into the water with a huge splash, another indication of its gigantic size. We could see it was indeed a 'horse'.

Lee was wearing his lucky clothes, a sleeveless fuchsia T-shirt and his blue and white flowered Hawaiian jams. This combination rarely failed to bring him something. Eventually he settled into wearing beige trousers of Pima cotton, 'Cheops Poplin', from Kerr's that were so lightweight they quickly dried after the inevitable drenching you got sitting in the chair. Instead of wearing less, we learned to cover up to stay cool. Lee wore the long-sleeved blue Levi work shirts our daughter Wendy embroidered for him. His favourite shirt had blue marlin jumping, hooks and stars in gold thread, the name of our boat *The Blue Hawaii* on the collar, and a sun rising over the sea on the pocket. A later shirt had a map of Australia in gold, 'Australia' in large letters and more jumping marlin. The state the shirts are in attests to how often they were worn and how Lee felt about them. They are now sleeveless, patched, burnt almost colorless by the sun; the material is tissue-thin, and though the stays

1 Robert Ward, *Rolling Stone*, September 1981.

are still in place, the lining has come through on most of the collar. He even wore the shirt in this condition while being filmed fishing by *60 Minutes of Australia.* We were never without the hats Lee bought for us. They were made from white sailcloth and named Golden Fleece by the woman who made them in Burbank. They wore like iron, never came off and gave you lots of shade.

As with almost all the marlin Lee and I ever caught, this first one was hooked in the hard part of the mouth, and as it should do, gave Lee a good fight. After the initial shock of seeing this mammoth fish, you settle down (hopefully) to the skilful work of angling, gaining line as steadily as possible. Lee seemingly knew everything there was to know about the reels and how best to work them: all his movements were steady and smooth. He was also very strong. At times, however, the fish pulled so hard that Lee had to let go of the rod and hold on to the chair with one or both hands to avoid being pulled up and even overboard. You are pulled right up out of the chair straight-legged. Your harness or belt is not, as some people think, attached to the chair, but snapped on to the rod. Whatever happens to it happens to you. The rod, made by Jack Erskin at Branford's Tackle Shop in Cairns, was a tough fibreglass one with a bent butt for a better angle. Dennis had talked us into using his equipment – even the Sugi line that Lee and I didn't much care for – but even this rod bowed deeply as the fish tried to sound. Lee would sometimes look at me, raise his eyebrows and utter a 'huummmmmm, hummmmmmm,' a comment on the exertion needed to stay in the chair. He recalled a line of Ernest Hemingway's on marlin fishing: 'For the first five minutes you think you've got him hooked . . . then you realize it's the other way around' – and *he* was with the striped guys off Cuba, three hundred seventy-five pounds maximum!

There is no way you can rehearse what happens at the back of the boat when the fish finally comes up to the leader wire: a wire of a specified length that the deckhand is allowed to grab to bring the fish in to be gaffed. Usually all hell breaks loose, the fish whipping its bill back and forth and furiously whacking its tail about. Water is everywhere. The person pulling the wire has to be very agile, to say the least, and must wrap it round his hands in such a way that it can be released without losing the hands or an arm, or even being cut in two. It is like seeing a violent ballet: the maneuver can be very beautiful, with intertwined, instantaneous reactions and acrobatic, rhythmic movements. Brian Reeves was one of the best wiremen we had ever seen, and most were courageous and determined. Brian had long curly blond hair, was very tanned and always seemed to be laughing: the Golden Boy. It almost made you feel as if tragedy was lurking somewhere. One night, as we all sat exhausted on the mother ship after-deck talking quietly, he pressed my fingers into two deep indentations in the top of his head. He told me about a surfing accident he had had at the age of eleven. He recalled only that a wave had hit him normally. He felt no pain but found himself lying face down in the water, unable to move his arms or move his head from side to side for a breath of air. When he was taken to hospital in a small country town in north Queensland, they found he had broken his neck in three places. The doctor bored two holes in his skull and he was suspended with wire pins and rested upright on a board. His parents were told that if he *did* survive, he would surely be paralyzed and would never walk again. He did recover, but never went back to school. Now we watched him at sea, bending and twisting, pulling in thousand-pound marlin, teasing us and keeping our spirits up while we sat in a chair fighting a fish.

Peter Fairburn also seemed to have been born with great tenacity and courage. Being on the 'fickle' sea, as Herman Melville describes it, can often put you in situations where these qualities are called upon. Peter, who had blue eyes, brown hair and a handlebar mustache, was very amusing in the way some people have when they aren't even trying to be. Peter once saved a friend's life when they were out in a small motor boat. They were ten miles out at sea between Green Island and Cairns when the outboard motor conked out. They drifted until dark, when the boat sprang a leak and sank. His friend, although himself a deckhand, could not swim, so Peter, by alternately teasing and bullying, kept the man afloat for nine and a half hours, eventually pulling him up on a rock near shore where another mate found them clinging near dawn. 'Christ!' he exclaimed, 'I found out later that half the way I could have walked in, it's that shallow there at low tide!' The first thing he did, of course, was rush to the old Pacific Hotel, his favourite haunt, and down several beers.

The sport fishing captains in Cairns were experienced, aggressive and professional, and Dennis was one of the most highly regarded of them. With his wife Yvonne, he has a plantation in Kuranda, up in the mountains behind Cairns. They both became our close friends.

'Like most of the other Australian women we met,' Lee commented admiringly, 'Yvonne is well up to what everyone thinks of as the Australian chauvinistic male, don't kid yourself. It might seem that the men have it all their way with their "mates at the bar", going their own way with the little lady at home by the hearth, but that ain't the way it is. They're just as gutsy, just as independent, and usually, like women everywhere, have the last word.' Here he would shoot me a squinting glance.

Although in describing Dennis to others, Lee would jokingly borrow an Australian expression, 'He's a piece of work!', he liked him very much. He also enjoyed the actor in him and his humor, the 'ocker' expressions he used – such as 'Now, now, don't get your tits in a tangle.' Your teeth were 'clackers', your nose a 'hooter', a true story was 'fair dinkum' and the ultimate sign of approval about anything was 'job's roight!' We had complete confidence in him at sea, even under the circumstances of bad weather and huge seas that we had on more than one occasion.

Lee caught this first 'grander', a thousand-pound marlin, within an hour. If it takes more than an hour and a half, as a general rule it will take ten or more – and then the line will probably break. Night will fall, which is dangerous in those reef-filled waters. Every second of that hour or two, or however long it does take, is packed with emotion. Just guiding the chair was thrilling. When Lee's marlin was just behind the boat, it did what every angler, deckhand and captain fears: it took a mighty leap out of the water. Brian had to release the wire immediately, throwing it away from himself to avoid being yanked overboard or losing an arm. Lee had released the drag, so the marlin fled harmlessly out without breaking line. More cranking by Lee and it was again alongside. When it did come up behind the boat and Lee had got past the double line to the lead wire, the deck became a wild place with Brian grabbing the wire and holding the thrashing fifteen-foot marlin. Peter rushed to gaff and Dennis appeared in an instant with his 'persuader' – a baseball bat – to subdue the giant fish.

'How he gets down those ladders so fast beats me!' Lee said. 'He spots the fish from the tuna tower, fights it from the flying bridge, and he's on the deck with the bat the second that gaff is in.'

The marlin had to be winched on to the boat through the transom door, and as soon as it was lying on deck the crew threw off their gloves and shook Lee's hand while he said, as he always did, 'Thank you, gentlemen.' Peter Fairburn snapped open a can of beer and drank deeply, while we all laughed at his pre-emptive celebration. Dennis called over the radio for the location of the *Coral Seatel*, one of the mother ships equipped with IGFA-approved scales, and we headed toward her to weigh the fish at sea. The marlin proved to be fifteen feet long including the bill, six feet four inches in girth, and weighed 1060 pounds. As it lay on deck, its dark purple color turning a shimmering bronze-brown, Lee examined the fish in minute detail. He showed me the different fins, the rigid pectoral fin of the black marlin and how it differed from the blue. He pointed out the vents in front of the anal fin and the fact that it was a female – as almost all the huge marlin caught are. They are magnificent beasts and catching them is like no other fishing experience. Like the shark, they are primordial, ancient, and roam the ocean depths without a natural enemy except for man: the Japanese long lines to catch them up and the pollution that pours from the rivers of the world. Although they are edible and fine-tasting fish, marlin are so full of mercury that only an ounce or two of the big ones can be safely consumed in a week.

The crew were as excited as we were, for Lee, for themselves and the boat. Fishing is a joint effort, in which a good captain and crew make a great difference, not only in finding the fish, trolling the bait properly, but in handling the boat, the wire and the gaff. A few captains believe in backing down the boat so fast on a fish that it does not even know it is hooked, bringing it immediately to gaff for the crew to do the actual catching. But not so Dennis, and we appreciated him for being more sportsmanlike; Lee would not have put up with that kind of fishing.

Lee caught five or six marlin in two days of fishing, and the next day, as the chair was again being set up for him, I called him over in private and quietly threw a fit. I told him that I too wanted to practice on small marlin, to prepare myself in case I should hook a large one, and said I hadn't come all the way down here just to watch *him*! His mouth flew open, and he hunched his shoulders in a cringing posture of surprised guilt. 'Oh, I'm sorry, sweetheart!' he said, hugging me. 'Jesus, I was just so excited I didn't think!' He quickly obliged, as did a marlin almost in the next breath.

'On the right!' sounded from Dennis again, and I ran for the rod, grabbed it, pointed it toward where I thought the fish was and went to the chair. I was not even aware that another marlin had taken the smaller bait on the left, and that Lee was fighting it while sitting on the side of the boat. I tightened the drag and struck the fish, and suddenly it jumped up out of the water. As it leapt up, with magnificent jumps, we could see that it was definitely a thousand pounds or more. Lee brought the smaller one in, released it and took over holding the chair for me. 'So this is my practice,' I thought to myself, wondering if perhaps it had been a mistake to wear *my* lucky pink and white checked shirt. We used a very heavy drag in those days, never backing off from fifty per cent, and on 130-pound test line at the half, it was around sixty pounds pressure on the fish and me. I inched the pressure on more and more whenever I could, or when Lee or the crew suggested it. The feeling you get, in addition to fright and awe, is that you are hooked to a locomotive that is trying to take you out of the boat and into the sea behind it. Your legs are all that keep you from being pulled out of the fighting chair. The foot rest had been set up for Lee's long legs, and when the marlin pulled I stood nearly straight up. We were using Sugi line, a clear monofilament, instead of our old favourite braided dacron; it crackled and cracked frighteningly – at every inch sounding as if it would break. Liquid soap was sloshed on to the seat of the fighting chair so that I could slide more easily up and back as I pumped the line in, then pushed with my legs back up as I brought the rod high and back. When I began to sag and feel tired, a bucket of seawater was poured over me and the weariness immediately and dramatically lessened. I had the fish up to the double line and almost to the wire three times. Each time it took the line back, I would lose hard-worked yardage. Suddenly – and this can be seen in the film Mutt Cobel was taking – the marlin gathered its forces and rushed toward us at great speed, making an attack on the boat. All 1030 pounds of it, with its vicious three foot long saber-like bill, would have been on top of me had its lower bill not caught under the lip of the gunwale. It did make a hole in the fibreglass just under the ledge. The boat shuddered with the impact and I saw this huge malevolent eye staring. It was trying to kill me, and had made a good attempt at doing so. I had never before been the object of this intention; I'm sure that the look from a water buffalo or elephant is similar. The deck hands wisely tried to get away – laughingly pointing out later, 'Well, it was *your* fish!' – but Lee stayed with the chair and me. The marlin was 1030 pounds, fifteen feet long, including the bill, and six feet in girth. I fought it for about an hour and twenty-five minutes.

Of course, it is a tremendous feeling to achieve something you have set out to do, and I felt very good about it as the gloves went down on the deck and *my* hand was being pumped this time. Lee was really hands-down proud, shaking his head and laughing as he kissed me congratulations. 'Do you realize that you are one of only four or five women in the world who have caught a marlin over a thousand pounds, including Kimberly Wiss with her world record?' This was the fifth marlin I had ever caught, and my fourth had been a world record. I caught the fish on 130–pound rod and line with a very heavy drag and no allowance for being a woman. I have to admit I was very happy about it, although I don't know why IGFA differentiates the women's from the men's records. Since then, a number of other women have done the same, including Sally Rice and Evans Frankenheimer.

'A Sea Monster,' Lee liked to quote from Herman Melville, 'is anything in the ocean that's bigger than you are.' We had ample opportunity to see these sea monsters over the next few days. We were now taking turns, and although I caught a few small ones, it was to Lee that the big ones kept coming. For some reason I was at times having trouble getting the twenty-five-pound rods out of the holders; I fell on deck three times with fish on the line, and I was once pulled to the bottom of the foot rest by a large marlin. We were all getting very tired; even the usually cheerful deckhands were getting weary. As fast as they could lace up the baits and put them out, something would take them or they would be chopped off by sharks. The joking was beginning to become strained. Brian would say after losing one after the other of his sewn-up baits,

'Sometimes I could tear my hair.' On the fourth day Lee caught a
1075-pound marlin, and the next two were over a thousand
pounds as well: 1020 and 1320 pounds respectively! The strain
was beginning to show on Dennis as well, and Lee looked nearly at
the point of exhaustion. It is always quiet when fishing is going on –
it is the unwritten law – but this silence now became one where
everyone was retreating into themselves. 'The doubts are creeping
in,' Lee said, 'What is this really about?'

One day, as Lee sat 'drifting' in his mind, as he described it, he
impaled me with a look, then glanced off to sea with a very odd
expression on his face. 'Oh,' he said, turning back to me, 'if you
only *knew* the things I've done.' I had no idea what he was alluding
to: the war, life or what? It was a troubling statement, and one that
he wouldn't explain. It left me upset, depressed and angry.

By now, when Lee had a strike he would walk to the chair with
stiff, almost disjointed movements. The heat was oppressive, and
we were having difficulty sleeping at night. I'd wake up and find
Lee gone from the bed, sitting on the back of the boat in the dark, a
cigarette glowing between his fingers. The more obsessed he got
with the fishing, the more I thought it was all getting out of hand; it
frightened me. I urged him to cut the trip short. It seemed to
concern something more than just fishing.

He talked about it in 'Marvin, as in Marlin,' an interview with
Roger Vaughn: 'It's like being in combat and you're hit. Uh, oh,
now you're fair game – anybody can walk up and stick it to you.'
He told Vaughn that he hadn't actually understood why he was so
upset during that fishing episode until he got back to the States:
'The correlation, the similarities between war experiences and this;
not being able to walk when my sciatic nerve was severed by the
bullet. Even the booze. When I got back to the beach in the war
they gave me brandy. I could hear the firing – the guys one hundred
yards away were shooting sharks.'

He wrote it out when we got home:

Phase III
Young outback Aussies – afraid of nothing – and the days
began. On a ten day charter for black marlin out of Cairns,
NQ, Australia, in November on a boat called *Sea Strike* . . . a

fine thirty-four foot fighting boat, extremely well-equipped for the task of big marlin and what a crew . . . We encountered some great fishing. The marlin were so large and frequent that I was overwhelmed and physically breaking down. We were celebrating at night, which is the Australian custom (as well as mine on a successful day). The fish kept coming and I felt a deep obligation to live up to the angler that I thought I was. The 'mother ship', a sixty-five footer named *Sea Fox*, was a beautiful ship, well-appointed, great food and lovely quarters with very congenial crew and host. Nothing in big game fishing could have been better – nothing! The hours slipped by or were endless, depending on whether I was in the fighting chair or not. At the start the joy was overwhelming, but as time went by my legs started to give out and pain me. This was about the fifth day and I was beginning to have doubts, an unknown fear was starting to build in me. Nobody to our knowledge had ever in big game history been hit so large and frequent – why us? *Me!* It was getting to the point where I was having difficulty transferring from the fighting boat to the mother ship morning and evening, my legs! Arms, shoulders, and back were fine – but my legs!

Then came the day when I had two huge fish in a row, fifteen minutes apart, much handshaking and back slapping and I knew I was through – they had done it, both the fish and the Australians had broken me, I had four more days to go.

It had all started earlier in August in Hawaii where my wife and I had fished our boat for forty-two days and she had put on a world record blue marlin. Of course we were all excited. One night during this time we were introduced to a young Australian captain on his way back from fishing the Bahamas – well, I found him to be terrific and knowledgeable – as the evening drew on our camaraderie and esprit grew and grew. Joyful challenges flew back and forth at a great rate finally culminating with his saying that if he had a cancellation in his charter season, September, October, and November of that year, he'd give me a phone call and I replied, 'You're on!' In October he called. I couldn't get out of it. We went.

I was so fatigued I had the dry heaves. I could keep nothing down. The host of *Sea Fox* suggested rum with a touch of port to settle my stomach. Nothing worked. I simply got more depressed. At bedtime I slept fitfully.

The mother ship was anchored right behind Opal Reef and rolled gently with the light lapping of the water against the hull and the low hum of the auxiliary generator. In and out of focus – sweating, then the chills – Gunshots! Wide awake! – Oh that's right, some of the other boats at anchor near us were night fishing for tiger sharks and were shooting them when they came to gaff. I went topside to the after deck where the beer cooler was, literally pulling myself up the stairwell. My legs were shot. This must have been about 3 a.m. Sitting with a cold beer in my hand I'd take a slug then crawl to the gunwale and heave it over – over and over again. I could not keep a drop down. The dark night, warm, humid breeze, gunshots. WHAT THE HELL IS WRONG WITH ME? Doze, shot, awake, doze. When I awoke my wife was looking at me. I mean really looking at me through and behind my eyes. I couldn't even smile to reassure her. It was close to dawn. A fighting boat idled slowly by very close to us. One of the men in the cockpit held up a huge tail of a marlin, all that was left of the fish after a night of shark fishing. Ropes behind the boat drug the bodies of six or seven twelve foot tigers they had killed that night. She told me I had to stop or I would die in that fighting chair – I knew she was right so I passed the instructions to take me in to the shore. In the first person, as I did not include my wife in my fear. After they had breakfast they loaded up and we said our good-byes and headed south to Cairns – but the water looked good. The seas were about six feet so the decision was to put out a couple of baits and there I stood – hanging on the chair again! The light was right and everything else – the captain on the tower, the two deckhands, and Pam on the flying bridge – all watching me in the pit. I knew if one came in I would have to take him. I wouldn't be able to say no. Time drifted by as we trolled South, the baits working well and clear as a bell, it was as if you were right on top of them you could see so well. Silence, no talking – there never was – just staring at the baits and the water around them. The steady rumbling of the twin engines – time – BANG!!!! EVERYBODY saw him at once – the deck hands hit the deck with a crash, Pam yelled, and the captain shouted over the p.a. 'On the left!' – thirty feet behind the left bait, all lit up to an electric blue easing in. One of the deck hands quietly said, 'Animal'. He was – one thousand five hundred plus. He eased up to the bait, put his eyeball right on it and without a movement I lifted my thoughts to Heaven and said, 'Please, if you are there, NO, NO, please.' Just as suddenly as he appeared he veered off to the left – a silent thanks and a quick turn to see the crew's reaction. Nobody – nobody was looking. What is wrong with me? Am I totally alone? A long pause, then over the p.a., 'OK, wind 'em up.' I cranked the left one in, while a deckhand got the right. When both were in, the engines came to a scream and we headed home at flank speed.

Although Lee claimed that the fish and the Australians had 'broken' him, he wasn't so wrecked that he didn't immediately go off the boat to Bransford's Tackle Shop for new fishing rods. He ordered custom rods for us both to be built by Jack Erskine for the following year's charter, for which Lee already had booked firm dates. He ordered two 130–pound class rods, light cream colored with navy blue wrappings, numbered '254 and 274 Erskine and Fitch 1974 for Lee Marvin' and two eighty-pound class for me with red wrappings, light cream colored, numbered '380 and 381 for Pam Marvin'.

Lee and I missed the real pioneering days of Cairns fishing. (Seven years before, George Bransford, owner of *Sea Baby I*, and his young crewman Richard Obach had hooked the first thousand-pound fish on eighty-pound test line.) Still, I think we were there at the best of times: from the early 1970s to 1983, when the boats and equipment were excellent, the captains practiced and professional, but the fishing still somewhat experimental. At that time, too, Cairns was an uncrowded seaport town surrounded by banana plantations and sugar cane fields which were set ablaze every November. Clouds of smoke were a constant backdrop, and a sweet, pungent smell pervaded the air. There were a few wide streets with stores, houses and two hotels, no high-rises and only a small domestic airport –

unlike today, when Cairns has its international airport and its first-class hotels. Even the historic Pacific Hotel, where world adventurers like Errol Flynn and Joseph Conrad stayed, has been replaced by the Pacific International Hotel.

When I won the world record for the marlin in Hawaii, Lee bought me a beautiful emerald-green tourmaline ring. He saw it in a display window of Harry Winston's in the Plaza Hotel in New York, and bought it for me because the color reminded him of the marlin 'lit up': the 'Christmas tree'. Now in Cairns, where opals abound, Lee celebrated my thousand-pound marlin catch by buying me a large stone from the Coober Pedy region. By good luck, or perhaps Lee's intuition, we walked into a jewellery shop and met Hilda Clausen, whose shop it was and with whom we later became good friends. Lee wanted the opal set in white gold, so he and a young German who worked with Hilda designed it together. There was always some reason behind each piece of jewellery Lee gave me: each meant something personal we had experienced together. 'Look,' I said to him this time, 'this is not the *easiest* way to come by jewels.'

Before we left Cairns in 1973 we visited a small aboriginal museum, which opened up a whole new area of mythology for Lee: the Aboriginal dream time. Having found a very good book store in Cairns, we loaded our suitcases with books: *The Dreamtime Book*, paintings and stories of myths by Ainslie Roberts and Charles P. Mountford, and whatever else we could find on the subject, along with histories of Australia. Lee also found books about Henry Lawson, who became one of his favourite poets. Born in a tent on a goldfield in 1867, Lawson became one of Australia's best-known authors with poems such as 'Ballad of the Drover' and 'The Never-Never Land':

> By homestead, hut and shearing shed
> By railroad, coach and track –
> By lonely graves where rest our dead,
> Up country and Out Back.

Far from ending anything, this first trip was just the beginning. Over the next ten years we had extraordinary experiences on land and sea: travels to the outback, meeting many people, being in violent storms in small boats, fishing for the great white shark in South Australia, and watching sharks eat each other in the tempest of the sea. Lee caught eleven marlin over a thousand pounds (1,060; 1,075; 1,320; 1,025; 1,218; 1,071; 1,012; 1,101; 1,148; 1,232; and 1,124) and several hundred other marlin that he tagged and released. He won the Angler of the Year award, and tagged and released more marlin in one year than any other fisherman in Australia. Some of these were not difficult to catch, some much harder, and one almost brought him to breaking point in a long, tough fight that went on well into the night.

Once home, Lee wrote a letter to Mutt Cobel discussing tackle and fishing, asking for information for use on our boat in Hawaii. He signs off with a sentiment that summed up his frame of mind and our feeling for the country:

> Our heads and hearts are still ringing with 'God, Australia,' and our eyes daily rise to the horizons of tomorrow. Pam sends her regards and I my thanks.
> Sincerely,
> Lee Marvin

10 Tucson, Arizona

We moved from Malibu, California, to the desert foothills of Tucson, Arizona, in late summer of 1974. Lee liked the south-west desert very much and so did I. From the 1950s throughout his career he had filmed on location in Nevada, Arizona and the deserts of California. *Gun Fury*, a western Lee made in 1952 with Rock Hudson, Donna Reed and Neville Brand, and directed by Raoul Walsh, was filmed in Sedona, Arizona. *Violent Saturday*, with Victor Mature, Ernest Borgnine and Lee, was shot in Bisbee, an old copper mining town. It was directed by Richard Fleischer; Lee said he spent most of the time trying to hide behind his own hand, turning his back or anything else he could do to disappear, he felt the movie was so bad. The television production of John Frankenheimer's *The American*, the story of Pima Indian Ira Hayes – one of the soldiers who raised the flag on Iwo Jima – was filmed on an Indian reservation near Tucson. *Monte Walsh*, one of Lee's favourite films, was shot mostly in Sonoita and Benson, Arizona, and *Pocket Money* was shot in Arizona and New Mexico.

Lee felt that he had 'worn out' Malibu. It had changed from how it was when he first moved there, when it had been home to less high-powered folk. Neighbours would come over for a talk on his porch, often writers or other people who were not quite so caught up in 'the Hollywood game' – as Lee called it – and lived a more casual life. And although acting was his life, the money aspect bored and annoyed him, and he hated to go into Beverly Hills for business meetings: 'When I park my car I have to have a martini to defend myself!' He couldn't wait to get home, tear off his tie and slacks, put on casual clothes, and shake off the wheelings and dealings of the corporate world.

Because most movies were now being filmed on location rather than on the backlots of Hollywood studios, we could live anywhere. We started house hunting up the coast: Point Dume, Trancas, California, and horse farms on the other side of the Pacific Coast Highway. We considered Clint Eastwood's suggestion that we move up to Pebble Beach or Carmel, but somehow didn't pursue the idea. Although Lee liked living on the ocean, he found the desert had a great similarity to it: the wide open skies and the feelings of space.

Other things prompted the move as well. Kerry was now thirteen and in junior high school. 'I don't believe in giving a kid a Mercedes,' Lee said. 'Here it's almost demanded.' And he liked peace. Confrontations and intrusions in our life disturbed him. 'Some people feel that they have a piece of me,' he said, and we seemed to have more of that problem than most people. We were being hounded by telephone calls from Michelle Triola and other bothersome people, and Lee preferred to absent himself from it.

We had moved from the Malibu Colony back to the smaller house on LaCosta Beach, but the noise of the pounding ocean at the front, plus the sirens and traffic noises of the Pacific Coast Highway at the back, made the house an island of conflicting sounds day and night. Never stagnant in his life or his career, and someone who was very aware of timing, Lee felt that it was now time to move on. I felt much the same, if not more so. Well aware of the essence of 'Hollywood', its history and foibles, Lee once said, 'You know, it really is a small town – a nasty little small town.'

We rented a house in Tucson at first to see how we liked it, and immediately bought horses for Kerry and me. She and I rode all over the desert, while Lee oversaw a massive clean-up of the grounds around the house, working alongside the gardeners. He loved that: what he liked doing best while waiting for the next movie to begin was working at some menial task or repairing something.

Chris, Cynthia and Claudia, Wendy and Jess (now six), Maury and Kerry were all with us at Christmas. Rod and Courtenay were busy elsewhere. We had a great time and picked big baskets of grapefruit from the trees in our grove, though Lee was hobbling around on crutches from twisting his knee playing tennis, and I, too, from a slight automobile accident in Lee's Chrysler Imperial. Lee was not happy about the accident, and quickly had the car fixed, refusing to give the insurance company my doctor's bills, accepting only the money for the garage bill: 'You're my wife, I can take care of *your* bills.' He so hated the readiness to bring a lawsuit so prevalent in his country that he signed away any claim immediately and firmly.

John and Christel Boorman and their four children came from Ireland for a visit – one we had looked forward to, after spending so much time with them in Ireland. When they were about to arrive, Lee said, 'I'm not sure what to do with an adult after the holidays here!'

Jack Palance came for dinner one night, dear man that he is. I tried to make home-made tortillas from corn flour. What a flop. Lee joked at my attempt: 'Oh, for God's sake! Only Mexican women can make those, and they pat them between their knees, whack, whack, fast as machine-gun fire.' Jack ate them none the less, declaring in a serious manner that they were really very good.

Lee liked to tease Jack, and this was particularly obvious when they talked about their movies together. They had been together in *Attack*, the 1957 movie about the Battle of the Bulge, and in 1969, *Monte Walsh*. Jack broke his ribs in a fall from a horse on this movie, and was all strapped up, resting on the couch in his trailer, when Lee burst in, startling him so much that he leapt up, causing searing pain. Like the roustabout cowboys they were playing, they both thought it was very funny – later. Again, during *Monte Walsh*, Mitch Ryan, Lee's adversary in the film, was with Lee one day at the studio, CBS in Los Angeles. After location shooting was over, Lee was given a huge, luxurious dressing room, the only one they had for the stars. He grabbed hold of Mitch, saying, 'Shhshh, come out here with me.' He opened the door to the backlot, but Mitch saw nothing, just the empty street. Lee just kept saying, 'Shhshh, wait.' Suddenly a door burst open, Jack Palance stormed out and threw a bunch of keys up into the air, swearing violently. Jack had been given a terrible dinky dressing room on the set, and Lee knew there would be some hot reaction.

Monte Walsh was a movie Lee and Mitch liked very much, as did Jack Palance, Matt Clark and the other actors. A sad, nostalgic tale of the demise of the American cowboy, it gave Lee one of the most poignant roles of his career.

Lee had a good deal to do with the production of the film. He had cast, script and director approval written into his contract. He wanted Jack Palance in the role of Monte's gentle partner, as opposed to Jack's usual casting as the heavy or the villain. He fought for Jack to be cast in this role, and when Jack held out for more money Lee insisted that the producers give it to him. He hadn't forgotten Jack's classic role in *Shane*, nor the fact that not too many years before he had been the bigger star commanding the higher salary.

Lee also approved the director, William A. Fraker, even though this was Fraker's first directorial attempt – he had been a cinematographer previously. Lee was ultimately disappointed in Fraker's direction, however, and felt *Monte Walsh* should have been a better movie, good though it was. Fraker couldn't seem to get beyond the viewpoint of a cameraman: he just didn't know what to do with the actors. In the end, however, the movie was saved by the editing. Lee was not small-minded, and he rarely criticized anyone in the industry, even to me, unless it was well-deserved – but he did have a disregard for Fraker. The producers, Hal Landers and Bobby Roberts, were so anxious to have Lee star in their film that they would have replaced Fraker with a more experienced director if Lee had objected. But by the time Lee realized what was happening, it was too late.

He was, however, very proud of having done *Monte Walsh*, and always felt very fondly about many of the people in the movie: Mitch became one of his closest friends, as did Matt Clark.

The two romantic leads were played by Lee and Jeanne Moreau, one of the tenderest roles Lee ever had. I later wondered whether the fact that Lee's character was called Montey – his father's nickname – and had a relationship with a French woman – as his father had done – affected Lee during this movie. It was well known that he and Jeanne Moreau had an affair during and after the filming. I do know how he felt afterwards, however. It was just before we were married, he had had several drinks, and he told me with boyish pride, 'Gee, sweetheart, I did it. Made love to Jeanne Moreau.' He had just put her on a plane back to France. 'She wanted me to come with her,' and then, pensively, 'but you know, of course, she wasn't for me.' Since he had come directly to my house and asked me to marry him, I couldn't be all that upset.

We left the rented house after nine months to go to Africa to film *Shout At The Devil*. But we liked Tucson so much that we decided we would stay there, so we bought a house before we left. When we got back, Lee threw himself into remodelling the house, which was designed in the 1930s by Joestler, a Swiss architect who fell in love with the area and its Spanish and American Indian influence. Lee spent years getting it just the way he wanted it, with the artists he admired working alongside him. He built a 'den', a large room for screening movies and displaying our fifteen foot long trophy marlin. It was somewhat similar to Will Rogers's game room at his house in Pacific Palisades, California; there was no entrance at all from the main house, but one door only from a courtyard instead. It had a big lock inside, so if he wanted to hide out, he could!

Lee designed much of the extensive remodelling with our architect Bob Taylor. He took everything back to what he felt Joestler had intended, or would have done himself had he had modern methods of heating and cooling. Lee added closets, something Joestler did not believe in, thinking that no one should have more clothes than would fit in one suitcase. This was some time before the rainforests were known to be depleted, so Lee built us each enormous bathrooms using teak for the open shower walls, designing teak slats over the Japanese blue floor tiles for mine, and giving my whole bathroom the feeling of being outside. Windows over my oversized tub brought the out of doors in – the cactus behind our house, the view of the mountains – as did an indoor planter filled with trees, ferns and Hawaiian plants.

The remodelling went on for more than two years, and Lee loved every minute of it (I can't say I did). He found the architect, the artists, the blacksmiths, the metalworkers. He had gates and doors hand-built by Forest Gist and brought him from Texas to hang them. He had blacksmith Tom Bredlow from 'down the hill' in Tucson to build others. Lee designed a courtyard, imported a massive fountain from Mexico, and added another enormous wing. He helped lay the tiny blue tiles in our swimming pool that make it look more like a piece of the ocean; he sat hour upon hour watching the men working and lending a hand himself. He knew where every pipe, pump and piece of wire was in the entire house, and he loved the place immensely.

Lee now had privacy, which he deeply appreciated. He bought a white pickup truck, mostly for going to the dump. He would spend hours at the local hardware store, which is where most people in Tucson ran into him. He helped me with a local charity I had joined, the Angel Charity For Children, televising ads for it and working as a 'celebrity croupier' on the gambling tables at the annual charity ball.

The white truck was also perfect if he didn't want to be found. He occasionally decided he wanted to go to a bar and drink, giving the rest of his family several hours of high anxiety. Some days I would spend hours driving around looking for him in great anxiety, imagining road accidents, following ambulances, hearing sirens. He didn't go to bars unless he was already quite drunk, and so the anxiety was real. Rod was usually able to find him, as he pretty much knew his routine. Once he found him at a bikers' bar, the Red Dog Saloon – which happened to be right next to Lee's chiropractor. Rod went in and found Lee surrounded by some pretty hairy, tough-looking fellows. When he came up to where Lee was sitting engrossed in 'great' conversation, one very big fellow named Tiny swung around to Rod glowering, 'Who wants to talk to 'em?' He was protecting Lee!

In between movies, Lee called himself the 'butler and the gardener', and he did spend a great deal of time taking care of not only 'our' desert near the house but also further washes and hills. He had some help from our grandson Jess, who recalls another favourite job of Lee's:

Once Lee recognized that I was big enough to do a good day's work, he offered to pay me for assisting him in some clean-up projects around the house. We would mostly trim the trees, pull weeds, and things of that nature. Lee always paid particular attention to the trees, and how they should be cared for. He would only trim a branch after careful consideration, and only if it was in the best interest of the tree's overall health and future growth. It was not uncommon for him to stare at a tree for over an hour, deciding what should be done. Every branch would be cut clean and fast, so that the tree wouldn't experience any unnecessary shock, then we would immediately paint a thick treatment on the exposed wound before moving on to the next tree. He did most of the cutting, and I dragged the debris to the truck.

His favourite part of the day was going to the dump – I don't know why, but he actually enjoyed the dump. We'd back up into a spot and get out to start unloading, and then the guy next to us would recognize him and usually try his best to strike up a conversation. He was always good with people who approached him when I was around, he'd say something funny and go about his business. If it got to be hectic, he would excuse himself and go talk to the person driving the bulldozer.

11 The Trial: 'Virulent Imagination'

'A Tangled Web'

After fishing in Australia, our next big adventure was the so-called 'palimony' trial. The trial is still, in the 1990s, given credence in some quarters: it is cited as one of the 'court cases of the century', and mere allegations are presented as facts. Some people even think Lee lost the case. I hope to set the record straight, not by putting down my own obviously biased point of view, but by giving the testimony presented in court by witnesses, attorneys and Lee, the findings of the judge and, most importantly, the words of the plaintiff herself.

MICHELLE TRIOLA MARVIN A.K.A. MICHELLE TRIOLA,
PLAINTIFF
VS.
LEE MARVIN, DEFENDANT

This was the daily heading of the case brought against Lee by a woman who had lived with him in the late 1960s. Advertised as a 'palimony' suit – the word was coined by the plaintiff's flamboyant lawyer Marvin Mitchelson – it proposed that a woman who lives with a man should have the same rights as a married woman. It asked that she be awarded alimony and, in this case, share in California community property rights, along with $1.8 million, or half of his purported income during the time they were supposedly living together.

The suit claimed that there were agreements to hold themselves as husband and wife and for all purposes to be husband and wife, but without the formality of marriage. Just to insure that this was upheld, Michelle Triola Marvin (she had legally changed her name to Marvin just days before the final termination of her relationship with Lee) and her attorney said that an oral agreement was executed by them in October 1964.

The parties 'would combine their efforts and earnings and would share equally any and all property accumulated as a result of their efforts whether individual or combined; motion picture rights; deferred earnings, options, etc.' This was formally amended, they claimed, in 1966 to say that Lee promised to provide for all of plaintiff's financial support and needs for the rest of her life. 'For ever,' nodded Michelle Triola.

In return, plaintiff would 'render her services as companion, homemaker, housekeeper and, at defendant's insistence, Plaintiff would give up her lucrative career as an entertainer/singer'. 'She did so,' it stated, 'and suffered irreparable financial loss by reason of her having so abandoned her prior career as a singer/entertainer.'

This fifty-fifty oral agreement was said to have been pledged just four months after they met, even though Lee was still married and living with his first wife and four children. It was true that his fourteen-year marriage was coming apart, but he was not happy or even sure about leaving his family. The idea that he would enter into a contract like this with someone he hardly knew was unlikely at best.

At the time in question, October 1964, Lee was already an established and well-known actor. He had been in at least thirty-four movies in featured, co-starring or starring roles, among them *The Wild One* with Marlon Brando, *Raintree County* with Elizabeth Taylor and Montgomery Clift, *Bad Day at Black Rock* with Spencer Tracey, *Not As a Stranger* with Robert Mitchum and Frank Sinatra, and two John Ford films, *The Man Who Shot Liberty Valance* with John Wayne and James Stewart and *Donovan's Reef*, also with John Wayne, with whom he had worked some years before in *The Comanchero*s. He had more than four hundred television shows to his credit, including three years of his own series *M Squad* and a nomination for an Emmy Award for *People Need People*. He had already filmed *Cat Ballou*, which earned him an Academy Award. He owned an expensive house in Rustic Canyon in Santa Monica and a large ski lodge in Wrightwood, California, in the San Gabriel Mountains.

Michelle Triola, on the other hand, had neither a career nor an income at the time – nor did she before or after. When they met in 1964 on the set of *Ship of Fools*, she was a stand-in for her 'roommate' Barbara Luna, who had a small part in the movie. (A stand-in is a person of approximately the same height as an actor or actress who takes their place so that the cameraman can measure the focal distance, set up the shot or focus the lighting when the actress or actor playing the role is resting or is not on the set at the time.)

The trial was held in the Superior Court of the State of California for the County of Los Angeles, under the Honorable Arthur K. Marshall. It lasted a few days shy of three months and cost hundreds of thousands of dollars. California taxpayers alone paid $30,000, much to Lee's chagrin and embarrassment. The rest he paid himself, except for the time, effort and expenses our own attorneys expended that could not have been paid for at any price. Our attorney Louis Goldman, respected as much for his humor and gentlemanliness as for his brilliance at law, developed diabetes during this stressful trial. Lee himself was plagued with colds and stomach flu, making this 'command performance' – having to look at all times attentive and self-possessed at his table – something of a physical chore on many occasions. Marvin Mitchelson himself was taken out on a stretcher after a particularly frustrating go-around with Lou Goldman. Mitchelson had taken the case on a contingency basis, rumored to be an unusual fifty per cent, and so Michelle Triola Marvin paid nothing, enjoying her notoriety at no price to herself at all.

Opening day was 9 January 1979 (nine *years* after Lee and I were married) and Judge Marshall rendered his decision on 18 April. More than eight thousand pages of testimony were taken from nearly seventy witnesses – roughly the same number as in the US Government's trial of Panama's Manuel Noriega.

Many of these witnesses were celebrities from the motion picture world and the entertainment industry, as well as stunt men, producers, agents, managers, pseudo-managers, gossip columnists, waitresses, publicists, *Playboy* employees, CPAs, accountants, bar owners, friends, neighbours, lovers, foes. Michelle Triola Marvin listed many other famous personalities in her testimony for what appeared to be little reason other than their publicity value: Paul Newman, Josh Logan, Milton Berle and others were mentioned but never called. Even the attorneys for the plaintiff and Lee were called by the opposing side to stand in the witness box, raise their right hands and swear to 'tell the truth, the whole truth and nothing but the truth, so help me God' – and the last 'new' witness called by the prosecution was me.

Because it was Lee Marvin on trial and the subject matter was touted as having far-reaching consequences, the daily testimony made headlines throughout the country and the world. Unmarried couples living together took pause; suitcases began to appear. We were the topic of the television news nightly throughout the entire trial and for some time after. Talk show hosts had a field day with the very accessible Michelle Triola and Marvin Mitchelson, who were seen on the *Phil Donahue Show* and many others. They gave interviews to most of the pulp magazines and tabloids, avidly soliciting the meetings and conducting them in Mitchelson's law office. For some of the interviews, Michelle was paid. Mitchelson pleaded his case in a book he wrote: 'Well, I took some poetic license.' To their credit, they were not only able to fabricate a case out of thin air, but to build up their story beforehand using the press, gossip writers and sensational magazine articles.

There was a great deal of manipulation of the press in the hallways of the court. Michelle Triola and Marvin Mitchelson, like two enthusiastic dairy farmers, grabbed each moment firmly and squeezed every drop of opportunity dry.

Lee, on the other hand, declined invitations for publicity, including one from Barbara Walters, who wanted to interview him and me. Johnny Carson, no stranger to the courtroom himself through several high-profile and expensive divorces, supplied some of the lighter moments with his nightly quips in support of Lee. Inside the courtroom, every aspect of Lee's purported life and personality were laid out before a packed courtroom and the public. His salaries, incomes, expenses, properties or anything he might possibly have owned were explored in depth. Slow-dragging hours turned into days as two opposing accountants armed with long pointers stabbed at boards and harangued the court over each line. Lee's daily life and habits, his alcohol consumption, his professional life, were painted with huge strokes in livid colors by an attorney and a woman who had a great deal to gain if the picture were believed. As the days progressed, the accusations became more and more sensational and demeaning. As each day ground on, it became more apparent that what Michelle Triola had threatened, and Lee had tried to avoid for many years, was coming to pass in spades.

Celebrities are often targets for legal action, and to avoid just such an embarrassing display the matter is often settled out of court. Mitchelson presented this option to Lee early on, in 1971, with the threat of adverse publicity. The letter sent to Lee through his attorney Louis Goldman warned: 'She [Michelle Triola] wishes me to assure you that it is her earnest desire to avoid unpleasant litigation, with the attendant publicity which is sure to follow because of Lee's status, if the action should go forward.' But by then Lee felt it had gone too far. To settle would imply guilt; also, Lee was not convinced that a settlement would stop what had become years of harassment. He felt he had to draw the line: 'I fought for the principle. I had to. These were false allegations. They slandered my character and my reputation.'

Roderick Mann said of Lee, 'In the extraordinary voice which Jean Seberg once likened to "rainwater gushing down a rusty pipe", he said, "The worst thing about it is it forces me to review a most unhappy period of my life."'[1]

As a movie star Lee was very much in the public eye, and his professional image was something he had spent many years building. Although some of his drinking extravaganzas did have a basis in fact, much of it was pure acting. He deliberately did nothing to refute the characterization. 'Ahhhh, I love it,' he said to Jerry Roberts in a news interview. In reality, Lee was a very private person. It took a good deal of courage to expose himself to such public scrutiny.

No one disputed the fact that Michelle Triola had lived with Lee. There was no reason to. There was no law against two consenting adults living together. Michelle Triola, however, claimed that they were just another happy couple and lived as if married. Lee said that quite the opposite was true: although he did like her at first, it quickly became a tempestuous, violent relationship that he soon tried to terminate. She moved into his house by degrees, despite his

[1] *Los Angeles Times*, Calender, 17 December 1978.

objections. He had asked her to leave, rented her apartments, and offered her money. There was her nearly fatal suicide attempt, threats of more attempts, and threats to harm his career and his children by publicly exposing their involvement together ('Was it blackmail?' her *own* attorney asked). During this period Lee was away working on movie locations for more than half of the time. This, however, was long enough to give her a credible foothold. She jumped upon his back and clung. Nothing anyone said could dislodge her. He asked friends and lawyers for solutions. One friend recalls Lee's exasperation, 'How do I get rid of this broad?' Their answers were, as Lee said, 'too physical for me – I couldn't lay a hand on her'. He had long since reined in his own violence after being in war, putting it on the screen instead. His frustration must have been immense – several bullet holes still in the floor of his house attest to that. Lee was also very preoccupied with his work. These were the busiest years of his acting life. And when he wasn't away on location, he drank a lot. 'Whenever I thought about her, I'd just get drunk. When I woke up and saw her still there, I'd get drunk again.' In that sense, he reverted to passive resistance. She was his worst nightmare because she found his frailties.

I can understand how Lee initially became involved with someone like Michelle Triola – breaking out of a cold, bitterly antagonistic marriage when his working life away from home was receiving such accolades. He was near the height of his career, recognized everywhere and pursued by women wherever he turned. It is hard to realize how avidly actors and celebrities are pursued unless you have lived it – married, unmarried, with someone, without, with your children at your side. Michelle Triola was not only available, she was aggressive, and she was also under the umbrella, falsely or not, of a movie company, a very close-knit band of people. It is Us against the Civilians; it's safe. This involvement was, Lee said, for both of them without commitment or emotional entanglement, one of 'fun, a relief'. I suppose it would be a rare man who would have done otherwise in the same situation; but I think it was a rare man who could get caught in it for so long.

Knowing that I would be as much affected by the proceedings as he, Lee asked if I could endure a trial of this personal nature. I knew it wasn't going to be pleasurable, but I did not feel unprepared. When the case came to trial, Lee and I had been married for nine years. I had known him since I was fifteen. I had seen him with his own parents and with mine, his children and my children, on a daily basis; I had witnessed him under every conceivable kind of pressure, pain and pleasure. He was not an angel, nor without complications, but I knew him predominantly as a sober, kind, extraordinarily responsible man of enormous sensitivity, and as an actor whose dedication and professionalism were deeply respected by the industry in which he worked. There was nothing anyone could tell me about Lee that would have surprised me. I knew what he was capable of and what he was not. He had my unconditional support and love throughout. I was a little angry on occasions perhaps, but only at what I thought of as stupidity on his part. 'How could any man be so *dumb*?' I recall thinking once or twice. And when testifying in court, he bent so far backwards in his attempts to be honest that he often gave the wrong impression, to the plaintiff's advantage. Even in the face of terrible lies and vicious accusations, he still had a sense of chivalry and largesse.

Although I had never met Michelle Triola, I had come to know her. Before Lee and I were married, all he told me – he was almost courtly when it came to women – was that he was having a difficult time trying to disentangle himself from a violent, volatile person. I found out for myself how obsessed and impossibly tenacious she was when pursuing something. Taken only a little further, it could have been a *Fatal Attraction*-type of pursuit; but hers was for money and fame, not really caring who supplied it. I think her opportunism did give Lee some pain at a certain level, along with some dismay over his own paralysis in dealing with her. And this wasn't because she was so clever, but more because Lee's own inner priorities and conflicts came together with her great tenacity and total lack of pride.

When the news came over the television that Lee and I had been married that evening in 1970, Michelle Triola called Lee before the newscast was finished. It was the first of hundreds of telephone calls we were to receive from her. She called in the day, in the evening and late at night, often when we were asleep. Michelle had a small poodle, and sometimes during these late night calls nothing but the sound of a small dog could be heard barking in the receiver. Lee, like many actors, had an aversion to answering the telephone, and so if I did not pick it up, one of the kids would. If it was Michelle Triola calling, we gave up in frustration and handed the telephone to Lee, even after we were told not to. To this day I cannot quite explain how she was able to keep someone engaged in an unwanted conversation. Somehow she would hold you with a 'Wait, wait, wait' or some hurried alarm: she had had an automobile accident, she needed her rent paid, she needed help. There was always a cry of emergency, or the threat that if Lee did not talk to her, she would call incessantly until he did. And she would. Lee would ask her not to call, listen interminably and then hang up wordlessly. Lee never sank to her level, never shouted, never changed his character. I would have – it might have been the sort of treatment she would respond to. As it was, it was *his* past relationship with her, not mine, and it was up to him. We thought of changing our number, but Lee said, 'Listen, believe me, if we change it, she'll have it the next day.' In order to stop the woman, you had to go against your own nature. She seemed to have an unerring and deadly instinct for what I suppose she thought of as one's weaknesses.

The calls continued years later when we were living in Tucson. A telephone operator called late one night, said there was an emergency call for Lee and gave him a number. It proved to be the home of the estranged wife of Dick Van Dyke. Lee was terribly embarrassed for having called, but Mrs Van Dyke assured him she was used to these kinds of call, and said, 'We all know who is behind them.'

Michelle Triola was rumored to be living with Dick Van Dyke during the trial, and articles about them began appearing in gossip columns: 'Dick Van Dyke split with his wife of 31 years'; 'Pals say Dick's moved into Michelle's Hollywood pad';[2] and so on.

Through his attorneys, Lee was giving Michelle money each month to stay away from him. He said he wanted to give her independence. For her part, she agreed to disassociate herself from

2 R. Couri Hay, 27 February 1979.

his life, not to use personal information she had gleaned from being in his confidence, and to stop feeding information to gossip columnists linking her name with his. All this she agreed to, but the promises were broken even before Lee and I were married. She gave self-serving interviews, rife with untruths, to movie magazines and gossip columnists, using Lee's name to solicit the interviews. Gossip columns began printing blurbs about our marriage: it was 'on the rocks'; Lee had 'fallen off the wagon with a resounding thump'. The articles invariably linked her name with this or that star, knowing that no one would give them credence by disputing them.

Michelle was not only planting articles and telling people that she was being 'kept' by Lee Marvin, but at the same time brought a suit for recovery of money against Bobby Roberts and Hal Landers, the producers of *Monte Walsh*. It claimed they had reneged on a promise to give her money in a secret 'deal' when she supposedly told them about a script she knew Lee was interested in doing. The deceit involved was monumental, and it involved Lee's work. She seemed to be on her feet again; as well as using the name Michelle Marvin, she was breaking all the agreements, so Lee had the payments stopped. To the threat of a lawsuit, Lee replied through his attorneys that he was ready to accept service. It was also apparent to Lee that paying the remaining money – about thirty thousand dollars by then – would only lead to some other future demand.

As promised, on 22 February 1972 Marvin Mitchelson and Michelle Triola filed a complaint. Trial date was set for 20 November 1973, but before the case came to court it turned into something quite different. It changed from asking for thirty thousand dollars to asking for half of everything Lee owned, or failing that, one hundred thousand dollars in damages. This was thrown unceremoniously out of court by the judge, who left the bench in anger, loudly ordering Marvin Mitchelson and Michelle Triola to 'get out of his court' as they hurried away. Unfortunately, the dismissal left the door open for an appeal. This eventually evolved into the case of Marvin v Marvin (which we were *not* personally involved in) and resulted in the 'Marvin Decision' handed down in 1976, which found that people who live together unmarried have the same rights as other persons: they can sue each other over contracts or oral agreements involving money or property just as people who *don't* live together can. Also, certain behaviour can lead to an *implied* contract being proven.

So this case never started out as championing 'palimony', women's rights or any noble cause at all. It grew by stages, taking on a life of its own, and by no stretch of the imagination could it be construed as altruistic.

It is ruefully ironic that of all Lee's accomplishments in his lifetime – a Purple Heart awarded for wounds received in battle, an Academy Award as best actor given by his fellow actors, and the many prestigious awards bestowed upon him by countries throughout the world – his name would be perpetuated in law books because of this inglorious case. It became known in legal shorthand as 'Marvin': 'Well, in Marvin it is said . . .' used as a point for or against an argument. Just as his Marine Corps training film trains young Marines, his acting techniques are studied by would-be actors, and his portrayal of a psychotic patient in the film *People Need People* is seen by psychiatry students, the Marvin Decision is now read by law students countrywide. 'Yeah,' Lee commented wryly, 'I can just hear it now: "I've been Marvined."'

By 1979, after the many depositions Marvin Mitchelson had taken from Lee and others and all the depositions Lee's attorneys had taken from Michelle Triola, we knew the tack they would be taking: low. And the more incompetent Lee was pictured to be, the more his success would be due to her help. We thought by this time we knew what we were in for – but even we couldn't imagine what was to come.

Instead of renting a house in California for the two or three months, Lee insisted upon our staying in a hotel: 'This is going to be difficult enough on you. I'm not going to have you spend every day in that courtroom listening to all that bullshit and then come home and have to worry about cooking or something.' So we moved into our favourite hotel in Beverly Hills, the Beverly Wilshire, for the duration. Nearly every Sunday afternoon, however, we were invited to dinner at the Malibu home of Lee's attorney and friend David Kagon. David's wife Dotty, an artist and magnificent cook, served us her own home-cooked and decidedly gourmet meals week after week after week. It gave us not only time to be with two good friends for brief discussions of the forthcoming trial proceedings, but also many hours of graciousness and civility during a very uncivil and ugly time.

The Beverly Wilshire too became our hearth and home for the next three months. We had daily moral support from the whole staff: Margaret Crowley (Peggy), the ever cheerful and loyal hostess of what was then Hernando's Hideaway; Hernando Courtright himself, 'El Padrino', the legendary owner of the hotel; managers, receptionists, bellmen, room service waiters (of whom we saw a great deal) and all the waitresses at breakfast, who guarded our table like hovering angels. After particularly draining days, we would walk down Beverly Boulevard to Nate 'n' Al's, the best Jewish delicatessen and restaurant west of New York, for bowls of comforting chicken soup or chicken in the pot. These waiters and waitresses rub elbows with Hollywood's celebrities every day, and as Lee said, 'They're in the know . . . they have seen just about everything human nature can dish up, and they cut through the junk at a glance.'

A few minutes before nine on the first day of the trial, 9 January 1971, we arrived at the courtroom door amid a bevy of television cameras, their operators rushing backwards as we walked. Newspaper reporters called out greetings and questions as we approached; bystanders or professional court watchers, many of whom had stood in line for several hours to get one of the twenty-five or thirty coveted seats, yelled words of encouragement to Lee or craned their necks to look as we passed. We met our attorneys, then filed into the room where we were to sit for the next few months. The press sat in rows directly behind us (me and whoever was with me on the day); behind them were the court watchers, the law students and the other attorneys who stopped by to observe. In front of us, Lee and his attorney A. David Kagon sat at one table, while Michelle Triola and Marvin Mitchelson sat at another, squared off for battle in front of balustrades separating the court arena from the spectators. Behind and above them was the raised pedestal of the judge's box, with the witness cubicle down on his left side. The atmosphere was charged: papers rustled, feet scuffled and people settled noisily into their seats, talking hurriedly in whispers. The armed bailiff called out a command to be silent and to rise as the black-robed judge strode in with all the confidence that his seventeen years on the bench had given him. It was all very intimidating, which is just what it is supposed to be.

With what became his daily greetings, the judge, the Honorable Arthur K. Marshall, looked over his glasses and nodded to each attorney, 'Good morning, counsel,' and they in turn replied, 'Good morning, Your Honor.' These pleasantries over, all sat down and waited expectantly. Except for when the attorneys or anyone else addressed the judge, this litany was usually the end of any civilized manners for the rest of the day.

The first day was an anticlimax. The lawyers went into chambers with the judge, where Marvin Mitchelson and his client decided to waive the right to a jury trial, preferring this judge instead. It was also decided which areas of Lee's finances and income would be explored (which they had a right to do, as they were asking for half of it). As we filed out to the popping of camera flash bulbs and the waiting television cameras filming our departure, Michelle Triola stopped and stood and cried.

Although Marvin Mitchelson was by no means as well known then as he was after the trial – which, as he noted joyfully, 'brought me publicity that I couldn't have bought for a million dollars' – he had already begun to build a reputation for himself in divorce circles. He enjoyed showing off his 'sexy' office, as it was sometimes described; he even invited our attorneys inside as he preened under his ceiling painting – a likeness of Botticelli's Venus. His sumptuous rooms boasted a private jacuzzi where he lounged between clients – or perhaps with clients – and piped-in classical music played soothingly. His desk was a massive wooden table, behind which sat his chair. Throne-like, it dwarfed all else in the room. It was covered in red velvet with elegantly carved arms and was high-backed; it took your eyes immediately ceilingward, where overhead was the much talked-of Venus. When you passed on the street far below at night, the painting could be seen glowing celestially.

Long before he gained notoriety as an attorney and long before she was introduced to Lee on a movie set, Marvin Mitchelson and Michelle Triola were friends. It was a fitting liaison. They met,

Mitchelson stated on the stand, in about 1959, when Triola lived in his mother's apartment building. Mitchelson obtained his license to practice law in the late 1950s and handled personal injury cases, some for Michelle Triola. He also represented her in a divorce action from her husband, Rufus King Ward, in 1962. He *thought* he remembered a lawsuit in 1964 or 1965, an automobile accident injury claim for Michelle. Marvin Mitchelson also handled Michelle Triola's personal injury case against the Regents of the University of California on 31 January 1967, where she used the name of Michelle Ward – although she later testified that she was not using that name any more at that time. (There had long been rumors that Marvin Mitchelson and Michelle staged accidents for profit early in their relationship.) Marvin Mitchelson also filed her petition for the change of name from Michelle Lenore Triola to Michelle Triola Marvin in 1970, thus speeding Lee's departure.

A large man with a somewhat flaccid face, Mitchelson sometimes came across as boyishly bounding, prankish and jovial, but most of the time he was insulting and deprecating, and would heatedly worry at a witness like a rat terrier jumping on flesh. Many of the accusations he made were so preposterous that it was difficult to believe he was being taken seriously. Surprisingly, every allegation had to be countered in court, and many of them were printed in newspapers as facts. When someone was testifying and he wanted to stop the direction they were taking, he would jump up to object, unleashing an unrelated torrent of words until he could get a line of thought going for himself – something that he would jokingly admit. He usually pandered to Judge Marshall, but would some- times forget himself and snap at him in disrespect, then catch himself and profusely apologize to the ever-patient judge. He was very adept at leading his witness, then screaming bloody murder and complaining to the judge that the opposing side was doing it. If things were not going his way he would complain that he was sick: he had a sore throat, he had been up all night preparing. It was indeed a performance, and if it hadn't involved people's lives, reputations and money, it might have been an amusing exercise in court histrionics.

By contrast, A. David Kagon, Lee's lawyer, was a trim, handsome, white-haired man – he looked like Paul Newman in

The Verdict – who was impeccably dressed and very much the gentleman. He didn't raise his voice; he was unflappable, unfailingly alert – a very intelligent, tough opponent. He and Louis Goldman, senior partners of the firm of Goldman and Kagon (whose junior partners were mostly their children), had been Lee's lawyers as well as his close friends for more than twenty years. Lou and his wife Judy visited us on movie locations around the world and came fishing with us in Hawaii on occasions.

Judge Arthur K. Marshall had a reputation in the legal profession as a fair and impartial man who took a scholarly approach to his constitutional interpretations. One could see that he loved the law, respected attorneys and gave them every benefit of the doubt, as well as much latitude. His patience in listening to what sometimes appeared to be awful logic and repetitive argument was extraordinary – only occasionally did he show irritation or frustration. When he heard testimony he found personally unpleasant, he demanded exactly the same scrutiny as everything else, ruling on these matters with courtesy and dignity. It was obvious that he did not want his court to be seen by the press – of which he and everyone else was acutely aware – or the world at large as anything but entirely proper. I worried a little about this aspect of him, thinking that he might not know about the baser instincts at times revealed in the case. He also prided himself on his ability to settle cases before they came to trial – but he was quite unsuccessful with this one.

When the judge, or 'the Court' as he is called, nodded and asked, 'Opening statements, gentlemen?' Marvin Mitchelson stood to deliver:

MARVIN MITCHELSON: Thank you, Your Honor. If it please the court and counsel, mindful, Your Honor, that this is a court trial and no longer a jury trial, I will do my very best not to allow my emotions to get the better of me in arguing and opening statements. I said, 'arguing and opening statement'; that was a Freudian slip to begin with, but I am sure Your Honor will indulge me with a little leeway, I only hope to acquaint this court with what I intend to prove, what I hope to prove, in this court in the days, weeks, I hope not months, ahead.

But it *was* months – and almost entirely because his own client was impossibly unresponsive to questioning, and because he had a habit of near-constant objections, dragging each issue out interminably. They had been building this case for many years and it was obvious that brevity was not what they desired.

Mitchelson often outlined his case in a very emotional way. He used words of his own that he attributed to Lee – from fourteen years previously – and quoted them as if verbatim. Mitchelson had to prove that an *implied* property agreement was made between Lee and Michelle Triola by their conduct, because there wasn't any other proof. He claimed the existence of an express contract between them in December 1964 (an oral contract: 'Don't work, come and live with me – we'll share fifty-fifty') which was modified in 1966 ('not only share fifty-fifty, but I'll take care of you for the rest of your life').

Mitchelson pictured his client as a singer, a Catholic girl heartbroken over her failed marriage to Skip Ward. She and her ex-husband were trying for a reconciliation, but Lee advised her against it, Mitchelson said. He talked of Lee's unhappy marriage and the meetings where the contract was made.

MITCHELSON: Now the parties commenced a series of
discussions, we are going to learn, that led to the making of a
contract between them. First, we have some meetings
between Michelle and Lee at a place called the African
Queen; this was an establishment over on Santa Monica
Boulevard at the time.

I thought for a moment he was joking. It sounded more like a line by W. C. Fields – the idea of anyone making such a serious contract in a bar.

MITCHELSON: They discussed their mutual unhappiness with
marriage . . . Lee Marvin had a picture which he had to do
some work on [*Mitchelson says in an understatement*] by the
name of *Cat Ballou* . . . Lee sort of disappeared for the
moment, because she knew he was going off working and she
wasn't in touch with him.

She was going to New York City to work in a musical called *Flower*

Drum Song, a wonderful job offered by Gene Kelly. Lee, however, talks her out of accepting the offer, and gets her to drop her singing work. He induces her instead to join him and a group of men from his fishing club and come to San Blas, Mexico, to 'talk about their relationship', he said.

MITCHELSON: Now, Mr Marvin by this time is paying for things, paying Michelle's rent, giving her, as he puts it, what she needs . . . Michelle is telling Lee that she doesn't know where she stands, he hasn't really left his wife in the sense of filing [for divorce], he hasn't made up his mind about a divorce, so they have that kind of discussion, and you will hear it in greater detail when Michelle takes the stand. Michelle breaks away from a singing engagement and goes down there. He is already there.

Now, Your Honor, you are going to hear Mr Marvin testify at this trial, not once but probably a dozen times, he never loved this woman, this lady who sits to my right. [*He turns sympathetically to her and she weeps*] You are also going to hear him testify that he told her he loved her, but he just didn't mean it. He liked her, but he didn't love her. You are also going to hear him testify, incredibly so, but testify nevertheless that . . . I may be getting ahead of myself, but that he tried to get rid of her many times, I don't know, fifty, sixty, seventy times a year.

During this unchallenged delivery, Michelle sat shooting alluring glances at the court artist. She was dressed in demure clothes and what lawyers have been advising their clients to wear on the stand for centuries: the little white Peter Pan collar. Apparently, however, she would not make any concessions about her oversized aviator's glasses, and the combination was incongruous. Her hands were small but plump, and her fingernails were noticeable with their deep red polish. Her facial expression was usually one of arrogance and scorn, sucking in her cheeks and looking disdainfully about, her eyes often roving over the spectators; at other times she wore a pursed-lipped smirk. At appropriate moments, however, she would draw out a handkerchief and cry softly, or pull Kleenex with exaggerated care from a large box on the table in front of her.

When Marvin Mitchelson read excerpts from a letter Lee had written to her thirteen years before, she began working up to another cry. However, her attorney's assistant Penelope Mercurio giggled out loud at one of the sentences being read. The giggle died quickly in her throat when Michelle stopped dabbing at her eyes, turned slowly around and silenced her with a withering 'You're fired' look.

At some point in the proceedings we broke for lunch, going to one of the nearby restaurants that caters to the legal crowd. We staked out what was to be our table for months ahead. With us were our attorneys – not only David Kagon and Louis Goldman, but Lou's sons Ken and Mark Goldman (who wrote the brilliant briefs), and the athletic young Barry Felson, who would very ably take over for David when there was a conflict, as did Berndt (Bernie) Lohr-Schmidt – the four who made up the defense team, along with Chris Fagan and any others who were either sitting in or had dashed down with some papers or files we needed (there always seemed to be a lot of running). At the same time the opposing team settled into *their* dining spot. I found it quite strange, eventually, to discover that there were times when the trial was enjoyable. Your heart pounds, you feel a sense of dread and you think, 'This can't really be happening to me.' But once it has happened, you just decide, 'OK, here I am, I am just going to get in there and do the best I can.' After a while you see that much of a trial is a game being played out – although one using words and rules that you, as a lay person, are not privy to. It is also terribly confusing, particularly if you are on the witness stand and the game is being played on *you*.

It is quite exciting at times. When you hear someone say something you know to be a lie, and you remember that they said something earlier that would refute it, you become agitated, thinking, 'Will that be remembered by our lawyer? Will the judge notice?' And you wait and wait, then see how skillfully, perhaps hours or days later, it is eventually revealed as what is called an 'inconsistency' – which of course is a euphemism for a lie. Little, if anything, went past David Kagon. It was also a shock to hear people lie after they had placed one hand on a Bible, raised their other one heavenwards and sworn they would not. I always thought you would go to jail, be fined or that something would happen to you. Following these parries and pitfalls, wins and losses, was to engage in an often very emotionally draining roller coaster ride.

Once back from lunch recess, Marvin Mitchelson took us back to a mythical time when Lee, having left his wife, moves into motels and is occasionally 'living' with Michelle; many bills came to the office of Lee's business manager and were paid for her. 'Your Honor, that is holding out [as married],' Mitchelson contended stoutly.

> MITCHELSON: Now let's move on. Now, Your Honor, I have to bring up something that is not pleasant, not pleasant at all, but you must understand the burden placed on this woman, what it was like to care for Lee Marvin, what kind of job it was, although she gladly did it. Mr Marvin had a drinking problem during the years of the relationship and indulged quite often and excessively. Miss Marvin had many moments where she had to extricate him from dangerous situations. She literally had to pick him off the floor and out of the street and places where he would fall down and maybe split his head open, and accidents he had, and so forth. [*This description of Lee was mild compared with what was to follow in the months to come*] But she did it because she promised she would take care of him. That was part of her agreement with him.

After some shuffling of papers he talked of Lee's damage to her career.

> MITCHELSON: Now in 1966 Michelle has still performed in her career. She has still worked, but not so much. There will be a witness who will testify that she saw Michelle Triola and Lee at a party and asked Michelle, 'How is your singing? How is your career coming?' at which Lee replied for her, '*I have become her career*.'

A glimmer of amusement flickered across Lee's otherwise studiously impassive countenance. I too could see that Marvin Mitchelson had gravely misunderstood Lee's remark.

At Lee's urging, his client de-phased her career: 'She has gotten a singing engagement in Hawaii while Lee was in England filming *The Dirty Dozen*.' During the seven months Lee was away he wrote 'nine or ten' letters, Mitchelson claimed, and one was crucial to their case. In it Lee is said to have given Michelle Triola an ultimatum: either give up her career to 'care' for him in England, or the entire agreement, the contract, is off. Unfortunately they were not able to put their hand on the letter. Marvin Mitchelson asked Lee if *he* had it. Having denied writing it in the first place, Lee said in exasperation, 'I'm not in the habit of saving letters I write to other people.' In various depositions and testimonies Michelle Triola asserted that (1) it had been mislaid, and she was looking for it, (2) it was already in past interrogatories, (3) it was a telephone call overheard by her manager, and finally (4) it was definitely a letter but was torn up in little bits by Lee in a fit of anger.

MITCHELSON: Now Mr Marvin will deny that, but there is one thing he will not deny from his own mouth. He will tell you that after she came back from Hawaii she never worked on her career until he broke up with her in 1970, in May of 1970, and sent her packing from his home. She never worked again. Conduct? Yes! Corroboration? Yes!

This, in his logic, proved the existence of a letter which could not be produced.

Mitchelson talked of Michelle Triola's change of name to Marvin, the 'breakup' or 'kick out' and Lee's decision to 'discard her'. She had gone to Lee's attorney 'begging him to tell her where Lee had gone, because he went off down the coast, and Mr Goldman said to her, "I can't tell you where he is; he is through with you, he wants you out of the *home*."' Another word might have been *house*, but that was avoided at all costs as not having the right connotation. 'Out at the *home* one night, Mr Kagon, Mr Goldman and Mr Marvin came to put her out, and Mr Kagon kept going to the phone and saying, "If you don't get out, I will call the police." This is Mr Marvin's testimony, he said that Michelle Marvin, hysterically crying, said, "What about the promises you made? What about the house, the babies I have lost, what about those?" She said it over and over again, and Mr Marvin will so testify, and not one word back to her in the face of promises.'

In one of the depositions taken by Marvin Mitchelson prior to the case coming to trial, Lee was asked to reiterate everything he remembered Michelle yelling when he and his attorneys asked her to leave the house. Lee was being searchingly honest, and when pressed recalled that she had said, among many other things, 'losing babies'. He didn't believe it to be true and attached no importance to it – but *they* did. In Michelle Triola's depositions, when asked what she had said, she replied, 'I don't recall what I said.' They had not even mentioned this subject before in their questions, complaints or suits. This one statement made in the 'hunting expedition' – which is what depositions are called – prompted the later allegations of abortions and sterility. This became one of the most sensational parts of the trial, and there was a heavy concentration on it in the newspaper accounts and television reports. Unwittingly, Lee had handed them the cudgel himself.

Marvin Mitchelson ended his opening statement with heavy sarcasm:

> MITCHELSON: Let me tell you why he stopped, and then I will
> really sit down. I will keep my promise – speaking of
> promises, he said she violated the agreement, she called his
> home and so on and so forth. But I will tell you why he really
> stopped, as the evidence will show. In October of 1971, he
> told his wife Pamela for the first time that he had been
> paying Michelle Marvin one thousand fifty dollars a month,
> and in November no check came, and that was the end.
> Coincidentally, the evidence will show that in the same
> month they made an arrangement with Betty [*Lee's first
> wife*], who is entitled to lifetime support, to pay her off
> within five years . . . The evidence will show that Mrs
> Marvin, in her business-like manner, the new Mrs Marvin,
> took things in hand and said, 'Let's cut off Michelle, and let's
> cut off the old wife, and go on with the three and a half
> million, plus more.' Thank you, Your Honor. I'm sorry I
> exceeded my time.

It was now the turn of the woman reporter sitting behind me to giggle – at my start of surprise at being called the culprit, I suppose

– and Michelle Triola shot her a baleful look as well. Mitchelson let it be known that I was to be his first witness, making me extremely nervous all night. He didn't call me to the stand, however; he called Michelle Triola instead. I suppose it was just his little joke – I was actually the *last* witness in their case.

Though Mitchelson had promised a short delivery, only forty-five minutes were left of the day. Lee's attorney David Kagon rose and gave his opening statements. He was dignified and to the point, and the press and the audience were very attentive as he outlined the defense, stressing the law rather than emotion, and countering Marvin Mitchelson's claims.

> DAVID KAGON: Your Honor, it would be impossible for me to refute each and every remark that Mr Mitchelson has made. Suffice it to say that 98 per cent of his factual statements are either totally fabricated or imagined. I can state that having read all the depositions not once, not twice, but several times, I fail to recognize any of the quotations therein which Mr Mitchelson attributes to Mr Marvin. Basically I am suggesting, and I submit, Your Honor, the true facts cannot be made to fit the law. Ironically, there are undoubtedly some 'good' Marvin-type cases, but this is not one of them.

He promised that the evidence would show there was 'no express contract, or agreement, or tacit understanding, to divide the defendant's property, or for plaintiff's support . . . Statements and conduct were such that *if* there were such agreements, she had breached them. And by virtue thereof, is not entitled to recover.'

He told the court of a meeting with Lee's attorney where 'Miss Triola Marvin', after consulting a lawyer of her own, made an agreement to accept money and to disassociate herself from Lee's life. He then asked Judge Marshall if, assuming she had an agreement to 'share' fifty-fifty, would she make this kind of agreement? Concerning the statements about Betty Marvin, Lee's first wife, she asked for the arrangement herself, wanting to remarry, but still retain alimony for seven years; Lee acquiesced.

Triola's marriage to Skip Ward, he corrected Marvin Mitchelson, was not one and a half years but four months and six days, and it was her husband who filed first for the divorce. She had no assets when she met Mr Marvin and she was low on cash. When she asked him for money he gave it to her, primarily for her rent or car payments.

KAGON: Mr Marvin was forty years of age at the time. He had been married for thirteen years and had four minor children. As Mr Mitchelson mentioned, his marriage was breaking up, primarily because, for sixteen years, he had devoted himself entirely to reaching that particular pinnacle of success, and it was significant.

It is under these circumstances, Your Honor, with a woman that he has known for not more than four and a half months, that the plaintiff and plaintiff's counsel would have us believe that Mr Marvin, who had not yet resolved his problems with his wife – as a matter of fact, he was still living with his wife – would make an arrangement whereby he would give Miss Triola, Miss Marvin, one half of everything that he made thereafter, and would take care of her for the rest of her life . . .

Miss Marvin will testify Mr Marvin asked her continually to marry him. Then why didn't she get married? The answer is abundantly clear, because no one asked her, Your Honor. The best evidence of that is that there was no marriage.

Mr Mitchelson has referred to a change of name. After the parties started living together, Miss Marvin began telling Mr Marvin that she would like to change her name, and he said to her in his deposition, 'I don't want you to change your name. It would be embarrassing to me, embarrassing to my children, and it's not your name.' . . . The name change actually occurred on 7 May. On 11 May, four days later, Mr Marvin got out.

An arrangement was made with Miss Marvin and Mr Goldman that she would remain in the house for a period of approximately one month, which would give her enough time to get another place.

Your Honor, at that time, on 20 May, and when Miss Marvin left the residence, no one threw her out. No one had been to the house at that time.

She thereafter received the monies and she obtained a place at the beach – and that is interesting in itself, because one of the conditions of the arrangement was that she divorce herself from his life. But she took a place a few houses down the beach, where if he walked up and down the beach, she would see him, and vice versa.

That house was rented by her *before* Mr Marvin returned. When Mr Marvin returned to the house on that day, he found Miss Marvin, and she refused to leave. It is true that she was asked to leave several times, many, many, times.

Now, we have heard very much today about the parties combining their efforts and earnings, and that they would share equally any and all property accumulated as a result of their efforts.

The net result of combining their earnings meant basically that she would receive one half of his earnings and property, but she had no earnings, Your Honor.

JUDGE: You say she had no earnings?

KAGON: She had no earnings. With all due respect to Miss Triola, she was just barely getting by – if at all.

Now we come to 'The plaintiff performed her part of the purported agreement', and this, of course, is an allegation that she must include, and prove, in order to obtain the relief she requests.

The burden wasn't very great, Your Honor. She had almost nothing to do . . . On location, Your Honor, Miss Marvin had women to do the cleaning, the cooking, at least five and six days a week.

In Los Angeles, living at the beach, she had women either two or three times a week.

[*Concerning mutual effort*] I submit to Your Honor that the two pictures which were the most successful during his entire career, from a box office point of view, *Cat Ballou* and *The Dirty Dozen*, Michelle Triola was not present on either, and he functioned rather well. He was on *The Dirty Dozen* for seven months. She was with him ten to fourteen days.

Purportedly Mr Marvin wrote to Miss Marvin – the most important element in this case – 'Leave your career and come with me.' That letter is not here, and I submit, Your Honor, that letter never existed.

The last item of the purported agreement is the allegation that she performed her part.

Miss Marvin testified that she entered into an agreement with two inexperienced producers, whereby she would advise them, not only as to what Lee then wanted to do, but whatever he wanted to do thereafter.

She further goes on, 'The arrangement that I made with them was made between us, between the three of us,' and the purported arrangement was that she was to get . . . 'a piece of them'; and she thereafter filed her complaint for recovery against the producers of Mr Marvin's picture known as *Monte Walsh*; her complaint was for $75,000, based upon all the information she had given to them . . .

Now, Your Honor, confidential relationship: if ever there was a breach of a confidence, that was it.

It shows, I think beyond any question, that the lady was going into business for herself. It is a clear indication that she had no understanding whatsoever about participating in half of his property, because if she had, why the machinations of making a separate deal with two producers? When it became apparent to her that the relationship was going to be terminated, she started to threaten him, and those threats took the form of 'If you try and get rid of me, I will tell everybody about our living together; I will ruin your career; this will hurt your children; this will hurt you; this will hurt everybody that is around you.' Now that, Your Honor, was not an idle threat.

She also threatened to commit suicide.

Miss Marvin is saying, 'All that I wanted to do was have the same arrangement as a wife; that was my understanding' – and yet she didn't get married at that time, but the deal she purportedly made was better than one that Mr Marvin would have made with her had he married her. Thank you, Your Honor.

The battle lines were drawn, and each attorney now had to prove his case with testimony from the 'principals' and their witnesses, and with his ability to convince the Judge.

The first witness was Michelle Triola. Lee had to sit at the table with his attorneys for the duration; on this day Jim Mahoney and Lee's daughters Cynthia and Claudia came to sit with me in the front row.

Michelle was on the stand for the entire day and many more to come. First she was under direct examination by her attorney and then under cross examination by Lee's. She tried very hard to look as though she were remembering the 'facts', but it seemed more as if she were trying to recall rehearsed answers. The time she took to answer the most rudimentary questions quickly became frustrating to everyone listening. She often wore an expression of boredom, but at other times she smirked, opening and closing her eyes slowly as she answered. After being sworn in, she was asked to state her name, 'Michelle Triola Marvin', and was then asked by the clerk to speak up please – the first of hundreds of such requests. She first met Lee, she said, on a film he was working on, *Ship of Fools*.

Now for the first time we heard real testimony rather than written accusations or attorney's arguments. She touched on a variety of subjects; abortions (she cried); Lee's drinking; her career.

MITCHELSON: What were you doing on that film?
MICHELLE: I was a stand-in. I was also kind of an extra dancer.
MITCHELSON: Is there anything else in that film that you did?
MICHELLE: I believe I had some lines.
MITCHELSON: Some lines?
MICHELLE: Yes.

Under Marvin Mitchelson's questioning she outlined – or he did and she filled in – her dancing in Las Vegas and Reno 'for The Barry Ashton Dance Troupe'.

MICHELLE: Yes, I was his partner.
MITCHELSON: His partner?
MICHELLE: Uh-hum.
JUDGE: What hotel, ma'am?
MICHELLE: Flamingo Hotel in Las Vegas, the El Rancho Hotel in Las Vegas, I believe, the Thunderbird, The Mapes in Reno,

and I believe Harrah's in Lake Tahoe . . . I believe I appeared
with Don Arder, a troupe during the Winter Olympics in
Lake Tahoe.

MITCHELSON: Anything else?

MICHELLE: And I believe that Arthur Murray took a troupe up
to Reno one summer. And I appeared. Yes.

MITCHELSON: All right, now, Miss Marvin, were you also a
singer?

MICHELLE: Yes.

MITCHELSON: When did you start singing professionally?

MICHELLE: I would say 1957.

MITCHELSON: In or about the time you met Mr Marvin on
Ship of Fools, were you singing professionally any place?

MICHELLE: Yes, I was singing at the Little Club. It's in Beverly
Hills, on Canon Drive. It was supper club kind of singing. I
think that particular time I was there four weeks. I worked at
Dino's Lodge two or three times before that on Sunset
Boulevard near La Cienega. I would usually go in for four
weeks and then maybe five months later another four weeks.

As this continued, at times she sounded pathetic, at others casual
and smug, but always the answers came agonizingly slowly. She
was at all times, she said, a featured performer; the work was
extensive, often with return engagements, and her 'option' was
constantly being picked up.

Having been taken through her domestic career, we approached
Europe and where she was appearing.

MICHELLE: At the Kit Kat Klub in Rome.

MITCHELSON: Tell us approximately how long you worked in
these places?

MICHELLE: Most of the places in Europe only had
entertainment on weekends.

JUDGE: Are we to assume you worked one weekend in this
place?

MICHELLE: No, no!

MITCHELSON: Tell us what you . . .

MICHELLE: I would say I worked four months at the Kit Kat
Klub.

MITCHELSON: On weekends?
MICHELLE: Uh-huh.

She believed she was reviewed in Europe, but did not have any copies. There were some heated exchanges between the attorneys about two reviews of her singing in a Los Angeles club, with David Kagon arguing that many of these so-called 'reviews' were planted ads.

MITCHELSON: Your Honor, at this time I would like to make a motion, respectfully so. My respect for Mr Kagon keeps me from saying what I would really like to say. But when Mr Kagon says an article is planted, and we know that these are planted, that goes in the same category as his opening statement in which he said ninety-eight per cent of what I had to say was fabricated. I'm going to make him eat every one of those percentage points.

JUDGE: Counsel, just a moment. No need to pass threats back and forth between you gentlemen. We are here to try to find out what the witnesses have to say about it. I presume we will have that testimony and that should be the end of it.

MITCHELSON: Thank you, Your Honor, I'm sorry. [*The first of many such apologies. Then to Michelle*] When did you first read the article?

MICHELLE: On 23 May 1962.

MITCHELSON: Did you save it?

MICHELLE: Yes, I did.

MITCHELSON: Why?

MICHELLE: I saved it because I wanted to include it in my ads.

MITCHELSON: Your ads? Is that what you said? [*Her lawyer didn't always get the answer he wanted*]

Marvin Mitchelson and Michelle then engaged in an exchange that was just a first example of the comfortable relationship they seemed to have with each other.

MITCHELSON: Do you know where I got it?

MICHELLE: Did you get it from me?

MITCHELSON: I'm not asking *you* to ask *me* a question.

MICHELLE: Noo-oh, I don't know *where* you got it.

Then testimony was given on 'compensation' in America.

MICHELLE: Dino's Lodge – scale.[3] And then they would
escalate it, but not very much.
MITCHELSON: Jerry Lewis's?
MICHELLE: The same sort of set up.
JUDGE: When you say scale, you mean what – $285 or
approximately?
MICHELLE: Whatever the scale rate was at the time.
JUDGE: Do you recall what it was at the time, ma'am?
MICHELLE: No, because they raised it soon after.

Judge Marshall raised his eyebrows and looked as though he had
missed something. Hours upon hours of court time were thus spent
in trying to establish that Michelle's career was extensive and
lucrative, and that Lee ruined it by insisting she give it up.

Other aspects of their case were introduced, including her first
meeting with Lee and the 'intimacy'. She knew him on the set of
Ship of Fools during June–July 1964 – and, she thought, also
August – and was intimate with Lee 'I'd say about two weeks after
we had known each other.' It was in dressing rooms on the set. 'He
told me he was not very happily married . . . that he adored his
children and that he loved his wife, but their relationship was . . .
seemingly lacking in communication.'

The day had started at nine and ended some time after 4 p.m.
Even with the morning and afternoon break and a lunch recess, it
was a dreadfully long day and therefore a great relief when court
was finally adjourned. We walked out into the waiting mob of press
and television cameras in the hallway, an everyday occurrence for
the next three months. Two women reporters came over to me and
privately said they felt very uncomfortable for me; they found the
situation very distasteful, but told me to keep my spirits up. Little
did we know that we had heard nothing yet.

In what became a regular routine, Lee and I drove immediately
back to the hotel and changed into more comfortable clothes. We
ordered a pot of hot tea and sat with our feet up watching the
evening news (much of it about us), usually nursing stress

3 Scale: the amount of compensation for performers which is set by the union.

headaches. We had quiet dinners alone, with friends, or with any members of the family who were with us at the time. We rose at six every morning to dress for our daily court and television appearances, and had breakfast in the hotel restaurant, Hernando's Hideaway, before the long ride to downtown Los Angeles in the morning rush hour.

Lee dressed for the court proceedings each day in one of his conservative, handsomely-tailored suits, either dark blue, black or a deep gray pin-stripe. He was very dignified and quiet throughout Mitchelson's rambling and insulting accounts of 'him'. I would have found it hard to be so composed under such descriptions of my life, my work, my honesty and my morality. He only once barked at Marvin Mitchelson, '*You* want to discuss *my* morals?' Even when Mitchelson was particularly goading, Lee would counter his accusations honestly and straightforwardly, rarely showing a glint of anger or engaging in sharp exchanges with him – something he could so well have excelled in over Mitchelson. He recognized the gravity not only of the situation but of the forum in which it was being played out, and quickly became accustomed to Mitchelson's manner and to court protocol as well. Who could have been more attuned to theatrics? It became immediately obvious that the lawyers – and the judge – had great latitude as 'officers of the court', and no matter what they called you, what they said of you and how they did it, you were cautioned not to react. They have the whole body of jurisprudence behind them (deservedly or not), and you ignore it at your peril. It's a wonderfully one-sided weapon, and attorneys such as Mitchelson use it like a meat axe.

David Kagon recently reminded me about the purchase of these suits of Lee's. Shortly before we were due in court for the first trial in 1973,[4] David remarked on Lee's fairly rustic wardrobe of slacks and sports jackets. Lee had given up the lifestyle that required fashionable dressing, and save for the occasional formal affair when only a tuxedo would do, he had only a suit or two from the old days. One favourite of his was a green suit – wardrobe from *Point Blank*, filmed in 1967. David suggested he wear something

4 The original complaint which was thrown out of court.

rather more conservative, the male counterpart of the Peter Pan collar. Lee gave him a long look and said, 'Gotcha.' We arrived at the courthouse on the day of the trial, and David was stunned by Lee's appearance. Not only had he taken his advice, but had gone one step further. He had had three very expensive and fine wool suits hand tailored for him by Lew Ritter in Beverly Hills. They were in impeccable taste, appropriate for the most proper occasion.

We went to trial and within a short time the case was thrown out of court. Everyone was elated and ready to leave when David noticed Lee still sitting in his chair, looking decidedly morose.

'What's the matter, Lee?' he asked. 'Don't you know we've won?'

And Lee, slowly shaking his head, replied, 'Dave, I got a problem.'

'What is it?' David asked, puzzled.

'What the fuck am I going to do with these suits?'

Of course he was joking, and he pulled them out again for this trial.

Since the plaintiff's case is presented first, and because the defense's cross examination must be kept within the confines of the subjects brought up by the plaintiff's side, their tune was the one we had to dance to. The career of Michelle Triola, along with other matters, was addressed by David Kagon the afternoon of the second day of the trial. Her answers about her singing engagements, their length and the compensation, were quite different from those of the previous day, but were delivered with equal assurance. It was an exercise in exasperation.

Not only Mitchelson but the news media as well made a great deal of the fact that Lee had forced her to give up a career. By the end of three months of searching testimony, however, it appeared she had herself flung her career away at the earliest opportunity, like a dog shaking off water.

She began singing seriously in 1959, although the day before she had said 1957 and on another occasion it was 1960. She also added, 'I would sing at weddings for twenty-five dollars.'

She had worked for the attorney Gregg Bautzer doing research. She had no legal background, 'believed' her salary was $125 a week, but that it was sporadic. She 'couldn't say' how many weeks she had worked for him. She was employed at Blue Cross in the coding room, but again 'couldn't say' how long or at what salary, or what other odd jobs she had had – which may have lasted only half a day.

In 1961 she had one performance with Barry Ashton, but no other jobs that year because 'I was getting ready to get married. I'm not clear on the date because I didn't work for a while while I was married.'

A series of questions about her European club appearances was answered slowly, with a bored expression but in a combative tone.

KAGON: After you left Rome, where did you seek employment?

MICHELLE: I never left Rome.

KAGON: I'm sorry. [*Puzzled expression*]

MICHELLE: I don't quite understand your question. Do you mean when did I leave Rome for ever and go to another country?

KAGON: No, when did you leave Rome to seek employment elsewhere in 1962?

MICHELLE: You mean *look* for employment?

KAGON: To look, fine. [*Concedes*]

MICHELLE: Or to *go* to work?

KAGON: To go to work. [*Concedes again*]

MICHELLE: I don't recall.

KAGON: During the time you were in Rome, you worked at the Kit Kat Klub?

MICHELLE: Yes, but not the whole time.

KAGON: Not the two months?

MICHELLE: No. [*Under Mitchelson's questioning she had stated she had worked at the club four months*]

She went on in this vein for a very long time. Coupled with her habit of exaggeratedly stressing some words and then pausing between others, the whole thing became extremely frustrating. I was fidgeting in my seat – or wanting to – and there were many sighs of exasperation in the room. Paul Wasserman, Lee's publicist with the James Mahoney agency, was sitting with me and fell asleep, snoring. Judge Marshall would look up sharply, trying to see who was doing such a thing in his court, and each time the bailiff would motion me to wake Wasserman up.

Trying as it was to listen to, David's questioning was slowly drawing out a long list of inconsistencies. I sat there wondering what the press and judge could possibly be thinking. One white-haired woman, a rather poorly-dressed court watcher, had sat there that day giving me withering glances, particularly when Michelle had been talking about 'the abortions'. And in the hallway she looked as though she would like to attack me with her umbrella, or at least vent her wrath at me some other way. I didn't notice her directing these same feelings toward Lee. (Later on, during the defense case, she flashed me a nice, warm change-of-heart smile.)

When David asked Michelle about her employment in Los Angeles before she met Lee, she answered, 'I don't think I worked that much because I was reconciled with my husband.'

KAGON: Did you return to live with Mr Ward in 1963?
MICHELLE: Yes.
KAGON: For how long?
MICHELLE: I really can't say . . . I really don't remember.
KAGON: Now, did your reconciliation with Mr Ward end in 1963?
MICHELLE: Yes, we were living with friends so I took a separate residence.

This served to impeach her claim that Lee had talked her out of a reconciliation with her ex-husband, as they hadn't even met until at least a year later.

Michelle spoke of being on a 'circuit' of Playboy clubs: 'It would be two weeks in one place, two weeks in another Playboy club, and then two weeks in another . . . You would rotate with another singer and sometimes there would be an added club.'

KAGON: To the best of your recollection, what was the first Playboy club you performed in?
MICHELLE: I believe it was Chicago.
KAGON: How long?
MICHELLE: I believe that one was three weeks.
KAGON: What other Playboy club?
MICHELLE: Tucson . . . excuse me, it was Phoenix. Two weeks. And next, I believe it was Miami. Two weeks. New York. All

the engagements were for two weeks except the original one.

KAGON: Any other?

MICHELLE: San Francisco.

KAGON: Any other Playboy clubs besides Chicago, Phoenix, Miami, New York, San Francisco?

MICHELLE: I really don't remember. I think there were no more than three others.

KAGON: A total of eight clubs? Over what period of time would that be?

MICHELLE: You know, I really don't know.

KAGON: You have no idea at all?

MICHELLE: Mr Kagon [*impatiently*], sometimes I would do two clubs, and then there was an opening, I would go home for six weeks, and then they would call me, and they would say, 'There's an opening in San Francisco,' and I would go there for two weeks. Then maybe I would have to go the next day to another place. That is what is considered a tour.

KAGON: Thank you. What did you receive as compensation – does it vary from club to club?

MICHELLE: I really don't know because it was scale, and scale in different states is different amounts . . . we always got our expenses paid.

KAGON: Did you have repeats?

MICHELLE: Yes.

KAGON: Which ones?

MICHELLE: Chicago. It may have been twice in Phoenix.

KAGON: In your opinion, were you well-received at all of these clubs?

MICHELLE: Yes, I was.

She was very specific about this work. Because she had met Lee in June or July 1964, her employment beginning in January 1964 was now addressed.

In an exchange typical of Michelle when left unguarded to her own ruminations, she explains to the court about scale, and says that really she made no money at all.

KAGON: How much did you receive when you say 'less than scale'?

MICHELLE: I don't know, because most of my salary was going
to the musicians.
KAGON: Oh, you were paying your own?
MICHELLE: No.
KAGON: Well, would you explain that?
MICHELLE: Two of my musicians were doing charts for me,
and I requested my salary go to them.
KAGON: What other employment in 1964?
MICHELLE: I worked on a film. Beginning of June. *Ship of Fools.*

She was completely unforthcoming about her income on the two
movies she claimed to have worked on.

KAGON: How much did you receive?
MICHELLE: I really can't say.
KAGON: You were working as an extra?
MICHELLE: I said I did not . . . I cannot pin down what I
received. Some days I received compensation as being
background. Another day I would receive compensation for
wearing my own clothes.
KAGON: Do you remember the maximum amount that you ever
received in any one day?
MICHELLE: No, I don't, *sir.*
KAGON: Any other work in 1964?
MICHELLE: I worked on another picture called *Synanon.* I
worked as Barbara Luna's stand-in. I worked background. I
worked . . . there was a part of a singer in the room. I did
that. I did that part, if you can call it a part. I had a few lines.
I did the same thing.

Again she had no recollection of her salary for this movie.

KAGON: How long were you employed at the Little Club?
MICHELLE: During that period, sometimes three days. The
Little Club is a place where you break in an act, and you do
it any time that you can get in.

She was forgetting that she had just said her employment was
initially for six weeks, then for another four weeks, and that it was
a supper-club kind of singing.

KAGON: You would pay your musicians, is that correct?

MICHELLE: Sometimes I would, sometimes I would send the bill to Mr Silver, Lee's business manager.

KAGON: When you paid your musicians, what happened to the balance of compensation that you received?

MICHELLE: There *was* no balance – of scale? [*Incredulously*]

KAGON: Where else did you work?

MICHELLE: I believe, but I'm not sure whether it was 1965, that I worked at the Holiday House on the Pacific Coast Highway in Malibu.

KAGON: What did you do with your compensation?

MICHELLE: I gave it to the piano player.

KAGON: So that once again, did you have any money left after you paid the piano player?

MICHELLE: No, no, I didn't have any left.

KAGON: What else did you do in 1965 for employment?

MICHELLE: I don't believe I had any more in 1965.

David next questioned her on her work in 1966.

MICHELLE: I made a record for Santana Records.

KAGON: Were you compensated?

MICHELLE: I don't believe so. No, I know I wasn't.

KAGON: When was the record made?

MICHELLE: I don't remember if it . . . I know that Lee won the Academy Award in April of that year, and I don't remember if he . . . if I recorded before he came back from London or afterwards . . . I don't remember. It could have been before or after.

KAGON: What other employment did you have in 1966?

MICHELLE: I had an engagement in Kauai.

By the day's end, more inconsistencies had come forth. Dino's Lodge was a club Michelle claimed to have worked in many times and for long engagements. When the defense put on its case, this claim was refuted when the owner of Dino's Lodge, Paul Wexler, was called to the stand. In answer to David Kagon's question about her employment in 1965, he replied, 'If I remember correctly, it was two weeks.' One two-week engagement.

KAGON: What was the reason for employing her?

PAUL WEXLER: She was recommended to us by a lady who was a frequent customer of ours, and . . . it was suggested that she had friends who would spend money, that Lee Marvin was her boyfriend, and he would bring in people and it would be good for business.

This two-week appearance in 1965 was never extended.

She had listed engagements at eight different Playboy clubs, and sometimes repeats. Two employees of the Playboy Club testified. Sam Distefano had been employed since 1960 as Director of Entertainment; he was the full-time music director, in charge of rehearsals, and the custodian of the business records. He had yellow cards for performers which rated them A, B, C, D or E – although he had never seen anyone get an E. His testimony was very upsetting to Marvin Mitchelson, who tried hard to keep it out. Even the Judge had to reprimand him, 'Counsel, you have interrupted twice and it is very difficult to get this down.' Upon looking up any cards for Michelle Triola, Michelle Triola Ward, Michelle Taylor, Sam Distefano found only one. This had her picture and the information that she had been hired for one two-week engagement on 8 April 1963 in Phoenix, Arizona. The press had access to these exhibits and informed the public that she was rated a D. Distefano's extensive records indicated that she had not worked in 1962 or in 1961, or at any time up to 1969, other than this once. She could not possibly have appeared at the San Francisco club either, as she had said, because it wasn't open at the time.

Noel Stein, general manager in charge of the clubs' openings, corroborated the testimony. Michelle's credibility was severely damaged. The caginess of her replies to questions about her work on *Ship of Fools* and *Synanon* was obvious, and from Lee's testimony it was clear she was a stand-in for Barbara Luna on *Ship of Fools*, not an extra and certainly not an actress with lines.

The second part of Michelle Triola's testimony about her career and the ruination of it concerned her job offer for *Flower Drum Song*.

When questioned by her attorney, she said that after her work on

Ship of Fools, she 'lost touch' with Lee. She had moved into a hotel, the Sunset Marquis, but there was a chance meeting. Lee followed her car and called her from the lobby; when he went up, she told him she was leaving for New York right after *Synanon* was finished. He asked her not to go – he didn't want her out of his life.

MITCHELSON: What did you tell him?

MICHELLE: I told him that I had been offered something in *Flower Drum Song*, and that I felt it was an escalation in my work, and I wanted to go.

MITCHELSON: Now, what did you do about New York and *Flower Drum Song*?

MICHELLE: I didn't go.

David Kagon's cross-examination asked more fully about this.

KAGON: *Flower Drum Song* was then being produced in New York, is that correct?

MICHELLE: Yes.

KAGON: Who hired you?

MICHELLE: Gene Kelly.

KAGON: Did you have a contract with Mr Kelly?

MICHELLE: No, because I never went.

KAGON: Now, let's narrow the span. Did you have a conversation with Mr Kelly at any time prior to the completion of *Ship of Fools*?

MICHELLE: I would say about three weeks before. I ran into him at Columbia and he said, 'You have Oriental features, you should try out for *Flower Drum Song*.' He said, 'I will call them, and if you want to go to New York, I'll set it up.'

KAGON: You testified that you told Mr Marvin about your desire to go and he dissuaded you from doing so, is that correct?

MICHELLE: Yes, he did.

KAGON: All right. You told him you had the job in New York? Did you?

MICHELLE: I *had* the job in New York.

KAGON: Miss Marvin, it was after that conversation with Mr Marvin that you called Mr Kelly, is that right?

MICHELLE: Mr Kelly called *me*. He asked me if I had decided to go to New York, and I said I couldn't make that decision yet. That occurred while I was making *Synanon*.

KAGON: When did you next talk to Mr Kelly?

MICHELLE: It was when Lee asked me not to make that decision. He came to my set. I was still working on the film, and he asked me to have a talk with him.

KAGON: Did you do so on the set?

MICHELLE: No, we went to Chez Jay's, which is a restaurant a few blocks from where we were shooting *Synanon*.

KAGON: And the two of you – he talked about your rejecting the offer, is that right?

MICHELLE: Yes.

KAGON: Did you thereafter talk to Mr Kelly?

MICHELLE: Yes, I did.

KAGON: Did you call him or did he call you?

MICHELLE: I called him.

KAGON: What did you tell him?

MICHELLE: I told him that maybe sometime later I would love a chance to be in *Flower Drum Song*, but that right now I had to stay in Los Angeles.

Her earlier testimony, given only days before, had cited a quite different time and location. The conversation, she then said, had taken place at the Sunset Marquis Hotel.

Gene Kelly was called to the stand on 15 February, when the defense had the opportunity to bring on witnesses. Not many people of his stature would have responded as gracefully as he did under the circumstances, and of course, we were all very interested to hear him talk about himself and his life.

KAGON: Mr Kelly, how long have you resided in Beverly Hills?

GENE KELLY: I first resided there in 1942, and outside of two years in the Navy – I was back in 1946 – I have lived there since.

KAGON: What is your profession or occupation?

GENE KELLY: Well, I was an actor, I was a director, I did a little writing, choreography. In 1956 I produced a film, and I directed a film also that very year, if it means anything.

Lee and Keenan Wynn racing in 1958. (Courtesy of Herb Ball, NBC.)

Playing Ira Hayes, the Pima Indian who was one of the soldiers who raised the flag at Iwo Jima, in John Frankenheimer's *The American* for N.B.C. Television, 1960.

Left: As Detective Lieutenant Frank Ballinger: *M Squad*, 1959.
In *Point Blank*, 1966.

Right: On the set of *The Dirty Dozen* with director Robert Aldrich, England, 1966.

John Wayne, Hank Aaron and Lee mugging it up in the background with John Ford on the set of *Donovan's Reef* in 1962.

Left: With John Boorman during the filming of *Point Blank* in San Francisco, 1966.   John Boorman and Lee in Palau, Micronesia, shooting *Hell In The Pacific* 1967–8. (Photograph by Orlando Suero.)

Right: As Ben Rumson in *Paint Your Wagon*, 1968.

Shooting *Monte Walsh* with Jeanne Moreau in 1969.

'The Cool-Sex Boys', as Candice Bergen called them. Paul Newman and Lee in *Pocket Money*, 1971. (Photograph by Terry O'Neill.)

Lee Marvin with William Hurt in *Gorky Park*.

Toasting our wedding on 18 October 1970 above the lights of Las Vegas. (Courtesy of Mahoney Communications.)

KAGON: During your career, Mr Kelly, how many motion pictures have you been involved in?

GENE KELLY: Frankly, I don't know. I would roughly guess, let's say a round number – fifty. I really don't know.

KAGON: In how many Broadway productions have you been involved?

GENE KELLY: Five, six, seven, eight.

KAGON: In what capacity?

GENE KELLY: Dancer, actor, choreographer, director.

KAGON: Are you familiar with the plaintiff?

GENE KELLY: Yes, I know Michelle very well.

KAGON: When did you first meet her?

GENE KELLY: Well, I think it was as far back as the late 1940s or maybe in the early 1950s, so I have known Michelle quite a while.

KAGON: What was the nature of your acquaintanceship with her?

GENE KELLY: Social, completely social.

KAGON: Calling your attention to *Flower Drum Song* – were you involved in *Flower Drum Song*?

GENE KELLY: Yes, I was the director of *Flower Drum Song*.

KAGON: Up until what period of time were you actively involved with *Flower Drum Song*?

GENE KELLY: Until 1 December 1958. It opened on Broadway, and when I came back from Europe on a trip in January, I visited there, as every director does, to check the progress of the show. I gave the stage manager some notes, made one more trip in the year 1959, and that was the end of that. I was really disassociated from it from 1 December 1958, when it opened.

KAGON: In 1963 or 1964, do you have any recollection of talking to Michelle about her taking a part in *Flower Drum Song*?

GENE KELLY: No, I never talked to anyone about it because the show was over for quite a few years.

KAGON: Do you ever recall at any time suggesting to Michelle that she go back east and try out for *Flower Drum Song*?

GENE KELLY: No, I don't recall that, no. Pardon me, I wouldn't suggest to *anyone* to go back east and try out for *Flower Drum Song* because it would be a terrific expense for them and I didn't have the authority to guarantee them a job.

KAGON: Now in 1964, did you know – or 1965, or 1963, did you know anything about Michelle Marvin's career?

GENE KELLY: No, no, I didn't. I knew she was connected in some way with motion pictures, but my understanding, which can be incorrect, was that she worked as an extra in pictures. But as I say, my understanding can be wrong, because the only thing – I must make a distinction there, she never auditioned for me for a role. That is all I can really tell you.

KAGON: Did you ever recommend to her that she audition for someone else?

GENE KELLY: No, never, I don't recall that.

Gene Kelly was then cross-examined by Marvin Mitchelson:

MITCHELSON: OK, Mr Kelly, you were connected with the motion picture *Marjorie Morningstar*, weren't you?

GENE KELLY: I certainly was, yes.

MITCHELSON: Will you jog your memory a little bit, because I know it has been many, many years? Don't you recall that Michelle tried out for a part in *Marjorie Morningstar*?

GENE KELLY: No, I don't.

MITCHELSON: You don't recall that. My client tells me that she actually worked on the film.

GENE KELLY: I was an actor in *Marjorie Morningstar*, so if Michelle did try out for it, she had to try out for someone else. I was only an actor and I had no authority to hire anyone, fire anyone, audition anyone, so Michelle is a little confused on that issue.

MITCHELSON: You remember she appeared in the picture?

GENE KELLY: No, I don't. But there were many, many girls in the picture. My goodness, many. As a matter of fact, I think all the girls were running across the street to see Errol Flynn during the breaks, and those of us who were working in the picture were left alone with our coffee.

MITCHELSON: Mr Kelly, wasn't *Flower Drum Song* playing some place in 1964, 1965?

GENE KELLY: I have no idea. You have to look that up.

MITCHELSON: Do you know a restaurant named Dominic's?

GENE KELLY: I certainly do.

MITCHELSON: All right. Now Michelle tells me that you ran into her there in 1964, and that she spoke to you. Do you recall ever talking to her at Dominic's?

GENE KELLY: No.

MITCHELSON: And she tells me further, Mr Kelly, that when she had the pleasure of seeing you at Dominic's and talking to you back in 1964, that she had mentioned that she wanted to go to New York for a possible audition in *Flower Drum Song* and that you suggested that she call a choreographer there, someone you knew?

GENE KELLY: No, no, I suggest Miss Triola is very confused about dates and the years of this show, and about her conversations about *Flower Drum Song*. I had nothing to do with *Flower Drum Song*. I couldn't advise her where to go or what to do. I didn't know where it was playing. I didn't know about any road shows. And to get that information you would have to call the Rodgers and Hammerstein estate and find it out.

More than a month later, in an attempt to refute Gene Kelly's testimony, Marvin Mitchelson questioned Michelle Triola.

MITCHELSON: Did you ever see Mr Gene Kelly in 1964?

MICHELLE: Yes, I had dinner with him a number of times.

MITCHELSON: All right. Did you ever have dinner at a place called Dominic's?

MICHELLE: Yes.

MITCHELSON: Did you ever discuss with Mr Kelly the subject of *Flower Drum Song*?

MICHELLE: Yes, I told Gene [*no more 'Mr Kelly'!*] that I was a Barry Ashton dancer . . . and I told him of my desire to go to New York and my desire to get on the stage in New York, and that I thought my chances were good in *Flower Drum Song* because I had Oriental looks.

MITCHELSON: Did you ever show a picture to Mr Gene Kelly?

MICHELLE: Yes.

MITCHELSON: Where were you when you showed it to him?

MICHELLE: It could have been at Dominic's because . . .

MITCHELSON: I don't want you to guess. Do you remember showing it to him at Dominic's?

MICHELLE: It may have been when he picked me up.

You testified against Michelle Triola at your peril: if she was going down, Gene Kelly was going down with her. This was a total departure from her earlier testimony – that she had run into him at Columbia or at Dominic's and during cross-examination she changed the name of the restaurant concerned to La Scala.

Guided by Marvin Mitchelson, Michelle told of the several other instances of the destruction of her career.

MITCHELSON: Now tell us about your working between the time that you started living with Mr Marvin . . . How often did you work during that one year and a half?

MICHELLE: I believe that I had one engagement, or possibly two, at Dino's Lodge, and I worked at the Holiday House in Malibu on weekends.

They overdid it in trying to disprove that her relationship with Lee was what got her the work in the first place. As they presented him, Lee was a hindrance.

MITCHELSON: Did anything unusual happen at the Holiday House that caused you to terminate your employment? In 1965? Did anything happen?

MICHELLE: Yes, I got fired.

MITCHELSON: Do you know why you got fired?

MICHELLE: Yes, because Lee used to come in drunk and yell in the middle of a song, 'Come on baby, let's go home now,' and the owners obviously didn't want that to happen any more.

Wally George, a witness who had worked at the Holiday House during her engagement, said this was not true. A television and radio producer of twenty-five years' standing, in 1965 he had a radio show based at the Holiday House. He was introduced to Michelle by the owner: 'He said he was going to use her as a substitute performer for about three weeks while the feature performer was on tour.' Mr George was present during the entire engagement of Miss Triola. 'And when the three weeks were up the regular singer returned.' A picture of Wally George, Michelle Triola and the owner accompanying an article about how she was 'filling in' for Mr LeMel was offered into evidence.

'I was there from quarter after nine in the evening until 1 a.m. Mr Marvin was there most every night.' Lee, he said, would 'encourage people to stick around for Michelle's program, and if he felt they were leaving . . . he would buy the bar a round of drinks. Many times he bought them round after round of drinks and they would stay to see Miss Triola.'

Oddly, Marvin Mitchelson's adversarial manner of questioning helped the defense more often than he intended.

MITCHELSON: Why did you come down here?

WALLY GEORGE: Because I was reading what Miss Triola was saying in the papers, and I knew from firsthand account that a lot of it was untrue. She was saying that Mr Marvin helped to get her fired at the Holiday House and that he was rowdy, and I knew that wasn't true at all.

MITCHELSON: Did you ever tell Mr Marvin that you thought Michelle was a mediocre singer?

WALLY GEORGE: Yes, I did.

MITCHELSON: You did? [*Ridiculing him*] What did he say?

WALLY GEORGE: He said to me, 'Well, I would very much appreciate it if you could do anything you can to help her, because I would like to see her be able to stand on her own two feet.'

MITCHELSON: Let me show you a record. The name of the record on one side is *Promise Me Your Love*, Michelle Triola, Santana Records [*the flip side is* The Boy Who Kisses Like A Man]. Ever listen to that record?

WALLY GEORGE: No, I have not. I have been a disc jockey since the age of sixteen, and I have never heard of the record label before.

MITCHELSON: Never heard it and you never played it?

WALLY GEORGE: Never heard it, and I never played it.

Lee had formed a company in March 1966 expressly to record Michelle Triola. He paid for everything: the forming of the company, the hire of musicians, the cost of cutting the record and of promotion, and the expenses of Michelle's so-called 'manager' Mimi Marleaux, and the songwriter (Marleaux's husband, whose name Michelle couldn't even remember). This was proved by not only financial records but by Michelle's testimony. Although created as a vehicle for Michelle, this company was used as one more example of the destruction of her career. When the record was printed, she claimed, he ruined her attempts at promoting it by the ultimatum (the letter or telephone call) to leave it and join him in London. This also forced her to leave a singing engagement in Kauai, Hawaii. Michelle told the court: 'I told Mr Marvin that I had taken the Hawaiian engagement in order to be working when my record was released, and then I received a letter from Lee telling me if I wasn't in London by 15 July, to forget it, and to forget the whole relationship, and the whole thing, and I told him that I had to go back to Los Angeles to promote my recording, and he didn't want me to do that.'

David Kagon read an excerpt from a book Marvin Mitchelson had written: 'Lee called her one morning and bluntly told her, "If you're not here in forty-eight hours, you can forget the whole thing. Michelle had no illusion about what was meant by the whole thing, and took the next flight to London."'

KAGON: Did you take the next flight to London?

MICHELLE: It sounds very dramatic, doesn't it? I say, it sounds very dramatic, Mr Kagon [*shaking her head back and forth at him*]. This is a *book*!

KAGON: Well, did you or did you not?

MICHELLE: No, I did *not* take the next flight to London. [*Without thinking*] I had to go home and see how the house was doing.

KAGON: You came back to Los Angeles?

MICHELLE: Yes, I did . . . yes, I did.

KAGON: Do you recall when you came back to Los Angeles?

MICHELLE: No, I don't.

KAGON: Do you recall how long you spent in Los Angeles?

MICHELLE: No, I don't because we stayed in Honolulu talking to disc jockeys [*again without thinking*].
KAGON: For how long?
MICHELLE: I don't recall.
KAGON: Incidentally, how many disc jockeys are in Hawaii?
MICHELLE: I really don't know.

Lee, then working in England, had got the job in Hawaii for her, calling his friend Dudley Child, President of International Island Resorts, and asking him if she might sing in one of his hotels. At first Michelle denied this. She had asked Mr Child herself, she said, or else he had heard her singing on a fishing boat once and he had asked her. Finally she admitted that Lee did make the telephone call for her, *but* at her suggestion, and she insisted that her manager Mimi Marleaux had arranged it. When Marleaux later took the stand, Marvin Mitchelson questioned her about this.

MITCHELSON: Did you go to Hawaii with Michelle?
MIMI MARLEAUX: Yes.
MITCHELSON: How did that come about?
MIMI MARLEAUX: The man owned some hotels there, his name is Dudley Child, and I guess he had contacted Michelle first and she said to me, 'Call him collect and discuss it.' And I did, and we wrapped it up on the phone.

She admitted that Santana [i.e. Lee] paid her and 'gave me some money to do some promo work after Hawaii', that she was with Michelle in Hawaii the whole time – 'Constantly, yes' – that Michelle sang twice a night, and 'they did a tremendous business'.

MITCHELSON: Generally full?
MIMI MARLEAUX: Yes, it held close to two hundred people – not large but not small.
MITCHELSON: Packed house? [*Nothing like leading a witness!*]
MIMI MARLEAUX: Yes, well, it was full enough they had to turn people away.

Michelle, supposedly a professional performer herself, didn't seem to have such a clear picture, particularly when she was being asked by Lee's attorney.

KAGON: What was the size of the Kauai Surf?

MICHELLE: I'm just a bad one to ask that, because I can't articulate the size of a room . . . when you have a light on you, you can't tell how far back the seats go.

KAGON: Well, you were there for at least a month, were you not?

MICHELLE: Yes, I was, but I was on the stage performing and I didn't hang out in the room afterwards.

In the end, however, the matter was laid to rest by a stipulation, accepted by all parties, that were Mr Dudley Child to come from Hawaii he would testify as follows: He was President of International Island Resorts, where Michelle Triola sang in 1966 at the Kauai Surf; he employed her because Lee Marvin asked him to; that he had no intention of extending her engagement. Furthermore, there were no employment discussions with her manager Mimi Marleaux; the capacity of the room where she sang was eighty-five; her performance was mediocre; and the audience reaction was mediocre. Hotel records supported the contention that she had a prearranged departure date. Four checks were drawn on the Inter-Island Resorts account and deposited in a bank in Beverly Hills in the name of Michelle Triola. Lee Marvin was not a signatory on the account. No sharing here.

This bank account belonging to Michelle proved to be important in another way. In July 1966, although she adamantly stated that she lived exclusively in Malibu with Lee ('I never had an apartment while I was living with Lee'), the address listed on the bank card is 8633 West Knoll, Apartment 201, Los Angeles. There would be more conversation about this apartment in due course.

No matter how the plaintiff tried to portray Lee in court, during Michelle's employment in Hawaii she invoked his name and their relationship over and over again in newspaper articles promoting her engagement at the Kauai Surf – even saying that she was his fiancée. Although she said it was important for her to be singing somewhere when her record was being promoted, she could not even remember when she cut the record: before or after April, before or after Lee won the Academy Award, only a scant two months before being in Hawaii. She and her manager claimed a huge success with the disc jockeys in Hawaii, but neither knew whether a single record had been sold. She could not remember how long she spent in London either, but however long, she claimed it was enough to destroy not only her record's chances, but her career as well. After its failure she never worked again. This was a major issue in her suit. She returned home from her stay in London with Lee after no more than two weeks.

KAGON: Why did you return from London at that time?
MICHELLE: Because he was drinking so heavily that I just didn't know what to do, and actually I had wanted to leave as soon as I got there for a day, because he was drinking so badly that . . .
KAGON: Was there any other reason?
MICHELLE: Not that I can think of.

However, when Michelle was asked in October 1978, 'Did anyone ask you to leave London?' her reply was different.

MICHELLE: My manager wanted me to come home.
KAGON: What was your manager's name?
MICHELLE: Mimi Marleaux.
KAGON: And you came home because she asked you to?
MICHELLE: I believe so, yes.
KAGON: Why?
MICHELLE: She wanted me to go out and promote my record.

Mimi Marleaux, brought in as a 'surprise' witness by Michelle and Marvin Mitchelson (the newspapers even printed the head-lines THE BIG SURPRISE IN MARVIN TRIAL), definitely caused a stir in the courtroom. It soon became obvious that, of the two women, Mimi was the star; Michelle was clearly pleased to have her as a witness, and smiled proudly as she entered. Mimi was an older woman, very tough-looking with flaming red hair. She wore a floor-length mink coat and dark sunglasses, and supported herself on a cane as she walked theatrically toward the witness box. Judge Marshall adjusted his glasses, peering over them and smiling, but with a decidedly quizzical expression. She spoke with a husky voice, at one moment pronouncing words in an almost affected English accent, the next lapsing into showbiz slang as

Marvin Mitchelson took her through her introduction.

She had been doing some publicity for the El Rancho Hotel in Las Vegas, she said – 'That was the first hotel on the strip in Las Vegas,' she purred – and she was there from late 1955 or early 1956 until it burned down in 1960. Mitchelson asked her what kind of attractions ('headliners')? She settled back comfortably in her witness chair: 'Well, people like Sophie Tucker, Milton Berle, Joe E. Lewis, Eartha Kitt – I mean, they ran the gamut.' In citing her qualifications as an 'expert' witness on talent, she observed, 'No, I mean, I had a bit of experience before I ever worked at the El Rancho. I worked with a lady named Martha Raye most of the years before that and we had big names on the *Colgate Comedy Hour* . . . I think I fairly much knew who had talent and who didn't . . . I consider myself . . .' But Marvin Mitchelson stopped her himself, 'All right.'

She had met Michelle Triola, she said, in 1957.

MITCHELSON: Now, Michelle was not a 'headliner' performer, was she?

MIMI MARLEAUX: No, she did special things with Barry Ashton. He used her as a specialty.

MITCHELSON: What kind of specialty?

MIMI MARLEAUX: Dancing.

MITCHELSON: Dancing?

MIMI MARLEAUX: Yes [*but quickly correcting herself*] – and now and then a little singing with it. I thought she had good projection. I thought she was a good dancer. She was a great showman, better than the dancing and singing. I thought she projected great showmanship.

MITCHELSON: Did you have occasion to see Michelle again?

MIMI MARLEAUX Well, I ran into her in Beverly Hills. I ran into her in Las Vegas, yes.

Marleaux said that she ran into her again in 1965, and that Michelle asked her to manage her. Mimi was 'married at the time' to a songwriter and she took Michelle on and became her personal manager; her husband wrote the song for the record Michelle made. She had read *all* Lee's letters to Michelle when they were in Hawaii, she said, and now recognized them when they were shown to her in court. She also said that she was in Michelle's room when Michelle got the telephone call from Lee giving her the ultimatum.

JUDGE: What did she say, ma'am?

MIMI MARLEAUX: She said words to that effect . . . I mean, I remember one part of the expression that she used was, 'Is this an ultimatum, Lee?'

When asked about the other clients she had represented, Mimi answered, 'I did some promo for a man named Trini Lopez, who had recorded one of my husband's songs . . . It was a difficult time because of the Beatles, so I was working with my husband.'

KAGON: In 1965 did you have any other clients besides the plaintiff?

MIMI MARLEAUX: In '65, no . . . not another one right then, no. I can't think of one.

KAGON: During the period of 1965 to 1970, did you have any employment?

MIMI MARLEAUX: I changed my life and business around 1970. I became involved in a divorce from the man that was writing music.

KAGON: You were no longer in the entertainment business?

MIMI MARLEAUX: Right.

In his closing brief Mark Goldman gave a summary of Michelle Triola Marvin's career, and showed it to be nearly non-existent. Her career prior to meeting Lee was 'suspect', he said. Appearances in Europe couldn't be checked at all, and other clubs she testified to – such as Peter Fairchild's Silver Cloud Room and Jerry Lewis's – no longer existed in California, and no records of any kind were available. The 'numerous appearances' at Playboy clubs could only be proved as one two-week engagement in Phoenix. She testified that she was hired by Gene Kelly to appear in *Flower Drum Song*, but Mr Kelly refuted the claim. She testified to 'twenty-four weeks' at Dino's Lodge, which was probably only one two-week engagement. The Little Club engagement changed in length from four weeks to any time she could get in, but was perhaps three days.

MARK GOLDMAN: The evidence establishes that plaintiff had

only worked a total of nine and one half weeks in the year and a half preceding the period when she allegedly gave up her career. If we subtract out those career events associated with Mr Marvin's name and his efforts, the evidence shows that plaintiff had no career at all independent of her association with Mr Marvin. Thus there was nothing for Plaintiff to give up which would serve as sufficient consideration for the very onerous obligation of support for life.

Michelle's 'Help on Movies'

Lee as a drunk who needed constant care to help him work was a theme chanted by Marvin Mitchelson and Michelle Triola like the chorus of a Greek tragedy.

'Plaintiff traveled with Defendant when he went on location,' the post-trial brief pleaded, 'in order to care for his needs. The evidence shows that Defendant suffered from a drinking problem although,' the brief concedes, 'the extent of the problem is in dispute.' ('It wasn't a problem to me,' Lee replied, tight-lipped.)

'. . . Plaintiff cared for him when he was sick from the drinking problem and saw to it that he was sober enough to go to work. These performances' (of her 'duties'), it went on, 'were directly responsible for his ability to work as a performer. . . Further, it was essential to Defendant's ability to work to have a quiet, non-Hollywood lifestyle which included living in a modest residence at the beach.'

The 'modest residence' at the beach, as they described it, was in Malibu, California, home of Hollywood celebrities, on one of the most expensive and beautiful stretches of beach in the entire country. It was a far cry from the Sunset Marquis Hotel or the other West Hollywood apartments, usually shared, that had been the previous abodes of the Plaintiff. Her sacrifice in coming to live in Malibu was difficult to appreciate when Marvin Mitchelson complained that she 'gave up her in-town lifestyle to devote herself to Defendant'.

And that isn't all. 'Plaintiff traveled with Defendant to London, England for filming and other less glamorous and comfortable locations such as the Island of Palau and Las Vegas' – although in previous testimony, appearing in Las Vegas was cited as a high point in Michelle Triola's career. The brief also neglected to mention that she was housed in suites in the best hotels, enjoyed first-class travel and was in the company of famous movie personalities: the kind of life that had certainly been beyond her grasp under her own efforts.

'She accompanied him on fishing vacations,' it complained, 'cheerfully.' These vacations were in the Hwaiian Islands and resort hotels in Mexico, so the complaint made one wonder if Penelope Mercurio, Mitchelson's assistant and writer of briefs, was secretly on our side. She added that Michelle Triola was Lee's buffer against the outside world, encouraged him as an actor and in his self-worth as a human being, was his confidante and discussed his fears about roles, the amount of money he made, and the direction of his career. 'He had the benefit of having someone accompany him as a traveling companion and escort to social functions which, pursuant to his profession, he was required to attend.'

Their description of Lee was of a man I did not know, either in the 1940s when we were young or later when he and I were married. With only the rarest of exceptions, Lee's public appearances, interviews with journalists or reporters, movie premières, publicity tours, and awards and honor ceremonies were without the benefit of her company, no matter what was claimed. She complained bitterly to Lee's publicity agent that she was not present during press interviews, previews, and publicity tours in America or Europe. In fact, she was specifically asked not to attend, and when Lee was asked in court, 'Did you ever ask the Plaintiff to accompany you to your father's home in Woodstock, New York?' Lee answered, 'No.'

The brief also did not mention the fact that Michelle Triola came to the movie locations she did attend at her own insistence or after repeated pleadings, and nearly always over Lee's adamant objections. Some of these visits were only brief, but they always meant trouble for Lee.

In Michelle's testimony she becomes more specific about the aid she gave – or tries to. Although her written complaints were very clearly expressed, when she came to verbal testimony she wasn't so forthcoming.

MITCHELSON: In your complaint you stated that you have reviewed literary properties submitted by third parties in order to determine their suitability for Defendant. Can you tell us . . . what scripts, literary properties did you review and look over for Mr Marvin's benefit during your relationship with him?

MICHELLE: Many.

MITCHELSON: Well, can you tell us? Does any come to mind? I realize it may be hard to pick one out, but does anything come to mind?

MICHELLE: I don't really understand the question.

MITCHELSON: Okay [*slowly, stressing every word*], I will give you another question. During your relationship with Mr Marvin did you review any scripts with him, with regard to how he would play the scene, or do a role? Do you understand the question?

MICHELLE: You are using the word review, which is not . . . [*She raises her eyebrows in thought*]

MITCHELSON: Did you discuss . . .' [*He tries again and she cuts him off*]

MICHELLE: – *read* them?

MITCHELSON: – read them?

MICHELLE: Yes. [*She stops again*]

MITCHELSON: All right. Tell us, what did you do to help in that regard? [*He is getting frustrated and stands in front of her, nodding his head*]

MICHELLE: Well, [*shaking her head as though to suggest Mitchelson just doesn't understand 'this movie business'*] I would *never* suggest his characterization.

MITCHELSON: Tell us what you *did* do.

MICHELLE: I would possibly read the lady's part, or other parts.

MITCHELSON: Did you ever read the lady's part? [*Valiantly trying to get something definite*]

MICHELLE: Yes.

MITCHELSON: All right.

MICHELLE: Yes. [*Nods*]

MITCHELSON: And what else would you do with regard to helping him with his work?

MICHELLE: He would ask me certain things – you know – how did I think a woman would react to a certain situation that had to do with his character?

MITCHELSON: And would you tell him when he would ask you?

MICHELLE: Yes.

MITCHELSON: [*Not having a great deal of success*] Did he ever ask your opinion with regard to a role that he was considering, or contracted to play?

MICHELLE: He would ask me an opinion only in one way.

MITCHELSON: Which way?

MICHELLE: As to the other – as to what the other character was. He *never* asked my opinion on how *he* should play a role.

MITCHELSON: Did you ever give him suggestions about his wardrobe?

David Kagon objected that Marvin Mitchelson was doing everything he could to help the witness. Mitchelson stopped his pacing, stood in front of Judge Marshall and raised his voice in protest.

But he *was* leading the witness and the objection was sustained. Considering that Lee had been a professional actor since the late 1940s – some twenty years before meeting her – had been in more than fifty stage plays, made hundreds of television appearances and had at least thirty-five movies to his credit, it was difficult to believe he would quite suddenly need the help of a person whose only experience in the field was as a stand-in on two movies.

Lee was now questioned on this matter by Marvin Mitchelson.

MITCHELSON: Did she discuss your work with you in any way whatsoever?

LEE: Well, she'd discuss it with me, but I was not discussing it with her. Let me make a statement that my work is a very private thing with me, and I really don't discuss it with anybody except possibly the director.

Michelle was more eloquent about her help with Lee's alcohol 'problem' while filming – or when not filming. She admitted too that he asked her to leave.

> MICHELLE: Early in 1966, but only because of his drinking. He asked me where I had put the liquor that he bought. And I said I threw it in the ocean. And he got very angry and said, you know, 'Get the hell out of here and don't ever come back.'
>
> MITCHELSON: Did you get the . . .? [*She cuts him off*]
>
> MICHELLE: No, I said, sure, sure.
>
> MITCHELSON: Did you take some liquor and put it in the ocean?
>
> MICHELLE: Yes.
>
> MITCHELSON: How did you accomplish that?
>
> MICHELLE: I took it out of the cupboard, walked down to the sand, and threw it in the ocean. [*Makes gesture of throwing a bottle away*]
>
> MITCHELSON: Did you ever float any liquor out to sea? [*She just said she did!*]
>
> MICHELLE: Yes, a lot of it.
>
> MITCHELSON: Is that liquor that you found in the house?
>
> MICHELLE: Yes – [*He cuts her off*]
>
> MITCHELSON: Don't cut in on me, please let me finish my question. [*Their familiarity with each other occasionally makes for curt exchanges*] During those times did Mr Marvin occasionally ask you to leave the home?
>
> MICHELLE: Yes.
>
> MITCHELSON: And did you?
>
> MICHELLE: No.
>
> MITCHELSON: Did you ever boil liquor to rid it of the alcohol content?
>
> MICHELLE: Yes.
>
> MITCHELSON: When?
>
> MICHELLE: In 1967.
>
> MITCHELSON: Why did you boil the liquor?
>
> MICHELLE: Because a chemist friend of mine showed me how to do it so the alcohol would no longer be in it.

Marvin Mitchelson also brought up the subject of alcohol with Lee.

MITCHELSON: Were you aware, Mr Marvin, that Michelle
went to an organization called Al-Anon?

LEE: No, I'm not.

MITCHELSON: Did that come as a surprise to you?

LEE: I'm not sure that I believe her.

MITCHELSON: Did she ever boil vodka to get rid of its
alcoholic content and mellow it down?

LEE: [*Incredulously*] You mean evaporate the alcohol out of it?

MITCHELSON: Yes, to evaporate the alcohol out of it.

LEE: If she had, I would have been the first to know it.

MITCHELSON: Do you ever remember her doing it?

LEE: No. I mean, you can't sit there and honestly believe I
would take a slug of vodka and know it hadn't been cut?

MITCHELSON: [*Baiting him*] Is that what happens to vodka if
you boil it?

LEE: I don't know what happens to vodka if you boil it – I
never had a boiled martini. This is really amusing. I hate to
waste your time in this discourse.

Lee sat there at his table with David Kagon, looking at Michelle
Triola and Marvin Mitchelson with his chin in his hands and
wondering how anyone could come up with something like that.
The courtroom was supposed to have decorum, but at times like
this it was hard to preserve it; people in the audience would look at
each other with silent amusement, rolling their eyes skyward. I had
to look attentive and serious at all times, but it was often a strain. I
felt like getting up and walking out, my stomach was in such knots.
It was a ludicrous situation, yet it was being taken so seriously. Lee
did drink, sporadically; he certainly did have a high tolerance of
alcohol, but this was well known to Michelle Triola from the
beginning. To use it now to benefit a lawsuit seemed disingenuous.
   Mitchelson again addressed Michelle.

MITCHELSON: All right. During your relationship with Mr
Marvin, did you ever have occasion to visit the set of a
picture he was working on during which time an argument
ensued between you and Mr Marvin?

MICHELLE: Yes.

When Michelle didn't stop to think, she sometimes said things that were actually true – if not particularly helpful to her case.

MICHELLE: It was on all the pictures.
MITCHELSON: Which pictures?
MICHELLE: *Hell in the Pacific.*
MITCHELSON: Did you have an argument with Mr Marvin down there?
MICHELLE: I think I misunderstood the question. I thought you said, did I ever have an argument with anyone on the set – not particularly Mr Marvin? [*She clearly thinks this isn't as bad*]
MITCHELSON: Who *did* you have an argument with on *Hell in the Pacific*?
MICHELLE: I had an argument with the doctor, the staff doctor. I asked the doctor not to give Lee any sedatives or Valium or any pill of that sort, because he was drinking heavily and I was afraid that the things would not mix.

It was very difficult to reconcile these assertions with overwhelming testimony to the contrary from Lee and nearly every other witness in the trial (including Michelle's own). With rare exceptions – such as Eddie Cantor's daughter Edna McHugh, or Ruth Berle, Milton Berle's wife (a rather salty ex-Marine herself, Lee told me) – they portrayed Michelle Triola as someone who made trouble wherever she went. She would alternate between ingratiating herself with Lee's co-workers, directors, producers and agents, and on the other hand causing dissension. As the girlfriend of a movie star, she was imperious in public, and on location she threw her weight around with the cast and crew, wearing Lee's mantle on her shoulders in a manner so different from his own. Whenever brought to account, she repeatedly managed to pull herself out of the fire with child-like reparations or promises to change in the future. She seemed to have a strong survival instinct. More often than not, Lee was not even present to witness this, being preoccupied with work or away. It's nearly impossible to separate Lee's working life from his daily life, especially in those days, which were the busiest of his professional career. Under scrutiny, the time they purportedly spent under the same roof shrank and rather than showing the contribution of Michelle Triola to Lee's life and work, it stands instead as testimonial to his tremendous creativity and success *despite* her presence, not because of it.

Lee filmed two movies during summer 1964, *Ship of Fools* and *Cat Ballou*, in both of which he had very demanding roles. Almost immediately after the completion of *Ship of Fools*, Lee went on location to Smith Valley, Colorado, for *Cat Ballou*. Again, his role – a dual role, actually, as he played both the heavy and the good guy – required concentration and focus. The entire location work was shot in just a month, and his fine acting earned him the Academy Award. During this same time he was having a lot of difficulty in his home life with Betty, and when he returned from Colorado in mid-October he 'just could not walk through that door. I slept on the lawn and the next morning caught a cab and went to work.'

The movie was being finished in the studio in Los Angeles, and Lee went to a motel.

LEE: There were a number of them. I moved around a lot because I felt more secure that way. My wife was rather distraught about my leaving, and so therefore the phone calls would disturb me at night, and I had a very heavy schedule at work and I would change my phone number by changing the abode. I would stay in the valley, near my work, which was being done at the Columbia back lot, and then in the Hollywood district, anything within a radius of that area of work.

Marvin Mitchelson contended that, during this period, being with Michelle Triola was the foremost thing in Lee's life, and that within a matter of a month or so he had pledged to support her for life and to live together as if married.

MITCHELSON: How long did you stay in motels?
LEE: Quite a while. I imagine until eventually I settled by renting a home.
MITCHELSON: Did you live in a dwelling during that period of time other than a motel or hotel?

LEE: Did I stay, or did I live?

MITCHELSON: Stay. 'Living' is a relative word.

LEE: Especially in Vietnam. [*Pause*] I don't recall the address, but there was an apartment on the south slope of the Sunset Strip . . . there was a house above the Sunset Strip. It was Michelle Triola's.

MITCHELSON: How long did you spend there approximately?

LEE: It was on a night-to-night basis. No span of time.

Lee used a motel at that same time, the Bel Air Sands, until he moved to Malibu and the beach house.

In December he went to San Blas, Mexico, with fourteen men from his fishing club for three weeks. He and his fishing companion Ray Accord drove there, towing a boat. The last week Michelle Triola came down to stay with him. This is when, Mitchelson contended, Lee and Michelle formed their contract.

MITCHELSON: Did he say anything about sharing?

MICHELLE: That what I have is yours and what you have is mine.

However, when she was asked this question by David Kagon some years earlier in a deposition, she gave different answers.

KAGON: What arrangements would be made in the event you did live with him?

MICHELLE: Everything he had was mine, you know.

KAGON: Everything?

MICHELLE: Everything.

KAGON: When did he tell you for the first time?

MICHELLE: In 1964. That was in San Blas.

KAGON: Wasn't he married at the time?

MICHELLE: Yes.

KAGON: Miss Marvin, I believe you testified that in your first marriage you had a religious ceremony?

MICHELLE: Yes, I did.

KAGON: Was that in a church?

MICHELLE: Pardon?

KAGON: Was that in a church?

MICHELLE: [*Pauses*] No.

Lee was asked about the Mexico trip by Marvin Mitchelson.

MITCHELSON: Did you think you were in love with her?

LEE: No.

MITCHELSON: What were your feelings about her?

LEE: I was coming from a very distraught relationship. It was light, airy, joyful, not deep, I guess light is the word. We were both at loose ends at the time. I think . . . generally . . . I'm trying to say something nice in that area. Yes, it started to go downhill almost immediately.

MITCHELSON: Did you discuss wanting to live with her?

LEE: Well, I believe *she* said something to the effect that she thought it might work out and be a good idea. I think that my response was that I didn't want to tie myself into an agreement of that nature. I objected to it because I wanted to be free. And I am sure that I must have said, 'Wouldn't it be better to visit each other?' Except more skillfully said at the time.

MITCHELSON: Now . . . how would you characterize your feelings concerning Michelle when you were leaving Mexico? Were you in love with her?

LEE: No, the fishing was bad. I know that sounds diverse. I was down there fishing with a group of men. The weather was bad . . . the whiskey was good. I don't know, really . . . in ten days you have to say something.

MITCHELSON: When did the next discussion occur relative to living together?

LEE: I would think it occurred after I rented the house at 21404 [Pacific Coast Highway, Malibu], when I found that she was not residing elsewhere.

MITCHELSON: Now she did come to live in the Malibu house on a permanent basis for a period of time – correct?

LEE: At a later date, yes. I'm not really clear on when she did, but I noticed that an awful lot of her clothes were appearing in my closet and I asked her to take them out.

MITCHELSON: Did you ever order her out of your home in 1965?

LEE: Yes. When I saw it was becoming a permanent situation on her part.

MITCHELSON: When did you first order her out?

LEE: When I realized that she was moving in. I didn't feel that I could just throw her clothes out on the street. And she said she had no place to stay; so I said, 'We have to work on that immediately.'

MITCHELSON: Did you work with her?

LEE: Yes, but I was alone. She said she was financially distraught and that she had no place to go.

MITCHELSON: Did you ask her again, after seeing the clothes, to leave that year?

LEE: Oh yes.

MITCHELSON: How often? More than twenty?

LEE: Yes, I would say in excess of fifty. Evicting a woman isn't . . . [*But he is interrupted*]

MITCHELSON: And did you physically throw her out?

LEE: Well, you are asking me to be a brute, aren't you?

At that point Lee himself left to go on location for a movie.

In her complaint, Michelle *said* that she was subjected to such location sites as Indio, California, Death Valley and Las Vegas while Lee was filming *The Professionals*. It was not mentioned that she arrived in Las Vegas over his objections.

But after several telephone calls from her asking to visit him at Furnace Creek, Death Valley, Lee said, 'Jump on a plane and come for the day or the night.' She came up one afternoon and left the following morning. But her general mood was 'hysterical' and, he said, when the production moved up to Las Vegas, 'I asked her not to show . . . she was harassing me in my work.'

MITCHELSON: What form would her hysteria take?

LEE: Misconduct and general harassment – her behavior in public places, shouting, things of that nature.

MITCHELSON: Prior to moving in, she also embarrassed you in public?

LEE: Not that I recall.

MITCHELSON: Did you feel, at the end of 1965 or in 1966, your relationship with Michelle as it existed – her living in your house, your spending money on her, going places with her, joining you on trips – infringing on your desire . . . to maintain independence and freedom?

LEE: Yes.

MITCHELSON: All right. Why did you do it?

That was the question many people would have asked – including me. Why couldn't he get out of this situation? Why did he, a motivated and strong man in so many other areas, allow someone to impinge so deeply upon his life and his work for such a long time? By the end of the trial the word 'irrepressible' had acquired a new meaning. It was clear that unless he was willing bodily to throw Michelle out, beat her or kill her, it would take more than mere words to get her to leave.

'I was trapped. She was a problem to deal with, and more often than not the easiest way for me was to accept the abuse,' was one laconic reply. He would be forced to say more during the coming months of the trial.

Michelle did come to Las Vegas for about two of the ten weeks Lee was filming *The Professionals* there. She did no cooking, cleaning or bedmaking on location – the 'caring for him' – he stayed in hotels. In fact, he quickly asked her to leave. 'On many occasions, I can't recall the exact number. I thought that she was being a detriment to my presence and to the rest of the stunt men and the cast, and said that I really would prefer she leave. Her response was basically anger and disagreement to my request, but yes, she did leave.'

The Professionals had been presented to Lee in March 1965 (just about the time he was asking Michelle to find a place to live). Meyer Mishkin, Lee's agent, and Richard Brooks, the director, author and producer, brought the book to him: 'It was titled *A Mule for the Marquesa*.' Lee did not ask Michelle's advice about the book. He did his own research into the role he was to play, as he had always done in the past and would do in the future.

LEE: It would be difficult to break down the hours. I read a lot of
books and photographs, history-type things from the . . .
Mexican border campaigns. And primarily I would also do a
lot of thinking. I would sit by myself or look at the beach, or
whatever you do, as I would visualize my part, my duty, my
relationship to the other characters in the story. On and off, all
day long. I would read, I would think, I would be diverted on

occasion. But it would inject itself no matter what I was thinking; you know, getting it tighter and tighter in my mind as to who I was . . . The contractual forms were agreed upon, and the movie was then called *The Professionals*. The other actors in the film were Mr Burt Lancaster, Mr Robert Ryan, Mr Woody Strode, Claudia Cardinale, Ralph Bellamy and Walter Jack Palance were the major stars. Walter Jack Palance – I'm sorry, Jack Palance – 'Walter Jack' to me because I love him.

During rehearsal, Lee testified, they started a little late in the mornings during the one week of rehearsals – about 8.30 a.m.

LEE: Then when we got to shooting, we had to get the magic-hour shot. That half in-between dark and half-between light, which is the sun coming up. We would get up around four, around that dark period – very dark, because it would take us an hour and a half to set up before the sun came up. We would return . . .

MITCHELSON: [*Interrupting*] Objection – immaterial! I think he testified that the plaintiff was there *one* day. Do we need his shooting schedule for the rest of the time?

Judge Marshall asked Marvin Mitchelson if he would like to make a stipulation that Lee does work hard at his profession; that he works hard and that it's physical work.

KAGON: I am agreeable.

MITCHELSON: I'm talking about when he's *able* to work, of course, and when he is *able* to work he does work hard.

JUDGE: [*Dryly*] Well, we have an erosion of the stipulation. Will you accept that, Counsel?

KAGON: No, I don't like the implication at all.

LEE: No, neither do I. Neither can I, thank you.

The company moved to Las Vegas for ten weeks, and Lee stayed in a suite in the Mint Hotel while there.

LEE: Then, just before Christmas, we terminated our shooting in Las Vegas and came into town for the week of Christmas and New Year, which were the only two holidays at that time of year. We were shooting at the studio in between and at the Columbia lot on Gower. That was for about a period of a week. We came down on Christmas Eve and left on New Year's Day. In town, shooting is five days a week, on location it is six. I would leave the house about seven or seven-thirty and eat at Oblath's. It's a kind of stage-door delicatessen and cantina, just in front of the Paramount gate. We were doing normal days, Christmas holidays, we would wrap around five-thirty, six. I would say six. I'd have breakfast at Oblath's and lunch depended . . . on wherever the rest of the cast and I would decide to go. On New Year's Day I drove over to Indio to be there for the final days of shooting. I believe I was in Indio five or six weeks.

MITCHELSON: Was the Plaintiff there with you?

LEE: Yes, she came down.

MITCHELSON: Did you ask her to come down?

LEE: No, she arrived about two or three days after I did.

MITCHELSON: Did you ask her to leave?

LEE: Yes. Her reply was no. [*Later testimony proved this to be an understatement* . . .]

MITCHELSON: Was the plaintiff doing any of your laundry? Cleaning the motel room? Cooking?

LEE: No.

Michelle Triola's reaction to Lee's request that she leave Indio during the filming was described by Lee's stand-in on the movie, Boyd Cabeen. He testified that he was a stand-in, a stunt man, an actor and a writer, and that he had known Lee for a number of years before, having been with him on *Ship of Fools*. Boyd Cabeen met Michelle Triola on that picture when she was standing in for Barbara Luna – with 'no other function on that film,' he testified.

Boyd introduced her to Lee at her request, and had a continuing friendship with her until half-way through the filming of *Paint Your Wagon*, when it abruptly ended.

Mitchelson questioned Boyd, pressing him, pacing and then stopping in front of the witness box and facing him.

MITCHELSON: Now, tell me, down in Indio, California, did you ever throw a glass at Michelle, cutting her in the face?

BOYD CABEEN: I threw a *drink* in her face. It was after she
swept the table in a booth in the restaurant, the bar, clean of
glasses. She was mad at Lee and she wiped out all the glasses,
and I had one and I said, 'Here, Michelle, you missed one.'
The glass flew over, apparently hitting a lady at the bar. She
later sued Lee. Michelle broke all the glasses. They were half
full – and ashtrays, a lot of glass around.

This was not a picture that Marvin Mitchelson was happy to have
elicited, so he tried to recoup.

MITCHELSON: All right, wasn't she protesting because you and
Lee were drinking, drinking, drinking . . . right?
BOYD CABEEN: No, she was drinking as much. Sweeping the
table clean had nothing to do with drinking. It was about
something else they were arguing about.

Of course, Marvin Mitchelson didn't ask him what they *were*
arguing about, but David Kagon, having been given the opportunity on redirect, did.

BOYD CABEEN: This particular time? I think it had something
to do with her . . . he preferred that she stayed away from
location, she was demanding to stay, and she swept away the
glasses off the table . . . we were drinking margaritas. She
couldn't handle tuaca. She would get kind of crazy on tuaca,
we had to . . . keep it away from her, but she mixed it with
whatever we were drinking at the time. Usually I would flee.

Glaring at him, Michelle threw her pencil noisily down on the table
where she was sitting making notes to hand to her attorney.
    During the filming of *The Professionals*, Lee was already
discussing the production of his next movie *The Dirty Dozen*: 'I
was talking to my agent Meyer Mishkin, Mr Robert Aldrich the
director, and another agent. We started talking the second or third
week in Indio.'
    In answer to David Kagon's question, Lee said that Michelle was
not present at these meetings, and her advice about whether or not
to do the film was not sought. The starting date of the film was 1
March 1966, a scant month after the termination of *The*

Professionals. He did not do much research for *The Dirty Dozen*: 'Just scanned some books, but no major work. There was very little research because the availability of it was limited to me. The title is very explanatory. It was about a bunch of bad guys that were utilized in a suicide mission to eliminate some high enemy brass. The picture was shot north of London at Borehamwood Studios. That is a subsidiary of MGM Studios.'

He arrived in March for 'basically seven months', and the plaintiff came over and stayed 'I believe, in July, for a period of about two weeks'. He had a maid who came in about two or three times a week. 'Did you have any meals in your flat?' In reply, Lee gestured toward the witness box he was sitting in: 'The kitchen in the flat was about one-third the size of this stand I am on. It was very small. No – two burners. We had coffee and tea.' (All movie locations have caterers providing meals.)

When Marvin Mitchelson asked Michelle about this period, she painted a different picture.

MICHELLE: He was drinking heavily. I used to get him home at
a decent hour, get some food into him, see to it that he didn't
drive [*Lee had a limousine driver on call twenty-four hours a
day*] and see to it that he had a decent breakfast in the
morning; make oyster stew, a special kind for him – with,
you know, crackers or something, eggs, bacon, toast . . . I
wouldn't call that special.

Lee was asked if he had had any conversations with the plaintiff about her coming to the location in London: 'Yes, it was prior to the time I left. It was a continuing series of conversations. In substance I said, "No, never again," and I said it was an ideal time for her to pursue her singing career.'

About a month into filming *The Dirty Dozen*, Lee was released to attend the Academy Awards ceremony on 15 April 1966: 'I returned to LA on Friday and left on a Sunday.'

KAGON: Did you have a conversation with the plaintiff about
her attending the Academy Awards?
LEE: I did.
KAGON: Would you please relate it?

LEE: I requested that she not join me because it was going to be a telecast . . . I knew my children would be watching, and I thought it might be improper and hurtful for them to see me with her . . . I asked her not to join me at that time, and she related that she had had a dress made for the occasion and said that if I didn't take her, that she would arrive at the theater in Santa Monica, the Civic, and make a scene that I would never forget. I took her that evening. I told Meyer, after talking with her, that I saw no way out of it.

MITCHELSON: Now isn't it the truth of the matter, sir, that you didn't want to appear on national television with Michelle only because you feared that your wife Betty . . . might see the two of you together, and that might interfere with the property settlement you were trying to work out with Betty? Wasn't that a fear of yours?

LEE: No, it was also my father and my family back East, people that didn't know her. And I felt with the children that if their mates were to see this, their playmates, they would say, 'Is that your mommy?' not having known the real mother maybe. In other words, the situation was one of a national situation there, which would bring queries to the children as to who that was.

MITCHELSON: You didn't want the children to see you out with another woman? [*Putting on his incredulous tone*] Is that what you are telling us?

LEE: [*Firmly*] I said I didn't want my children to be accosted by questions from unknowing people.

MITCHELSON: Well, we won't argue about it. [*Sounding like a pugnacious child*] Nevertheless, you took Michelle, right?

LEE: Yes.

Lee was quite angry, I could see, but he was able to readjust quickly.

As the star of *The Dirty Dozen*, Lee carried a great deal of responsibility every day of the filming: six days (or nights) a week for more than seven months.

Marvin Mitchelson and Michelle Triola would have had the court believe that most of Lee's time was spent writing letters. They spent many hours of court time exploring Lee's feelings for Michelle Triola at that period, by dissecting eight letters he wrote to her. This was an attempt to prove an implied contract through love and affection.

MITCHELSON: Fair to say when you left for England you were enamored of Michelle?

LEE: Not at all at that time.

MITCHELSON: When you got back to England, did you realize you were enamored with Michelle?

LEE: No.

MITCHELSON: I suggest to you, sir, that in the month of June you felt great love for this girl. Would you disagree with me?

LEE: Yes.

MITCHELSON: Is it true that you did not want her to come to London in May or June?

LEE: It is true that I wanted her to come in July.

MITCHELSON: [*In his accusing and 'I'm about to trap you' tone*] You wrote her some letters, didn't you, sir?

LEE: Yes, I did.

MITCHELSON: You told her you missed her, didn't you? [*Holding copies of these letters, he stops in front of Lee in the witness box*]

LEE: Yes, I did.

Mitchelson begins to read his question and then Lee's answers in a previous deposition.

MITCHELSON: You said you missed her . . . in the letters, and you did miss her, didn't you?

LEE: You are delving into a subject matter that I think the whole thing is about. No, I didn't miss her.

MITCHELSON: Why did you tell her you did?

LEE: To keep her content in her job. What I'm saying is that I was very glad she was working.

MITCHELSON: Were you glad that she was away from you?

LEE: Well, I was away from her. Yes, I was glad.

Mitchelson stops reading the deposition and turns again to Lee. 'Now I'm going to look at Exhibit Number 10,' and he began reading aloud Lee's letters to Michelle. All were written within a few weeks of each other from London to Michelle Triola in Hawaii.

I don't believe these letters had ever been tied up with a pink ribbon, kept in a small cedar box or anything sentimental like that. They were probably kept in a vault with other negotiable items – or so it would seem, hearing them thrashed over in such detail here. If they had ever had any sentimental meaning, if they had ever stirred fond memories of a bygone moment, it would have been hard to imagine had one seen the swift readiness with which they were now turned over as Exhibit Numbers 10 to 18. Sliced out of their envelopes, spreadeagled on a Xerox machine, the juicy titbits underlined with red pen, they were now no longer personal possessions – words written by one person privately to another – but instead became just another piece of evidence for public record that anyone with just a passing interest had a right to contemplate (or not, as they chose).

Mitchelson strode back and forth, brandishing the letters dramatically in his hand, reading them and putting in inflections where he wanted, stopping in front of Lee to ask what he meant here or there. Michelle seemed to be working in concert with the lines, dabbing at her eyes now and then; at other times looking at me with a half-smile, hoping perhaps they would bother me. Hearing them read aloud in the courtroom, they seemed more lustful than fond. One that Mitchelson was particularly fond of had Lee writing about a fictitious character – himself – 'The first man in history that was guilty of robbing a thirty-three-year-old cradle.' In a court the man is found guilty and accepts the verdict, but asks, 'Will the jury please get out of the cradle?'

When the trial was over these letters prompted Lee to advise Jimmy Breslin of the *New York Daily News*, 'Never give an actor a typewriter'.

In answer to one question, Lee answered, 'I don't know. This is in response to a letter, I believe, so I don't have that cue sheet with me.'

MITCHELSON: All right. We're not working from cue sheets.

We're working off letters you wrote back in 1966. Speaking

of cue sheets . . . didn't you tell a reporter about two days
ago out in the hallway, that the best script here will win?

LEE: Yes, that's the truth.

MITCHELSON: One moment, we'll get into that later.

LEE: You are reading, Counselor, my letters, but your emphasis
might not be the right one.

Marvin Mitchelson asked Lee if he loved Michelle, to which he
answered, 'No.' '*I do, however, spend a lot of time thinking of you
with kindness,*' Marvin Mitchelson read out. Lee retorted, 'I don't
think the content is that heavy.' He also said that many of the
letters were in response to queries or telephone calls from her.

A letter was read out where Lee tells her that he has a plane ticket
for her to come to London . . . tells her to pick the departure date
that best suits her (this does not sound like an ultimatum) and that
she should bring empty suitcases so she could shop and fill them up
at his expense. He is also having his driver meet her. He has got her
a first class ticket: '*I thought it over and came to the conclusion that
the difference is not worth the discomfort.*' Rather nice of him, I'd
say, as he usually flew coach himself; it seemed so ironic that such
letters were being read out in a courtroom to prove what a bastard
he was.

In a quick change of pace, Mitchelson stood in front of Lee and
read from the *Herald Examiner* of 24 January 1979. He had asked
permission from Judge Marshall to approach Lee, which was
granted. No one in a court setting asks permission from the
defendant: it is one of those procedures designed to show how few
rights a person has here and how subordinate they are to the court.

ACTOR LEE MARVIN, COMPARING HIS TRIAL TO A THEA-
TRICAL PERFORMANCE YESTERDAY, SAID THE JUDGE
WOULD PICK A WINNER ON THE BASIS OF WHICH SIDE
HAD THE BEST SCRIPT.

These cases are staged as a good script. Lines have been
thought out for years. He said that he felt the 'script was more
important than the actors involved'. The actors? 'Oh, the
Judge has seen thousands of those,' he said.

'Then it went on,' Mitchelson continued, trying to arouse the

Judge's ire, 'to say what the case was about. And then it says, in the fourth column: "*Gee, I got the Award once,*" he said, "*do you think I will win another? Do you think that's not going to be considered? People will say, that SOB, he's an actor, but you only get one chance . . .?*"'

> LEE: [*Interrupting*] No, it says 'here': 'But *here* you only get one chance.'
> MITCHELSON: Now do you still feel the same way? You read those quotes. Are they accurate?
> LEE: They are fairly accurate.
> MITCHELSON: Anything inaccurate?

Mitchelson adored using the press, but throughout his professional career Lee was always very aware of what he had or had not said to the media.

> LEE: Well, yes, I'm sure some of the words are inaccurate.
> MITCHELSON: Show me.
> LEE: '*Actor Lee Marvin compared his trial to a theatrical performance.*' Incorrect, I did not compare anything. They compared it.
> MITCHELSON: OK.
> LEE: '*. . . and said the judge would pick the winner on the basis of which side had the best script.*' I said that. It is not quoted. '*These cases are staged as a good script. The lines have been thought out for years.*' I didn't say '*a good script*' . . . '*They are staged. These lines have been thought out for years.*' That is both sides, right. '*And, he said, adding that he felt that the script was more important than the actors involved.*' Meaning I have read thousands of scripts that I have rejected. If they are not good, or I don't believe they state an honest thing, I discard them, and I am comparing the two sides of this case to being fictitious, which unfortunately [*looking directly at Marvin Mitchelson*] is your side, and the truthful side . . . [*Loud laughter from the courtroom forces him to stop*]
> MITCHELSON: Did you work that line out for yourself, Mr Marvin?

Lee was not amused, and had not been laughing himself.

LEE: Let me finish it out . . . '*and the truthful side is mine, so hence the judge will decide on the scripts.*' Thank you [*in deadly earnest, Lee now instructs* him]. Continue.

MITCHELSON: '*People will think, that SOB, he is an actor, but here you only get one chance.*'

LEE: The content of that line is that having won the award at one time, people will say, 'What an advantage for him to be on the witness stand against an amateur,' and that I am the professional actor.

MITCHELSON: Is the amateur me? [*Sounding like a kid with his sleeves rolled up and fists ready*]

LEE: No, the amateur is the Plaintiff.

MITCHELSON: All right, she's the amateur and you're the pro?

LEE: That's correct – as an actor.

MITCHELSON: Keep talkin'.

LEE: I am. I think that's a very honest statement. [*Sits back in his chair in the witness box*]

MITCHELSON: [*addressing Judge Marshall grandly*] On that nuance, may we have a recess?

JUDGE: Let's continue another ten minutes, Counsel. We started a little late.

So, robbed of his dramatic conclusion, Mitchelson went back to the pile of letters and asked Lee when he had last read them.

LEE: I am reading them now, yes, sir. I didn't see any content. I thought they were rather silly letters, so I wasn't looking for any specific content. I don't know what we are looking for.

MITCHELSON: Well, maybe we'll find out we are looking for the truth.

LEE: [*incredulously*] In *these* letters?

By the end of the third day on his letters, it became apparent that Michelle's aid was not in her presence but rather her absense. These were fantasy musings, written to someone who was well over twelve thousand miles away.

When Michelle was on the stand, she quoted some of the sentences from the letters.

MICHELLE: He said that his work was almost unbearable to him, and that he was still interested when a project started, and that he was holding up the whole project himself – if the movie failed it would be the Lee Marvin picture that was not selling tickets . . . and he said that he found that the pressure of being a movie star . . . not an actor, you know . . . he said, 'I still love my work,' and then he said sometimes, 'I don't like my work.' And then I would say to him, 'Oh, come on Lee, you like . . . don't tell me you don't like your work.' And he would be very serious. And he would say, 'What makes you think I like my work?' And then I said to him, 'Well, what makes me think that you don't like your work?' And he was drinking out of fear, too. He said . . .

MITCHELSON: All right. What would you tell him?

MICHELLE: He told me many, many times he drank because of his experience in the war.

MITCHELSON: What would you say to Mr Marvin in reply to these expressions to you?

MICHELLE: When he would talk about the war, in the beginning I couldn't relate to them because I didn't know much about World War Two.

MITCHELSON: Tell us what you did say, Miss Marvin.

MICHELLE: I didn't say very much.

Once again, it seemed that most of the help Michelle Triola claimed to have given Lee on *The Dirty Dozen* could not easily be identified.

It wasn't until the trial was in progress that the defense team heard anything about an apartment Michelle had apparently maintained for more than a year and a half during the time when she had sworn, under oath, she had lived exclusively with Lee and nowhere else.

The trial received enormous coverage in the newspapers and on television. Watching and reading the reports was the woman owner of an apartment building. She decided to come forward after hearing Michelle Triola and Marvin Mitchelson declare that Michelle lived exclusively with Lee from 1965 (sometimes they said 1964) until May 1970. She knew otherwise. Upset by what she felt were falsehoods, she contacted Lee's attorneys. Michelle, she said, had rented an apartment from her for more than a year and a half – from 1965 to 1966 – and thereafter took it on a month-to-month basis. In the middle of the case for the defense, David Kagon questioned Michelle about this apartment. In her case she had made a great effort to prove that she and Lee had moved into the beach house together.

KAGON: Now you heard Mr Marvin testify that in 1965 he asked you on several occasions to get yourself an apartment, did you not?

MICHELLE: No.

KAGON: He never asked you that?

MICHELLE: I don't believe so.

KAGON: Did you ever get yourself an apartment?

MICHELLE: No, I think Mr Goldman rented me an apartment one time. I never . . .

KAGON: When was that?

MICHELLE: In 1967, I believe it was.

KAGON: That was the only apartment you are referring to?

MICHELLE: I believe so. I never had an apartment while I was with Lee.

KAGON: [*Asking permission to approach the witness*] Miss Marvin, I'll show you what purports to be an apartment lease.

MICHELLE: What date is this?

KAGON: 1 May 1965, Murray N. Nelson and Michelle Triola Ward. Do you recall the duration of that lease?

MICHELLE: No, I don't, because I never read it until this day. Your Honor, may I explain?

JUDGE: You may indeed.

MICHELLE: I signed this lease for Miss Marleaux because she had been a resident in another state, and the landlord would not issue her a lease.

KAGON: Did you advise Mr Marvin that you had executed the lease for the apartment?

MICHELLE: Yes, I did.

KAGON: When?

MICHELLE: I mentioned that I was going to do that for Mimi because after I signed the lease, I thought that maybe I would get stuck with it, you know – in other words, if she decided to move, wherever she moved. I didn't like the fact that I had signed the lease, but Mr Nelson knows that I never lived there. I never lived in that apartment, Mr Kagon.

KAGON: Did you make any payments on the rental?

MICHELLE: No, I did not.

Marvin Mitchelson fought ferociously to deny that his client had had this apartment: 'Your Honor, she did not occupy the apartment, that's number one; and number two, she lived with Lee Marvin, and he says so and everyone else says so.' He contended that bringing up the apartment was done for 'sexist' reasons, to hint that it was used for illicit purposes. David Kagon replied that he had never alluded to anything sexist: 'If counsel believes there is one, it's in his mind and he will have to struggle with that. During this period of time, Your Honor, Mr Marvin was not present in Los Angeles. In the later part of 1965 he was on location doing *The Professionals*; the early part of 1966 he was on location doing *The Professionals*. The only testimony we have to where the plaintiff resided was her testimony.'

KAGON: Miss Marvin, did you have a telephone at that address?

MICHELLE: I would imagine that there was a telephone in there, but as I have explained, Miss Marleaux was from out of state . . .

JUDGE: Is your answer yes or no?

MICHELLE: Yes.

KAGON: Was that telephone registered in your name?

MICHELLE: It could have been.

JUDGE: It could have been what?

MICHELLE: It could have been registered in my name. I don't have a recollection, though.

KAGON: Were you on an answering service?

MICHELLE: I could have been . . . I mean in other words, I could have gotten an answering service, but I don't believe that I got messages there.

JUDGE: What? Does that mean you did or did not?

MICHELLE: Can I explain?

JUDGE: That answer is not clear: yes or no?

MICHELLE: No, I don't recollect whether I had one in my name. If I could explain . . . Miss Marleaux was from out of state and I could have had the utilities in my name in lieu of deposits . . . but this landlord knew that I never stayed there. I may have had some music there. And I may have had some rehearsal clothing or a gown or something that I didn't want to lug into Dino's. But I didn't have . . . my belongings were not there.

KAGON: When was your last engagement at Dino's?

MICHELLE: 1965. Mr Kagon, I was working with my manager, and I'm not sure that I had music there and bits of clothing, maybe some drawing material. Maybe I left a dog there. I don't know.

A next door neighbour of Lee's in Malibu now came forward. She and her husband became aware that Lee Marvin had moved there in 1965. A few months later the existence of the plaintiff also became known to them. She came over and introduced herself as Michelle Triola. She told Mrs Munich that she was 'visiting Lee Marvin' for a few days, and wondered if she could borrow some shampoo.

They liked Lee very much, Mrs Munich said, and when he moved next door they were surprised to see him sitting alone having coffee at six o'clock in the mornings: 'I didn't think actors got up that early in the morning.' Michelle told Mrs Munich in 1966, when Lee was away in London, that she had spent time at 'her apartment in Beverly Hills' (embellishing the apartment by moving it from West Hollywood to Beverly Hills). Asked if Michelle had ever discussed her relationship with Lee, Mrs Munich replied that she had. At this point Michelle Triola started to interrupt, yelling out, pounding on the table, and crying loudly to Judge Marshall that she had just seen one of our lawyers, Barry Felsen, laughing at her. She started to cry so loudly that she was ordered out of the courtroom. She wailed, 'Don't laugh, Barry. It's not funny. I'm tired. I can't take this any more. I don't even know her. She's lying.' She was escorted out by the bailiff as Barry, shocked and surprised, protested his innocence.

Mrs Munich testified that in 'perhaps a half dozen conversations' Michelle had told her she was trying to get Lee Marvin to marry her, and that later on she told her that they *had* got married and that, as Mrs Lee Marvin, she now could sign checks in that name.

The most damaging witness for Michelle Triola's testimony was the owner of the apartment. Mrs Erem owned it jointly with her husband and was in charge of collecting the rentals. The apartment was unfurnished.

> MRS EREM: She came to the office to say that she was going to Hawaii for several months and she couldn't afford to keep the apartment while she was away, so a friend of hers was going to stay in the apartment while she was away. Later she came back and said that she was going to London, and that her friend was going to stay on.

Michelle, she continued, personally paid the rent several times, and she saw Michelle in the apartment six to twelve times: 'The lease was for one year and thereafter on a month-to-month basis.'

Seeing Michelle move out with her furniture in December 1966, Mrs Erem went to see her in the apartment: 'There was another girl with her and there were movers.'

She told Michelle that she hadn't given thirty days' notice, and that because it was after the 15th she owed another month's rent. 'She said to me, "Don't worry. I'm going to marry Lee Marvin and the rent will be taken care of."' It wasn't.

Mrs Erem also refuted Michelle's claim that she rented the apartment for Mimi Marleaux because she was from out of town: 'We would have rented to anybody. There was a big vacancy factor in the city at the time and we were desperate. Anyone residing in an apartment has to sign the lease.'

By the end of the trial, Michelle Triola had yet another story: 'I have thought about that, and I *could* have paid the rent on the apartment.'

When asked by her attorney why she paid the rent, Michelle now recalled the circumstances.

MICHELLE: Mimi was spending a tremendous amount of time with me. She was not basically getting paid. We had what between us we called a kind of a running account. She would run errands for me. She would personally hem gowns for me. I mean, she just did so many personal things for me. She would do my hair. She would run short, and sometimes . . . if I had some money . . . I would give her some of what I had. And I bought her some clothing sometimes. I bought her a dress for the opening.

KAGON: Opening of what?

MICHELLE: Dino's . . . I told you I have never seen that woman . . . Your Honor, may I explain something? I believe that woman said that I was going to – oh, I can't – that I was to go to Hawaii for an indefinite engagement. Well, at the time that I was going to Hawaii, I didn't – I didn't know – I mean, I was going for a two-week period. And I believe that woman said – I might be extended or something, and I couldn't possibly have even known that when I was going to Hawaii. I was going to Hawaii to – to promote my record for two weeks, and I never had a conversation with that woman, ever.

After only a few weeks of the trial, Mr Rodin, Marvin Mitchelson's associate, came to David Kagon and proposed a settlement. His client Michelle Triola would settle the case for $100,000. David answered that he was doubtful, but would bring it up with Lee. When asked, Lee said, 'I can tell you in two words.' 'What are they?' David asked – and Lee told him.

Kagon went back to Rodin and said his client had only two words in reply. Mr Rodin asked him expectantly, 'Does the first one start with an F?' To which David said – you never could anticipate what Lee would do – 'No . . . the two words are No Thanks.'

Sitting in court listening to the two sides, the plaintiff's case and the defense, is like hearing the ebb and flow of tides: first one wave, the attack, then the other, the defense. Then would come the parade of expert witnesses to prove or disprove what had been contended. We heard at great length from the plaintiff's side that Michelle Triola's record could have been a success but for Lee's intervention.

Both sides presented witnesses with various opinions on how to promote this record or a hypothetical one – and much of this discussion was hypothetical. Supposing Michelle Triola's record *had* been played by all the disc jockeys in Hawaii with heavy coverage: *if* that were the case and *if* Lee had forced her to leave this promotion by demanding she come to London for a brief visit, what would the effect have been on her success? Many days were taken up with such seemingly irrelevant testimony, but it did give us in the gallery a lot of information about the record industry – though it had nothing to do with Michelle Triola. We heard from Joseph Smith, chairman of the board of Elektra-Asylum Records, who had been president of Warner Brothers Records for seven years.

We heard about the impact of the Beatles, the careers of Tony Bennett, Steve Lawrence and Edie Gorme, their successes and their problems. All very interesting – essentially, the history of popular recording from 1961 to 1966 – but having little to do with the case at hand. Under the defense's questioning, Mr Smith agreed that even if you did bombard the whole Hawaiian island chain with a record, it would not necessarily become known to disc jockeys elsewhere in the US, and that to leave off promoting for two weeks or a month would have had no impact at all.

To refute Smith's testimony, the prosecution brought on Mel Torme (renowned as The Velvet Fog), a client of Marvin Mitchelson's, as expert witness. He was asked, 'Do you have any feelings of ill will against Mr Marvin?' 'Absolutely not, I am a great admirer.' When asked what he had done to promote his music when he was an unknown back in 1945, Torme told of visiting disc jockeys and librarians of music.

MEL TORME: If the record was believed in, and there was a will
to promote it, I think an unknown performer [in the late
1960s] would have to quadruple his efforts to combat not
only the new kind of music that was coming at that time, but
also the rest of the well-known MOR [middle-of-the-road]
artists like myself, Steve & Edie, and Jack Jones. I mean,
there was a plethora of MOR artists who were having
trouble getting records played. Therefore, I think to promote

that specific record at that specific time would have taken a
very huge effort on the part of the artist and perhaps the
recording company on a nationwide basis.

This was clearly a criticism of Lee for not personally promoting
Michelle Triola's record. 'I am not a promoter,' Lee replied, 'and
this is not my field. That is what managers are for, I thought.'

Singer Trini Lopez was also called as a witness for the plaintiff.
This was a mistake, as he refuted Mimi Marleaux's earlier
statements that she had done publicity for him, and also said that,
rather than ruining Michelle's career, Lee was attempting to help it.
Trini listed his hit songs: 'If I Had a Hammer', 'Michael Row the
Boat Ashore' ,'La Bamba' and many more. He had been
subpoenaed to appear in court and stated that he knew Lee: 'Yes,
he is a good friend.' Lee had brought a record to him when they
were in London filming *The Dirty Dozen* together, and asked him
to listen to it and give his opinion.

> TRINI LOPEZ: I told him it was pretty good and that her voice
> was pretty good –
> MITCHELSON: [*Interrupting*] All right.
> KAGON: Did you tell him that you liked it?
> TRINI LOPEZ: Can I say I liked it pretty good?
> JUDGE: [*To laughter*] He should have been a lawyer, I think.
> TRINI LOPEZ: I was trying to be courteous to Lee by saying
> that I thought Michelle had a pretty good voice, you know.
> KAGON: Did you mean it?
> TRINI LOPEZ: Well, I meant it . . . yes, I meant it not to offend
> Lee by saying the record was pretty good. Well, let's say she
> had a fair voice.

By the time this point was reached, the subject was more than
exhausted, and good, bad or indifferent, the recording had been
more talked-about than any hit record. It seemed clear, even with
Michelle's testimony, that Lee was the only one who was interested
in making a success of it.

When the defense began to put its case, one of the questions Lee
was asked concerned his record,'Wand'rin Star'. David Kagon
called Lee to the stand to ask about his own success in recording.

'Must I?' Lee asked, not considering himself the world's greatest singer, even though his one recording outsold the Beatles – who collectively sent him a tongue-in-cheek telegram telling him to watch out as they were going to knock him off the charts. (They also took the name Beatles from a line Lee had in the movie *The Wild One*.)

During the defense case Lee was questioned on the subject of ruining Michelle's career.

KAGON: Mr Marvin, did you ever give the plaintiff an
    ultimatum to quit her career?
LEE: Never.
KAGON: Did you tell her to terminate whatever she was doing
    in Hawaii and join you?
LEE: Never.

When asked if he had ever called her in Hawaii from London, Lee said, 'I don't believe I ever phoned her, no – in Hawaii,' but he recalled telephone calls she made to him: 'I would have said, generally, a number.'

David Kagon presented a record of incoming calls, receipts charged to Lee's number in London from Lihue, Hawaii, from Michelle Triola. There were *none* outgoing, thus disputing the ultimatum claim.

KAGON: Did the plaintiff ask you if she could come to Europe
    in a telephone call when you were in London?
LEE: I don't remember the specific phone call, but I'm sure it
    was discussed at the time nearing her arrival, yes.
KAGON: Mr Marvin, how long did she stay in London?
LEE: I really don't have a sharp recollection of that, so I'll just
    say for about two weeks.
KAGON: Did you have any conversations with the plaintiff after
    you returned from London with reference to her record?
LEE: Yes. To the best of my recollection, I asked her had she
    done the other DJ visits that she was going to do up and
    down the coast, and I don't recall her answer, except I think
    that it was a negative answer – I imagine a number of them.

Far from dissuading Michelle Triola from having a career, it appeared Lee was flogging a dead horse in trying to encourage her to *get* one.

In Michelle Triola's deposition taken by David Kagon in May 1972, the subject of pregnancies came up for the first time.

> KAGON: During the time that you were living together, were you ever pregnant?
> MICHELLE: [*Quickly*] Yes.
> KAGON: When?
> MICHELLE: [*More slowly*] I don't remember. I know that I had one pregnancy, I went and had shots, and another I miscarried, I believe.

By 1 January 1979, seven years later, this had become three pregnancies: the second had miraculously appeared as an abortion that made her sterile, then in a later testimony it was the third and done at Lee's insistence. The memory of it was now terrible, very clear and very traumatic. Crying bitterly in court that the abortion had left her sterile – she could not remember the name of the doctor who told her she was sterile or in what year ('1968 or 1969, I don't remember'), but she remembered with clarity the name and spelling of the doctor who recommended him: her old friend Dr Tristam Coffin Colkett III.

As far as the alleged abortion was concerned, she did not make any of the arrangements, pay anyone or do anything herself – but her 'best friend Pat Dean Hulsman, H-u-l-s-m-a-n, did it'. And Lee must have given Pat the money, $600 for *Pat* to pay the doctor. Which would have been illegal in those days, if true. During the defense case, Pat Hulsman firmly denied this or ever hearing about any pregnancy whatsoever.

> MITCHELSON: Miss Marvin, I have to ask you a couple of personal questions here – which I regret, but I must do it. During your relationship with Mr Marvin, did you ever become pregnant as a result of relationships you had with him?
> MICHELLE: Yes.
> MITCHELSON: On approximately how many occasions?
> MICHELLE: [*Without hesitation*] Three.

MITCHELSON: Let's take the first one. Approximately when did that occur?

MICHELLE: [*After a pause*] 1965.

MITCHELSON: All right, now was there a second time you became pregnant during your relationship with Mr Marvin? Yes or no?

MICHELLE: Yes.

MITCHELSON: Give us the year,

MICHELLE: I believe that was 1967.

MITCHELSON: What conversation ensued in 1967 between you and Mr Marvin with regard to your becoming pregnant?

MICHELLE: He wanted me to have an abortion.

MITCHELSON: What did you tell him?

MICHELLE: I told him I would probably like to have a child.

MITCHELSON: Did he tell you to have an abortion?

MICHELLE: Yes.

MITCHELSON: Did you?

MICHELLE: Yes.

MITCHELSON: All right. As a result of that abortion, do you know whether or not you are able to have children?

MICHELLE: It's that I have scars. [*Sobs*]

MITCHELSON: [*Much louder*] You what?

MICHELLE: [*Hastily*] And I can't have children.

There was a long pause while this thought was left to sink in.

MITCHELSON: Was there another pregnancy thereafter?

MICHELLE: Yes.

MITCHELSON: When did that occur?

MICHELLE: You mean after the abortion?

MITCHELSON: Yes.

MICHELLE: No.

MITCHELSON: I'm sorry. Was there another occasion on which you became pregnant? The answer is no?

MICHELLE: No, there were two occasions before the abortion.

MITCHELSON: Excuse me. The abortion occurred immediately after the second, is that correct?

MICHELLE: No, the abortion occurred . . . the abortion was the third pregnancy . . . The second one was, I believe, I don't know, 1966 . . . and the third may have been in 1968. I'm not sure on the dates of those. I know that there was a year in between, in between the miscarriage and the abortion.

MITCHELSON: Miscarriage? When?

MICHELLE: I believe in 1967.

Five days later, under David Kagon's cross examination, a similar question is asked.

KAGON: Did you have three pregnancies?

MICHELLE: Yes, I believe in 1967 is when I had the abortion, and the miscarriage was before that.

KAGON: Did this abortion make a very firm impression on your mind?

MICHELLE: Yesss, it did. I believe I had the abortion late in 1967, or it might have been early. I really cannot recall that. It was very traumatic for me and I do not remember . . .

KAGON: But *do* you remember the abortion? [*He reads aloud from her deposition in May 1972*] 'During the time you were living together, were you ever pregnant?'

MICHELLE: Yes.

KAGON: When?

MICHELLE: I don't remember. I know I had one pregnancy, I went and had shots, and another pregnancy I miscarried, I believe.

She had not recalled an abortion at that time. I noticed the Judge writing something on his pad.

This sensational topic of abortions was given much media attention. It was further brought to the attention of the court and the world by the excruciatingly detailed testimony of a doctor who appeared as a witness for the plaintiff. With no advance warning to the court or the defense, Michelle Triola went into hospital in the middle of the trial and had tests performed in an attempt to support her statements about her supposed pregnancies, abortion and resulting sterility. Judge Marshall had intended to appoint an impartial physician of his own to study all the proffered medical reports; however, the matter was not only taken out of his hands pre-emptively, but voluntarily taken to far greater lengths.

Michelle went into St John's Hospital in Santa Monica one Friday after the court proceedings of the day, and over the weekend subjected herself to anaesthesia and a laparoscopy, along with a number of other invasive tests. We, in our turn, were subjected to hours of descriptions of the minutiae of these procedures and in-depth reports of their results.

Where they had found a doctor who would do these tests over a weekend and testify in the manner he did became obvious during the cross examination by Lee's defense attorney. He was, it turned out, a friend of Dr Tristam Coffin Colkett III, MD, an Alcoholic Anonymous dropout and an old friend of Lee's (and more recently Michelle's) from his beach days in Malibu.

Dr Robert Scott, the friend of the friend, settled confidently into his seat in the witness box and proceeded to give us many more intimate details about women's internal organs – in particular, Michelle Triola's – than any of us wanted to hear.

He spoke with exuberant clarity, completely comfortable about discussing his 'patient's' reproductive arrangements in a courtroom packed with members of the public and the press. Marvin Mitchelson had only to ask him a question and the floodgates opened. Not once were we spared. I guess that was the point – nothing less than a vivid description would do. By the time he stepped down, nearly every woman in the audience had a flushed face and sweaty palms. Everyone, it seemed, but Michelle Triola, who sat through most of it looking beatific, validated possibly by being the object of such interest. At times she cocked her head to listen more closely, furrowing her brow or nodding in under-standing. She seemed to be taking it all in with impersonal interest, as if it were a lecture on plants, perhaps, or the sex life of the Gambole quail.

Dr Scott had a perfect recollection of having seen this patient once before, he said – nine years previously, on 12 May 1970 – even though Michelle never recalled seeing him herself or whether this were the same doctor.

She first came to see him in May 1970 and he could recall much of his findings and her history at the time. This was several days after her change of name and one day after Lee's departure.

In her history, Dr Scott tells us, Michelle wrote that she had had an abortion in 1967 which resulted in a terrible infection – the one she had forgotten by 1972 and did not remember until 1979. She was distraught and tense, he remembers, because she was going to Al-Anon to help with her husband's alcohol problem; her husband was Lee Marvin. If she really had gone to him and written these things down, it would appear that plans were being laid long before for this court case; if not, there must have been a lot of hasty writing recently.

He told of his examination when he saw her again in January of this year. 'What did you observe?' Marvin Mitchelson asked, and Dr Scott told us and told us and told us, giving us what he saw and the background – the usual and unusual findings of internal examinations of the healthy and the diseased, and how each manifests itself – using mental images we could have done without. He also explained to her the different tests he could perform if she wanted.

Mitchelson told the court that his client was here today in great discomfort, but gamely so because she didn't want to miss the proceedings. At the end of the day we knew exactly why and where she had the discomfort!

> MITCHELSON: All right, now tell us, *Doctor* [*using the title as often as possible*], what procedure did you perform on Michelle Marvin on Saturday?
> DR SCOTT: Shall I take them in order?
> MITCHELSON: [*In his most courtly manner*] Please do.

Scott told of four procedures and their findings in considerable depth: 'OK, she was taken into surgery.' He then went on about uteruses and other bits and pieces. Finally, he talked of the positive findings and listed the negative.

> MITCHELSON: [*Hardly able to contain himself*] All right. Describe, please. Tell us what you did next.
> DR SCOTT: I don't like to tell this where you ladies can hear.

But tell he did. He even told Michelle, right there in the courtroom, the results of one test: 'I was a bit alarmed – what if we find an early cancer etc – when I saw that abnormal tissue.' He turned, addressing Michelle directly, 'Everything is normal, there is *no* malignancy,' reassuringly nodding his head up and down to her, to the press, to us all. Michelle looked wide-eyed with concern, then smiled in relief, glancing around the room to include us all in her good news.

If we thought he had finished, we were sadly mistaken. He was going on unchecked, his nose was in the wind. We then heard what she did have, what she didn't have, and some uncalled-for and putrescent descriptions of what she *could* have.

At last came the payoff.

MITCHELSON: *Doctor*, as a result of these tests that you performed last weekend at St John's Hospital . . . Sterile or not sterile?

DR SCOTT: My conclusion, with the history I have and with my findings, is that she is sterile.

As these words rang through the courtroom, Michelle bowed her head and cried into a Kleenex, but Marvin Mitchelson was on his feet in triumph. He dramatically threw his hand out toward David Kagon, palms up, finger pointing in his direction. You expected to hear trumpets blare. 'Cross-examine!' he commanded.

It fell rather flat, however, because Kagon was not even looking at him at that moment. He was studying his notes, and looked up to see Mitchelson still holding his dramatic posture well after he should have done. David acknowledged his finish and addressed Judge Marshall. He moved to strike the entire testimony of Dr Scott on the grounds that he had no independent findings himself about any abortions other than what the plaintiff *told* him.

Unfortunately, the motion was denied by the judge. So David began his cross-examination by asking to see Dr Scott's records. One small card was in the doctor's own handwriting, but five long pages were filled out by 'the patient at home'. The doctor said, 'It's someone other than myself. I don't know whether she filled this out alone or had help, or what.'

Asked about the writings on his card, he confessed, 'I can't read my writing. I'm sorry.' 'You are not alone, Doctor,' David retorted.

KAGON: Predicated on the examination you made in May 1970, would it be your opinion that you could have made a diagnosis that the patient was infertile?

DR SCOTT: Could you repeat that for me, please? [*The court reporter reads the question again*] Not a firm diagnosis, not with that small amount of information.

KAGON: Now, between 1970 and 1979 [the present time] many things could have occurred that would have contributed to the condition that you found now in 1979, isn't that correct?

DR SCOTT: I would only be guessing. Yes, it is within the realm of possibility.

Once this subject had been brought up with a 'professional witness', it had to be 'plumbed to its depths' as Judge Marshall was wont to say. And plumbed it was – though Dr Scott was not nearly so loquacious as he was when testifying under Marvin Mitchelson.

KAGON: Don't your records indicate in *1977* there was a D and C?

DR SCOTT: Yes, they do. That was simply history furnished by the patient with no name, no place.

KAGON: In 1970 you attributed nothing unusual to her condition?

DR SCOTT: [*Reluctantly*] I think that is correct.

KAGON: Are you telling us now that, in 1979, the *only* contributing factor that you found at the moment, you could trace back to the abortion?

DR SCOTT: No.

KAGON: You are *not* saying that?

DR SCOTT: My inference is I know of a history and I have a finding and I know nothing else.

Much as he was trying to testify for the plaintiff, Scott still made it very clear that he based his conclusions on the history Michelle Triola told him: 'If I am asked if those *are* all the facts, then I would say that is one of the main causes.' 'I have no further questions,' said David Kagon.

But Marvin Mitchelson certainly did – beginning, innocently enough, by asking who referred Miss Marvin to him.

DR SCOTT: Tris Colkett?

MITCHELSON: Who is Tris Colkett?

DR SCOTT: Tris Colkett is a very nice man that I met some
years ago through some other patients, and a friend of Lee
Marvin.

He didn't say he was a doctor – perhaps by that time he wasn't. So
finally, after sixty-seven transcript pages of dialogue of the most
graphic kind, and a promise of copies of hospital records, we were
off to the next witness.

It isn't difficult to imagine the headlines in many of the
newspapers at the end of that day. One example is this truncated
version of the proceedings published in the *New York Post* for 15
February 1979. The heading proclaimed, in bold black letters,
MICHELLE STERILE: ABORTION BLAMED. Directly underneath
was a large photograph of Lee. The smaller print of the story read:

Los Angeles (UPS). A gynecologist testified yesterday that
Michelle Marvin cannot bear children and that as far as he
can determine her sterility was caused by an abortion when
she was living with actor Lee Marvin twelve years ago.

This article gives not one hint that these were merely allegations,
and that what Dr Scott testified to was information given to him by
Michelle Triola. Even if one didn't read the article, just seeing the
heading with Lee's picture underneath made an inference no one
could possibly miss.

What was *never* printed, however, or even heard in the
courtroom was that this entire subject – all claims of sterility, all
testimony about any abortion or pregnancy *whatsoever* – was
completely dropped by Marvin Mitchelson and Michelle Triola. It
was withdrawn as a complaint, stricken from the court issue, and
all testimony pertaining to it was dropped from the court's
'recollection' – wiped clean as if it had never been contended.

This change of plan came about after Dr Scott's testimony, on the
evening of the day before doctors testifying for the defense were to
appear – and very much behind closed doors, in the Judge's
chambers. There was to be testimony proving she was 'fertile' in
1977, seven years after the end of the 'relationship'. Served with
notice of this testimony, Marvin Mitchelson visited the law offices
of Goldman and Kagon and asked to see what these doctors were

going to say. When he did see the transcripts, he decided the better part of valor was discretion and suggested the matter be dropped. This was brought up to Judge Marshall the following day, but in chambers. It was interesting to see what these men thought about the allegations.

MITCHELSON: Now, Your Honor, we have a situation that threatens to create such a *time* problem in this case. [*He was the one who first brought it up!*] I regard whether or not my client is barren is really a collateral kind of matter . . . It was brought up because there is a question – Mr Kagon openly questioned whether Michelle Marvin was just making up a story as to whether or not she could have children. Now *is this* something that happened *since*; or is it something that happened *back then* through some other means or method? But we now have, Your Honor – if we are going to get into this issue – we have five or six doctors' records to take a look at.

KAGON: Your Honor, I am trying to prove a negative here – the only way that I can prove that she was not infertile during that period of time is perhaps by showing that subsequent to 1970, something occurred which showed she was *not* infertile during that period of time. [*'i.e. fertile,' adds Bernie Lohr-Schmidt, capping the sentence*]

JUDGE: [*Well versed in Mitchelson's approach by now*] Would you so stipulate that you withdraw any contention that she was rendered infertile by anything that occurred during the period they were living together? If so, then that will take the entire thing out of the domain of this particular lawsuit, and I think it is a minimal point to start with. I permitted testimony about it because it was a point, *but it is certainly not a factor of any great consequence, one way or the other.*

MITCHELSON: Well, I didn't think it was, Your Honor.

If Michelle hadn't been such an enthusiastic party to this lie, I might have felt pity. As it was, I had an overwhelming sense of indignation that we had been subjected to any of this.

JUDGE: I know you share my view on that. I think also Mr

Kagon shares our view. Now, the question is, do you wish to withdraw the point, of not very great significance, this allegation? Then we will be permitted to proceed to some things of greater moment.

MITCHELSON: OK. Then let's strike out all of the testimony and be done with it.

JUDGE: I think you are saving everybody a lot of work.

KAGON: Absolutely.

JUDGE: On a minimal issue really –

MITCHELSON: I do want to –

JUDGE: – of no significance.

LOHR-SCHMIDT: We discussed it in our office. Mr Mitchelson was up to read those portions of the transcript and he did say that he didn't consider it a great issue, and I told him, 'Well, why did you bring it up?' and when he left the room, he was considering withdrawing it.

JUDGE: Then the matter is removed from this case. Testimony to abortions is out. Let's see. [*Thinks*] What else?

KAGON: And that would apply to the pregnancies and the whole issue?

JUDGE: Yes, all the material goes out.

MITCHELSON: I think if there is going to be any statement by the court on it –

JUDGE: I wasn't going to make it –

MITCHELSON: Let's just drop it. Otherwise we have to go into the reasons why.

LOHR-SCHMIDT: Well, with all due respect to counsel and court, the matter is on record. It will take a motion to strike. It is all over the newspapers.

MITCHELSON: They aren't talking about it any more.

JUDGE: No, I am not concerned about the newspapers. First of all, the newspapers have discussed it and already dropped it. It is past, it is no longer news and there is no need to resurrect it.

Although Marvin Mitchelson and Michelle Triola had everything to gain from leaving things as they were, it would have been far better for Lee's reputation if it had never been alleged in the first place. But since it had been, and so dramatically, the fact that these allegations were being withdrawn because they were about to be disputed by medical testimony the public should have been told that the allegation of pregnancy was a lie.

Judge Marshall was happy that time was being lopped off this lengthy trial, Marvin Mitchelson was happy because his client was no longer in danger of being impeached on this issue, and Lee and his attorneys were happy to have it behind them.

David Kagon asked the judge, 'Will that include Dr Scott's testimony, Your Honor?' The judge asked, 'Who?' – after all those hours of Scott! 'Dr Scott,' David repeated. 'Oh yes,' Judge Marshall remembered, 'because that is all he testified to.'

With that, Judge Marshall imposed a 'gag order' on all concerned. No one could talk about this to the press or anyone else. What Michelle Triola contended, what Marvin Mitchelson accused, what the newspapers printed and TV reporters announced, what archives held on this subject, *that* is what stood. Only the allegations were preserved in print or in people's memories. The defense of these was never presented and, moreover, never discussed in public again. Even in the 1990s I hear about it from people and it is still given credence in television specials (for instance, Bill Kurtis on A&E television in 1996). I was also surprised to see how much erroneous material was printed even in publications such as the *New York Times* and what choices reporters made about the testimony – what to emphasize and what to omit. The assertions took on a life of their own. Whether it was just from repetition, poor reporting or Mitchelson's manipulation, I don't know, but 'giving up her career' seemed to seep into the consciousness of even the supposedly more responsible writers. A writer covering the proceedings observed, 'Nothing is too trashy or trivial for this trial.' And he was right. This is exactly what Lee had been trying to avoid all along, but his manner of doing so was to try and entice Michelle to leave on her own accord. Others might have been more direct.

I could see why Lee had taken Michelle Triola's threats so seriously. As each day unfolded, more evidence of the darkness of her nature was revealed – something that Lee had probably realized quickly. With testimony she knew to be false, even having given it herself – *especially* having given it herself – she would cry or laugh or be irate about the supposed injustice. It went well beyond acting. She is difficult to describe because, fortunately, so few people have anyone like her in their lives.

One of the ironies of this trial – already filled with such self-promotion and sensationalism – was the appearance of the women's rights activist Gloria Allred. Amid a small flurry of tipped-off news people, she and three others marched down the courthouse hallway arm in arm with Michelle Triola, rallying to the cause.

As a woman myself and by extension the target of their protest, my first feeling – after 'they must be kidding' – was one of regret and some despair as I thought of the more deserving issues they could be addressing. They had to be either people of enormous naïveté, which was excusable, or of such an opportunistic bent that they were able to use Lee's celebrity status to further the cause of women's equality. Here they were carrying the colors in defense of someone they described as being treated like a 'rape victim'.[1]

Ms Allred felt, 'Unquestionably Ms Marvin has been demeaned in the courtroom. There's sexual slant in this trial.'

These women striding down the corridors for their photo-op had not sat in the court listening to the testimony themselves. It was Michelle's unproven accusations, not the facts, that they were echoing. Lee's defense arguments had not even started, and as far as a 'sexual slant' in the trial was concerned, I would say there was certainly that . . .

Marvin Mitchelson was probably the ultimate user of women, and Michelle Triola his female counterpart. No matter what the case claimed, she was in my estimation about as far as you can get from the ideals of women's liberation. What she swore under oath in a court of law was proved to be 'without merit', that is, untrue – that is, she was lying. A case was concocted against someone so that she could be awarded a great deal of money: half what a man had earned by his own talent, labor and creativity.

Marvin Mitchelson, 'the champion of women' as he would have us believe, used Michelle Triola, though she was an all too willing

---

1 *Los Angeles Herald Examiner*, Ann Salisbury, staff writer.

tool. He orchestrated the case – suggested it even, as he himself said. He concocted stories and tried to rewrite history to fit the needs of the case. What kind of a man would subject a woman to the testimony he elicited from Michelle or from Dr Scott about her medical procedures? He wanted to win money and fame for himself to further his career on the back of Lee's.

The real irony is that, of all of them, Lee was the romantic, the giver, the caretaker. He gave a woman kindness and respect that she didn't deserve . . . and he was probably the only man in her life who ever did.

Before the end of the day of Dr Scott's testimony – and the last day before the defense case – Marvin Mitchelson called me to the stand. I was nervous and had to take some deep breaths, but it wasn't long before I began to feel angry. Marvin Mitchelson had a threatening attitude and tried to change what I said to confuse me. It wasn't a very important testimony, so I suppose he put me on the stand to annoy Lee.

His questions seemed pointless, designed to show that this case was a result of my interference in an agreement between his client and Lee. Primarily, he tried to pin me down on when I was told about the payments to her. He yelled and demanded a copy of my testimony, but he was just wrong – which the transcripts proved anyway.

In 1976 the 'Marvin Decision' had ruled that an implied property agreement between unmarried persons living together may be inferred by their conduct. Michelle Triola Marvin and Marvin Mitchelson wanted the court to interpret this to include 'love and affection' as a promise to share property. Perhaps it was for this reason that Michelle claimed she and Lee had become engaged at the home of Keenan and Sharley Wynn.

KAGON: Did he ever ask you to marry him in the presence of a third party?

MICHELLE: Would that include engaged?

KAGON: Yes, if he asked you to become engaged.

MICHELLE: Yes, he asked me to become engaged in front of Keenan and Sharley Wynn . . . To the best of my knowledge, I would think it would have been late in 1965. At the Wynns'

residence. I believe one of their little girls was in the room.
Yes. And we called my parents.

KAGON: Did you get an engagement ring?

MICHELLE: No, I got a coat.

KAGON: What kind of coat?

MICHELLE: A mink coat.

KAGON: Who ordered the coat?

MICHELLE: I don't recall. I would imagine Mr Marvin . . . It was
my engagement present so I mean, I don't know. It wasn't me.

KAGON: What was your state of mind at the time as to why you
rejected the engagement ring?

MICHELLE: I already had an engagement from my husband,
and I didn't wish to have another ring. I didn't – at that time
my state of mind did not symbolize an engagement ring as
anything, it could have just been an engagement present, but
not necessarily . . . [*Her voice trails off*] . . . just didn't want
a ring.

KAGON: You stated Mr Marvin called your parents. Were the
Wynns present when he called your parents?

MICHELLE: Yes, they were.

KAGON: And they could have overheard the conversation, is
that correct?

MICHELLE: They *heard* the conversation, not 'could have' –
unless they are deaf.

Keenan Wynn came to court to give moral support to Lee as well as
his wife Sharley, who was to testify. The Wynns' appearance
created a great hubbub among the press and the courtroom
audience, with flashbulbs popping and cameras whirring.

Lee and Keenan greeted each other with a hearty embrace, and
Lee bowed slightly and kissed Sharley's hand.

Sharley, a very attractive, slim and well-dressed woman, was
nervously smoking and tapping her cigarette holder on the ashtray
in the hallway as we waited to go into court. She is energetic and
lively at the best of times, and her impending appearance on the
witness stand was making her really jittery. It is a terrible experience
for most people, and having done it myself, I could deeply empathize
with her. Once on the stand, she was so straightforwardly unused to

court procedure and so human in an inhumane situation, she immediately had the sympathy of the audience.

Under questioning she testified that she had met Michelle Triola some time in 1965, having been introduced to her by Lee. Sharley and Keenan lived in Brentwood, and Lee and Michelle would stop by two or three times a week when Lee was in town. Michelle came over more often than Lee, and would stay for dinner. Keenan and Sharley were never invited for dinner at 'Mr Marvin's' house: 'No, never had dinner there.'

Marvin Mitchelson objected repeatedly, and when at one point Sharley failed to realize she was supposed to stop talking, he complained to the Judge: 'Your Honor, if I'm not allowed to object, I guess I'll go off in a corner and mumble to myself.' 'That's the last thing I would expect you to do,' Judge Marshall replied. 'Tell me what the objection was; you just said, "Excuse me."'

Marvin Mitchelson, quite excited himself by this point, was becoming garbled and talking in shorthand fashion until Judge Marshall observed, 'You seem to be amusing Mrs Wynn considerably.'

The next time David Kagon asked her a question she was silent, and he looked at her questioningly. 'I'm waiting for him,' she said, nodding in anticipation toward Marvin Mitchelson, and thus eliciting many a stifled chuckle.

JUDGE: Perhaps I can instruct the witness. Mrs Wynn, are you calm?

SHARLEY WYNN: Yes.

JUDGE: All right. Just relax and wait for the question, and make no comments thereon and no intermediate remarks. Answer the question directly and answer no more than the question. [*Although his words sounded firm, he looked at her over his glasses and smiled*]

SHARLEY WYNN: OK, got it.

JUDGE: Lean back in your chair and remember, nobody here is going to do anything to you while Mr Wynn is in the courtroom. [*A reference to Keenan's enormous and well-documented strength*]

People in the courtroom burst into laughter, and after everyone had quietened down, Keenan himself laughed. Judge Marshall looked over at him saying, 'I didn't know there would be a delayed reaction.' At which everyone laughed again. Knowing Keenan *was* hard of hearing, I had just told him what the judge had said. David Kagon asked, 'Mrs Wynn, do you recall whether that took place early in the relationship?' He was asking her about something that had been asked of her before, but which she must by now have forgotten. 'What are you talking about?' Sharley asked him in alarm. There was yet another eruption of laughter, and Judge Marshall, grinning, said, 'I guess we'd better start again.'

In the end they got used to her way of answering before the question had been entirely posed, instead of the other way around. More seriously, she did dispute Michelle's statements. She had introduced to Lee the decorator who did the beach house, opposing Michelle's contention that *she* had found the decorator. Sharley answered with a firm 'No' when asked if she were present at any time when a telephone call was purportedly made about a engagement of marriage.

Mitchelson became very aggressive toward her during cross-examination, trying to rattle her by posing a series of fast and insulting questions.

MITCHELSON: Did you ever see Mr Marvin consume alcohol?
SHARLEY WYNN: Consume? Yes.
MITCHELSON: As a matter of fact, I suggest to you that Mr Keenan Wynn, your husband, and Mr Marvin used to drink to the point where they fell down on the floor, is that right?
SHARLEY WYNN: No.
MITCHELSON: Over and over again?
SHARLEY WYNN: No.

Mitchelson usually made it such a disagreeable experience to come forward for the defense that few people wanted to do it. This made Lee very reluctant to subject any of his friends to it – but they did so over his protests.

MITCHELSON: Regardless of what sobriety, I won't touch upon that, don't you ever remember Mr Marvin making a telephone call, or purporting to make a telephone call, to Michelle's family?

SHARLEY WYNN: No, I don't remember.

MITCHELSON: Don't you recall him, in one of those moments of drinking frivolity, mention something about getting engaged to Michelle?

SHARLEY WYNN: No.

Snapping, snarling and scolding, he was still unable to shake her. Drunk, sober, high, he asked her repeatedly, but she had heard nothing about this engagement. I don't know why this kind of brutality is allowed in a court. It is hardly a civil way to extract information.

David Kagon asked Lee about his friendship with the Wynns during the time in question. He replied that they were indeed friends: he saw them a lot in 1965, but he was away almost the entire year of 1966.

LEE: I was in town for maybe a month, I believe.

KAGON: Mr Marvin, did you ever ask the plaintiff to marry you?

LEE: No.

KAGON: Did she ever ask you to marry *her*?

LEE: No.

KAGON: Did you ever ask her to become engaged to marry you?

LEE: No.

KAGON: Did she ever ask you to become engaged to her?

LEE: No.

On the last day of the trial, 27 March, Michelle Triola and Marvin Mitchelson were back to characterizing witnesses, this time Keenan and Sharley Wynn.

MITCHELSON: Was Sharley Wynn a friend of yours at one time?

MICHELLE: Yes.

MITCHELSON: Let me ask you this. Would you see her as much as two or three times a week when you were in town?

MICHELLE: No, I would see her possibly once a week . . .

MITCHELSON: Did you ever see Mr Marvin and/or Mr Wynn, after drinking together, affected to any degree by what they had drunk? Out of control?

MICHELLE: Yes, on many occasions.

MITCHELSON: All right. Was there ever an incident that happened in Malibu concerning Mr Wynn being put in jail?

MICHELLE: Yes.

MITCHELSON: Tell us what happened.

MICHELLE: Keenan had come down to the beach. It was during the Christmas holidays. And Keenan came down to the beach house very early in the morning. It was either Christmas Eve or Christmas Day. And there was – as I remember – either a landslide or a fire or something. And when he went to go home, he had been drinking, and Lee had asked him not to drive, because Lee was not drinking on that occasion. And he had asked Keenan not to drive along the highway. And when Keenan got to, I believe it was Sunset and Pacific Coast Highway, he saw the disturbance. There was a road block. And he got out of his car and went over to the police car and stuck his head in the police car, and they put handcuffs on him and took him away.

MITCHELSON: Now, did you have a conversation with Mrs Wynn?

MICHELLE: Yes, we called her – I called her and I said, 'Sharley, you have got to go down and get Keenan.' And she was furious and said, 'Let him stay in jail,' you know. And I said it was Christmas.

MITCHELSON: Is that the words she used?

MICHELLE: Well, she used profanity. I don't want to use profanity.

The enormity of this remark was not lost on those who knew Michelle. One story told by numerous sources leaps to mind. Lee was on a publicity tour of one of his movies and Michelle had joined him in New York for a dinner at Danny's Hideaway. In the party were a number of Lee's publicists, attorney F. Lee Bailey with a female guest, and others. As Lee walked through the door, an actor he had known in the early days of his career in New York was sitting there and called out to him, 'Well, if it isn't the big Hollywood star Lee Marvin.' In *Billy Budd* with Lee on Broadway, he was still plugging away as a stage actor while Lee was now at the height of his career in movies. Lee stopped to speak to him, but it was obvious the comment affected him. It didn't take a lot to get his feelings of guilt going. Once seated, Lee began drinking his famous 'double martini . . . straight up' while Michelle, sitting next to F. Lee Bailey, was discussing 'the law' with him. While Lee got more drunk, Michelle's accent became more and more British: 'Ever since I was a little girl, I've wanted to appear before the bahr of justice . . . I've always been fascinated by the courts of lawh' etc. When she was at her fanciest, Lee somehow accidentally spilled his martini on to her dress. She jumped up, and just as one of those silences that sometimes happen came over the room, she screamed at him, 'You've humiliated me in public for the laahst time . . . you cocksucker!' Knives and forks clattered all over the restaurant. Later, she was still outraged: 'This isn't one of my schmatta dresses, you know – it's designer.'

I can well understand why Mitchelson apparently agreed: 'I don't want you to use profanity. Did she call him a name of some kind?'

MICHELLE: Well, she just used an expression, let's put it that way . . . And she was very angry and . . .

MITCHELSON: Let's move on.

The most traumatic part of the trial came as a surprise to Lee. A young actor friend, about the same age as Lee's son and mine, came forward to reveal a long-standing sexual liaison with Michelle Triola during the time she was living with Lee. It was painful for all concerned, particularly for the young man who had so wrestled with his conscience in speaking out.

JUDGE: Can we proceed to the sexual thing?

KAGON: I would ask her if she had sexual relations with anyone during that time other than Mr Marvin.

JUDGE: All right. If she says no, what are you going to do?

KAGON: I may call some witnesses, Your Honor.

MITCHELSON: That is the very thing, Your Honor, that

outrages me, just outrages me . . . shameful, and I mean it.

KAGON: Your Honor, please, before we get into a lengthy
diatribe, may we comment on the issues?

The argument as to whether to admit this evidence was thrashed
out emotionally, loudly and at David Kagon's request, out of
earshot in the judge's chambers.

MITCHELSON: They know they have not a shred of evidence
. . . They are trying to sort of work around, and bring out
something sensational in this trial.

JUDGE: I don't see it as a moralistic issue . . . If true, she
couldn't be a companion to this man to the extent that she is
stating.

MITCHELSON: Wait. It takes me a while to get wound up. She
could be a very loving companion and could have engaged in
a sexual incident with another person. That would be a
matter of degree, Your Honor. If my client were a call girl,
yes.

JUDGE: If there is a single isolated instance, the court will
ascribe to it the weight that should be ascribed, Counsel. For
all I know, a dozen instances.

KAGON: We are taking the plaintiff at her word. She has
pleaded a contract. I have no desire whatsoever – none,
believe me – for sensationalism. And let's not talk about
sensationalism. We both know . . .

MITCHELSON: [*Interrupts in his most pugilistic tone*] We both
know what?

KAGON: Let's not talk about that. But being accused of
sensationalism, Your Honor, is probably the most absurd
accusation that has ever been leveled at me. I'm not usually
given to having my temperature rising.

JUDGE: Let me ask you this, sir. Do you have in hand testimony
with respect to more than one sexual misconduct?

KAGON: I do, Your Honor.

JUDGE: More than one?

KAGON: It could be many, Your Honor. The reason I say that
. . . I don't want to compromise my witness, because I may
not use him. [*In an attempt to preserve some decorum*] Your

Honor, I would be happy to have the witness testify in chambers.

MITCHELSON: I wouldn't, and I want to tell you this, Your Honor . . . I don't know who he is talking about. The only thing I could be thinking about is possibly a stand-in drunk of Lee Marvin's which it may . . .

JUDGE: It may be that it will all be stricken, but the sexual conduct, Counsel, if it is of the degree, perhaps not of a call girl, but were of a greater degree than a few isolated instances . . . it may erode the alleged consideration of companion, full-time, loving companion.

Never let it be said that Mitchelson gave up on anything easily!

MITCHELSON: Well, you see, the problem we have in this case is that Mr Marvin does not assert a contractual relationship.

JUDGE: But *you* do, Counsel. [*Quieting him up for a brief pause*]

MITCHELSON: I assume most men go off and have affairs.

KAGON: Speak for yourself.

The day before this witness was to testify in the judge's chambers, Michelle Triola and Marvin Mitchelson filed an amendment to their complaint accusing Lee of fraud: 'Defendant Lee Marvin tricked Plaintiff into devoting six years of her life to his benefit, he ought to suffer punitive damages in the amount of one million dollars or in a greater amount according to proof of his wealth.'

The next day the testimony of the 'confidential witness' was heard in judge's chambers and lasted for two long days. Dick Doughty was a young man in his early twenties who was in the Peace Corps in Palau when Lee went there to build a fishing boat in 1969. It was a small island and their paths crossed often. He was outgoing and popular, and when he came to California, he quickly became friends with Lee's daughters and his son Chris. After Lee and I were married, he was a welcome guest at our house. He would often come over for the day, or for dinner in Malibu. He had a small role in one of Lee's movies, *Emperor of the North*.

Knowing how much Dick admired Lee, we knew that this admission must have been torture for him. He sat in the judge's chambers in intimate proximity to Lee, Michelle Triola, the interrogating attorneys, a stern-looking, black-robed judge and a court stenographer taking down his every word. While David Kagon tried to elicit the information gently and impassively, Marvin Mitchelson outdid even himself, demanding the most sexually explicit descriptions and raining insults down upon Doughty's head. When the press later heard of the testimony, his photograph was on the front page of newspapers all over the country, his admissions headlines. Some of the press castigated him for 'kissing and telling', and one television commentator in particular blasted his youthful indiscretion with such fury one would have thought he had committed high treason.

The witness was sworn in and cautioned by the Judge not to reveal any proceedings until the Court did. The witness answered: 'Right, yes.'

He tells the court he is an actor, and that he first met both plaintiff and defendant in Palau ten years before in 1969. He was in the Peace Corps, working for the Micronesian fisheries program as a research biologist and diver. He had been there fifteen or sixteen months. He graduated from college with a BA in zoology and minors in chemistry, botany and geology.

KAGON: Now, after the first time that you met the Plaintiff, did you go on a picnic with the Plaintiff soon after you first met her?

DICK DOUGHTY: Yes, I was working at the fisheries office and I met Michelle earlier, and she came in and asked Pete Wilson, who was my boss over there . . .

MITCHELSON: Hearsay! [*The first of many objections*]

DICK DOUGHTY: She asked Pete if I could have the afternoon off to take her out to a picnic at the beach where they shot *Hell in the Pacific*. Mr Wilson said yes; I said yes, I would go. There was a Palauian, a local boatman. He was just operating the boat.

KAGON: During the course of that episode, were you and the plaintiff intimate?

DICK DOUGHTY: Yes.

MITCHELSON: The testimony is vague.

JUDGE: Counsel wishes you to be more specific, Counsel.

KAGON: During the course of that picnic, did you and the plaintiff have sexual intercourse?

DICK DOUGHTY: Yes.

KAGON: During that two-and-a-half month period, did you have sexual intercourse with the plaintiff?

DICK DOUGHTY: Yes.

KAGON: How often?

DICK DOUGHTY: Just about every day.

Under questioning, he said that she told him she was not married and that she was living with Lee.

He talked of the possibility of employment on a motion picture with the plaintiff and then with Lee.

DICK DOUGHTY: She said there was a chance that I might be able to get a job on *Monte Walsh*, working as Lee's stand-in. She said she had discussed this with him and that there was a good possibility that I might get the job.

KAGON: Did you thereafter discuss that with Mr Marvin?

DICK DOUGHTY: Yes. He brought it up . . . later he said maybe a stand-in wouldn't be the best job because I really wouldn't have an opportunity to see what was going on on the set as well as I might in another position. Then Bill Fraker came down a couple of weeks before they left the island. He was the director. I don't think Michelle was present at these conversations. I think just Bill, Lee and I. Well, they said that I had the job.

KAGON: How many people, Americans, were there on the island when you were present?

DICK DOUGHTY: There must have been at least a hundred or more because Palau is the district head, it's the seat of government for the District of Palau, so there are a lot of American government workers there, and there were quite a few Peace Corps worker volunteers in the area, teaching school, fisheries, some working in the local hospital. Things like that.

KAGON: Did you ever hear Mr Marvin introduce her as Michelle Marvin?

DICK DOUGHTY: No.

KAGON: Ever hear Mr Marvin introduce her as his wife?

DICK DOUGHTY: No. Never.

Doughty was asked by David Kagon what he did after leaving Palau.

DICK DOUGHTY: When I left I went to Saipan to be mustered out, and then to Hawaii and on to Los Angeles.

Lee and Michelle met him at the airport. He stayed with them for several days in Lee's beach house, and right away Michelle asked him to go to a motel with her.

DICK DOUGHTY: I told her . . . that since I was living with them now, and that either one or the other of them was responsible for getting me a job, I would rather not have any more physical contact with her. But shortly after that, we went to Cabo San Lucas to go fishing for about five or six days, and right after that we went down to Tucson.

KAGON: Did you have sexual intercourse in Cabo San Lucas?

DICK DOUGHTY: Yes, it was late at night, or early in the morning, however you like to phrase it – after midnight. We had been fishing – the three of us – had dinner, had some drinks, and retired for the night; and Michelle came down to my room.

KAGON: Did you ask her to come to your room?

DICK DOUGHTY: No.

In Tucson, he said, the movie company rented the house for him to live in and I resided in the house the entire length of the shoot in Tucson.

KAGON: Did you ever have sexual intercourse during that period of time with plaintiff?

DICK DOUGHTY: Yes.

KAGON: Was it at your request or her request?

DICK DOUGHTY: It was at her request. At that time I was feeling more and more guilty about what I was doing. I was trying to limit it as much as I could at that time.

The witness was then asked about a conversation he had had with Michelle.

KAGON: With regard to continuing your sexual intercourse with her, I ask you to relay that conversation, if you will, please?

DICK DOUGHTY: I was told in a very angry manner that the only reason I was brought over from Palau was to 'make love to her' and that if I didn't continue, I would be fired from the movie. She would get me fired, that is more accurate . . . if I didn't continue.

KAGON: Did you believe her?

DICK DOUGHTY: Well, I guess I did, yes.

He moved to an apartment and the plaintiff visited him there once, not at his invitation: she called and asked to come. Once more he went to her apartment off Sunset Boulevard – just before the case was thrown out the first time.

KAGON: All right, did she invite you to come to her apartment on that occasion?

DICK DOUGHTY: Yes.

KAGON: To the best of your recollection would you please relate the conversation?

DICK DOUGHTY: First, I was asked if I had any negatives to any pictures that I had taken of she and Lee when I was in Palau. I was told that she had a book she wanted to publish after the trial, after she won the trial. That was the intention and she wanted the pictures for this book. Secondly, I was asked not to testify about our sexual conduct. She said that since I was such a good friend of Lee's it would be very embarrassing to him, and it would hurt him deeply if he found out that someone who was living with him, as I was at that time, was making love to his girlfriend. I agreed not to testify on the material. Also, she was then working for William Morris Agency; she said she might be able to get me an agent with William Morris.

KAGON: Did you have any discussions with plaintiff about the Roberts and Landers matter?

DICK DOUGHTY: She told me she was involved with Landers and Roberts in giving them information that would be beneficial to them as far as presenting the film project *Monte Walsh* to Lee. She also said not to tell Lee this, not to mention it to him, that he would be very angry to find this out.

KAGON: Did you ever tell Mr Marvin?

DICK DOUGHTY: No.

KAGON: Did you observe Defendant and Plaintiff during the two to two and a half months in Tucson?

DICK DOUGHTY: Yes, every night. They were fighting a lot. Lee and I left the house just after daybreak, six or six-thirty . . . most of the arguments were in the evening . . . five or six times a week. Arguments about Betty, Lee's ex-wife, arguments about his children, there would be arguments about his drinking, about me being there. I left two weeks after the film ended.

KAGON: Your Honor, may we approach? [*Re the other affairs of the Plaintiff*] I have no more desire to put the names of other people on the record . . . I would suggest, Your Honor, that if these names are mentioned, that we stipulate that they may be stricken from this record, from the public record.

JUDGE: Well, I'm sure Mr Mitchelson will be agreeable at least that amount.

MITCHELSON: I'm sorry, Your Honor, to be so emotional about it, and I apologize for that.

KAGON: Had plaintiff ever told you about any other sexual relations that she had with other men during the time she was residing with Mr Marvin?

JUDGE: Without naming names. Do you understand that? [*One was a well-known, and married, movie star*]

DICK DOUGHTY: Yes.

JUDGE: Go ahead . . .What did she say?

DICK DOUGHTY: She said she was seeing a person sexually and that she went with him on his motorcycle. The other incident took place in Tucson.

KAGON: Nothing further.

Marvin Mitchelson began his cross-examination with a statement to the court designed to denigrate the witness and make him ill at ease.

MITCHELSON: I would like to sit at a position where I can face this witness and look him in the eye and not be too close to him . . . I take it that up to October–November 1974, you never told Lee Marvin that you had a sexual relationship with Michelle, had you, sir?

DICK DOUGHTY: I hadn't told him until yesterday.

MITCHELSON: What made you change your mind on 26–28 November, whatever date it was when you say Mr Kagon asked about sex that you had with Michelle – allegedly had – with Michelle?

DICK DOUGHTY: I am thirty-four years old now, and I am more willing to accept responsibility for things I do and have done. [*At the time of the affair, Michelle was thirty-seven and he was in his early twenties*] And despite the embarrassment to my family that this testimony will cause, I understand there's a lot worse things can happen to you than to have to tell the truth.

MITCHELSON: Any other reasons?

DICK DOUGHTY: This is a marginal reason. I have seen you on television an awful lot recently just by happenstance, and from your demeanor I feel that you are trying to railroad something through Lee, and that makes me feel . . . makes me more than willing to speak up . . . but that is a minor reason.

MITCHELSON: Any other reason, *sir*?

DICK DOUGHTY: No.

MITCHELSON: Now, besides telling Mr Kagon about these alleged sexual incidents, did you ever tell anyone else, any other human being in the world, about them?

DICK DOUGHTY: No, I was told that Michelle told some other people about it, by one of the other people.

MITCHELSON: Now did you talk to the other person?

DICK DOUGHTY: I listened. I was told this, I said.

MITCHELSON: Who was the other person who talked to you?

281

DICK DOUGHTY: Mitchell Ryan.

MITCHELSON: Did you talk to Mitchell Ryan when? When did you talk to him?

DICK DOUGHTY: The last time I talked to him was about the third week in December, right before the Christmas holidays. I was just finishing up the student movie that I broke my nose and cheek on.

MITCHELSON: Just tell us about when the last time you talked to him. Don't tell us about your illnesses . . . And did Mr Ryan tell you he was going to be a witness?

DICK DOUGHTY: He did not. [*Ryan later offered to come and testify to confirm this, but Lee talked him out of it*]

MITCHELSON: You said nothing, right?

DICK DOUGHTY: I didn't admit a thing to him, that's correct.

MITCHELSON: Now when you had these alleged incidents, did you notice anything peculiar about Plaintiff's – Michelle's – her stomach, any peculiar markings?

DICK DOUGHTY: I did not.

MITCHELSON: Notice anything unusual on her back?

DICK DOUGHTY: What do you mean by unusual? Like a growth, a bump, what?

MITCHELSON: Anything unusual?

KAGON: I think the witness is entitled to know what he means.

DICK DOUGHTY: A wart? A mole?

MITCHELSON: Anything unusual, Mr Kagon, includes anything unusual.

JUDGE: [*Admonishing Mitchelson*] All right, Counsel. [*Addressing Dick Doughty*] Do you understand now?

DICK DOUGHTY: Well, Your Honor, I do, but warts and moles and freckles, at least from a biological standpoint, aren't unusual at all. Nothing like that stood out in my mind, no.

MITCHELSON: How about when you had this alleged sexual intercourse with Michelle? [*Asks for intimate details and graphic descriptions*]

DICK DOUGHTY: What do you mean, unusual or how?

JUDGE: Counsel . . . [*They have an off-the-record discussion*]

MITCHELSON: Let's go back to the question.

Mitchelson had apparently talked Judge Marshall into letting him pursue this descriptive questioning for reasons of 'later impeachment'. I found it very hard to understand why these questions were allowed to be asked at all. They were, however, and you must answer the 'officer of the court'. After the subject was thoroughly exhausted, Mitchelson made a quick change.

MITCHELSON: You were kicked out of the Peace Corps, weren't you?

DICK DOUGHTY: That is absolutely incorrect.

MITCHELSON: What kind of discharge did you receive?

DICK DOUGHTY: Totally honorable.

MITCHELSON: Weren't you accused of sexually molesting native women over there?

DICK DOUGHTY: That is absolutely untrue.

Changing tack again, Mitchelson and Michelle then attempted to imply that Doughty was homosexual. They had him followed by a detective who would be willing to testify that he saw Dick go into a bar frequented by homosexuals. If brought back, Dick would vigorously deny the characterization. There was nothing too underhanded for this duo.

MITCHELSON: Did you feel that Lee Marvin was a friend of yours after you met him?

DICK DOUGHTY: No.

MITCHELSON: Didn't you like him?

DICK DOUGHTY: I grew to, yes. As a matter of fact, my regard for him increased the more I got to know him . . . so, it would be after.

MITCHELSON: I see. Did you feel guilty about the sexual incidents? Yes or no, sir?

DICK DOUGHTY: At the time I was in Palau, no, I did not. When I was leaving to come back to America, the idea came to my mind that it might be better for me, as a person, not to do this.

JUDGE: I am going to put off the reporters. I don't think we will be able to do it today.

The press as one body was clamouring at the gates, but there would be no word for several days of the Court's decision on whether to admit this testimony as evidence.

MITCHELSON: You know Mr Marvin had a drinking problem?

DICK DOUGHTY: I wouldn't say that, no. I would say drinking doesn't cause the problems – problems cause the drinking, in my mind.

MITCHELSON: As a matter of fact, you from time to time gave him a bottle of liquor, did you not?

DICK DOUGHTY: Never.

MITCHELSON: Never gave him one?

DICK DOUGHTY: I never gave him any whiskey.

The judge now admonished Mitchelson because he was yelling at the witness in loud and hectoring tones.

MITCHELSON: Sorry, Your Honor. Were you in love with Michelle?

DICK DOUGHTY: No.

MITCHELSON: Have you ever been infatuated with her?

DICK DOUGHTY: The idea that the girlfriend of a movie star would be interested in me did inflate my ego a little bit.

MITCHELSON: I want you to tell us what kind of guilt you felt. Describe it.

DICK DOUGHTY: Oh, there were two things. I felt guilty about one, staying in the same house, and two, I felt guilty about not just saying, "Look, forget it, I don't care about the job. If you want to get me fired, get me fired." I felt guilty about not being able to stand up and just say, "Take the job and do whatever you want with it." I was troubled by my own inability to end the situation sooner than I did.

MITCHELSON: Let's go to Palau, and I want you to recount for me as best as you can each and every time you had a sexual intimacy with my client. I want you to tell me how long it lasted.

KAGON: Your Honor, I object to this.

JUDGE: How long what lasted, Counsel?

MITCHELSON: The act of intimacy, from the time it started until the time they parted company. Your Honor, may the

witness walk out for a moment because there is a very
important thing here? I want to make a record of it.

JUDGE: [*Wearily*] Yes, step out. [*Dick Doughty leaves*]

MITCHELSON: Your Honor, let me submit to the Court that in
a little while I'll want to argue to this court that the time
spent with Michelle, if it's true . . . which I doubt very much
. . . is minimal. The question for this court to consider, and
the only question for the court to consider, is whether or not
there is such a loss of companionship and homemaking here,
and cooking, such an infringement upon it that the Court
feels that Michelle Marvin did not fill her end of the express
contract. That wasn't part of the agreement.

JUDGE: Well, Counsel, let's stop right there. What you are after
is to secure from this witness a statement as to how much
time was involved in these various sexual incidents?

MITCHELSON: Yes.

Judge Marshall had a very high threshold of tolerance, and at times
I found this deplorable.

JUDGE: I have no objection to your inquiry. Let's get the
witness, please.

MITCHELSON: Is it fair to say that when you had the sexual
encounters with Michelle, they were brief encounters?

DICK DOUGHTY: [*Not having heard the conversation about the
importance of the length of time*] I think that they were
normal encounters. I don't know about brief.

MITCHELSON: Were they brief, most of them? Were they . . .
you didn't spend hours and hours making love, did you?

KAGON: Objection, Your Honor.

JUDGE: Overruled.

DICK DOUGHTY: [*Incredulously*] That was overruled?

JUDGE: Yes.

DICK DOUGHTY: Well, in the act, no. Sometimes we were
together for more than a few hours.

MITCHELSON: Most of the time you were together for less than
a few hours, weren't you, in all fairness?

DICK DOUGHTY: I would say most of them were under an
hour, yes.

MITCHELSON: [*Warming to the chase*] OK, let's go to Malibu when you came over here. I think you decided that you weren't going to have any sexual encounters in Malibu, is that right? How many sexual encounters in Malibu before *Monte Walsh*?

DICK DOUGHTY: None.

MITCHELSON: OK, in Tucson?

DICK DOUGHTY: Approximately five.

MITCHELSON: Is it fair to say they were rather brief? Under an hour?

DICK DOUGHTY: Yes.

MITCHELSON: And thereafter I think you said a Mexican town?

DICK DOUGHTY: Yes.

MITCHELSON: Very brief encounter, wasn't it?

KAGON: Objection to the brief encounter . . . whatever that means.

MITCHELSON: It was a brief encounter, wasn't it?

DICK DOUGHTY: [*Getting exasperated*] I think in humans or animals that almost all sexual encounters are less than an hour. I think that is quite normal.

MITCHELSON: In Cabo San Lucas and in Malibu after *Monte Walsh*. Less than an hour?

DICK DOUGHTY: [*Now acquiescent*] Yes.

MITCHELSON: All right. When Michelle allegedly came down to your place in Venice – 19th Street – that was only for a little while, wasn't it?

DICK DOUGHTY: I would say less than an hour.

MITCHELSON: You told me how she came to your room. Did you not try to resist her?

DICK DOUGHTY: That is correct.

MITCHELSON: Were you afraid of her in any way?

DICK DOUGHTY: I gave credence to the fact that she might be able to get me fired.

MITCHELSON: Did you think she had that kind of power with reference to your state of mind?

DICK DOUGHTY: My state of mind didn't have anything to do with it. I saw her go into Bobby Robert's office and get me a fifty-dollar raise just by talking to him. I assumed she could do the reverse.

MITCHELSON: You liked Lee Marvin in Tucson better than you liked Michelle, didn't you?

DICK DOUGHTY: I thought he treated me in a more humane and a more genteel manner, yes. I said, too, that Michelle told me that she would take monies from the household expenses and put it away in a personal account of her own. They were cash monies. They came from Lee.

MITCHELSON: Does it make you feel guilty, sir, to come in here and tell this court what you told them concerning your alleged intimacies with Miss Marvin? How does it make you feel?

DICK DOUGHTY: I'm trying to make the best of an unpleasant situation. I am trying to be as honest as I can . . .

MITCHELSON: You said this morning you had the impression that I am trying to railroad Lee, remember that?

DICK DOUGHTY: I do. It seems that you are just trying to create a new type of law practice – a new area that you can specialize in.

MITCHELSON: So you decided you would come in here and you would help stop it, sir, by making up a cock and bull story, getting together with Mr Kagon.

JUDGE: You are arguing.

DICK DOUGHTY: No, that is totally untrue.

After the witness had been excused, Marvin Mitchelson began an impassioned argument to the Court.

MITCHELSON: What have you heard that prevented her from really fulfilling these duties that should allow us to take this lady into open court and have this stuff go into the record?

A married woman, Your Honor, can go and have affairs with twelve neighbors down the block, and let the dishes pile up in the sink. She gets half the property.

We heard Mr Doughty say it took him less than an hour each time only, the whole thing. I mean, even if it happened, maybe thirty hours out of a six-year relationship – or five and a half years, as they like to put it.

You want to do a little multiplication? Three hundred sixty
– how many? – twenty-four hours a day. I guess we are
dealing with several tens of thousands of hours. Thirty hours
out of their life together, and she should suffer this kind of
humiliation, and this kind of degradation. It's just outrageous
to even think about it.

Bernie Lohr-Schmidt, speaking for the defense, argued for the
inclusion of the testimony. Beginning with the sensible custom of
complimenting the judge on his equanimity and brilliance, he
moved on to the relevance of Doughty's testimony and then argued:

LOHR-SCHMIDT: It's on the record at least three or four times,
she did *not* have third-party sexual contact.

On the issue of credibility alone, I believe Your Honor
should let this matter stand on the record . . . Counsel has
made an argument that thirty hours, if Mr Doughty's
testimony is true, was spent in third-party sexual conduct . . .
And in Mr Mitchelson's eyes, this is rather insignificant,
possibly even minuscule.

The other thing is, this took place over the course of
approximately nine months, a year.

It was at the repeated urging of Mr Mitchelson that Your
Honor has to consider the *quality* of the relationship . . .

Defendant vigorously contends that it wasn't a full-time,
loving relationship, and this conduct and with others,
demonstrated that in the plaintiff's own mind she didn't
consider this a full-time, loving relationship . . .

The other point I would like to address myself to is the
issue of Mr Doughty's credibility.

Mr Doughty – I just heard a snicker from Counsel's table –
you have to look at the fact that this man was fresh out of
college.

Counsel has made much of the fact that Mr Doughty
didn't tell Mr Kagon about that when they met in 1973
before the first trial.

But let's look at that.

We have Mr Doughty, who doesn't know Mr Kagon from
Adam, knows that Mr Kagon is Mr Marvin's lawyer, and

sees Mr Kagon only after the plaintiff has already gotten to him and compromised him and gotten him to promise not to talk about sex, sex that he had with the plaintiff.

At that time after plaintiff's urging him, he chose not to tell a stranger, about something that was very touchy to him.

Five years or six years passed and he finally does tell Mr Kagon. All these reasons, in our estimation, are very creditable, very believable, and we submit, are the truth. Thank you, Your Honor.

MITCHELSON: Your Honor, Miss Marvin has clearly testified part of the agreement was simply companionship, homemaking, cooking, housekeeping. Faithfulness was not a part of the contract, and that Lee couldn't have cared less if she wound up in the bushes where she wound up.

JUDGE: [*Breaking his patient silence*] You elicited considerable testimony about the love and affection that existed between the two persons. Are you contending that love and affection that was extended by the plaintiff to the defendant was also subject to the proviso that neither need be faithful?

MITCHELSON: Why is it, Your Honor, that people who are husbands and wives with a license, do not have to be held to this standard? Why is it, Your Honor?

JUDGE: We are not talking about standards, that's why, Counsel. We are talking about a contract.

The following proceedings were held in open court.

JUDGE: The Court has given considerable thought and attention to testimony elicited in the Court's chambers, testimony by a witness for the defendant. The Court is of the opinion that it *is* admissible. [*Pauses*] There is going to be available to the reporters a reading of the transcript of testimony. It will probably be at noon.

At the appointed time the testimony was read by two stalwart court reporters taking turns, while pencils scribbled for the waiting world.

To corroborate the testimony about the affair with Michelle Triola, Carol Clark, a young mother and the wife of actor Matt

Clark, came to testify in Lee's defense. She came to the court hallway with her husband and their two-month-old baby. I didn't hear her on the stand – only Marvin Mitchelson's voice as he yelled questions at her – because I was in a jury room off the court holding the baby. She was a beautiful child: her bright-eyed presence lifted our spirits to a far loftier plane for the several days she was there. Under David Kagon, Carol testified that she had known Michelle for eight years, having met her while her husband was on the film *Monte Walsh*. She knew her for two or three months in Tucson and later in Malibu, and she had helped her move.

KAGON: Did you become very friendly with her?
CAROL CLARK: Yes.
KAGON: Did you exchange confidences with her?
CAROL CLARK: Yes.

The two women usually shopped for clothes for Michelle. Early on in their acquaintance, Carol was told about Dick Doughty.

CAROL CLARK: We were in a car and Michelle was driving. She
    told me that when she and Lee were in Palau . . . she met an
    oceanographer, Dick Doughty, and that they started to have
    an affair together, and that she arranged for him to get on
    the film *Monte Walsh* and that she was worried that he had
    given up his career in oceanography, and she had meddled in
    that, and she didn't feel he might become an actor, or a
    successful actor.

We then broke for lunch, and Mitchelson asked the Judge, 'Your Honor . . . I would like the benefit of hearing the rest of the testimony before the reporters get a hold of her. She is certainly going to be besieged. I would like to be able to at least cross-examine her first.'

When we returned, David Kagon asked to be heard in judge's chambers: two other witnesses, Mr and Mrs Munich, would testify to other affairs.

Miss Marvin had told Lee's neighbour, Mrs Munich, about five affairs, including the one with the movie star – with whom she had a motorcycle accident. This almost got into the newspapers, had it not been for some quick work by the actor's publicist. His two attorneys called at the beginning of the trial to ask if his name would be mentioned; Lee decided that it would not, that he would take this on by himself.

Judge Marshall advised Mitchelson that the testimony from Mrs Munich would be more damaging than it might be from someone who claimed to have participated in the affairs. The judge then made his decision: 'You already have in evidence Mr Doughty, Mrs Clark. The Court will refuse this testimony on these grounds: one, that I think it is cumulative . . .'

Cumulative it was certainly becoming. This kind of testimony about Michelle's activities was beginning to reveal qualities that most of us would rather not have heard so much about – particularly not Lee.

Michelle Triola, as rebuttal witness at the end of the trial, painted a quite different picture of her relationship with Carol.

MITCHELSON: Next subject, Carol Clark. Now did you at any time ever discuss Dick Doughty with Carol Clark?

MICHELLE: Yes, I did. I believe, to the best of my recollection, it was at the hotel or motel in Tucson. I believe that we were having a sandwich in the coffee shop.

MITCHELSON: Did Dick Doughty live in your house in Tucson?

MICHELLE: No, not to my knowledge. I do remember that he was around there sometimes.

MITCHELSON: Around there when?

MICHELLE: During the shooting of the film. But I have racked my brain, and he used to . . . drive with Lee's driver to come and pick Lee up.

MITCHELSON: In the morning?

MICHELLE: Yes. [*Inexplicably, after having denied Doughty stayed there*] And we had other house guests.

MITCHELSON: Let's go back to Carol . . . Did you ever tell Carol Clark you had an affair with Dick Doughty?

MICHELLE: Absolutely not.

MITCHELSON: Ever talk to her about anything of a confidential nature?

MICHELLE: No – and, Your Honor, may I explain that, please?

JUDGE: Not unless your attorney . . .

MITCHELSON: [*Taking a flyer*] Go ahead.

MICHELLE: I knew Carol Clark, but Carol . . . was quite a bit younger than myself, and I really found no common philosophy with Carol.

We went shopping. We had a very light kind of an existence, you know . . . the friendship. It was a very surface kind of – it was a typical movie relationship. Her husband was working on the film. I was with Lee. Lee was the star of the movie. So I thought that Carol was kind of ingratiating herself to me, and she was nice [*damning with faint praise*], but we never had . . . a common ground for any kind of deep philosophical conversation . . .

MITCHELSON: [*Interrupts*] I think you have explained it.

MICHELLE: Yes.

MITCHELSON: Next subject: how did you meet Dick Doughty?

MICHELLE: Mr Marvin, the Defendant, introduced me.

MITCHELSON: Who brought him round?

MICHELLE: Lee.

MITCHELSON: What did Lee tell you about him? Anything?

MICHELLE: That he worked for the Peace Corps and that he was interested in fish.

Mitchelson asked to approach the bench, requesting a stipulation from our attorneys. If we thought we had heard the last of Michelle's innards, we were quite mistaken. We were now told that Miss Marvin has a certain gland – the B-A-R-T-H-O-L-I-N gland, actually – and we were back to spelling the name of body parts. We were told that it is inside the vagina. If asked, Michelle would testify to what it does and that hers is different: 'It causes a certain secretion.' One of hers doesn't even work at all. We were also told what one had to do in order to have intercourse with Miss Marvin, and that the witness had already testified that he didn't do this (proof number one).

And lo and behold, there is a prominent mole on her body – 'under the left breast and left side of her back' – and the witness had also said that he did not notice anything unusual on her (proof number two).

David Kagon said he distinctly recalled Mr Doughty saying that, if she had moles, that would not have made an impression on him. 'With regard to the rest of it, Your Honor, if Counsel wants to open up that Pandora's box, I am going to have to have her examined by a doctor with reference to that, Your Honor.'

I had never in my life before come across people who were so anxious to lay bare someone's most intimate organs. True or untrue, it didn't appear to matter as long as the exposure proved some point that could be used to win this case. There was nothing they wouldn't say or do, apparently – but happily for us all, the court agreed.

Mitchelson defended his request by saying, 'It's just weight, anyway' – weight being accumulated evidence. When the judge decided against him, he went back to Michelle Triola.

MITCHELSON: Ever go on a picnic with Dick Doughty?

MICHELLE: Yes, but there were a lot of other people, you know, with us.

MITCHELSON: Ever have sexual relations with Dick Doughty?

MICHELLE: Absolutely not.

MITCHELSON: Did you ever have a discussion about a repayment of the loan from Mr Doughty to Lee?

MICHELLE: I may have, yes. Yes, I did.

MITCHELSON: When and where?

MICHELLE: When we got back from Tucson. I kind of wanted – I asked how long he would be staying with us and how he was going to – how he figured he was going to repay Lee for all the things Lee had done. He told me he had already paid Lee back a certain amount of money. I don't remember what it was.

MITCHELSON: Did you say anything about it should go to you instead?

MICHELLE: No, I did not.

MITCHELSON: [*Referring to the location of* Monte Walsh] You said Mr Marvin's driver would show up in the morning with Dick Doughty in the car – and would Mr Doughty come in the house and would Mr Marvin customarily have breakfast?

MICHELLE: Yes, I would fix it – but he wouldn't eat it all the time.

MITCHELSON: Did you find out about anything that was happening to the breakfast? What was happening?

MICHELLE: I don't know if it was happening to the breakfast. I just know that invariably Dick Doughty would come in with a pint of bourbon, and Lee would spike his coffee with it. Now I don't know whether that is why he didn't eat breakfast some times or not.

MITCHELSON: Did you ever talk to Dick Doughty about it?

MICHELLE: I said to Dick . . . I asked him . . . why he found it necessary to ride in the car to the set with Lee, that why he didn't he just – you know, as long as he was trying to break into the business – why didn't he become part of the crew instead of riding to the set every day with the *star* of the movie. [*Looks about with a pained air*] And he said to me, 'Well, what do you care?' And I said, 'Well, I don't care. The impression that you give your fellow workers is just that I would appreciate you not starting the day this way.' And I asked him please do not bring any booze in this house.

MITCHELSON: How about the part where . . . [*But Kagon objects to this leading question and Mitchelson is stopped by Judge Marshall*] All right. While in Palau, did you at any time ever see Dick Doughty in the company of another woman alone?

MICHELLE: Never.

Referring to that contention later, David Kagon commented, 'If what he said was true, why would he?'

A few days before the end of the trial, the subject was again brought up when Mitchelson called Lee to the stand.

MITCHELSON: Did you think the boy had a bright future? I'll reframe the question. What was your state of mind as to any future he might have, if he had one?

LEE: I don't think I had one.

MITCHELSON: Did you ask Mr Mishkin at some point to . . . talk to Mr Doughty about becoming a client of his?

LEE: A client? No, no. After the filming of *Monte Walsh* and in view of his relationship with the crew and the cast, and he expressing his desire to continue along the line of motion pictures, I suggested to him that *he* talk to Meyer Mishkin about the pitfalls and the problems . . . so he could get a clear, more concise view of what he was headed for.

MITCHELSON: He was just working with the crew, right?

LEE: No, he was the dialogue director.

MITCHELSON: Well, he didn't do any acting, did he?

LEE: Yes, he did. Off camera, with dialogue. As the dialogue director, his job was, at the request of the actors, to run lines with them or rehearse scenes, and he would play the missing characters, or he would read that dialogue with them, and as a number of the scenes were rather large, encompassing maybe three, four or five actors with speaking roles, I noticed eventually his timing and that he was sensitive to the other actors when they were not up on their lines. He didn't jump right in and throw them the line. The way he would relate to the other actors, I found to be very great . . . impressed me tremendously.

Mitchelson now insisted upon a general review of the topics of discussion between Lee and Dick Doughty during the latter's social visits to our house. Ridiculous as it sounds, this request was upheld by Judge Marshall.

LEE: [*Thinks for a moment*] The Pacific, boats . . .

MITCHELSON: [*Incredulously*] The ocean?

LEE: All of it, yes. Just general. Fishing, boats, acting, stars, fame, failure, and on down the line.

MITCHELSON: You say stars. Do you mean stars in the Heavens or stars in films? [*What a silly question at the end of this excruciatingly long trial!*]

LEE: [*Tersely*] Films.

So with that, the 'bombshell' topic of Dick Doughty, read aloud in court by the two clerks with dispassionate voices, was laid to rest, to be resurrected later when Judge Marshall delivered his opinion. The 'love and affection' part of the plaintiff's case had been not only refuted in painful detail, but the testimony had been corroborated by one other witness. This was enough for the judge: the other witnesses were not called.

When it was all over – when Lee had won, the hullabaloo had faded, and Lee and I went back to our normal lives at home or away on location – Dick left Los Angeles and the acting profession in which he had spent ten years of his life, a career that Lee always felt held a good deal of promise for him. (If the case had happened in the 1990s instead of the 1970s, it would have been an enormous *boost* to his career, had he wanted it.) He could have left things as they were and not come forward; he could have just stayed silent. No one else would have told Lee about it. He followed his conscience and suffered the consequences without complaint or asking forgiveness. We were very thankful for his courage in coming forth. Dick Doughty is now married, the father of three children, and has a career outside the movie industry.

Point Blank

Marvin Mitchelson now began testimony on Michelle's claim that she had helped Lee with his films; this was in order to prove an implied agreement of 'partnership or joint venture'. The first film to come under the spotlight was *Point Blank*.

> MITCHELSON: Miss Marvin, Mr Marvin testified that he didn't recall your discussing his motion picture work with him. The reference I'm going to ask you about deals with anything you had to do with any suggestions or discussions concerning motion pictures that Mr Marvin appeared in.

As David Kagon pointed out, this question managed to be leading, compound (i.e. several questions at once) and suggestive all at the same time. I nearly jumped up myself to object – we were by now getting quite astute at law ourselves.

> MITCHELSON: All right. With regard to *Point Blank*, did you have any discussion about Angie Dickinson with Mr Marvin?
> MICHELLE: Yes.
> MITCHELSON: What did you say, what did he say?

MICHELLE: Well, he . . . said John Boorman is having . . . some problems with her picking wardrobe.

MITCHELSON: What did you say?

MICHELLE: I said, 'Why?' And he said, 'Well, she . . . has to be very one color in this because John is shooting a new form in films where everything is the same color, but you don't visually know that it is. And Angie seemed to want to wear . . .'

MITCHELSON: Did you make any suggestions to Mr Marvin?

MICHELLE: Yes.

MITCHELSON: What did you suggest to Mr Marvin?

MICHELLE: Well, Lee asked me . . .

MITCHELSON: [*Cutting her short*] Just tell me what you suggested to him, ma'am, please.

MICHELLE: OK, I suggested – after he asked me if I knew a designer that she should wear – a dress called Pucci, P-U-C-C-I.

MITCHELSON: Eventually, did she do so?

MICHELLE: Yes.

MITCHELSON: Now, did you ever work on any of the scenes with Mr Marvin for any of the movies? Did you?

MICHELLE: I don't understand what you mean by 'working'.

MITCHELSON: Did you talk to him about the scenes of the movies he was to play?

MICHELLE: Yes.

MITCHELSON: Which ones?

MICHELLE: I can't remember exactly which ones, but sometimes Lee would come home in the evening and say, 'Do you remember that scene in say *The Professionals*? Well, it isn't . . . working.' And I would say, 'Well, why isn't it working?'

MITCHELSON: Don't go into the dialogue. Did you discuss scenes with him?

MICHELLE: Yes.

MITCHELSON: How often?

MICHELLE: Very often.

Mitchelson and Triola had repeatedly attempted to prove that Lee was usually too drunk to perform without her aid. On cross examination, David Kagon pursued the matter.

KAGON: Miss Marvin, do you know if Mr Marvin ever lost any work on any of the pictures that he was making during the time you were living with him?

MICHELLE: I don't understand the question.

KAGON: Did Mr Marvin, by virtue of his drinking, lose any time from his work on any picture on which he was working during the time you were living with him?

MICHELLE: [*Sarcastically*] Do you mean . . . if the set had to close down?

KAGON: Did he ever miss a call?

MICHELLE: Did he miss a call? Yes, he did.

KAGON: Which ones?

MICHELLE: *Paint Your Wagon*, many.

KAGON: Any others?

MICHELLE: *Point Blank*. I also wanted to ask you [*with even more sarcasm*], does it mean standing on your feet missing a call? Is that what you mean? If you are just standing there in your marks and they can't shoot . . .

KAGON: Was he unable to respond to a call to work?

MICHELLE: Was he on the premises? I don't know what you are referring to.

KAGON: [*Addressing the judge*] Your Honor, it's quite clear she doesn't know.

MICHELLE: [*Breaks in*] Yes, I do. I know what you are trying to infer.

Work on the movie *Point Blank* began in December 1966, almost immediately after Lee had returned from location on *The Dirty Dozen*. Testimony from Lee, John Boorman, Boyd Cabeen, Patricia Hulsman and Michelle Triola herself revealed what kind of aid it was that she supplied during those months. This was quite the opposite of what she asserted; in fact, midway through the filming she was rushed to the Cedars of Lebanon Hospital after a near-fatal suicide attempt. Very fortunately for her, she was found unconscious by John Boorman when Lee and John had been rehearsing the next week's work. Whether or not she had really intended to die, or just wanted the attention, she would have succeeded but for this stroke of luck.

The climate in which Lee worked was brought out by his testimony and that of his director John Boorman, with whom he was closely associated for two movies in a row, encompassing more than a year and a half in total. At about the same time, on 13 January 1967, Lee's divorce decree from Betty was granted.

KAGON: During 1967, do you recall if you had any conversations with the plaintiff regarding what would happen in the event the relationship terminated?

LEE: Yes, on my return from San Francisco. I said she would have to prepare for the future. She would have to get herself a job or learn a trade, something of that effect, and her discussion was that she would not leave the relationship, and that if she were forced to do so, she would reveal certain private matters, items to the press and the public at large, and she would tell of my problems with my ex-family and those of my children; of my fears, my worries, my self-doubts. Generally saying that it would not be worth my while to have her leave at this time.

KAGON: Did you believe her?

LEE: I did.

KAGON: Did she mention suicide?

LEE: She mentioned that on a number of occasions.

KAGON: What did she say?

LEE: Say? That she would do bodily harm to herself.

MITCHELSON: Now, Mr Marvin, you just told us something I found rather fascinating. You, in 1967, during the filming of *Point Blank*, you told her that she would have to go get a job, right? Become gainfully employed, is that right?

LEE: Feed herself, or whatever.

MITCHELSON: [*Takes a different tack*] Now, you weren't fearful of her doing physical harm to you in any way, were you, considering the size difference between you?

LEE: [*Unable to hide his sarcasm*] Not when I was awake.

MITCHELSON: All right. This morning you told us that you discussed her leaving a lot, but it was always followed by offers of assistance or money . . . That is what you told her in 1967, didn't you, before she threatened you?

LEE: No.

MITCHELSON: No?

LEE: No, I got her an apartment, and of course, told her she would have to get a job.

MITCHELSON: I'm talking about 1967, sir.

LEE: [*With finality*] 1967.

MITCHELSON: [*Apparently confused*] There was an incident where Ed Silver and Mr Goldman, I think, rented an apartment for Michelle in Pacific Palisades, wasn't there?

LEE: That's correct. *Before* that incident where she was hospitalized. I was asking her to leave at that time and said there was an apartment available for her.

MITCHELSON: [*In his most scornful manner*] I see. You weren't so frightened any more, huh?

LEE: [*Raising his voice*] I was frightened if a woman comes out with a shotgun in her hand and two shells in her other hand and says, 'How do you load this fucking thing?' [*He left the F-word out in court, but it was in an earlier deposition*] I would think I would be very cautious, and that would come under the consideration of being frightened.

MITCHELSON: OK, was this something she just sprung on you suddenly or . . .

LEE: [*Interrupts him*] I was sitting there in the living room and she appeared in the bedroom door with this riot gun I had made for tigers, and she had two shells in this hand [*mimes her gesture*], and she said, 'How do you load this so and so thing?'

MITCHELSON: [*Trying to minimize the impact*] And you are pointing with your hands sideways as though to show that a gun is pointed over in a direction to your right or left . . . right?

LEE: [*Angry at Mitchelson's attempts to downplay the incident*] I'm saying this is a shotgun that is capable of blowing people away.

MITCHELSON: [*Cajolingly*] Mr Marvin, come on now. You

weren't worried that Michelle walked into this doorway and said, 'How do you load a gun?'

LEE: [*Squinting angrily at Mitchelson*] I wasn't? I *was*. I removed all the guns from the house the next day, which was quite a considerable collection I had, and took them completely out of the area.

MITCHELSON: One of your gun collection, right?

LEE: They were usable weapons, not a collection.

MITCHELSON: OK. Did you rent her an apartment after she threatened to expose you to the world?

LEE: Yes.

MITCHELSON: And then you took her back into your house?

LEE: No, there is a progression you are leaving out.

MITCHELSON: When did you decide to take her back?

LEE: I didn't decide to take her back. It was after the suicide incident and she pleaded with me and apologized. I guess I had too much forgiveness.

MITCHELSON: And you loved her?

LEE: I did not love her.

MITCHELSON: But you forgave her and took her back?

LEE: I forgave her because I had seen both sides of the coin. Because of the human elements involved and the torture she must have gone through and the fear that must accompany an act like that.

MITCHELSON: What act? The gun . . .

LEE: No, her pill event. When she took the overdose. I was trying to get her out of my life – not *leave* the life.

Little did Lee know then that he could have avoided all this misery had he kept to his resolve. On the other hand, after briefly thinking how dumb he was to have fallen for this, I had to admire him for this same lack of resolve – his desire not to take a chance. He had seen death in the war, he had caused it and he was still living with the consequences. Although Michelle's behaviour seemed like some kind of melodramatic ploy to me, he knew her uncontrolled irrationality and violent temperament. Some inner guilt always seemed to be part of Lee's thinking, and because of this, he would blame himself.

Lee had also been unaware of the conversation between her and his stand-in Boyd Cabeen. After her suicide attempt she went to Boyd's house – not the apartment Lee's lawyers had rented for her – and asked for his help. Cabeen said, 'I came back from location on *Point Blank* from San Francisco, and she said to me, "It looks like it's all over between us. Can you do something?" And she said, "Can you do anything or can you introduce me to another celebrity?"'

Marvin Mitchelson took this up at the next opportunity, asking sarcastically, 'And did she have any particular celebrity in mind?'

Cabeen replied, 'She didn't mention a name, no. She would have settled with anyone at that stage,' a remark which was stricken by the court but not lost on the press.

Such was Lee's life during the filming of *Point Blank* – illustrating just how helpful Michelle's presence was to his ability to concentrate on a highly demanding film. His heavy involvement in the production was fully documented by John Boorman when he appeared in the courtroom. It was an extraordinary movie, still recognized as the model for many subsequent attempts. Filmed partly in the island prison of Alcatraz, it is powerful and violent, providing Lee with one of his most intriguing and brilliant roles.

At the time of the trial, John Boorman had come to the US to work on a new film of his, *Excalibur*, and was thus able to testify on Lee's behalf. I think Judge Marshall, a cultured man, very much enjoyed having him in the courtroom.

John's testimony refuted any claim of help by Michelle Triola, instead describing her propensity for interfering in Lee's work. It also gave us all an insight into the making of *Point Blank* and *Hell in the Pacific*.

KAGON: Mr Boorman, when did you first meet Mr Marvin?
JOHN BOORMAN: I met him in London in 1966 when he was making a film called *The Dirty Dozen*.
MITCHELSON: Objection.

Despite an extraordinary number of objections from Marvin Mitchelson, Boorman eventually was able to answer the defense's questions.

JOHN BOORMAN: I was introduced to him by a producer who had given me a script and also given it to Mr Marvin, with the idea that we could make a film together. The script was called *Point Blank*.

KAGON: During that time . . . By the way, did you have an opportunity to meet with the plaintiff, Miss Marvin?

JOHN BOORMAN: No, I didn't.

KAGON: What was the purpose of your coming to the United States?

JOHN BOORMAN: To make the film we had been talking about.

KAGON: During that time did you have any communications with Mr Marvin?

JOHN BOORMAN: Yes, of course, on a daily basis. For the most part I was calling on him. There was already a script in existence, which we completely rewrote, and during that period of three weeks, much of that writing was done, and I was working closely in collaboration with Mr Marvin on a daily basis.

KAGON: During that period of time did you have an occasion to meet Miss Marvin?

JOHN BOORMAN: Yes, well, I think the first – as far as I recall, the first time that we met was at Mr Marvin's house in Malibu. I didn't know of her until I arrived in Los Angeles.

KAGON: Now, on those occasions when you came to the house to discuss the story material with Mr Marvin, did Miss Marvin participate in any of those discussions?

JOHN BOORMAN: No.

KAGON: OK. Prior to the time that you commenced shooting, do you recall any telephone conversations during that period of time with the plaintiff?

JOHN BOORMAN: Yes, there were several conversations. During the preproduction period, I did receive a number of telephone calls from Michelle. On one occasion Michelle said that, when we were beginning to cast, she said that Lee was unhappy about an actor that I was proposing to cast in the film. She said that Lee was unhappy about it and that I – that I shouldn't tell Lee that she had called. But she wanted me to know he was unhappy and that she could – she would do what she could to help talk him around, and that she was on my side in the matter. On the next occasion that we met, I was slightly alarmed because Lee and I had a very close, open, and frank relationship of . . .

MITCHELSON: Objection, Your Honor.

KAGON: Your Honor, the relevancy is we are going to show a continued practice of interference in Mr Marvin's business affairs to ingratiate herself on these people. Why was he suddenly receiving a telephone call from Michelle; wouldn't he be talking to Lee on a very intimate basis about what they were doing? Mr Boorman, did you thereafter discuss that telephone call with Lee Marvin?

JOHN BOORMAN: No, but I discussed the substance of it, without referring to the telephone conversation, with Mr Marvin. I was surprised because . . . it was inconceivable to me that Lee would not mention any problem or difficulty that he had . . .

JUDGE: Did you reach a conclusion as to whether it was true or false?

JOHN BOORMAN: It was untrue.

KAGON: Were there any other conversations that you had with Miss Marvin that you recall with reference to the motion picture *Point Blank*?

JOHN BOORMAN: Yes. It was a similar conversation to the previous one. She said that Lee was distressed about a new scene that I had written. And she said she liked it, but he didn't; she would try and talk him around, but I should know that he was unhappy, and also that I shouldn't tell him that she had called. It wasn't true. I discussed the scene with Mr Marvin.

KAGON: Was Mr Marvin present on each and every day of shooting?

JOHN BOORMAN: I think there were, as I recall, two days during the course of the schedule that he was not required to be present.

KAGON: On those occasions when he was present, was he there during the entire shooting period?

JOHN BOORMAN: Yes, and more often than not we would confer during the evening, because we had a lot of things to discuss. We shot five days a week during the time that we were on location in the studio in MGM, in Los Angeles, and then a six-day schedule when we were outside the Los Angeles area. We worked most of the weekends on rehearsal and script revisions. He was a close collaborator on all aspects of the making of the film. He was very much involved in the script, in casting, all aspects of production . . . so that during these weekends, we were revising and rewriting and rehearsing with other actors. [*Thus refuting Michelle's testimony that Lee was so drunk 'he missed many calls on* Point Blank']

KAGON: Was the plaintiff ever present at any of those meetings or the editing process?

JOHN BOORMAN: No.

KAGON: When did you start discussing *Hell in the Pacific* with Mr Marvin?

JOHN BOORMAN: On my return from London to complete the film in September, we resumed the relationship which we had had on *Point Blank*, which was a continuous and daily collaboration. Including weekends.

Lee was now called to the stand to answer questions about his subsequent film. After discussing Michelle's pill overdose and Lee's inability to extricate himself from her presence, Marvin Mitchelson proceeded in a bland manner, blunting any impact Lee might have made with what he had said about his feelings after the suicide attempt.

MITCHELSON: OK. When did you decide to put her out again?

LEE: [*Looking at the ceiling and thinking aloud*] March, April, completed *Point Blank*. May, June, working again. September [*looking at Mitchelson*], I asked her not to accompany me on the next film, which was Palau, which would have been in the October sequence of 1967 . . . She refused to respond to my request.

MITCHELSON: Why did you have to take her, Mr Marvin?

LEE: Because of her conduct. She threatened me again with

these types of acts and I could not concentrate on my work – well, suffer under those constant bombardments of dialogue . . . I was extremely lacking in the educational ability to handle it – to get rid of her would be to exchange one set of horrors for another . . . I felt trapped, the lesser of two recourses would have been to take her. Her verbal and physical activity would be such that it became unbearable. She would break things in the house and scream and cry and kick, you know, very childlike activities saying, 'If you don't take me, I'll do something horrible.' She would kill herself, wreck my career, make statements to the press, things of that nature. She would cause deep embarrassment to me and my children.

MITCHELSON: You weren't married to her. Did she have a hold on you?

LEE: Obviously I wasn't able to throw her out. She had private information of my feelings, my nature, of my make-up that I didn't want disclosed. She would tell my business affairs, investments. I felt that I had sunk so low in the eyes of my friends and family that the only place to go from where I was at would be lower . . . and I wasn't willing to destroy myself.

MITCHELSON: You mean 'sunk so low' in the eyes of your family and friends because you were with Michelle? Living with Michelle?

LEE: Yes.

Hell in the Pacific

Michelle Triola's 'mutual effort' on the film *Hell in the Pacific* was the next to be explored.

Of all the movies of Lee's career, *Hell in the Pacific* was undoubtedly the most important to him on a personal level. In it he was reliving, exploring and resolving his feelings about his war, and putting the results on the screen. This was not something he had done before, and he was not to do it again with such complete openness. He was back on islands in the Pacific theater of operations where he had fought, and the only other actor in the entire film was the Japanese star Toshiro Mifune. At the same time that Lee was serving in the US Marine Corps fighting for his country, Toshiro Mifune was in the Japanese Imperial Army fighting for his. Working this out twenty-odd years later was an opportunity not many ex-soldiers have, and I know that for Lee it was of extreme importance. (Just after Lee and I were married he had the movie run for me. It was the only time he did this; and he told me privately that it was his favourite. He did not like publicly to admit to having a favourite, and when asked in interviews, his standard answer was, 'The next one.')

Because of the close collaboration between John Boorman and Lee on this movie, they scouted for the location together. The month-long search ended on the tiny, remote islands of the Palaus situated between New Guinea and the Philippines. Coming back to Los Angeles, they began working together on the story. In the courtroom, John and Lee explained in some detail what the working conditions were like and how much physical effort by all concerned went into the filming. Lee stopped by to see me at my house in Woodstock after he completed the movie, and I saw for myself the toll it had taken: he was noticeably gaunt and thin.

The island where they did the shooting was deceptive and rugged. Dense jungle curled down to the ocean. The beach where most of the action took place was thick with living coral outcrops that cut and infected the skin. Sub-tropical rains poured down and reduced the ground to a steaming swamp, making shooting impossible for days at a time. The gruelling four months of work – along with the two or three weeks of preparation and rehearsal – reduced the strongest constitution to near-exhaustion. Lee lost forty pounds in that short time, and John Boorman was out of commission and delirious for several days because of a coral infection of his leg.

Shooting for *Hell in the Pacific* began early in December 1967. The massive amounts of equipment – generators, lights, cameras, small boats, everything – had to come in by ship or plane. A cumbersome vintage DC-4 which landed there twice a week was the only lifeline to the outside world. The plane took the dailies back for processing and review, brought letters in and out, and carried the rare visitor from the studio, along with needed parts or equipment.

KAGON: How much of your time and attention were you devoting to the preproduction stage of *Hell in the Pacific*?

MITCHELSON: Your Honor, excuse me, I don't know, it might save some time if Mr Marvin, in narrative form, explained what he did on each of these pictures.

JUDGE: The court is happy to agree with you gentlemen and permit Mr Marvin to do so. Well, you finished your acting chores with *Point Blank*. What else did you do in connection with that film?

LEE: Well, at that time Mr Boorman was cutting *Point Blank* at Metro . . . I would go in and look at the sequences or reels . . . During the cutting process, when I no longer was in the rags, the wardrobe or on the payroll, John and I could step out from a cutting room or a projection room and generally talk about the future.

The discussions consisted of – we had no script or no story at the time and no idea of a proper story. We knew that Toshiro Mifune was the other actor – it was going to be a two-man project, two actors involved – and we tried to formulate in our conversations some kind of a situation that we could put these two extremely foreign people in, that would tell our feeling about the content, against war or extreme relations, and how that could in some way be conveyed to an audience with understanding.

I was doing a lot of Memory Lane-type thinking. I had been in the Pacific during the war, and I was recreating in my mind my feelings about those times, rereading a lot of old division books, and things of that nature . . . accounts of the various battles that I was involved in, and using them to conjure up my memories, or the ones that I had put away.

I read a lot more of other situations that I was not involved in, like *Baba Black Sheep* by Pappy Boyington, who was a Marine flier, and I figured that the furthest you could get away from the Marines would be a flier, to live on an aircraft carrier, in clean sheets or with hot meals, or in an airfield – this is just an assumption, naturally, of a scout sniper . . . a footslogger or a Marine . . .

JUDGE: Is that what you were?

LEE: . . . a rifleman, yes, and we also looked at any other form of military with secret envy, but not being able to attain that position, we thought they were kind of pussy-footers. But the extremes I was looking for had to be discussed in this manner. So I assumed, in my thinking, that it would have to be, if I were playing the role, a Marine pilot in a stressful situation.

Now what would be equal to that in the Japanese form – because they were fantastic troops – so I thought the most extreme thing in the Pacific of a Japanese soldier would be a naval officer. In other words, taking both of those men out of that position, and abandoning them on an island. However they got there is immaterial at this point – how would they behave?

MITCHELSON: I am going to have to object, Your Honor.

JUDGE: All right, Counsel, if you object, we will return to question and answer.

KAGON: Thank you, Your Honor. Mr Marvin, during the summer or the fall of 1967, was the plaintiff with you during that location tour?

LEE: She was not.

KAGON: Where did you go?

LEE: We went to Hawaii first of all, so we hit all the major islands there, the five. They did not impress us because they were too beautiful.

KAGON: What location did you eventually decide upon for the picture?

LEE: The island of Koror and surrounding territory, and the Palau district of Trust Territory of the Pacific Islands.

Lee said that the movie company lived for a short time at the Royal Palauian Hotel, a grand name considering its rusty, island simplicity. 'A Quonset hut with tin wall divisions,' he told the court. Their permanent quarters, when it arrived, became a Chinese ship, the MV *Oriental Hero*, which was then anchored offshore.

LEE: The ship was built in Germany, of Chinese registry out of either Hong Kong or Singapore. It had a Chinese crew and there were thirty-two staterooms on the ship for us, the movie company. It was a freighter-transport combination, a rather nice ship. It was built in 1958. Some of the crew, the movie crew, doubled up – that is, including the Japanese crew – for the Toshiro half of the film. And so whoever was on the film of foreign extraction, except for Mr Boorman and one or two other people, lived in those staterooms . . . There was a common dining room, for all meals aboard ship.

KAGON: Mr Marvin, who did the cooking for you and the plaintiff?

LEE: The Chinese crew.

KAGON: Was any cooking done in your room?

LEE: No.

KAGON: Who did the laundry for you and plaintiff? [*Because of the plaintiff's claim in the lawsuit, even the laundry had to be argued in this case*]

LEE: The Chinese crew.

KAGON: How far from Palau or the ship were the various locations that you went to?

LEE: From about half an hour to say – we had two speedboats for the principals. They could go very fast. So the furthest location would be about an hour forty-five minutes. They were rock islands, small beach, dense jungle.

KAGON: What time would you leave in the morning in order to get to the location?

LEE: Depending on the production of the day, of course, you would get up at the first light. We are close to the Equator, about six degrees above the Equator. So it would be about half night and half day. So, say, between five-thirty and six the sun would rise – and would set at the same time.

KAGON: When did you return from the set generally?

LEE: When we lost the light.

KAGON: How many days a week did you work?

LEE: Consistently six, except for weather provisions, and occasionally a seventh day.

KAGON: Do you know of your own knowledge what the plaintiff was doing during the time you were working?

LEE: Not really.

KAGON: Do you remember an episode where someone went out shark hunting during the period of time you were there?

LEE: No, I don't.

KAGON: Did you ever go out hunting for sharks?

LEE: I did not.

KAGON: Mr Marvin, do you recall any episode where you fell from a fifteen- or eighteen-foot cliff and hurt your head?

LEE: No.

KAGON: Do you recall any episode where you skinned your knees or legs on the coral?

LEE: Many times.

KAGON: Did you have any arguments with the plaintiff while you were there?

LEE: Many.

KAGON: What was the subject matter, to the best of your recollection, of those arguments?

LEE: Generally speaking, they were in conjunction with discussions that she would bring up concerning members of the company, and I would oppose that as not being in her jurisdiction, and requested that she didn't, you know, indulge in those conversations, with them or with me.

KAGON: Now, on your return from Palau were you then preparing for another film?

LEE: Yes, *Paint Your Wagon* . . . scheduled to start in June of that year. [*A short month and a half later*]

From Michelle Triola's testimony during the trial, we heard her version of what being on the location for *Hell in the Pacific* meant to her. Michelle's 'activities', as Lee called them, seemed to attain new heights – or depths – not to mention the things she apparently perceived because of her bizarre, often twisted, sense of reality. This came out not only in her testimony, but in a series of letters she fired back to Lee's agent Meyer Mishkin. With her taste for secrecy, Michelle asked Meyer not to tell Lee about these letters – and until the trial, Lee was unaware of them.

With Marvin Mitchelson questioning, Michelle Triola held that the film was another example of their 'mutual effort' in his professional career. She described her 'duties', as she called them.

MICHELLE: Well, we were living on a ship, and he was
    shooting a film, and the same duties I had in Malibu, or
    London, or wherever I was to be with him.
MITCHELSON: What services did you render?
MICHELLE: I cleaned the stateroom. And I cooked, believe it or
    not.
MITCHELSON: Where did you cook?
MICHELLE: I cooked in the galley.

In her deposition of 1972 she said she had cooked in the galley 'at
least ten times', but by the beginning of the trial she had changed
her mind once again, saying, 'No, no, not on that trip. We were on
an ocean liner so there was a dining room.'

Against all odds, Michelle would say anything that came into her
mind. In answer to her attorney's question, 'Let's take Palau – did
you do any of his laundry?' she answered, 'Yes, I picked up his
clothes, I sewed buttons on his clothes, I washed his shirts, washed
his shorts, his socks.'

It is hard to imagine her going into the galley of a large ocean
liner whose crew spoke only Chinese and puttering around with
pots and pans, and also that she would do the laundry – especially
on a movie location, where everything is done for the principals
and everyone else. Where would you hang the clothes? A little line
strung across the stateroom in the humid tropics? Lee was also a
fastidious person. I never saw him take off a jacket or shirt without
folding it very neatly over a silent butler or the back of a chair. I can
imagine how difficult it was for Lee to sit so calmly hour after hour
listening to such descriptions, and far worse.

Michelle was asked by Kagon if it were a fact that Lee preferred
to be alone on locations. Her answer was, 'Well, if he preferred
being alone, I never knew about it.'

It was a loaded question, of course, because she was asked to read
a letter she had written to Meyer Mishkin dated 14 February 1968.
She read it to herself, paused, and said to Kagon, 'I get the point.' He
then read aloud an excerpt from the letter: 'I have decided to go into
Honolulu anyway for a ten day change of scenery. Surprising
enough, Lee doesn't want me to go, but I think this time I'll use some
good sense and take a leave of absence. Usually he can't wait to be

alone,' and, 'He is starting to make those classic Marvin remarks to Boorman and John doesn't like it at all.'

On redirect Mitchelson picked up the letter Kagon had quoted and asked her to elaborate – to repair the damage.

MITCHELSON: [*Letter in hand*] 'Usually he can't wait to be alone.' What did you mean by that?

MICHELLE: Usually he can't wait to be alone to drink.

MITCHELSON: Was he drinking at that time?

MICHELLE: Yes.

MITCHELSON: 'By this time we haven't had the usual disagreements.' Were you referring to the liquor?

MICHELLE: Yes.

MITCHELSON: 'And I think he likes the idea that I have been able to stick it out this long.' Were you referring to the liquor again?

MICHELLE: Well, just everything. I mean, it was a very hard location; he was drinking, the doctor was drinking . . .

MITCHELSON: [*Interrupts*] Don't pound the table. We can't hear you when the table is being pounded.

MICHELLE: I'm sorry. The stuntmen were drinking; they were going straight out to sea, doing dangerous things, smashed, and it was difficult – it was difficult. I just felt that I would go into Honolulu to just get off the subject. I mean I . . .

MITCHELSON: [*Trying to stem the tide*] All right. One moment, please . . .

MICHELLE: [*Unstemmable*] I had to find a new tactic . . .

MITCHELSON: [*Interrupts her again*] New subject. Mr Mishkin – you wrote a few letters down there, didn't you? Now, did you write other letters to Mishkin and complain about Lee's drinking?

MICHELLE: Yes, many.

MITCHELSON: Here is another one. 'February 5, 1968,' he reads, 'Lee into heavy drinking . . .' and another one, 'February 18, 1969, Lee having a breakdown over drinking . . .' [*Continues with the leading questions*] Did you ever implore Mr Mishkin to do something about helping you out with Lee's drinking?

MICHELLE: Yes, I did.

MITCHELSON: Did you beg him to do so?

MICHELLE: Yes.

MITCHELSON: Did he help you out?

MICHELLE: No. [*Mitchelson's aide Penelope Mercurio is reading and hastily handing each letter to him*]

MITCHELSON: Here's one, a letter dated 26 December 1967 – the stamp at the top is the Orient Overseas Line *Oriental Hero* – and the last one is a letter that starts off, 'January 1967, Dear Meyer, they are into their second week of shooting, if you can call it that . . .'

These must have been very worrying letters for an actor's agent to receive, particularly from a remote location more than ten thousand miles away. In her first letter to Meyer Mishkin, on 2 January 1968, when *Hell in the Pacific* was being shot, she ingratiatingly promised to give him 'inside' information about Lee: 'I have no idea how or when the mail gets to the States, but I will give you information as to Lee . . .'

When Meyer was a witness, Marvin Mitchelson asked him, 'And did she keep you up to date as to what was happening in Palau?' Meyer replied, 'From *her* point of view.' (I felt from the beginning that Meyer was not an unwilling recipient of Michelle's information about Lee, whether he believed it or not.)

Lee heard these letters read in court. He had not seen or heard of them before, and all he could say after court was, 'For Christ's sake!'

Another December letter to Meyer from Michelle reads: 'Christmas eve, late in the afternoon, stoned out of his head, they sent him out fishing for sharks alone. At the last minute I jumped in the boat with Lee and this crazy Palauian, and after losing our way in the dark a half-dozen times, we finally saw some lights around ten o'clock.' Next line: 'I was furious at John for sending Lee out like that, and told him so.'

MITCHELSON: What did you say to Mr Boorman and what did he say to you at the time it happened?

MICHELLE: John was standing on the dock. I said, 'John, help me get Lee off the boat before it takes off,' and he wouldn't help. I said, 'John, you can see that Lee has been drinking, and will you help me get him off the boat? I'm afraid that he will fall in the water.'

MITCHELSON: What did John Boorman say to you?

MICHELLE: This was at the start of – I don't believe that they were shooting yet, and I had heard . . .

MITCHELSON: [*Interrupts*] No, just tell me what you said, Miss Marvin.

MICHELLE: They said that the Palauians didn't know how to swim, and I asked John to help me get Lee off the boat – and he said, 'I can't get Lee off the boat.'

MITCHELSON: All right . . .

MICHELLE: . . . so I jumped on the boat.

MITCHELSON: You jumped on the boat, and what did you do?

MICHELLE: . . . and just got lost at sea, and just, you know, saw that Lee didn't get too near the edge.

MITCHELSON: Now, let me go back to the letter: 'Lee was in total agreement with me, and thought that John should have known better.' Did you discuss this with Mr Marvin and what did you say?

MICHELLE: Well, from what Lee said to me, he didn't really know that they were going out looking for sharks.

MITCHELSON: All right. Then the letter says: 'Lee was too stoned to even remember he had been on a boat . . . I told John that I was going to write to you and tell you what had happened.' And did you write to Meyer?

KAGON: The letter speaks for itself, Your Honor.

MITCHELSON: Well, Your Honor, that may be true, and I submit to you that she tried to save the man's life, and was concerned with him falling overboard amongst a pool of sharks. Further, I intend to show that Mr Marvin shared the same complaints about Mr Boorman that Miss Marvin wrote to Mr Mishkin about hoarding of food, and everything else. Very well, I will ask her instead of reading. Did you ever have any discussion at all with Mr Marvin about Mr Boorman's wife Christel, concerning food?

MICHELLE: Lee asked *me* if Christel was taking – this was at the beginning of the trip – if Christel Boorman was taking food off the ship, and I told Lee that I didn't know whether she was or not, and he asked me to speak to the production manager, to get the right story, and I forget the production manager's name, so I spoke to the gentleman . . . I told Lee that what I had found out was that the Ibedul [the island chief] had spoken on the ship . . . that he didn't want the price of food to go up on the small island, because the Ibedul said that Mrs Boorman was going into the bakery shop and paying four dollars a loaf of bread, and naturally the person baking the bread would rather give the loaf of bread to Mrs Boorman than one of the Palauians.

MITCHELSON: This *you* told *Lee*?

MICHELLE: Yes, and then he – he didn't want that to start happening on the island, and that is where that hoarding of food – I mean – I told Lee that she was buying a fruit called King Kong, and that when I opened her refrigerator they all came rolling out.

When on the witness stand, John Boorman spoke about the filming from the director's point of view, again describing a pattern of intense work and long hours every day, with no involvement of the plaintiff.

KAGON: Now, during the shooting of *Hell in the Pacific*, did you have any meetings with the plaintiff Miss Marvin, any conversations with her with regard to the production of the film?

JOHN BOORMAN: No, and in point of fact, within a week or two of the commencement of the location, she ceased to address me at all.

KAGON: Mr Boorman, will you please describe the event following which the plaintiff ceased to address you?

JOHN BOORMAN: Well, the occasion was a certain confrontation between Michelle, Lee, myself and the owner of a store in Palau. The incident concerned an accusation that had been made . . . I said to Miss Marvin, 'You have accused me and my wife of buying things in the store and charging them to the account of Mr Marvin.' [*That would hardly qualify as constructive help with a movie: accusing the director and his wife of theft!*] I asked the storekeeper to say this was not true, which he did.

KAGON: What did Miss Marvin say at that time?

JOHN BOORMAN: She was confused. She said that . . . well, that she had been told that this is what I have been doing or my wife had been doing.

KAGON: What did the storekeeper say?

JOHN BOORMAN: He said that not only had I not done that, nor had my wife, but that nobody did it in his store because he didn't even take a check.

KAGON: On any of those occasions, do you recall whether the plaintiff was present on the shooting location?

JOHN BOORMAN: Not at all, I don't think. There were no extraneous people on the beach.

KAGON: Was Mr Marvin present each day that the shooting occurred?

JOHN BOORMAN: He was.

KAGON: Did you observe the relationship between the plaintiff and the defendant while they were on the ship?

JOHN BOORMAN: Of course, yes. What did I observe of their relationship? It was erratic and strained.

KAGON: Mr Boorman, I show you a letter dated 11 December 1967, Exhibit 81. Mr Boorman, did you ever have Lee – meaning Lee Marvin – fall off a fifteen-foot cliff 'while in the state that he was in'?

JOHN BOORMAN: Did I have him fall off a cliff? No, not in any state.

KAGON: Do you recollect, was he all cut up on his back and head?

JOHN BOORMAN: He was not.

KAGON: I have no further questions of this witness, Your Honor.

JUDGE: Cross-examine.

MITCHELSON: Thank you, Your Honor. Mr Boorman, last evening you looked at some letters, didn't you, sir?

JOHN BOORMAN: Yes.

MITCHELSON: These were a total surprise to you?

JOHN BOORMAN: Yes.

MITCHELSON: Now when you looked at Exhibit 77 and you read the following: 'Now John came in tonight' – that is you – 'and says he wants to reshoot the whole picture. Lee came in the stateroom a few minutes ago and is very depressed. He won't admit it to himself that the crew doesn't dig Boorman and that they are not moving as fast as they would for someone that they really liked.' That upset you to read that, didn't it, sir?

JOHN BOORMAN: No.

MITCHELSON: You didn't like it, though, did you?

JOHN BOORMAN: It didn't upset me. Because that is the kind of talk you get around film units of every kind.

MITCHELSON: Now, how about Exhibit 59? It says – let's see – 'stoned out of his head, they sent him out fishing for sharks alone'. Did you know what Michelle was talking about when you read that?

JOHN BOORMAN: No, I don't recall this incident. I do recall that I never sent him out on a boat to fish for sharks because there would have been absolutely no point in that. I had no interest in sending him out to fish for sharks or anything else.

MITCHELSON: Now it says, 'Lloyd told the Boormans . . .' Who is Lloyd?

JOHN BOORMAN: Lloyd Anderson, production manager.

MITCHELSON: All right. He told the Boormans that 'everything they had charged to the company they would have to pay for out of their expense money and they were shocked. John had ordered all Swedish modern furniture from Tokyo to put in the house they rented here and charged it to Selmur as necessary to their comfort here in Palau, and when they found out they had to pay for it out of their own money, they have sent a wire trying to cancel it.' Well, did anything like that happen?

JOHN BOORMAN: No.

MITCHELSON: Did you order some furniture?

JOHN BOORMAN: No. I mean I have never heard of anybody ordering furniture for a location.

MITCHELSON: Were you in Tokyo before you came to Palau?

JOHN BOORMAN: Yes, I was.

MITCHELSON: Did you ever look at some Swedish modern furniture?

JOHN BOORMAN: Tokyo is not the place where I would buy Swedish furniture.

MITCHELSON: I can think of a good one, but I'll pass on it. The answer is no?

JOHN BOORMAN: The answer is no, sir.

MITCHELSON: Now, did that upset you when you read that last night?

JOHN BOORMAN: No, it didn't upset me because I just thought it was rather ludicrous.

MITCHELSON: Well, do you think Michelle just made that up out of whole cloth?

JOHN BOORMAN: Well, certainly her imagination seems to be virulent.

John later recounted that Michelle had succeeded in convincing Lee that he and Christel were charging to his account. Lee came to John quite distraught and said, 'John, are you having money problems? Please let me help you. I can give you anything you need.'

It pained John greatly to think that Lee must have believed her whisperings. He was so enraged by these terrible lies that he took her literally by the throat and marched her up to Lee, making her retract her accusations.

She also spread rumors that John was always pestering her to get drugs: heroin. 'I don't mind a little marijuana,' she would complain, 'but heroin is too much.' John felt she was either so vicious that she could make these things up and say them without a second thought, or was simply insane.

LaVerna Hogan was called for the defense and testified that she was present during the filming of *Hell in the Pacific* because her husband was production manager on the second unit.

LAVERNA HOGAN: I was simply a wife that went along. I would relieve the production secretary at times.

KAGON: Mrs Hogan, while you were on board ship, who did the cooking, who did the laundry?

LAVERNA HOGAN: The Chinese nationalists that were the crew of the ship.

KAGON: Where did you eat while you were on board ship?

LAVERNA HOGAN: The principals and the main part of our crew took over the Captain's table, because we would discuss the picture, what was happening the next day, what had happened.

KAGON: Now did the plaintiff and the defendant also eat at the Captain's table?

LAVERNA HOGAN: Yes, they did.

KAGON: How frequently would you see them?

LAVERNA HOGAN: Daily.

KAGON: Based upon your observation, what was the nature of the demeanor of the plaintiff and the defendant toward each other?

LAVERNA HOGAN: Argumentative.

KAGON: Did they appear to be friendly from time to time?

LAVERNA HOGAN: From time to time they were friendly.

KAGON: I have no further questions, Your Honor.

JUDGE: Cross-examine.

MITCHELSON: [*Showing Mrs Hogan a letter dated 5 February 1968 from Michelle to Meyer Mishkin*] You know Mr Mishkin, don't you?

LAVERNA HOGAN: No sir, I never met him.

MITCHELSON: He's the gentleman in the first row next to Mrs Marvin. Now I'm going to read from the third paragraph, and then I'll stop and ask you a question. This was written from Palau on or about February 5: 'I feel very dubious about leaving Lee here by himself. By that, I don't mean because of women or anything, I mean there is no one that understands the problem, and sometimes he doesn't eat for days at a time.' Does that help refresh your recollection that you seldom saw him sitting at the Captain's table on the ship *Oriental*?

LAVERNA HOGAN: I know he visited the other tables and talked to the other people, would sit down with them. But I don't remember one night he did *not* eat at the Captain's table.

MITCHELSON: Now let me go on: 'I panic that he will fall down when he's stoned or fall off one of the decks or a million things that people around here think are so funny.'

Now, you have seen Lee Marvin fall down on to the ground after having drinks, didn't you?

LAVERNA HOGAN: I have never seen him fall.

MITCHELSON: Have you ever seen him stumble?

LAVERNA HOGAN: I never saw him stumble.

MITCHELSON: [*Reads from letter*] 'Then they really laugh at him behind his back and say, "Isn't it too bad." If I could know that there was someone that would watch him from a distance, or something, I would feel a lot better.' All right. Let me go on: 'Now the new thing is "See that Mr Marvin has a bottle of vodka at the breakfast table."' I suggest that every morning, for a period of two weeks almost, there was a bottle of vodka sitting at his table for breakfast in the morning.

LAVERNA HOGAN: Not when I was there.

MITCHELSON: [*Reads from letter*] 'I happen to know that Lee never asked for one and was quite shocked when they brought it to him, and proceeded in downing the whole thing . . . He has been very good up till now, and it really makes me mad that most of the people around here think it's quite funny to see him walking around drunk.'

LAVERNA HOGAN: Again, I have never seen him in this condition.

MITCHELSON: A little more: 'Meyer, I have nothing more to say on this subject. Maybe you can clue Selmur in on your end.' Now you know that the picture was made by Selmur Productions. You don't remember Michelle telling you something like that, Mrs Hogan?

LAVERNA HOGAN: No, I don't, but nobody on a show that has charge of it is going to get their principal star smashed.

MITCHELSON: I ask that that be stricken, Your Honor, as being a conclusion.

It boggles the mind searching for some purpose behind what Michelle was writing to Lee's agent and asking him to tell the movie's producers. Even if her stories of Lee's drinking and behaviour had been true, what end would it serve for her to notify the studio? And why, if these things were really happening, did not the director or the on-site production company – the professionals who were hardly likely to stand by while the star destroyed their film – complain about Lee? Michelle was not writing personal letters to a girlfriend or a member of her family, she was firing off letter after letter to Lee's agent asking him to notify the studio executives.

Instead of proving her point, it seemed to confirm the opposite: she was a detriment to Lee's career, interfering with his professional life to an unpardonable degree.

Also, most of the witnesses disputed Michelle's assertion that she was known as Lee's wife, 'held out as married'. Nowhere in the world, it seems, is there a place so remote that you can say anything you want. An attorney from the Los Angeles County offices came forward to swear – against almost hysterical objections from Marvin Mitchelson – that he had been in Palau in early 1968 when *Hell in the Pacific* was being filmed. A volunteer in the Peace Corps in his official capacity, he spoke Palauian and was assigned to the Trust Territory to carry out land management and serve on the legislative council for Yap Island. Later he was with the US Department of Interior.

Mr Farrell testified that he knew many people there, native and non-native, including the chiefs. People spoke to him about Lee Marvin and Michelle Triola 'who lived with him', which contradicts Michelle's contention that she was held to be his wife in Palau. He was present when a benefit performance by the cast of *Hell in the Pacific* was put on in the auditorium of the Catholic School at Koror. The announcer told the three or four hundred people assembled that there was 'an error in the program. It was not Mr and Mrs Lee Marvin, or Mrs Marvin, it was Lee Marvin and Michelle Triola.'

Since he knew neither the plaintiff nor the defendant, Farrell had no axe to grind. He was the perfect witness.

Paint Your Wagon

The court's exploration of how Michelle had helped Lee with his career now reached *Paint Your Wagon*. Lee was asked what preparations he had made for this movie.

LEE: Again, reading up on the gold rush, musical rehearsals, wardrobe and actual rehearsals of about two weeks.

Paint Your Wagon was a movie Lee really enjoyed doing: the men, the partners, the romance of the gold rush. It was a long movie to make and an extravagant one. The starting date was just two months after he returned from Palau, and it wrapped in November.

The film was shot high in the mountains outside Baker, Oregon, and meant hard outdoor work from early morning until dark six days a week. Lee spent a good deal of time falling into cold mountain streams, digging for gold, and slogging through the spring mud. He loved the wooded wilderness, however, and very much liked his co-stars, his friend Clint Eastwood and Jean Seberg (who he felt was sweet-natured and naïve, easily taken in by the different organizations she tried to help – such as the Black Panthers). It was also the beginning of his lifelong friendship with Josh and Nedda Logan. The subject matter and the large, congenial cast gave him a lively enthusiasm for the project. His son Christopher, now aged fifteen, was with him to keep him company and earn a little money working in the wardrobe department. His three daughters also came for a week's visit – one of the few times they did, as he and his children were estranged during the time Michelle was with him.

Lee watched every scene of the filming and gave a brief summary of it himself.

LEE: It was about the gold strike in California in 1850, the major one up in the Feather River district. The cast was very large. It was tremendous, a very big picture. On locations we had 450 extras up in the mountains, in the camp itself, in the town we built, and then we had about 35 or 40 major principals and, I imagine, around 100 bits. There were close to a thousand involved. The actual shooting location was in the Willowa Whitman Wilderness area and was on the East Eagle Creek. I don't know how far from town it was as the crow flies, but by car, which I generally took, it would be an hour fifteen, hour and a half.

He would get up at 5 a.m., he said, have coffee at his house, eat breakfast on the set, and have his main meal at lunchtime on the set. He returned home at anywhere from 6.30 to 7.30 each night.

Lee's preparation for this film was thorough: he researched the gold rush of 1850, metallurgy, mining techniques, the era and the costumes. He became well acquainted with the subject, and put this to good use when we bought our own gold mine later. As usual, he enjoyed the ride to work while at the same time concentrating on the day's work schedule.

Michelle Triola was there in Baker, Oregon, too, but her testimony under oath presented a much darker picture of Lee at the end of his rope, almost incapacitated from drinking, and 'frightened'.

> MICHELLE: Again I would say to him – I asked him one time why he was the only one driving to the set: 'Is it because you want that time to drink and you need that time to drink on the way coming home?' . . . Because it was a two-and-a-half hour drive on a winding mountainous road, I asked him if he was frightened to fly, and he said that sometimes he was frightened to fly, that we are all going to crash one of these days and that the money aspect of this film was consuming him. I asked him, 'What do you mean about the money aspect?' and he said, 'Well, do you see that jet coming in with a salami on it every day?' [*Her rambling is stopped by an objection from Kagon*]

Michelle Triola's testimony revealed the bitter arguments she had had with many people in the company, and outside, during the filming: Lee's driver, a housekeeper (who quit and then sued her and Lee), various stunt men and Lee's stand-in and stuntman Boyd Cabeen.

Although Cabeen had once been one of her closest friends and confidants – he and Pat Hulsman had taken Michelle in after her suicide attempt – she reserved for him one of her most scathing attacks of the trial after he testified in Lee's defense.

> KAGON: Did you ever ask Mr Marvin to discontinue his friendship with Mr Cabeen?
> MICHELLE: Absolutely, yes.

KAGON: Because Mr Cabeen was under the influence of alcohol, as far as you were concerned?

MICHELLE: That was one of the reasons, but that was one of the lesser reasons. Mr Cabeen never liked Mr Marvin and used to talk about him behind his back, and it made me sick when I saw him here . . . Mr Cabeen is a thief, he is a liar, he is a parasite, and I can't even describe what that man is . . . yes, I did not like Tyrone Cabeen from the minute I saw him stealing chips from Lee, who was drunk, and Mr Cabeen and I had a running gun battle the whole time that I was with Mr Marvin.

KAGON: And yet you did go to Mr Cabeen's house when you came out of the hospital in 1967?

MICHELLE: I went there to see Mrs Cabeen – Pat Hulsman. I never asked Mr Cabeen to do anything for me. The man lied.

At the trial's end she spun a sinister and highly imaginative tale about Boyd beating Pat so badly that she had 'lesions all over her body' and then hiding, drunk, in a tiny woodshed. Michelle came and saved the day once more.

Boyd Cabeen was now asked about his friendship with Michelle Triola.

KAGON: Do you recall any conversations with the plaintiff, during the filming of the motion picture *Paint Your Wagon*, regarding a change of name?

BOYD CABEEN: Yes.

KAGON: Was anyone else present?

BOYD CABEEN: No, we usually talked alone. Well, let's see – there was a chauffeur, Mr Marvin's driver and chauffeur, and Michelle asked me to fire the chauffeur and I said, 'Why do you want me to fire him?' I thought he was a good man. I said, 'Why?' and she said, 'Because he called me "Michelle".' I said, 'Oh? What do you want him to call you?' 'Well, Mrs Marvin. I want to have some respect.' 'He is calling you by the name he knows,' I said. 'If you want to be known as Mrs Marvin, the next time you are in Hollywood, for twenty-five dollars you can go to court and have your name changed to Marvin.' It was in jest, and about three weeks later I was standing with a group of actors and I moved away when she approached me. She had just come back from a trip to Hollywood and she said she did what I told her, and I asked, 'What is that?' She said, 'About changing the name.'

Perhaps this was the germ of an idea that she did not act on until later. But for whatever reason, Michelle took a trip to Los Angeles during the filming of *Paint Your Wagon* and went directly to Lee's attorney Louis Goldman. Mr Goldman was therefore called by Marvin Mitchelson to the witness stand.

Testimony from Lee's theatrical attorneys, his agent and his publicists explained in detail not only their own professions but by extension Lee's. The three professions were Lee's base of support. Most actors and other creative people don't like to have much to do with the business end, preferring – and needing – other people to take charge of it. (Though they are by no means always successful in getting trustworthy aid, particularly when a lot of money is involved.) The people he chose to surround himself with were, in most cases, extremely articulate, highly-principled professionals who became his close personal friends as well as enjoying long-enduring partnerships; this was the case with Louis Goldman and David Kagon.

Mitchelson questioned Goldman in a pugnacious manner, pacing up and down in front of him, and adding an exaggerated 'sir' at the end of each question. Though both men were attorneys, the differences between them were marked. Louis Goldman was probably in his early seventies, kindly-looking, tall, conservatively dressed, neatly groomed, and with a look of great good humor. He was comfortably straightforward and totally unflappable in the face of Mitchelson's increasingly antagonistic approach. By contrast, Mitchelson appeared unkempt, no matter how hard he tried to wear his three-piece suits nattily. At times he was thrown by Louis' answers, which were given in a conversational tone with a 'helpfully getting to the bottom of it' delivery. Louis was an absolute gentleman with a very firm grasp of the facts, and he proved to be far better than Marvin Mitchelson at legal duelling – which of course drove Mitchelson crazy.

On the other hand, since Goldman was an attorney, and

therefore used to being on the other side of the box, he had some trouble conforming to the rules of the game. At one point, Mitchelson asked him if there was a reason why he had not taken notes at a certain meeting with Michelle.

LOUIS GOLDMAN: I think there possibly was. It was not an adversary meeting, it was a meeting which . . .

MITCHELSON: [*Interrupting*] Excuse me, is the answer yes?

LOUIS GOLDMAN: Well, I've got to answer the question . . .

MITCHELSON: [*Sharply*] No, you can answer the question yes or no, sir, like any other witness, please.

JUDGE: [*Interjecting more pleasantly*] Mr Goldman, I know lawyers who take the witness stand have . . .

LOUIS GOLDMAN: [*Helpfully*] Difficulty?

JUDGE: . . . unusual ideas as to how a witness should testify, but one of the usual ideas, that you must practice as anybody else, is when you are asked a question that calls for or can be answered yes or no, that you do so. Then if you have some explanation to make thereafter, you may make it.

LOUIS GOLDMAN: Your Honor . . .

JUDGE: [*Paying no attention*] But first, will you precede it with a yea or nay so that the questioning lawyer knows in which direction you are going?

LOUIS GOLDMAN: [*Trying again*] Your Honor . . .

JUDGE: Will you do that?

LOUIS GOLDMAN: Yes, I can – but did you know that I think he asked me *why*?

JUDGE: I didn't recollect that.

There was an almost complete breakdown of protocol by the end, with everyone talking at once. Our lawyer Bernie Lohr-Schmidt jumped in, saying, 'Give him a yes or no to his question.' Louis then replied directly to his own attorney (which was way against the rules): 'The question about my notes?' Judge Marshall cried out, 'Just a moment, just a moment,' trying to call a halt now that both Bernie Lohr-Schmidt and Marvin Mitchelson were attempting to lead him. Finally, with a scolding from the judge, we all got back on track.

JUDGE: He is not going to give anyone anything, he is going to answer truthfully as best he can. Now we will go back to the question. Put it again.

Those of us who had experienced the rigours of court procedure ourselves – and been frightened or embarrassed because of our ignorance – enjoyed seeing someone tangle it up so comprehensively and yet suffer no ill consequences.

MITCHELSON: I had asked you, and I will ask you again, was there some reason you did not take any notes? You can answer that yes or no.

LOUIS GOLDMAN: Oh, I see, I understand. Yes.

MITCHELSON: [*After much ado about nothing*] What *was* the reason you took no notes?

Goldman then repeated exactly the answer he had given before, and which had been so strenuously objected to.

Kagon asked Goldman about the visit from Michelle.

LOUIS GOLDMAN: Michelle called me on the telephone, either from Oregon or Los Angeles, she wanted to talk to me about something. I checked with my wife and then invited Michelle to my house for dinner.

She asked me if it was much trouble to have her name changed from Triola to Marvin. I asked her whether or not she had discussed this with Lee, and she said it was Lee's *idea* . . . Later in the evening she took me aside and she said, 'Lou, I would like you to do me a favor. Could you contact Lee and see whether or not Lee could put some property in my name? I have nothing specific in mind; maybe the house, or something else. Perhaps a lump sum.' She said, 'You know I have to watch out for myself. I don't know whether or not this relationship with Lee will last for ever.' I said, 'Well, why don't you talk to Lee about it instead of me?'

She also said that Lee had a great deal of respect for me and that if I advised him that it was the right thing to do, that perhaps he would do so, I could change his mind. I told her I didn't exercise that influence over Lee.

KAGON: After the dinner meeting, did you have a discussion

with Mr Marvin regarding the subject of the name change?

LOUIS GOLDMAN: Yes. As soon as I could reach him in Oregon by telephone . . . he absolutely refused to accede to her wishes.

MITCHELSON: [*Taking a different tack*] As a matter of fact, she told you that Lee was intoxicated a lot up in Baker, Oregon, didn't she?

LOUIS GOLDMAN: No, she didn't, Mr Mitchelson. Not a word of that.

MITCHELSON: [*Skeptically*] Uh-hum.

LOUIS GOLDMAN: No, she did not.

MITCHELSON: [*Irritated by Goldman's assertion that he had no influence over Lee in personal matters*] Now, as a matter of fact, you were amused by the fact that Michelle thought you had any influence over Lee Marvin, weren't you?

LOUIS GOLDMAN: I was, and I would like to explain.

JUDGE: Go ahead.

LOUIS GOLDMAN: I was amused because Michelle – not once, but fifty times – told me how much she was doing for Lee. Because I had nothing to do with her relationship with Lee.

Mitchelson was frustrated at not being able to force Lee's attorney to reveal privileged attorney-client conversation. But the more he lost his temper, the worse things became for him.

MITCHELSON: May I make a motion now? I'm going to move in the interest of justice that every single line of this man's testimony be stricken from this trial. And I appeal to the court to please give me some relief from it and strike Mr Goldman's testimony. It's not fair.

JUDGE: I don't know what you are doing right now, Counsel, making a motion of some kind. The motion is denied.

MITCHELSON: Now you said before, Mr Goldman, that Michelle about fifty times would just keep telling you how good she was for Lee and talking about the drinking problem, right?

LOUIS GOLDMAN: Yes.

MITCHELSON: And you wouldn't even answer her on those occasions, would you?

LOUIS GOLDMAN: No, but I would like to explain my answer.

JUDGE: You may.

MITCHELSON: What does he have to explain about a 'no' answer? May I suggest, it does allow Mr Goldman a forum to lecture. If Your Honor wants to permit it, I can't stop it.

JUDGE: [*Showing rare annoyance*] Now, Counsel, the forum is granted to him by the law and the constitution of this United States.

LOUIS GOLDMAN: All right. On more than one occasion Michelle told me that Lee was intoxicated, and I could not talk to him. Because later, within an hour or less, I called back to talk to Michelle, and Lee answered the phone, and I found out he was not intoxicated, that's what I found out . . .

MITCHELSON: [*Interrupting*] You never told us that in the deposition.

LOUIS GOLDMAN: You never asked me.

MITCHELSON: Of course, but I didn't ask you now either [*laughter in the courtroom*]. I'm sorry, Your Honor, I couldn't suppress it.

JUDGE: I can see how that would slip out, Counsel.

But this was only a brief respite. Mitchelson returned to the attack.

MITCHELSON: That night when Michelle was at your home, did she tell you it was reported by a local columnist that the film was held up because of Lee's drinking?

LOUIS GOLDMAN: No. She wasn't complaining about Lee. She was talking about trying to get something put in her name.

MITCHELSON: [*Coughing*] Your Honor, I need a drink of water.

JUDGE: Go ahead.

MITCHELSON: [*Temporarily recovering*] In connection with the property, Mr Goldman, didn't you tell Michelle also that she was getting along fine and Lee was treating her pretty good and not to worry about property, something like that?

LOUIS GOLDMAN: Nothing like that, Mr Mitchelson. Nothing.

MITCHELSON: [*Almost choking but reluctant to give up his line of questioning*] Did you tell her when she said to you . . .
JUDGE: [*Concerned*] Go get yourself some more water.

He left the room. A few minutes later Judge Marshall instructed Mitchelson's aide Penelope Mercurio to go and see what he was doing.

PENELOPE MERCURIO: I think he is just coughing.
JUDGE: I can hear him out here. [*After a pause*] We will take the afternoon recess at this time – ten minutes.

But it proved to be the end of the day. We were standing outside in the hall when the paramedics arrived. They bundled Marvin Mitchelson on to a stretcher, put an oxygen mask over his face, and were rushing him out as Michelle pooh-poohed the incident to the press: 'Oh, he always gets that way when he's frustrated.'

Michelle's version of her meeting with Mr Goldman was decidedly different when the court reconvened days later. It had been an urgent mercy mission, undertaken at her own risk to get help for Lee. She spoke with disgust when describing Lee's 'drunkenness' and the chauffeurs.

MITCHELSON: Miss Marvin, did you ever have any problems with the crew on any production that Mr Marvin worked on?
MICHELLE: No. I mean, unless you would call Lee's stand-in and driver part of the crew. I don't consider them part of the crew.
MITCHELSON: Chauffeur – referring to who?
MICHELLE: The chauffeur, whomever the chauffeur was. I used to have problems with the drivers.
MITCHELSON: Why did you have problems with the drivers?
MICHELLE: Because they would always have . . . not always, but invariably they would have liquor in the trunk of their cars. [*Apparently dismissing the 'addressing her as Michelle' incident*]

She flew to Los Angeles, she said, risking her life in a storm, to see Lee's attorney.

MICHELLE: I called Mr Goldman from Baker. I called Lou and I said I had to see him right away, that evening. He asked me what was the matter, and I said I had to talk to him immediately and that I was coming down.

MITCHELSON: Did any of your conversation, any bit of it, involve a discussion of a change of name?

MICHELLE: No, I said to Lou, 'Lou, you've got to convince Meyer that Lee had got to seek some professional help,' because I just – I was tired, and I needed help. I needed help with Lee.

MITCHELSON: What else?

MICHELLE: I said that Lee was in the middle of the street in Baker, Oregon, kicking cars that were parked at stop signs, and that he was just impossible. He wouldn't – I didn't know whether to – I mean, he couldn't work a lot, and I didn't know – I needed help. I was calling Meyer to ask . . . whether I should put him in the car, stand him on his marks – could they sue him? There was talk that if he didn't get to work that there would be a lawsuit. There was talk . . .

MITCHELSON: Continue.

MICHELLE: There had been things in the newspaper that Lee was unhappy with the director. There was an article in the newspaper that the director was being replaced at Lee's request. And then Mr Logan had come over and talked to Lee personally.

MITCHELSON: Was this what you told Mr Goldman?

MICHELLE: Yes, yes . . . And I told Lou that – that it was impossible for me to be able to make the kind of decisions that I was making then. I didn't know if I was doing the right thing in telling people that Lee had the flu. I didn't know. I needed help. I needed help and I wanted to see if – I – I regarded Lou as . . .

She would start out on a thought, but it would suddenly change in the middle. She'd run out of steam and eventually start on some other topic.

MITCHELSON: Just tell us what you told him.

MICHELLE: He said that he – he would try, that he would

332

speak to Meyer. And he tried to calm me down. And I kept – I kept on saying that . . . if something wasn't done, in my opinion at that time there wouldn't – that there wouldn't *be* a Lee Marvin.

Kagon put one question to Lee on this subject, 'Were you on location every day?' Lee answered firmly, 'I can't think of when I was not.'

When the court turned to the matter of Michelle Triola's aid to Lee on the movie *Monte Walsh*, this started to look more like perfidy than help. The end result of her involvement was a suit she and Marvin Mitchelson brought against the producers of the movie, Bobby Roberts and Hal Landers, demanding payment of $75,000. Her complaint alleged that on 15 March 1968 she entered into an oral agreement with the defendants, Roberts and Landers, concerning a private 'deal' she claimed she had made with them when she passed information on to them about Lee's interest in the project.

Her deposition, taken by attorneys for Roberts and Landers, and her later testimony in the trial against Lee were so contradictory that trying to follow any given statement was as confusing as a trip through the Coney Island maze. She baffled even the logical minds of trained attorneys, as well as the usually clear-headed Judge Marshall, who looked as close to scratching his head as anyone had ever seen him. His pencil wrote, erased, scribbled again and fell limp in his hand. There were so many different answers to the same question that preserving any continuity was tortuously hard, if not impossible.

In Michelle's deposition, taken under oath by Michael R. Shapiro, the lawyer for Roberts and Landers, she told of her alleged meetings with these producers and of their arrangement.

MICHAEL SHAPIRO: Would you please state your full name?
MICHELLE: Michelle Marvin – Michelle Triola Marvin.
MICHAEL SHAPIRO: Is that Miss or Mrs?
MICHELLE: Miss.
MICHAEL SHAPIRO: Where did this meeting take place on or about 15 March 1968?
MICHELLE: In their office. I believe it was on Beverly Drive – here.

It was in the afternoon, she believed, some time after lunch – a working day, she thought, and there had been an appointment.

MICHELLE: Mr Roberts made it known to me that he just . . . had sold Dunhill Records . . . and that they were very interested in going into production, and if ever I came across a property that I knew that Lee wanted to do to please let them know, and that I would have a piece of them. I said that I did have a project that I knew he wanted to do, although I did not tell them about it that day.

MICHAEL SHAPIRO: Were there any other details discussed?

MICHELLE: Only that . . . I understood that a Lee Marvin picture would absolutely put them on the map. In those words. It would be a feather in their cap, you know, that sort of thing.

There were many other meetings, she said, but this was the first with Mr Landers and Mr Roberts.

MICHELLE: Yes. With a meeting soon after, I believe in their office, because that is when I brought the script over . . . within a month of the first meeting.

. . . And we decided that – in other words, that I did not want – in other words, a percentage from the studio. We decided between the three of us, that I would have *half* of them. I mean – in other words – that we would – it was between the three of us. It had nothing to do financially with the grosses of the picture.

Bobby suggested that they could squeeze it into the budget of the picture – in other words, my half, or what have you. And I said, 'No, I do not want it that way' . . . I did not want to be put on the payroll or anything like this. In other words, that I would not go along with it unless it was an agreement between the three of us.

MICHAEL SHAPIRO: Were there other meetings after this second one?

MICHELLE: Many, many, many.

MICHAEL SHAPIRO: You alleged that on or about 22 September 1969, you demanded your fees? Where did this demand take place?

MICHELLE: Well, I don't understand the word 'demand' – I
   don't, you know. Are you correlating 'demand' with asking?
   You know, I couldn't get an appointment. They evaded me.

Eventually she said she had three meetings with them, but to no
avail.

MICHELLE: . . . I mean, I just couldn't believe it, and then Mr
   Landers leaned over the desk, and he said, 'We are not
   going to pay you. We are just not going to pay you,
   Michelle.' And I said, 'Well, you have to pay me,' and I was
   – I don't really know what – I was in a state of shock and
   was crying. I couldn't believe that this had happened to me
   because I – I just never – and they said, 'Well, you know,
   you don't have a leg to stand on. You have nothing in
   writing, you know?'
MICHAEL SHAPIRO: Who said it?
MICHELLE: I don't recall.

They did not pay her, she said, and in 1971 she filed suit against
them.
   By the time it came to the lawsuit against Lee eight years later,
Michelle's memory had improved, and she recalled various things
about her conversations with Bobby Roberts and now with Lee as
well. On the witness stand she said that Lee had known of the
arrangement all along.

MICHELLE: I told him way before the movie started. I believe I
   told Mr Marvin after Bobby Roberts and Hal Landers
   acquired the property . . .
      Then he said to me, 'Oh my God, Meyer is going to kill
   you.' I said, 'Well, I can't understand why Meyer is going to
   be angry. I really have nothing to do with this. I merely told
   someone about the script.' And I said, 'Also now they are so
   grateful because – you know – they had you in mind, and
   they want to give me a Rolls-Royce.'
      And Lee said, 'You cannot accept a Rolls-Royce from
   Landers and Roberts.' He said, 'It just wouldn't be right,'
   and he was angry.

There was also a different version of her first meeting with Roberts and Landers.

MICHELLE: I never went to see Bobby Roberts and Hal Landers. [*So no meeting in their office*]

KAGON: Where did you meet them?

MICHELLE: I called them – where did I meet them? Bobby is a good friend of mine. And I called Bobby. I happened to be sitting on the beach one day and Bobby and Milton Berle walked by. And Bobby said to me, 'I loved Lee's last picture, and I just sold Dunhill Records, and I would love to do a film with him.' And I said, 'Call his agent.' And he said, 'Well, I don't have a property in mind, and I've got this money.'

I didn't tell Lee because I didn't know whether – whether Mr Roberts and Hal Landers would acquire the property. I just said that I heard that the option was being dropped . . . I called Mr Roberts on the telephone and I said, 'There is a project that Lee would love to do.'

KAGON: Did you have an agreement with Mr Roberts and their company?

MICHELLE: In the beginning, no.

KAGON: After he acquired the property, did you have a meeting with him?

MICHELLE: No.

KAGON: Did you ever give them the book or a screen treatment?

MICHELLE: No.

KAGON: You were not to participate by way of salary?

MICHELLE: No, of course not. It was never brought up.

KAGON: Did you discuss the casting of the picture with Roberts and Landers?

MICHELLE: No, I think I discussed the casting of the picture with Mr Marvin, and sometimes I would relate to Bobby what Lee felt about the casting, in conversation.

KAGON: Your Honor, the whole thrust of our argument here is that *none* of this was disclosed to Mr Marvin. [*To Michelle*] Where did you get the script?

MICHELLE: There were . . . there were a few copies of the
script at our home. [*In other words, Lee had them*] I believe
that script was submitted . . . by Bob Altman. No, Bob
Aldrich. Bob Aldrich was a producer-director.

She earlier testified that Lee had angrily insisted she call the union
and find out what a 'finder's fee' would be. She said she was told it
was ten per cent.

KAGON: What was the reason you gave Mr Marvin for the ten
per cent finder's fee?
MICHELLE: Because I found the script for Bobby Roberts.
KAGON: Didn't you say earlier that the script had been on the
fireplace for years?
MICHELLE: I let them know about the script. Lee was signed to
do that script. It had nothing to do with Mr Marvin. That
script was on our mantel since 1966. There were many
people offered that script.

Once this piece of logic had sunk into the by now almost numb
gallery of listeners, David asked if there was anything else she had
done, any other suggestions she had made.

MICHELLE: I believe he asked me . . . he called and said that he
understood that he had heard from someone else that Lee
admired Jeanne Moreau as an actress very much, and what
did I think of that. I believe I said, 'Well, I believe Lee thinks
she's a good actress, but you're going to have to discuss that
with him.' I may have had a few other discussions strictly as
a layman.

Michelle's memory was at best faulty. On the last day or two of the
trial, under questioning by her own attorney, she testified that it
was *she* who had suggested this casting to Lee.

MICHELLE: I suggested Jeanne Moreau.
MITCHELSON: To whom did you make this suggestion?
MICHELLE: To Lee.
MITCHELSON: Did you suggest anyone else for the movie?
MICHELLE: Jack Palance.

MITCHELSON: What did Mr Marvin say to you when you suggested Jack Palance?

MICHELLE: [*Apparently forgetting what she had just said*] Palance?

MITCHELSON: Palance.

MICHELLE: He had worked with Jack.

MITCHELSON: What did he *say*?

MICHELLE: [*After a pause*] He said that he had worked with Jack before and that it was interesting that someone could think of Jack in the part of a good guy. He seemed to like it. He told me that . . . he smiled and . . . I don't know what he said. I don't remember what he said.

This kind of testimony makes one realize how easily someone in Lee's household could listen to his business meetings and later repeat – even claiming as their own – his ideas, his conversations with others, his musings out loud.

When Lee was asked about what help she might have been to him, he replied firmly.

LEE: She wasn't helpful to me when I was working. By all her activities, basically her behavior was erratic . . . erratic is too general for you? Non-reliability, is that better for you? She was not trustworthy. She revealed the privacy of the household to outsiders. She was a doper, and I couldn't count on her. She revealed to other parties material that had been submitted to me for my eyes only and with . . . *Monte Walsh* and, on lesser levels . . . minor infringement of the privacy of the relationship to other people, too numerous to count. I couldn't pin them down to make them worth repeating. The interjecting of herself into the work . . . disturbed me extremely . . . repeatedly over the whole period . . . in most of the films I worked on. I'm not saying she went to the extremes that she did in *Monte Walsh*, but she would interfere with my daily work habits.

MITCHELSON: Would you say that she wanted to know what was going on with you in regard to your work and just . . .

LEE: No, I think she was doing it for her financial gain.

MITCHELSON: You said she was a 'doper'. What did you mean by that, what were you referring to?

LEE: I was referring to pills and marijuana, to the best of my knowledge . . . Percodan, the other name slips me. I'm not that familiar with drugs.

Michelle testified on numerous occasions that a friend at Twentieth Century Fox had told her about their dropping the option on *Monte Walsh*, not 'Mr Marvin'.

KAGON: You were aware, were you not, that Mr Marvin had been talking to Mr Aldrich about doing *Monte Walsh*?

MICHELLE: Yes, I was . . . Your Honor, I was aware that he was talking to Bob Aldrich and I was aware also that he decided not to do the project with Mr Aldrich, and I believe Mr Aldrich could not get the deal at Twentieth, and that's why the option was being dropped.

KAGON: And Mr Marvin told you that?

MICHELLE: Yes, sir.

KAGON: So that you *did* become aware that the option was being dropped by virtue of a conversation you had with Mr Marvin.

Michelle never took it to heart when these 'inconsistencies' were demonstrated: she just went right on, though perhaps a little sullenly. She had something irrepressible about her – coming back determinedly, relentlessly, like a breaker on a rising tide.

Not surprisingly, when Bobby Roberts, producer of *Monte Walsh*, was called to the stand, he had a different story to tell.

BOBBY ROBERTS: I met Michelle . . . gee, I met Michelle when I was working as a performer at a café in Las Vegas, at the El Rancho. I would say in excess of twenty years ago.

He was working, he said, as a dancer in a group he called the Dunhills that was working with Milton Berle at El Rancho: 'She was performing in a show, working as one of the so-called chorus girls in the show.'

KAGON: Was she a featured dancer?

BOBBY ROBERTS: No.

339

KAGON: Now, Mr Roberts, did you meet the plaintiff again some time in 1967?

BOBBY ROBERTS: Yes, at the beach in Malibu.

KAGON: Who was present?

BOBBY ROBERTS: I think the only one that was present at that conversation was Michelle and myself.

KAGON: Was Mr Marvin present?

BOBBY ROBERTS: Definitely not, no. I asked Michelle if there was anything that Lee was interested in doing. That was my question. And she told me about a piece of material called *Sunset Trails* (*Monte Walsh*), that Lee was quite excited about.

KAGON: Did you ever talk to Lee Marvin about that?

BOBBY ROBERTS: I never talked to Lee Marvin about that. Michelle asked me not to discuss it with Lee Marvin. I never discussed it with Lee Marvin.

Kagon brought up the document, the complaint for money, and asked him if the lawsuit was ever settled. It was, but before he could answer, Marvin Mitchelson suddenly recalled that the amount they settled for was $750, not $7500 as he and Michelle had stated.

KAGON: Did you ever speak to her about an automobile?

BOBBY ROBERTS: Never. Never did that.

KAGON: Did you ever talk to Michelle about a producer's fee?

BOBBY ROBERTS: I never did.

But he did thank her, he said, and offered her a suede suit she had admired. She refused it.

MITCHELSON: [*Cross-examines*] All right. Do you know Barry Ashton – who is he?

BOBBY ROBERTS: I think he is a producer and a choreographer of shows that work in Las Vegas and Reno and cafés.

MITCHELSON: All right. Do you know whether or not plaintiff ever was with Barry Ashton?

BOBBY ROBERTS: I never saw her. I don't know that as a fact.

MITCHELSON: Do you remember, did you have an opinion as to Michelle's performance, whether she was a good dancer or a mediocre dancer or . . .

Lee and me on the fishing boat in Australia, 1974.
(Courtesy of John Mondora.)

Left: Lee and me on our boat *The Blue Hawaii*, Kailua-Kona, Hawaii,
1972. (Photograph by Orlando Suero.)   I've just won the world record
marlin. Kailua-Kona, Hawaii, 1973. (Photograph by Jerry Seely.)

Right: Lee on a difficult marlin in
Australian waters, 1980.

Below: Lee's boat in Palau, Micronesia,
1969.

Our fishing boat off the coast of Kailua-
Kona, 1972. (Photograph by Orlando
Suero.)

Left: Captain Dennis Wallace, Lee with his 1,148-pound marlin catch, Erroll 'Snudge' Schembri, deckhand, and Emmett 'Mutt' Coble. Australia, 1976. (Photograph by John Mondora.)

Dennis Wallace, his wife Yvonne, Lee, me and Eddie Lauter on location for the movie *Death Hunt* in Banff, Canada, 1980.

Lee presenting a copy of the script of *The Missouri Traveler* to President Harry S. Truman in 1958.

Left: With Dr Harry A. Wilmer during the International Psychiatric Film Festival in San Antonio, Texas, 1974.   Addressing the International Film Festival of Culture and Psychiatry in 1976. (Photographs by James S. Waldron, University of Texas Health Science Center.)

Attorney Mark Goldman, me and Lee in the courthouse hallway
during the trial in 1979.

Lee's daughter Cynthia outside the courthouse, 1979. (Photograph by
Michael Dobo.)

In Lee's den with a 1,232-pound marlin on the wall. (Photograph by
David Steen, Scope Features.)

Constructing a painting in his workshop. (Kerry took the picture.)

Just some of us. Front row (left to right): Lee, Trevor, me, Emily, Morgan, Jess and John. Back row: our niece Mara, Kerry, Wendy with baby Pamela, Rod and his wife Hideko. (Photograph by Graham MacCarter.)

Baby-sitting for grandsons John and Morgan, 1982. (Photograph by Graham MacCarter.)

At home in the Malibu Colony in 1973. (Photograph by Raymond Depardon – Magnum Photos.)

BOBBY ROBERTS: Michelle was not a good dancer.

MITCHELSON: I see. Did you ever hear her sing?

BOBBY ROBERTS: Yes.

MITCHELSON: OK, I won't ask you that.

Marvin Mitchelson now called Lee to the stand to talk about *Monte Walsh*.

MITCHELSON: OK now, Mr Marvin, during your relationship with Michelle, when you made the picture *Monte Walsh*, I suggest to you that you indeed knew that Michelle was claiming that she had been instrumental in having gotten you the part in the film, correct?

LEE: No.

MITCHELSON: You did know before you broke up with her that Mr Roberts and perhaps Mr Landers wanted to give her a car for her help and aid in the film, or she *told* you that, is that right?

LEE: She told me that that is what they wanted to do, yes, at that time.

MITCHELSON: All right. Now did that arouse some suspicion in your mind?

LEE: No more than anything else she would say to me.

MITCHELSON: All right. Did you ever ask Landers and Roberts what Michelle had done to help?

LEE: No, the film was over.

MITCHELSON: All right. Did you end up buying her a car?

LEE: I bought her a car.

MITCHELSON: Did she tell you they wanted to give her a Rolls-Royce?

LEE: No.

MITCHELSON: Did she tell you what kind of car it was to be?

LEE: Yes, a Mercedes. I ended up giving it to her.

MITCHELSON: Now, when you heard that they wanted to give her a car, with reference to your state of mind, what did you think Roberts and Landers wanted to give her a car for?

LEE: Because they were very sweet men, and also they had sold a very wealthy company, and being in the record business, that is a kind of a nothing gift to people in that end of the business, in that they are very big wheeler-dealers in a very nice way. I cannot say too much about how free and gratifying . . . they would do anything that my actors asked of them. They were more than willing to see to our comfort, so I just took this all as part of this very grandiose operation that they had.

MITCHELSON: So I take it that when you broke up with Michelle you hadn't the slightest idea that she was going to sue Roberts and Landers some year and half later?

LEE: No.

The testimonies of Dick Doughty, Carol Clark and Michelle herself about her fights with Lee had between them painted a picture of a pretty miserable time during *Monte Walsh*.

If Michelle Triola's behaviour in Palau was, as Lee said, 'very difficult but tolerable', and on *Monte Walsh*, 'suspect', during the period immediately after that film it became a nightmare. She offered, Lee testified, to get out of his life for $50,000 cash. While Lee mulled this over, it was quickly upped to $100,000.

Marvin Mitchelson asked Lee about the situation at the end of 1969.

MITCHELSON: Did you feel, in your state of mind, that Michelle was trying to blackmail you into continuing the relationship?

LEE: Yes.

MITCHELSON: Did she say she wanted cash?

LEE: Well, I'm sure she wasn't going to take a credit card. You know . . . yes, she wanted it boom, boom. Fifty thousand dollars to consummate a deal and she would leave. Shortly after, maybe a two-month period, I believe she said that the price had gone up. She said she would get out of my life and I would never hear from her again but the price was now $100,000. Prior to that offer she discussed going to Europe.

MITCHELSON: That was pretty far away. What did you say?

LEE: I said, 'By all means.' Then she would say, when I agreed to that, that she would need ten thousand, or again fifteen thousand, a month to sustain herself, and I felt that was beyond my means.

MITCHELSON: Did you make a counter offer?

LEE: No, hers was a token offer. That, in other words, 'you cannot get rid of me'.

While these negotiations were going on, Michelle and Marvin Mitchelson quietly filed an application for a change of name from Michelle Triola to Michelle Marvin and published it in an obscure newspaper. On 7 May Michelle and Mitchelson went to the courthouse together and the change of name was granted. She walked down the steps with a new name – Lee's. By 11 May, Lee was gone.

In their court case against Lee, a very important part of their suit – 'The Evidence On Which Plaintiff Primarily Relies To Establish An Implied Agreement' – was this name change. But however profusely the change was used as evidence by Michelle Triola Marvin, she could not actually recall doing it until driven to the wall, and could, with only the greatest reluctance, remember the date or let it pass her lips: the month, day, even the year it was either applied for or granted. To admit the date might suggest ulterior motives.

KAGON: Do you recall what was your reason for wanting to change your name?

MICHELLE: I had no reason.

KAGON: Did you ever ask Mr Mahoney to introduce you as Michelle Marvin?

MICHELLE: I may have.

KAGON: Mr Mishkin?

MICHELLE: Never.

KAGON: Mr Wasserman?

MICHELLE: Never.

But Paul Wasserman, Lee's publicist with the Jim Mahoney Agency, testified differently. He and Michelle had a friendly, bantering type of relationship, and she was very anxious to have him refer to her as Michelle Marvin in columns. He tried to stay out of all of his clients' personal lives, he said, but Michelle talked to him a great deal: 'She called many times.'

She would often be angry when Paul submitted something for a column: 'I usually identified her as Michelle Triola. She would usually phone me.'

Lee, he said, rarely if ever read columns, interviews or publicity. Even his notes to Lee went unread and were often used to light the fire in the fireplace. It was Michelle who was interested in having her name in print, he said.

Lee adamantly denied asking her to change her name. When she brought the subject up with him, he said, 'I told her not to do it. I didn't think that she could. I said if you're going to change it, why don't you change it to a *big* name, yes – Gary Cooper or someone.'

KAGON: Did you ever use the name Marvin professionally?
MICHELLE: Never.

Although Michelle was usually cautious about making such adamant statements, this time she put her foot in it. In response, Kagon presented a paper to the court.

KAGON: Your Honor, for identification this is a petition for change of name. This is a photocopy of the application of Michelle Lenore Triola. It is dated 26 March 1970. The signature thereon is Michelle Lenore Triola, on page two; Marvin Mitchelson, also on page two. I would ask the witness to read paragraph five: 'The reason for the proposed change is that the petitioner is an entertainer, presently under contract, and has been known professionally by the name of "Michelle Marvin" which she has used extensively throughout her career . . ."'

When Lee learned of the name change, he had a meeting with Lou Goldman at Lou's office in Beverly Hills. Despairing of getting her to leave, he packed a bag and departed himself in his car.

LEE: I would say it was roughly a six-week period. I went from place to place in the seaport towns of southern California.

Trying to track Lee down, Michelle made hundreds of telephone calls and tried to hire a private detective through Guy Ward, an attorney.

MICHELLE: There was a time where I was having a problem

344

finding Lee. One of the questions I was asking – going to ask
– Mr Ward was if he knew of a detective, in other words, to
keep it kind of silent. I was trying to find Lee.

She called Louis Goldman and asked for an appointment.

LOUIS GOLDMAN: She wanted to meet me on 12 May. She
wanted to determine the whereabouts of Lee Marvin. I
agreed to see her.

MITCHELSON: And she promised you that if you would tell her
where he was, she wouldn't even go after him and look for
him, didn't she?

LOUIS GOLDMAN: Yes, that's right.

MITCHELSON: OK. Well, Mr Goldman, you understood her
when she said that she was concerned about Lee, that she
was concerned about his safety? You understood her to mean
that, didn't you?

LOUIS GOLDMAN: I really didn't. I didn't understand her to
mean that at all. I knew that is what she said. No question
about it. I think that she wanted me to give her the
information which I was instructed not to give her, and she
would do anything, she would say anything that came to her
mind, to induce me to give her that information – and, of
course, I didn't give it to her.

MITCHELSON: She called a few days later?

LOUIS GOLDMAN: Every day, every day. During that period of
time there were many, many calls from Michelle to me.

Unfortunately, she somehow managed to get information about
Lee's whereabouts and 'ran into him' on the streets of LaJolla. At
one point in her testimony she hinted that Meyer Mishkin might
have told her a general vicinity but made her promise she would
not contact him.

MITCHELSON: All right. Now you went to LaJolla. She found
you at the Valencia Hotel in LaJolla; is that right?

LEE: She found me on a *street* of LaJolla.

Michelle, in her inimitable way, recounted the events blow by blow:

MICHELLE: I guess what I am trying to say is that I called Mr

345

Mishkin. 'Meyer,' I said, 'where is he?' And he said that he had called him and said he was south of San Onofre. I said, 'Is he all right?' and he said he was. A couple of days later, I hadn't heard anything and I kept on calling to see if anyone had heard from him. I called Mr Mishkin and I said, 'Have you talked to him?' and he said, 'Yes, I have talked to him.' I said, 'Where is he?' and he said, 'I can't tell you that.' And I said, 'Meyer, I am just being courteous, because you know, I will find him.' So Mr Mishkin said, 'Let me take care of it. Just promise me one thing, that you will not call him or call around town trying to find him so that he won't think you are looking for him and then leave from place to place . . . and drink.' So I said, 'OK, you have my word,' but I didn't give my word that I wouldn't get in my car and find him, which I did. I found him in LaJolla. I tried to remember what he had been talking about – and he was talking about the war and the Marines and I just knew that he was down that way and I stopped in Oceanside where the Marine Corps Base was and he had been there. He had gone – he had stopped in Laguna.

KAGON: How did you know that?

MICHELLE: Because I used to live in Laguna and I know people there. He was just in town, in the bars, and they had seen him there. So then I called the head of the tuna fleet whom I had met because the tuna were running and I thought maybe he was going to go down and do some tuna fishing and he said that he had not seen Lee. So I remembered that he had once done a play in LaJolla. He has spoken a lot about LaJolla and a hotel there, but I couldn't remember the name of the hotel. I just went to LaJolla and checked into a hotel and went down into the lobby and the bellman was talking about Lee and I knew he was there.

Lee's recollection of the event was not quite so gay.

LEE: She pursued my absence and found me in LaJolla, California, in the La Valencia Hotel. She took a room there under the name of Marvin and found me on the street coming home from the movies; she said she wanted to talk to me. I knew it was useless, so I made a date to meet her at five o'clock the following afternoon at the house for one hour.

MITCHELSON: And she returned in her car, or a car?

LEE: I don't know how she returned.

Lee was asked about the following day's meeting.

KAGON: Mr Marvin, had the plaintiff, in so far as you were able to observe, been drinking?

LEE: Yes, she had.

KAGON: Was she under control at that time?

LEE: No.

MITCHELSON: Did you tell Michelle that you wanted her to leave this time?

LEE: Yes, I had been telling her that for a long time, yes.

MITCHELSON: Well now, was there an incident where Michelle was arrested, to your knowledge?

LEE: Yes, that same evening.

MITCHELSON: How did that come about?

LEE: I returned to the house from LaJolla, and we had a discussion, at which one time she left the house for a moment and returned shortly thereafter. I excused myself and went out to get into my car and drive away, and it was gone. I realized that she had done something with it. And I wasn't going back into the house.

So I started to walk down the road toward Santa Monica. And then she came out and got into her car. And then she pursued me with her vehicle – making harassment for the traffic on the highway.

I could avoid it because I was on foot. There were telephone poles and parked cars. But her erratic behavior on the road was deadly. Until I saw a sheriff's car go by. He stopped and backed up. And I said, 'Can you give me a hand here?'

I said, 'Well, he better do something because this girl is going to kill herself,' at which he utilized his radio and in a few moments I noticed the Highway Patrol car parked down across the street watching. Eventually they came over. When I had succeeded in reaching in the car and taking the keys

347

out, she was stopped in the inside lane of traffic . . . I said, 'Well, there is nothing I can seem to do here.' And so they proceeded to ask Michelle to get out of the vehicle. I gave them the keys. She wouldn't do so. So they opened the door and bodily took her out of the car. She resisted them and tore part of the steering wheel off the horn ring, and they took her over to the police vehicle. And one of them said, 'What do you want to do about this?' And I said, 'Well, whatever the least is to retain her until she straightens out,' because she was really out of hand.

MITCHELSON: Now, Mr Marvin, you told us this harrowing tale of Michelle chasing you down the highway, the Pacific Coast Highway, in which I think you told us that you could dodge that because you were on foot. You didn't feel that she would run you over, right?

LEE: [*Grimly*] I was doing my best to avoid it.

To pin down the date of this fracas, Kagon presented a copy of the arrest complaint of the sheriff's department. Marvin Mitchelson was 'outraged'.

MITCHELSON: It says '2020 hours', that is, eight o'clock . . . I have no quarrel with the date. The circumstances don't bother me.

JUDGE: What does bother you?

MITCHELSON: Charge 647 PC: Disorderly Conduct. And they have underneath it 'drunk'.

That night Lee departed once again. Jim Mahoney came to the house, drove him to the airport and Lee flew to Hawaii. The next day, 21 May, Michelle, out of jail, was already on the telephone to Lou Goldman.

MICHELLE: I asked him where Lee was. He said that Lee wanted me out of the house. He said, 'Lee wants you out of the house and he would like to provide you with some money so that you can get started again.' I kept saying that I wanted to speak to Lee directly. My main concern was to speak to Lee directly. And he wouldn't tell me. He told me that Lee would give me eight hundred and something dollars for five years – every month – but that I was to leave the house. I told him I couldn't believe that I – I told him that – that Betty Marvin was well provided for, and I'd – I just didn't see how I could even – how I could even exist on that.

Marvin Mitchelson questioned Louis Goldman about this conversation.

LOUIS GOLDMAN: We talked about a place for her to live. I said, 'How much time do you want?' She said, 'I want a month's time.' I said, 'Fine.'

MITCHELSON: Did you ask her to give you a list of furniture she wanted from the house?

LOUIS GOLDMAN: Yes, I did.

KAGON: Let me ask you, what was your arrangement with Lou Goldman?

MICHELLE: I don't remember at the moment . . . I refused it and walked out of the office very upset.

KAGON: How much were you receiving per month?

MICHELLE: One thousand fifty dollars a month, with taxes deducted. Net was eight hundred plus dollars.

Although Michelle said she refused this offer of money, refused the arrangement and did not agree to leave the house, she immediately began accepting the checks and rented a house several doors down on the small curved beach known as LaCosta.

Kagon paid Michelle's disorderly conduct charges to the Sheriff's department. Some time later, Lee came back.

LEE: I came back from Hawaii and then in the end of June, I returned to the house.

MITCHELSON: And who did you find when you returned?

By this point, no one in the courtroom was surprised by Lee's answer.

LEE: Michelle.

MITCHELSON: Michelle said she would not leave, is that true?

LEE: That's what she said . . . I just went to the phone and picked it up and called Mr Kagon, and it took him and

Lou, I would say, forty-five minutes to an hour to get there.

MITCHELSON: Now, by the end of May or June you were no longer fearful Michelle would go out and tell the world?

LEE: 'No longer fearful'? I think the climate had risen beyond that. At that time, I *had* to get rid of her.

MITCHELSON: I see. Well, *is* the answer you were no longer fearful?

LEE: I think the sum – it had to come to a halt. Events had gone as far as they could go in maintaining any kind of civil obedience . . . She said she would not leave. A lot of verbal abuse to the people there: ganging up on her, 'getting the silk suiters in'. They maintained a tremendous decorum as gentlemen under the abuse . . . and when she finally stopped, they said, 'Our position is the same.'

Marvin Mitchelson asked Michelle about the events of that day.

MITCHELSON: And did you go that night?

MICHELLE: I don't believe I did.

LEE: Yes, she *did* leave, by way of the beach. She had walked down, came into the house when I arrived, and then left the same way.

LaJolla had proved too close . . . and he now thought Hawaii was too. So the following day Lee was on a plane to Guam. And he was right. Although Michelle was finally out of his house and it was over for him, this was by no means the last of her.

While he was in Palau and Guam, she gave Rona Barret an interview discussing her 'life with Lee'. When he returned to his beach house she began telephoning him. He again got into his car and this time drove all over the west, the south-west and Colorado. (We later discovered that he and I had been driving in the same areas of the country at the same time.) In some ways, rather than being the end, this was just the beginning. The battlefield simply shifted to the public arena: from the gossip columns and the tabloids (as threatened) to the law offices of Marvin Mitchelson and eventually to the courtroom.

At long last, the final day of testimony arrived, 27 March. We all anxiously watched the clock, hoping against hope that nothing would prevent this from being the end.

For his last words, Marvin Mitchelson brought to the Judge's attention his client's financial predicament. She was on unemployment, it had run out, and prior to that she had lived on disability insurance (she had had yet another accident).

Judge Marshall then ended the proceedings in the same way as he had opened them – only this time with many eloquently, if weary, expressions of relief.

> JUDGE: Do you gentlemen have anything further to contribute? I gather not. Well, thank you, Counsel.
> KAGON: Our thanks, Your Honor.
> MITCHELSON: Thank you, Your Honor.
> JUDGE: . . . and all parties for going through a difficult case in many respects for all these months. My goodness, it is 'months', isn't it? Is it the twelfth week?
> CLERK: Yes.
> JUDGE: Well, I don't know, maybe we ought to look at Shakespeare and see what he says about this.
> MITCHELSON: *Twelfth Night*?
> JUDGE: That's the twelfth *night*, isn't it? That won't help us very much.
> KAGON: I trust it was not *Love's Labours Lost*.
> JUDGE: Thank you, Counsel.
> MITCHELSON: Or *Much Ado About Nothing*.

After all this good-natured quipping Judge Marshall said:

> JUDGE: You will now have some time to submit briefs, and on the tenth we will argue the case. May I say a couple of words to the reporters? [*Addressing the press corps*] On behalf of the court, I do want to thank the reporters, the press, for the accuracy of the reporting. I thought that you ladies and gentlemen did a fine job, for your orderly and highly-disciplined decorum; also, despite the many demands of your calling, requiring you to go in and out, nevertheless quiet reigned on that side of the room and the court appreciated it. The court artists aren't here, but please thank them for the

court. They certainly did professional work and did their best with the judicial countenance as one can do under the circumstances.

And so, if you gentlemen have nothing further to contribute to the common weal, we will adjourn.

And so, with that pleasing speech of good fellowship to one and all, the court went into recess. You almost expected the cast to take a bow.

On 10 April the Oral Closing Arguments were presented by Kagon and Marvin Mitchelson. It took the entire day. Marvin Mitchelson began, then Kagon argued for two hours.

He listed 'impeachments and inconsistencies' in massive numbers. He harked back to Michelle's testimony, 'in which the Plaintiff has testified uniformly in this matter, and demonstrates a rather unrestrained imagination or, as Mr Boorman sometimes referred to it, as a virulent imagination'.

JUDGE: Virulent usually refers to a disease, Counsel.
KAGON: Yes, a diseased imagination. Now . . .
MITCHELSON: Your Honor, I don't think he has a right to comment on anyone's medical condition, assume it, without any facts in evidence.
JUDGE: Well, this isn't meant to be a comment on a medical condition.

Then David Kagon brought his lengthy oral argument to a conclusion.

KAGON: I only submit, Your Honor, at this time. It has been a long road. I am most grateful to Your Honor, the Court, the officers of the Court, employees of the Court for the courtesies that have been extended to me, my associates, my partners, to my client and I thank Counsel and his staff for his courtesies. Thank you, Your Honor.

These were noble sentiments, I thought – especially after the lying, rudeness and deprecating remarks that characterized the way Marvin Mitchelson pleaded his case.

Mitchelson himself finished as emotionally as he had begun.

After some impassioned statements,'his blood boiling', about how a drunken Lee had knocked people off their bar stools and so on, he too at long last drew to a close, throwing himself on the mercy of the court as regards finances.

MITCHELSON: A fair division of property is all we're asking the court to do – be *fair* with us . . . OK, now I am almost done, Your Honor. Just two more minutes, please. Your Honor, when you pose the question, 'What about $50 million; do you think it would be fair to give her something?' How about three and one-half million? That's how much it's worth now. Do you think it's fair to give her something, a million and a half dollars? Everything is relative, isn't it? The Marvin Decision says, 'Treat her fairly.' And I implore the Court to treat her fairly. That is all I ask of you – treat her fairly. She gave something to this man. She gave something to his life. She gave something to the acquisition of that property and I urge and I implore you to do equity, Your Honor.

That's all I have to say, and I thank you for one of the great experiences of my life – to participate in this trial.

So, with yet more bonhomie, all the arguments were concluded – leaving the defendant, his witnesses and family (probably even the Plaintiff's witnesses) feeling sullied, torn to shreds, swirled around and spat out by the wheels of justice.

We packed our bags and went home to Tucson. Our personal life, as well as the publicity for *The Big Red One*, had been put on hold pending the outcome of this lengthy trial. We stayed at home, poised to depart for New York, awaiting the decision of Judge Marshall. It came in a memorandum on 18 April. A call from Kagon gave us the gist: Lee was not guilty on all counts. Along with his decision, Judge Marshall made some comments. He said that it was not Lee's testimony, nor the testimony of any other person, but Michelle Triola's alone that 'hung her' – though of course he couched it in far loftier terms.

Regarding Michelle's career, he commented:

The plaintiff's career, never very brisk paced, was sputtering and not because of any act of defendant; it came to an end unmourned and unattended by plaintiff who made no attempt to breathe life into it.

The plaintiff's testimony as to defendant's drinking habits would indicate that he was virtually awash with alcohol, yet during this same period defendant starred in several major films, all demanding of him physical stamina, a high degree of alertness and verbal as well as physical concentration. Her portrayal of large-scale and all pervasive inebriation raises doubt as to her accuracy of observation.

Regarding the name change, Judge Marshall observed:

Coming at a time so close to the date of separation and after some indication of difficulties between the parties, the change of name does raise a question whether plaintiff sought relief from embarrassment or whether she wished to acquire the right to use defendant's name after separation.

Finding no contract, the testimony of Doughty is not evaluated as that relates to an alleged breach of contract. [*All that misery for nothing!*]

It may be contended that as the defendant did not need to expend funds to secure homemaking services elsewhere, she thereby enhanced the financial base of the defendant and enabled him to increase his property purchase. Such alleged enhancement, however, would appear to be offset by the considerable flow of economic benefits in the other direction. Those benefits include payments for goods and services for plaintiff up to $72,900 for the period from 1967–1970 . . . Further, defendant made a substantial financial effort to launch plaintiff's career as a recording singer.

The defendant earned the money by means of his own effort, skill, and reputation. The money was then invested in the properties now held by him. It cannot be said in good conscience that such properties do not belong to him.

The judge did however consider Marvin Mitchelson's plea for financial aid.

The court is aware that footnote 25, Marvin v. Marvin, supra, page 684, urges the trial court to employ whatever equitable remedy may be proper under the circumstances. The court is also aware of the recent resort of plaintiff to unemployment insurance benefits to support herself and of the fact that a return of plaintiff to a career as a singer is doubtful . . .

In view of these circumstances, the court in equity awards plaintiff $104,000 for rehabilitation purposes so that she may have the economic means to reeducate herself, to learn new employable skills or to refurbish those utilized so that she may return from her status as companion of a motion picture star to a separate, independent, but perhaps, more prosaic existence.

ARTHUR K MARSHALL
Judge of the Superior Court

Fair though Judge Marshall may have felt this award to be, it had absolutely no basis in law. Lee had been found not guilty on each and every count. As one attorney was heard to comment, 'He threw her a bone to please everyone a little.'

Our house was surrounded by members of the press corps from all over the world with cameras and television crews. Lee made it known we were not giving interviews in or near our home. Barry Bono, a young friend of ours from Brooklyn and something of an actor himself, smilingly gave the impression that there was some lurking threat behind his demeanour and informed them all: 'No cameras.' Kim Mariner, a newscaster from Los Angeles, was an exception. We had promised him an interview and Lee made good his word. Lee did, however, hold a press conference for everyone in a conference room at Tucson airport just before our flight to New York.

Although Judge Marshall was unaware of it, Michelle Triola Marvin had already rehabilitated herself: as the companion of television actor Dick Van Dyke. Although Michelle and Marvin Mitchelson had accused Lee over and over again of excessive drinking, Dick Van Dyke's wrestle with alcohol addiction was widely known; he had talked publicly about his problem.

The decision once again brought forth headlines and photographs in all the newspapers. There were declarations of victory by both sides; there were comments from other leading attorneys throughout the country, from celebrities, humorists and vocal feminists. Paul Simon wrote a song, 'There Must Be Fifty Ways to Leave Your Lover – Just Turn in the Key, Lee,' and the sale of 'Free Lee Marvin' T-shirts on the courthouse steps was brisk.

Michelle opted to stick with the 'I did it for all womankind' image, and she and Marvin Mitchelson exuberantly held a 'winning' press conference on the courthouse steps. 'I am proud to have paved the way for other unmarried women,' Miss Marvin said, 'I'm happy about it.' She added, 'But no amount of money can give me back those years.'[2]

Under the heading TOTAL VICTORY TO MARVIN, Lindsey wrote:

> 'I'm absolutely excited about the decision,' Mr Marvin said. 'I could not have hoped for more. They lost on every charge, on every one. It'll probably make a leading man out of me when in reality I just want to do some of those good westerns.'

The front page of the *New York Daily News* was almost entirely taken up by the headlines and photos of Lee and Michelle Triola. At the bottom of the page, taking up only about half an inch and completely overshadowed, was 'Copter Crash Kills Three at Newark Plus 15 Injured'.

Feminist Gloria Steinem had a written statement prepared almost immediately: 'Lee Marvin seems to be the one who needs rehabilitating – in the form of a short course in truth-telling.' A puzzling observation on her part.

It was hard to believe that Gloria Steinem, a high-profile spokesperson, did not understand the power of publicity, the frailties of the press and the manipulation of reporters. She seemed instead to harbour little doubt about the truth of Michelle Triola's testimony, without having spent a single day in the courtroom. The 'feminists' jumping on the bandwagon to denigrate Lee affected me more than some because of my own standards. I have probably been as independent-minded and self-sufficient as any woman. I also happen to like men – a lot. I don't think a man is a chauvinist simply because he's male and that every woman is a victim because she is female. I

2 Robert Lindsey's Special to the *AP New York Daily News*, 23 April 1979.

am a believer in women's dignity and the right to control one's own body, but I can't for the life of me make a determination about justice or truth on the basis of one's gender. Lee was a gentleman throughout the entire trial . . . perhaps a subtlety unrecognized by Ms Steinem.

Lauren Bacall said, 'I think it sounds pretty fair, just off the top of my head' – then added, with a familiar snap, 'I think everybody ought to work for a living – if she can go to school and learn to work. But I don't know who is going to see to that!'

Art Buchwald, who had written many amusing articles about the case, commented: 'It seems to be a victory for everybody.' He growled, 'I don't know what they are going to retrain her for – remedial marriage?' Buchwald jokingly agreed, however, that the decision would make him more careful were he 'tempted to indiscretion. I've always been against splitting 50–50 with your wife, much less your girlfriend.'

There were many interviews with attorneys, much scholarly opinion offered, much practical advice and interpretation, but whatever might have been said for or against on television or in the written word, in the eyes of the public Lee was very much a hero.

We arrived at New York's Kennedy Airport from Tucson on the day of the decision and had to be wrestled away through the cheering mobs by New York's finest, the NYPD. I had never been in a mob before, and although this was a joyous one, it was crushing, surging and quite frightening. We were whisked off through private corridors and hurriedly helped into a limousine or taxi – probably a taxi, which Lee preferred. Wherever we went people shook Lee's hand, congratulated him with victory signs, applause; cab drivers yelled out 'Hurrah, Lee' as they raced by. Lee was always well loved by the public. People felt a kinship with him, he was one of their own. (Later, on the beach in Malibu, the cry was 'Yo, Lee!')

We had gone to New York to see the opening night performance of our friend Mitchell Ryan in Arthur Miller's play *The Price*. The *New York Post* reported, under a large photograph of Lee with utility workers and a smaller one with Arthur Miller at dinner later:

Lee Marvin could probably run for mayor and win these days. He was so big in the city last night that he sweet-talked a bunch of utility workers into abstaining from the use of their jackhammers so the audience could hear the lines inside the Harold Clurman Theater.[3]

There was so much press about the case that we only had to keep an eye on the newspapers to see how things were progressing in California. In this way we learned that Marvin Mitchelson was threatening yet another lawsuit. One heading warned LOOK OUT, LEE: 'Marvin Mitchelson is coming up with a wild twist. He's now planning to sue Lee . . .'[4] He didn't, but he did petition the court for $500,000 asking that Lee pay their court costs, but David Kagon successfully argued against this. In fact, *they* should have paid Lee's costs.

After dinner with Mitchell Ryan, Arthur Miller and the cast, Lee, Mitchell and I went to our hotel and talked the night away; we caught up, drinking a few happy toasts. Lee and I went to bed probably just before dawn.

The day before, a letter had been delivered to our rooms at the St Regis Hotel from Jimmy Breslin asking, as only he can, to meet up:

Daily News
Lee,
As I never read court stories involving people I know, I was one of the two or three Americans who knew nothing of your case. But then last night at the bar, Fat Andy, the boss of the East New York unit, organized crime, got into a major fight with his woman friend about your case. I didn't know Fat Andy knew how to read. He and the woman threatened each other with violence known only to the most desperate of people. At 1 a.m. Fat Andy, carrying your banner, kicked the glass out of the door of the Tutto Bene bar and walked off into the night.

At that point I decided that your case transcends gossip and is now sociology. If possible, could I stop by and say hello?
Take care.
Jimmy Breslin

Who could ignore such a note? Besides, Lee and Jimmy were old

---

3 A. Fayette, *New York Post*, 20 April 1979.
4 *New York Daily News*, 23 April 1979; Phil Roura and Tom Poston.

friends. I had met him only once before. Lee and I had gone to Sardi's for dinner, and after dinner to the Sardi's bar. Who should we run into but Jimmy? – in the days when we drank a bit. We went with him to his usual haunts, and then to breakfast – lots of conversation on 8th Avenue in the wee hours of the morning. Jimmy knew all the short-order cooks, the bookies and everybody else who was important. It was wonderful.

Breslin arrived at around eleven o'clock in the morning. Having had only a few hours of sleep, I was exhausted and trying to prepare myself mentally for going to Josh and Nedda Logan's apartment for lunch. Lee, who had hardly slept at all, jumped up, ready for the day. During the long months of the trial, and right up to the previous night, no drink had passed his lips. Now, however, he was in the state we always called his 'high-speed wobble': he was raring to go. A bit wild of eye, but spiffily dressed. I had little faith in the outcome of this day, and sneaked into the bedroom where I phoned Nedda and called off the lunch – or so I thought. Lee was chomping at the bit to go, and had pressed Jimmy into going along too. He didn't need much pressing: no one in his right mind would turn down a luncheon with Josh and Nedda Logan – which says something about me. They were extraordinary people, and their apartment on East 52nd Street was also extraordinary – there had been a great deal of entertaining there throughout the years.

I told Lee that the date had been changed to the following day. 'By whom?' he demanded, knowing full well – and they were off, the elevator door sliding tightly shut as I protested. I was left behind in the hallway without the room key, my jacket or my purse, and by the time I found a housekeeper to let me in they were long gone. I called Nedda to tell her that lunch was somehow on but without me, and she just laughed merrily. 'Oh, we know Lee,' she said. 'We love Lee. He'll be all the more spirited.' Which of course he was – as I sat by myself feeling foolish in a hotel suite in New York in the spring.

I leave it to Jimmy to tell of that day, because I wasn't there. Who could have predicted that it would spark off another Marvin Mitchelson court opportunity – one he leapt at with alacrity?

KEY TO DOING COURTROOM DRAMA IS LYING, SAYS LEE

'The only thing that I really got out of it was that I learned how to lie. You had to. Everybody lied. Witnesses, lawyers, I never knew that's how they do it.' His hands made weaving motions as he imitated how lawyers prepare people to testify in court, 'Not just this and not just that, and not this . . .' he kept saying . . .

Just before he stepped into Josh Logan's apartment, Marvin shook his head and shucked off the night before and walked into the living room as a steady and warm friend paying a call. And Logan pushed his glasses up on top of his head and said to Marvin with a sad smile, 'You're not famous in this country until you make it in the hay.'[5]

At the same time as the newspapers were informing us of Marvin Mitchelson's maneuvers, he was following Lee's press in New York. No sooner did this article come out than Mitchelson filed an objection to Judge Marshall's decision:

. . . IN VIEW OF THE DEFENDANT MARVIN'S POST TRIAL ADMISSION THAT HIS LAWYERS PREPARED HIM TO COMMIT AND THAT HE COMMITTED PERJURY.

'Lee Marvin,' he said, 'boasted of his success in defrauding "The Honorable Court",' and duly presented the judge with the Jimmy Breslin article.

Back to the Los Angeles courthouse we went, with Marvin Mitchelson taking every press opportunity – 'Lee Marvin is certainly not the George Washington of the acting profession'[6] – and yelling perjury.

The *New York Post*, as well as many other newspapers, followed the story:

Palimony king . . . Marvin, in his affidavit, said his words were misunderstood and that all he meant was that witnesses do not tell the whole story. What a shock.[7]

---

5 Jimmy Breslin, *New York Daily News*, Sunday, 22 April 1979.
6 *Herald Examiner*, Milt Policzer, Wednesday, 27 June 1979.
7 *New York Post*, A. Fayette, 27 June 1979.

Lee and Jimmy were called upon to give a sworn affidavit. The District Attorney's office was ordered to investigate, but found nothing to prove perjury. Joe Smith, in the *New York Times* of 20 July, put the matter straight:

'She lost on all points,' said Judge Marshall. And that his ruling was based 'virtually not at all' on Lee's testimony (i.e. *Michelle's* testimony was responsible for the decision against her).

Marvin Mitchelson and Michelle Triola continued to declare their victory, so Lee decided there had to be a definitive end to the case. He was guilty of nothing, legally or ethically, and the accusation that he would have taken advantage of anyone, least of all Michelle Triola, was repellent to him. So in September 1979 he appealed the $104,000 rehabilitation: 'I don't know what she is being rehabilitated *from*,' he observed.

The Court of Appeals agreed: the award of $104,000 to Michelle Triola was vigorously overturned. She received nothing. Marvin Mitchelson received nothing. Taken to the California Supreme Court, it was denied without comment. *Now* at last, in October 1981, it was all over, after nearly ten years of court actions.

In spite of this, the misconceptions persist:

Fiction: Michelle Triola Marvin and Marvin Mitchelson won and she received $104,000.
Fact: Lee, was, as defendant, found not guilty on all counts and Michelle Triola (Marvin) did not receive $104,000 or even one penny.

What Michelle Triola and Marvin Mitchelson did was knowingly wrong: it was a scam, it was reprehensible, it should have been punished. She was the guilty party: she made allegations, in sworn testimony, that were not true. What happened was that they *didn't win*. Lee was exonerated by the court that heard the case. It cost him a great deal of money – and some damage in terms of the impression that lingers in people's minds. Not his real fans, not the people who knew him, but some of the public.

Lee was once again mentioned in the press in September 1980, more than a year after the trial, when Michelle Triola Marvin (the name was now hers, like it or not) was arrested for shoplifting at Robinson's in Beverly Hills: 'Apprehended with three sweaters and two bras stashed away in her bag.' From that time, nearly every account of an unmarried couple suing each other – most recently Sandra Locke's case against Clint Eastwood – carries the obligatory mention of Lee and 'palimony'.

In 1993, nearly six years after Lee's death and fourteen years after the trial, his picture and name were still in the headlines, accompanying articles about Marvin Mitchelson: this time, Mitchelson's conviction for failing to report $2 million dollars on his federal income tax returns. He was sentenced to two and a half years in jail for tax fraud and for 'spinning what federal prosecutors called "a web of deceit" to fund a luxurious lifestyle,' which included a house described as a castle.[8]

Cindy Adams, the *New York Post* gossip columnist, admitted something rather rare in her poignant article headed DIVORCE LAWYER TO THE STARS SPEAKS OUT IN HIS OWN DEFENSE. She describes Marvin Mitchelson as 'the man who handed me many a scoop'. What was the photograph heading the page? 'Lee Marvin and his wife Pamela during a break in the landmark palimony trial – WHERE IT ALL BEGAN.'[9]

There must be people around the country who are not very upset by this turn of events: people who were treated with gross disregard, lack of fair play and paucity of dignity. Some might think that jail is Marvin Mitchelson's just reward.

The wheels of justice grind slowly and often excruciatingly painfully. By the time it's all over, you're often too spent emotionally to feel any jubilation. You're just left with a feeling of 'aha' – and a certain amount of surprise that the system *does* seem to work eventually, no matter how tortuously the decisions may have been reached.

8 *LA Times*, 10 February 1993.
9 *New York Post*, 3 June 1993.

12 The Last Battle

It didn't take us long to put the trial behind us. We had much to do: finishing the remodelling of the house, celebrating the births of more grandchildren, fulfilling our publicity commitments, making more movies – and of course, our yearly fishing trip to Australia. But although Lee always seemed invincible, no matter what the challenge, ahead of us loomed something we had not predicted – and this was a battle Lee did not win.

It began with an asthma attack just as we were getting ready to go to Helsinki for the shooting of *Gorky Park* in 1983. Any actor worth his salt usually starts a film in a state of high anxiety, and Lee was no exception. Whether this, coupled with a cold, contributed to the attack, who knows, but in the middle of the night before leaving for location we had to go to the hospital in Tucson where he had treatment for his breathing – the first of many thereafter.

Although we had moved to Tucson, we still saw Lee's doctor Martin Covel in Beverly Hills for yearly check-ups. (The last time we saw Sam Peckinpah was in Covel's waiting room after he had suffered a heart attack.) Lee had his usual excellent report, but for one thing. He was quite pleased with himself for his 'handle on the drinking'. 'Well,' Dr Covel said, pricking Lee's balloon, 'go *back* to drinking and quit the *smoking*.' Lee tried. We both did. I succeeded, he didn't.

Lee was immediately better after the few hours in hospital. He, Kerry and I packed; Lee, pencil clenched between his teeth, made his usual list, packing then checking things off.

We flew by Finnair from New York, the Finnish pilots getting us directly into the mood of the country, and landed at Helsinki in what we came to know as typical Nordic flying weather: impenetrable fog.

The producer of the film, Howard Koch Jr, met us and took us to our hotel, where we slept for several hours. A welcoming dinner had been arranged for that evening with Howard, the movie's director Michael Apted, William Hurt, the English screenwriter Dennis Potter and his wife Margaret, Kerry, Lee and me.

We were barely into our potato and salmon soup and reindeer chops before we were treated to a sample of Dennis Potter's saber-sharp wit which, as the weeks went by, was to keep our spirits up and our minds piqued. He was not only extremely amusing but piercingly brilliant, murderously caustic; and also warm and affectionate. He smoked ferociously, teased his wife mercilessly, but had the good sense to appreciate her own zinging retorts. All his good humor was in spite of a condition which left him in excruciating pain, at times keeping him awake many hours of the night: 'All I can do is pace up and down and smoke,' he told us. He later fictionalized his own physical pain in his play (and later television series) *The Singing Detective*, where he gives the condition – psoriatic arthritis, a painful and crippling disease of the skin and bone – to his character Marlow. Lee, Kerry and I immediately became Dennis Potter-philes. Along with the *Gorky Park* script, we had seen his films *Pennies from Heaven* and *Brimstone and Treacle*. Shortly after the making of *Gorky Park* Dennis wrote *Track 29*, asking Lee to do the forthcoming movie. Lee liked the script enormously, and to his pleasure and mine Vanessa Redgrave was to play opposite him. Unfortunately, the director became sick and the film was shelved. Dennis and Lee spent a good deal of time together talking, laughing and smoking. Kerry too had a laser wit, which Dennis enjoyed right off the bat. At the end of the film he offered her a job, which she was unfortunately not able to accept.

At this first evening's dinner we also met Bill Hurt. You don't come away from an encounter with William Hurt – even a light-hearted preliminary meeting in a social setting – without strong feelings and many doubts as to the wavelength he might be on. Kerry, whom Lee described to the press as 'a real student of film', was roughly the same generation as Bill and was an ardent fan of his work. Lee thought her a discerning critic, and would often send her out to see films for him, comfortable that he would share her opinion. She wasn't excited by very many stars, but William Hurt was an exception. By this dinner's end – after hearing at length from Bill himself that Dennis Potter obviously did not like him but greatly admired his work – we weren't sure we weren't in the same boat. This uncertainty persisted for a short time, but then quickly and irrevocably turned into admiration.

Lee left the dinner early because he did not feel well. In an aside to me, he said he would leave as soon as he could politely manage it, and eventually excused himself, asking us to continue. When I came up later he was coughing and uncomfortable, and at five or six in the morning he woke me. He was having a terrible time getting his breath, and he asked me to call first Dr Covel in California – whom we couldn't reach – and then Howard Koch Jr and the company doctor. They came very quickly, and Dr Cedarberg immediately pronounced 'hospital'. When the ambulance arrived, Lee could not even lie down on the stretcher and was carried out sitting upright. We came out of the elevator doors to find the lobby filled with members of the cast and crew waiting to leave for the day's filming. Conversation petered out into dead silence as everyone watched Lee – whose arrival had been much awaited, I'm sure – being carted out on a stretcher on his first morning in Helsinki. What an entrance – or exit, as it were. He managed a smart tongue-in-cheek salute as he was rushed out of the door. This tableau must have added considerably to the anxiety not only of Bill Hurt, who was deeply entrenched in the making of the film, but of the entire company, particularly the producers responsible for the money.

We sped in the tiny ambulance to the emergency room of the Helsinki University Hospital. It appeared very efficient: the long hall leading to the emergency room was busy with beds coming and going, pushed in a quietly-ordered, fast quadrille. The young doctors, I was happy to find, spoke English, as did one of the nurses; all of them wore white uniforms and rubber-soled clogs. Lee was immediately hooked up to oxygen and intravenous cortisone. He couldn't lie down, but had to crouch on his knees and elbows to get air. It took two or three hours before his breathing became easier. He then had X-rays, ECGs and blood taken from the artery in his groin; all this was frightening to me, but didn't seem to concern Lee. Many Finns smoke like stovepipes, so it was quite crowded in this large, well-equipped room. The people on either side of Lee wore oxygen masks: a long thin man on one side, a plump woman on the other. Undressing was very casual for both men and women: just short screens in front of the beds, which were mostly ignored anyway. When Lee eventually seemed to be out of the woods, he took his mask off for long enough to urge me to go back to the hotel and reassure the movie producers that he was OK. Even then his thoughts were for the project, and he didn't want to worry them. I was also quite in the way in this busy hospital. I went out into the gray afternoon to find that it was not snowing, as might be expected, but raining. The sidewalks were filled with women pushing baby carriages, the infants bundled up and kept dry, red-cheeked and warm behind plastic flaps. Finland is bitterly cold and snow-laden for many months of the year, but these children are out in it all the time; it occurred to me how healthy they must be. I reflected then on the scene I had just left behind in the emergency room – people gasping for breath – and on what a waste it all was. I hailed a taxi and explained in sign language that I had no Finn marks. We had not even been there a whole day and I hadn't had time to change money. By that evening Kerry and I had Lee's driver Ari, a handsome, pleasant young man (who later served in the UN buffer zone between Israel and Syria), to drive us, so we went back to see Lee. To my great relief, he was much improved and now had his own room, number 51, in the special lung area. Inside this modern, futuristic-looking hospital the rooms were tiny but extraordinarily well-equipped, with all the medical apparatus neatly recessed. Everything was white and glass, blue trim, flowers at every station. Finns smoke so heavily that they are very much on top of this area of medicine.

By the second day, Lee was much better. While he languished reluctantly in his bed he had visitors – among them William Hurt and the director – and bedside meetings.

After four days in hospital Lee was out, with the local and foreign press in attendance. 'Old war wound kicking up,' Lee declared straight-faced from the hospital steps. Luckily he had arrived a week early on location and no time was lost with the filming; which he jumped right into a day later. Sable-hatted, driving over the snow in a Russian troika, he joked to a visiting journalist, 'I've given up falling off horses; yet the first day here they stick me in a troika, and I spend the day staring up at a horse's backside! Yeah, but not just one – *three* of them. Jesus, I've gone up in the world. I think they are trying to tell me something. Where am I? What am I doing here? Will someone please tell me?'

Much of the shooting was done outdoors in Finland's winter cold. I know now it must have been physically tough on Lee – but he didn't show it. He appeared to have recovered well after the spell in hospital.

William Hurt really had the lion's share of the work in the film. Lee and Bill became close collaborators during the shooting, although what happens on a movie set can be a very complicated thing for some actors. They are deeply committed to the work: 'the movie', the project as a whole. In this film Lee and Bill were as deadly adversaries, each fighting for his life. They are also professionals, who have to keep what they're doing in perspective. There was a contest between their characters in the movie, and the acting was also something of a contest as well. Later Bill was to say of Lee, 'Lee Marvin acted the hell out of his scenes. He acted better than I did. Instead of trying to beat him, which was, of course, not my job, I wanted to let this person teach me. Let me be Good and him be Evil, and my goodness will be how much I can learn from him. Because he's going to shoot at me every precious thing he ever learned. And he did; on so many levels you wouldn't believe.'[1]

Lee said of their working together, 'He's a dangerous actor' – a compliment, and one he didn't hand out often. 'But he didn't scare me. I've always operated under the same philosophy: know your lines and defend yourself.'[2]

Describing Bill to Army Archerd, Lee said, 'It was like working with Brando or Jimmy Dean in the old days. He's very intelligent, not a fooling-around actor.'[3] And Lee not only admired his work, but enjoyed his company. Few people were as pleased as Lee when Bill won the Academy Award for his role in *Kiss of the Spider Woman*, and we were both very happy to be there to witness the event.

1 *Esquire Magazine*, October 1986, Jack Kroll.
2 Saturday, 31 December 1983, AP from Beverly Hills, Arts Mexico City News.
3 28 April 1983.

I wrote to Bill Hurt and asked if he would consider writing down his reflections about Lee and *Gorky Park* for inclusion in this book. Within the week, from the location where he was filming a movie, he answered. I will forever be in his debt for his insight, his great generosity and his brilliant turn of the pen:

10/17/91
Buenos Aires, Argentina
I don't really know how to say this without sounding a bit meagre in the feeling department, but: I don't miss many people gone the way I miss him. He was 'real'. I think many people feel actors are not, that their feelings are somehow manufactured, that they are fake. But acting is about telling the truth, if you're really an actor. And he was. I loved him. Instantly and truly. I frankly hardly ever took to anyone the way I did to him. I think about him often and the pangs of missing him cut deep. He was a pro in the best sense, the real sense, the honorable and loving sense. No BS, generous, clear, honest.

I remember the first time I met him. We were in Helsinki and I got the word that Lee would like to meet me and I said, with some fear, 'Fine, where?' 'Well,' came the reply, 'he's in the hospital.' 'Oh . . .' I thought, 'he's going to die right here, now, before I get a chance to work with him.' I don't mean to be crude, Pam, but it's what I thought. I really wanted to know him, and I didn't want to get that close to it and lose out. 'Or,' I thought, 'he's finding some excuse not to work with a patsy like me and he's looking for an out. He saw some dailies or something and is dumping it.' I don't know what I thought, exactly, except I thought I was about to be disappointed. I went to a hospital; Michael Apted was with me. I was nervous. I think his work in *Cat Ballou* and others is genius, pure and simple. And he was head and tails above most others, not only in his 'genre', if that's what it ought to be called. He pulled serious fun and style out of every minute, every second. His humor was fathomless. Panache. So we get to this kind of not-so-clean-looking floor in a strange hospital, and walk down the hall, an endless hall with lots of small doors; it looked like a very inactive place. And we get to a door and Michael looks at me and says, 'Ready?' I say, 'Sure.' We go in. Real nervous, now. So, I look around from behind Michael who is saying, 'Lee, would you like to meet with Bill Hurt now?' The voice: 'YEAH, SURE, BRING HIM ON IN.' I come in and there is this long, thin mantis man sitting on his knees in the middle of the bed bending forward over about six books, one of which I see right off is the script, and he's still trying to concentrate on the last paragraph of whatever page, with his white-white hair dipping in a quarter moon around his red forehead. And we stand there for a second. He doesn't look up. He's wearing white pajamas. Then he curls a leg, really lithe, around underneath him and assumes a half cross-legged sitting position, all with his head motionless, fixed in concentration, takes a pause, a large, large breath, holds it for a long second, and lets it out slowly and fully and deliberately. Then he sits back, raises his head with his eyes pinched closed and head tilted back, concentrating real hard on what he just read, letting it sink in, and suddenly his eyes slam open under those twirled eyebrows in that face forever amazed, and he looks at the ceiling for a second, seeing the image, opens his impossibly cavernous mouth, sucks in a bunch of air fast through clenched teeth, and looks at me. He blinks, seeing nothing for a second, focuses, and lunges forward, rolling over onto his leg with his right hand stretched way out and says: 'HI THERE! GOOD SCRIPT, ISN'T IT? I'M LEE!'

This guy had rhythm. Really. I fell for him right there, finito, I was gone. We talked and talked. About the script, life (scripts are supposed to be about life, I think sometimes people forget that). I was astounded to learn about his life, considering I was laboring under some of the hazy illusions about macho that much of the world was. I was stunned, at first, but then not at all as I began to look at it more clearly, at how well read he was. It's impossible to act well if you're uneducated, I feel. It doesn't have to be Yale, but it has to be something. We had flyfishing in common. He told me about mornings *before* he went to the job that he had (to pay for his education), *before* he went to college classes, when in the dawn he would creep up on 'them little trout' in the cold mists. He put them back alive before it was common to do it. He would make this little sipping sound with his teeth and lips when he described it that used to put me on the floor laughing. I loved this guy.

One time, the first day we actually were on the set together, he arrived. Now, I had been having a bit of a time of it with some of the English crew and cast. There were a few I was not getting along with at all, and they were screwing around with me. Little stuff but aggravating. I was really the only American involved, and there was a good deal of resistance to me socially. It was OK, but difficult at times. He came in quietly, in his suit, looking very dapper and *in character* (he was so much more of an actor than, I think, typically, he was given credit for: he did what he did so well you couldn't tell he was doing it. In some of his work he made such fun of the macho so beautifully that the subject of the artistry of it didn't come up too often. We were laughing *with* him too hard, I guess.) He was very quiet, sitting comfortably in a chair on the set, readying for his scene. At one point he comes up to me (I was more nervous in those days though I am still high-strung, I try to concentrate hard and don't like to be distracted). He quickly leans to my ear, very 'conspiratorially', with a couple of those over-the-shoulder, 'don't let anyone know what I'm about to say' looks, and he says, 'HOW LONG HAVE YOU BEEN PUTTING UP WITH THIS CRAP???' I said, taken aback that anyone would notice let alone seem to care, 'Six weeks.' He said, 'WHOA!' like he had just been given a head count of the enemy surrounding our foxhole, and was planning the master counterattack. 'OK,' he said, 'WHILE I'M HERE, YOU GO AHEAD AND TRY TO ACT – I'LL GUARD YOUR FLANK!' And you know what? He did. He really did it. Nobody pulled any of the little numbers while he was around. He was a good friend to actors.

He was the most 'set-savvy' actor I ever met, and it was all for the betterment of the work. He knew more about film than most of the people he worked with and he shared his knowledge when asked, and when not asked (usually people are too proud and foolish to ask a lot of questions when they're acting in film; they're too busy trying to make it look like they know something) he would help out in lots of little ways that few if any noticed. He policed the set for distractions and tried to stop it. Often there are people who look like they know their job, but don't know how to keep out of the way when someone really needs to work hard. There are many things that happen on a set that an unpracticed eye would be completely unaware of; this is true in any craft. It is unfortunately true that many powerful people in the 'industry' know as little about the artisanship of film-making as the average viewer. I thought professionals were supposed to know more about their work than 'lay' persons, but . . .? He honestly cared about other actors' working conditions and the quality of the whole. And acting with him was . . . just exciting, just a joy. He was always 'there'. Some actors are never 'there', they show up, point their eyes, point their ears, but never see and never 'listen'. They're too scared to learn to do anything but the minimum requirements. He always saw and always listened. Acting demands courage. Some are not ready. Some are hired for the very reason that they are not ready, it helps dilute the contribution he/she might make imperceptibly in the never-ending whittling away at character and detail. He was so vivid. His subtext was strong and clear. And he had . . . bravado. I loved every minute of working with him and was sad when a scene between us was over. One of the important scenes between us was cut from the film, it was a disappointment to me because it was good, and I thought it was important to the film, but 'them's the breaks', as he might have said.

At one point he was supposed to fall into and 'die' in a bunch of mud. It was very cold, outdoors, very damp, he was sick. He lay there for a long time without letting anyone help him up so as not to destroy the continuity while they set up another angle, never a complaint.

He didn't travel with an entourage, as you know. Just came to work, on his own feet, no board of directors. He was proud of his work. He was not commonly apportioned an appropriate credit, I felt. He used to tell me how some other actors got 'big' and started to travel around with their lots of people. Not him, he said. He was him, he was the package, he knew his work, he did his work. I learned a lot from him, a whole lot.

I remember the night I was given the Academy Award, he was the only person of all the hundreds of hundreds of people that night who said anything that I remember or am proud of that made sense and could be distinguished as honest. Not that some other people did not say anything meaningful, it's just such a frenzy that it's impossible to say whether anyone means it. People are nervous. He said something wonderful to me and I'll never forget it and I'll be forever grateful to him for saying it. I'll be forever grateful to him anyway. You were standing there next to him, you were both sitting quietly at a table and you were quiet and unassuming and he stood up and said something I will treasure all my life.

One time, you and I and Lee were sitting in that bar/restaurant in the lobby of the hotel in Stockholm, and he said, I think out of the blue or maybe I had asked him for another story, 'You want to know what life is all about?' 'Yes, I do.'

'OK.' And he reached behind him and pulled his wallet from his back pocket. He took a battered photo out of it and held it in his hand while he spoke, not showing it till the time was right and purposeful to his theme.

He says: 'You know I like to fish, right?'

'Right,' I say.

'And you know I like to fish on the Great Barrier Reef for Black Marlin, right?'

'Right.' I had wondered if there wasn't some relationship between the great Black Marlin and the great White Marvin. 'OK, well . . .' he said, 'once I was out there, with the forty footer, and the Aussie crew (and they're a tough bunch, I can tell ya) and one day we were out there, and we saw "it". And we all knew when we saw "it" that it was The One; it was the record. And we all knew this. By the size of its sail. The spotter knew it up where he was in his perch, and we all knew it, even on the deck, we had glimpses, because the thing was huge, man – and the hunt was *on*, if you know what I mean.'

I knew what it meant to him. Though I personally disagreed with the act, it was from a different perspective. He was from another time, and the event was different for him. I also knew that he had the ability which some people don't, to learn from

events, and even and especially from pain. I remember that
reporter who asked him, after the palimony trial, 'Mr Marvin,
do you think you've learned anything from all this?' And he
said, 'Knowing me? No.' Well, anyone who can say that has
learned something very important. 'I got into the chair,' he said
(the fighting chair) and his hands started working. He threw his
hands out of his cuffs like he was getting down to 'the work'
right there at the table in the lobby. 'I grabbed that rod – and
waited. "Talk to me!" I shouted to the top-man. "Tell me when
it's close."'

When Lee told a story, you were with him when the story
happened. He stops, pauses, lingers, remembers, fingers the
memory like 'fine agate marble', as a playwright named
Corinne Jacker said it in a wonderful play called *My Life*,
which I had the privilege of doing.

He did that – he played with his memories like fine agate
marble. I waited. He waited. I broke the pause, 'Well, what
happened?' 'He closed on it,' he said. 'He tapped it with his
"bill" once, twice, gave it a lash, and took.'

Pause.

'What happened?'

'Nothing.'

I waited.

'What do you mean? Was he hooked?'

'Yah, he was hooked.'

'And?'

'I've never felt a weight like that,' he said. 'But it was very
strange. Very. He didn't do anything. I couldn't budge him, not
an inch. If we moved the boat forward he would come forward
that much, if we backed down on him he backed down, just
that much and always the same pressure, immovable. He didn't
sound, he didn't run, he didn't charge, didn't rise, didn't do
anything. He just hung there, down under the waves, real still,
and like a rock. Couldn't budge him.'

I waited.

'It was like that for almost an hour,' he said.

Lee's face looked like a cliff, staring, expecting me to
understand something. He was waiting under his unkempt

falcons' wings, furrowed brow, head tilted with an eternal 'Well, do you understand?' I didn't.

'My arms were falling off,' he said, 'Couldn't move; and I've never asked anyone to take a rod from me in my life, but I was about to. We were all spooked; my arms were numb, I wanted to throw up. And then, suddenly, there was a great, huge tug on the rod and it almost flew out of my hands or pulled me with the harness and the chair out of its roots in the deck, and . . . it was gone. Nothing. No pressure. I pulled a bit but even the weight of the line was too much for me, I was shaking that much from it all, and I asked a guy to reel in for me. I knew we'd lost him, no pride lost in the deckhand reeling in nothing.'

He looked at me one more time to see if I'd figured anything out, yet. He leaned forward and picked up the picture now, which he had placed earlier face down on the table. He held it cupped in his hand where I still couldn't see it.

'Later,' he said, 'I was at the rail up forward, having a beer, feeling my arms come back onto my body, but I still could hardly raise the can. And one of the crew comes up and casually says, "What'd you think of it?" I asked him, "What?" He said, "What was on the hook." I said, "What was on the hook?" He looks at me like he can't believe what I'm saying and says, "You mean you don't know?" "*What*?" I say. He tells me to come with him and he drags me to the back of the boat, till we're looking at a big ice chest cooler. He stops me and says to his mate, "He doesn't know." The guy looks strangely at me and goes over to the ice chest and opens it. And puts his hand in and pulls out . . .' (And here he hands me the picture.) 'The eye.'

I looked at this snapshot, and it's a picture of a guy holding something big, like almost the size of a bowling ball. It was the eye of the creature. Attached to it were the nerve endings and blood vessel stems that had torn away as the fish, which had been what they call 'foul hooked' (hooked badly) in the eye, had been forced to decide to wrench its own eye out of the socket rather than lose its life and freedom.

This is what Lee had meant when he said, 'You want to know what life is all about?' That there are some very tough decisions to be made, sometimes.

The ever-present glint, the Big Wink, in his eye was that much more of a masterstroke now to me, seeing the realizations he had had to endure and out of which he had managed to salvage his dignity. He had managed to save his joy of life from experiences of great difficulty. It's a rare triumph, an inspiration to see someone save their joy from the inevitable sadnesses and disillusions of life, to see the choice where others would reject a choice. He was one of the ones who knew there was always a choice, that sometimes it was not between alternatives either, any of which one would choose, but . . . 'them's the breaks'.

I remember the impossibly low voice falling out of his jaw, great jaw, oddly fine forehead, his odd handsomeness, and the ever conspiratorial joke upon macho itself. He was a deadpan. He told a lifelong joke about how seriously we all tend to take ourselves and how ridiculous and touching we all are as we do it. He seemed to be forever saying, 'Oh, c'mon. You really *believe* this? *Do* you? You *don't*? Well, you *should.*'

The market is more mockery now, than anything really funny. One rarely laughs 'with' anymore, one laughs 'at' – it's really pretty pathetic that we can't think of ourselves as forgivably funny. He was a fine tragedian, too.

I remember lots of other things. I remember every detail of his face and features, mannerisms, etc. I remember these things about people, sometimes, but not with the love I remember him with. Maybe I should have loved more people, but there are not many who I find as honest as him, and it's hard for me to enjoy loving a dishonest person. Loving a dishonest person is different from loving a person who enjoys life, with all their faults, and everybody has them. He was one of the rare ones who could get past them. Maybe not eradicate them, certainly not, but – transcend them, clearly, he did.

I expect, hope him to be at the Gates for my Interview. I have a hope, an imagining, that as my transgressions are counted endlessly and laboriously, he will sit there in the lobby, legs crossed, watching the angels flapping around, seemingly disinterested, till finally bored, stand and say, 'Look, Pete. This guy is a friend of mine, and I know he's fullashit and you know he's fullashit and he knows he's fullashit, but can we cut this shit? Just let me take him under my wing and I'll straighten his sorry ass out for him and get him outta your hair. Thanks a lot.' And, without waiting for a response, just looking up with that 'Oh, Brrrotherr!' look, he puts his hand between my shoulder blades and pushes me into heaven despite myself, me and Peter too dumbfounded with his sheer style to do anything about the regulations.

I think Lee knew a lot more about the regulations than a lot of tightasses do. Lee was not a tightass. There are some things I wish had happened for him, but that's my problem. There was nothing about him that he couldn't handle, and that he wouldn't take the rap for if it was his responsibility to take it.

I really loved him. And thank you for this opportunity to reminisce about a man I treasured and treasure, and miss, in a real, surprisingly and consistently fresh way. He was such a delight that I enjoy missing him.

I know I am effusive.

I remember how, whenever I saw the two of you sitting anywhere, that you always seemed to be a quiet couple. People did not bother you, you did not seem to need cheap attention, you minded your own business. I met you both not that long before he died. I met you after you had rediscovered each other and seemed to have found something very simple and beautiful, after some of life's battles, I imagine. I am fortunate to have met you and Lee.

'While I'm here, you go ahead and try to act; I'll guard your flank.' I'd have him on my flank or in my company anywhere, anytime. A Thorny Critter, with a heart of mother of pearl. People with his . . . sense of and deep, funny compassion for what fools we all are, are rare. That line, from Shakespeare, 'a Fool, a Fool, I met a Fool i' the forest!' And Jaques can't stop laughing with the great relief of having discovered someone, out there 'in the woods', who sees us, as we are, and can wink. 'All the world's a stage, and the men and women merely players.'

He was a great clown, and an actor, and a stylish man.

Pam, you're wonderful to write a book, for all of us who were his pals and for all the people who might get a glimpse into what he was really all about. I'll be standing on line waiting for it.

He 'nailed' Lee – as Lee himself would say – in his descriptions during this time, and they will stand unrivalled in my estimation before or since.

13 Fighting a Good Fight

Two short months after the wrap of *Gorky Park* we were in Paris preparing for the film *Canicule*. 'Mounted up' again, as Lee would say.

He particularly liked the idea of making a French film, 'a French *French* film'. The actors and actresses were all French except for Lee, who spoke his lines in English and they were later dubbed.

We were ensconced in Paris in the extremely comfortable Hotel de la Tremoille, just off avenue George V, where I immediately fell into bed with jet lag. Lee, rarely bothered by fatigue of any kind, closed my curtains and went off to lunch and meetings with Norbert Saada, the film's producer, and the director Yves Boisset. The location was in and around Orléans in the Loire valley, but the preliminary work was in Paris for a week or so before shooting began.

Three days into the wardrobe fittings, haircuts and new pages for the script, Lee developed a bad cough. We went to the hospital for diagnosis: 'A lovely case of pneumonia,' declared the doctor, Professor Even, so back we went to the hotel, where Lee had been ordered to bed, much to his annoyance.

A nurse came in and gave him penicillin shots. He slept a lot and forced himself to drink broth or whatever I ordered for him, and took handfuls of vitamins. Lee was always a very active participant in his own cures, no matter how sick he was. He seemed mentally separated from this bothersome body; the physical state had nothing to do with *him*. He would sleep or rest, whether he wanted to or not, all the while mustering his forces.

Lee was still quite sick the day we were due to leave for Orléans. We weren't traveling until late in the afternoon, so Christel Boorman, who was in Paris at the time, and I went to Saint-Germain to shop. Later we sat at an outdoor café having coffee and *croque-monsieurs* and talking the time happily away. It was after five when I looked at my watch. I fled, while Christel walked away down the sidewalk barefoot, her shoes in her hand, sore from all our enthusiastic walking. I got back to the hotel just in time to meet Lee coming out of the elevator. He was quite properly annoyed with me. 'I'm leaving,' he said shortly. 'You can come if and when you're ready to.' Then he drove off with the producer. He did leave his driver Hubert Gauthier, however, to bring Kerry and me. I packed like a madwoman, rushing here and there from closet to closet while the cleaning maids waited unhappily out in the hall. Of course, I felt very guilty, and wanted to get to the hotel in Orléans as quickly after Lee as possible.

As we were leaving Paris through the Arc de Triomphe, there was a wreath-laying ceremony being held at the grave of the Unknown Soldier from World War Two. It made me think of my father, who had died the year before, and about the wars that had been fought through those shadowed green woods we were now driving through. My father had probably been in them, and my first husband Mac undoubtedly. I struggled to hide my tears for most of the hour and a half ride to Orléans. I didn't want to think about it, but I was beginning to worry about Lee's health – particularly his starting off with pneumonia at the beginning of another action movie. However, instead of being in the cold Nordic winter, he was now in the sultry heat of the Beauce, the 'bread basket' of France, in summer.

On Friday morning, Lee rose for his first two days of work. He was given ampicillin shots twice a day on set by a nurse, and still looked quite ill and thin, but game as usual. After a day in bed on Sunday, he was noticeably better on Monday and had good scenes, running through fields of wheat with the young actor David Bennent. I was still very concerned about him. He was pale under the flush of physical activity, but he strove hard to hide his shortness of breath after the scene; sitting down and leaning over, resting on his elbows as if concentrating, head down. Sitting together, it would look as if he and I were talking about something privately; he also developed a trick of pushing himself up from the chair with his legs so that it looked effortless. After two weeks we went back to Paris to see Professor Even. Lee's lungs were clear and he was declared fit: working, even running through hot fields, was good for him, I guess. Lee was extremely happy about the filming of this movie, and was impressed not only by the other actors and actresses but the whole production. Then, after more than two months away – including an appearance at the Deauville Film Festival, where he was being honored (*Point Blank* was shown) – we were back in Tucson.

As a result of these episodes of asthma, bronchitis and now pneumonia, Lee began going to Dr Benjamin Burrows, a well-known lung specialist. They talked about his smoking (and the doctor's, who was having his own problems quitting). We stocked up on antibiotics and spancils of prednisone whenever we went on location out of the country, and Lee did cut down to a pack of cigarettes a day – which was as far as he could go at the time.

Lee and I had settled in as full-time parents of two grandchildren: seven-year-old Trevor (whose middle name is Lee) and Emily, who had just turned six the month he began work on his next film, *The Dirty Dozen: Next Mission*. Their strikingly beautiful mother Maury, so capable on the one hand, so vulnerable on the other, had more in her life than she could possibly cope with: trying to work, care for a young infant and endure an abusive marriage. One morning she was taken to hospital in upstate New York. We heard about it.

'What will we do?' I asked Lee.

'Get the kids out here.'

'What about the baby?'

'*And* the baby,' Lee said without hesitation.

That evening they were in our house in Tucson and I was in New York with my daughter.

Lee and I had deliberately not had children after we were married. First of all we were too old – I was forty and he forty-six – and between us we already had eight.

'That's a lot of phone calls,' Lee liked to growl on television shows. 'And they are all gainfully *un*employed,' he would joke, whether they were or not.

We already had one grandchild when we were married; three-year-old Jess, who came to live with us at Malibu when his mother Wendy moved in to take care of the house and our respective children when we went away on locations. Being around all the kids was a lifestyle Lee liked: it was one of the reasons for our getting married when we did. As for me, nothing could have made me happier: everyone was safe and well cared for, yet we could still go off filming whenever Lee chose. Being married to Lee, whom I loved very much and had for most of my life, and having my children and his with us – all now totally secure – was a fulfillment of my existence that I could scarcely have dreamed of (though of course I did).

As most people would at this stage of the game, I imagine, Lee liked the situation up to a point. By the time he died, we had ten grandchildren. Lee became well known for getting through the main course of a big holiday dinner – Christmas, Thanksgiving, birthdays, we had them all at our ten-foot-long dining room table – and then, raising his eyebrows and putting on a forced 'I've had it' smile, he would excuse himself from the clamour to go down the hall to our bedroom and read.

Lee was very straightforward with the children and treated them like small people; people who made him recall things about his own early life. He didn't go to Trevor's Cub Scout meetings – I did – but he did help him to make the wooden cars or the other required projects, taking him out to his workshop with its saws, sandpaper and paint. He gave him *The American Boy's Handy Book: What To Do And How To Do It*, and he went to Emily's first-grade class on 'parents' day', where he sat in the middle of the room and explained to a circle of six-year-olds what he did for a living. When Emily was very young she wrote down some memories of Lee:

> I remember something Lee said.
> (wen) he went to the hsopital once. He said he didn't want to room with anyone there or it would be, 'bifuurbbb . . . ops sorry pal' And another time he said (wen) we were making penut butter he said 'Looks like a doggie doing something.
> Love,
> Emily

Emily recalls Lee explaining to her in great detail about the compound eye of a fly, the different birds and cactus.

He was very big on showing up for the babies' births, going to the hospital and giving moral support in the labor room. He made sure the nurses and staff knew he was there, and everyone got lots of attention and the best of care – and he was there to congratulate the fathers. The weddings were held at our house, in the living room in front of the flower-bedecked mantelpiece of the big white fireplace – with the exception of Cynthia's, which was held in a small hotel.

By taking on two grandchildren, Lee became the backbone of support for me, even though he very much liked a quiet, hibernating sort of life in between movie-making. He enjoyed the freedom of being able to go off at a moment's notice to Australia or anywhere else in the world, even to view a movie in LA, but more than anything else just to be alone with me in our house. He was almost sixty when the kids came to us, and I was fifty-four.

Now that he had a role of such responsibility, his occasional drinking bouts began to worry him. 'What if we get *the* phone call in the middle of the night – a wreck or something – and I can't make it'; no doubt a recollection of his motorcycling days or of life on the accident-strewn Pacific Coast Highway – or of his own close calls and great good luck. We were also reminded of this in Tucson. Although we lived in a secluded area in the desert, the road not far away from our house wound through the foothills to the nearby mountains, and its curves were a favourite for glissading drivers dropping down toward town in the night. We were often wakened by a squeal of brakes in the silence. We'd wait. If they didn't make it, we could hear the thud into a palo verde tree or mesquite tree or the crackling of greasewood bushes and cactus being plowed over. Lee would say, 'Uh-oh,' jump into his clothes, grab a flashlight and be gone. Mostly they were young drivers, but not always. One night he came back shaking his head and laughing. 'I don't know how they made it. The car was upside down and these two older guys, black, were dead drunk. I got them in my car and drove them to Tucson General. When they got out, they saw me and one of them said, "Man oh man, I must really be drunk. I'm seeing things. You look just like some movie star."' When we moved to Tucson, Lee bought our grandson Jess a dirt bike and gave him rigorous training, also laying down the rules: 'Never ride without all your gear and never two on a bike.' He also bought three other bikes: a

500 TT Yamaha four-stroke for himself and two 175s, one for me and one for Rod, Kerry or whoever was to ride with us. He bought all the boots (Italian Alpine Stars) and the helmets; he already had the white pickup truck to cart us all out to the desert. He took his bike out alone several times, and suddenly one day, after all my hopeful questions about when we were going to go with him, the other bikes were gone, sold back to the store he had bought them from. No matter how romantic an idea it had been, he apparently didn't trust us not to kill ourselves.

The Dirty Dozen: Next Mission was shot in England in winter 1984. It was a movie for NBC television, so the filming schedule was only six or seven weeks. At first the location was to be Yugoslavia, but Lee said no. The winter weather in England was bad enough, he said, without combining it with the notoriously rustic accommodation and food in Yugoslavia at that time. 'I hate cabbage soup,' he summed up. 'What will I do about Trevor and Emily?' I asked Lee. 'Have someone to come and take care of them?' Lee had already thought about it. 'No, we'll take them with us and get a nanny in England.'

The weather *was* really raw, cold and raining a good deal, and this was an action film, most of it set out of doors. The interiors were cold as well, as an empty, unheated stone building was used as the general's offices. I was concerned about Lee's recent propensity for contracting pneumonia or asthma, so had got the name of a doctor at the famed Brompton Chest Clinic in London. Lee hadn't forgotten the shooting of the original *The Dirty Dozen* in 1967, where so many of the actors and crew had been laid low by colds and pneumonia – and they had all been *younger* then.

During the first part of shooting near London I rarely went to the set with Lee. 'Don't come out,' he'd say, 'there's just nowhere to get warm.' I never saw Ernie Borgnine at all, as all his scenes were done in or around London.

We were at the Dorchester only a week before we moved north to an old inn outside Peterborough for the flying scenes. The flat lands of East Anglia were dotted with small airfields, and one was used for the German aircraft in the movie, a three-engined Junkers 52. The weather was mostly gray, wet and cold, but the kids and I (no nanny here) spent our days with Lee. It was very exciting for them, of course, with the plane and the fake explosions and lots of machine-gun fire. They were very popular with the actors, and loved to hang on Lee and follow him around after the shots. Lee's brother Robert had spent World War Two at a similar airfield not far from where we were. There was a lot of action and a lot of lying in cold mud for Lee. His trailer was warm, but nothing is very comfortable when you are wet.

After returning to London, the company moved once more, southwards to Hayward Heath for the railroad . . . and more cold, wet weather. Lee finally succumbed to a cold, or should I say succumbed in his own fashion: working and coughing.

Lee was on antibiotics by the time we got back to our house in London. He kept himself under tight control mentally and physically. He moved into another bedroom, one with a big four-poster, and immediately after work and dinner, which was usually no more than soup, he would go to bed, bundled up under an eiderdown. His whole focus was on the work – something he did so well on movies in any circumstances – and on getting through it. He made it, but not before losing fourteen pounds. We had a couple of relaxed days before an afternoon of looping, and we were home before Christmas, laden with ginger cakes from Harrods.

The sun of Arizona soon had Lee feeling fit again, and by February we were in LA, where he was doing the round of publicity for the television debut. We spent the day with Ernie Borgnine, Richard Jaeckel, Kenny Wahl, Larry Wilcox, Andrew McLaglen, Harry Sherman and the others from the film; we moved to our 'home away from home', the Beverly Wilshire, for more rounds of interviews. A tribute to Sam Peckinpah was organized at this time, and Lee had been asked to speak about him.

It was during the shooting of *The Dirty Dozen: Next Mission* that Lee saw the monument to the Polish flyers who fought with the RAF in the Battle of Britain in 1940. He wrote it down on the back of his call sheet in England, and after looking it up in the Bible in the hotel, quoted it at Sam's memorial:

> I have fought a good fight,
> I have finished my course,
> I have kept the faith.

14 Finishing My Course

Shortly after *The Dirty Dozen: Next Mission* was finished, the Israeli producers Menachem Golan and Yorum Globus sent a script to Lee. The movie was *Delta Force*, and it was to co-star the popular martial arts professional and actor Chuck Norris. The Globus production company, the Cannon Group Inc, had been very successful with a string of action films: *Invasion USA* and *Missing In Action* with Chuck Norris; the *Ninja* series; and the Charles Bronson sequels *Death Wish II* and *Death Wish III*. (Lee had been offered the part in one of the *Death Wish* sequels, but turned it down flat. 'That's Charlie's role,' he said, leaving no room for negotiation. He also suspected they were trying to negotiate Charlie's salary down, or get some other compromise from him.)

Delta Force clearly resembled the hijacking of TWA Flight 847, which had so stirred the emotions of the American public and the rest of the world. It recounted the painfully long standoff; the killing of the young man who was in the US Navy; and the unbending stoicism of the plane's pilot. It was fiction with a strong basis in fact, but had a near-perfect happy ending.

Lee's role was to be that of a colonel, the commander of an élite group of commandos and anti-terrorists, the Delta Force. He and Chuck Norris, who gets to display his karate expertise and some high-tech weapons, head up the successful, explosion-filled rescue mission.

Lee described it as 'Hollywood fantasy' and stated publicly his own personal view that diplomacy, not violence, was the only solution to the dilemmas of the world. He did think, however, that the story brought to the big screen the anguish and discomfort of hostages everywhere, and in its own way went right to the basics. 'A close-up of conditions . . . bad enough on *any* long flight,' he said. 'Add to that the facilities breaking down. Just imagine a bathroom after three or four days in the heat.'

The starting date for *Delta Force* was September 1985, and the movie would be filmed entirely in Israel. Besides all the usual concerns connected with accepting a movie offer, Lee had to think about whether he wanted to make a purely action entertainment, a 'martial arts' film, at this stage in his career. It would also mean that for the second year in a row, he would have to forgo our annual fishing trip to Australia. Ordinarily, he would refuse a movie which interfered with our fishing dates. Lastly, and most importantly, he was having difficulty breathing whenever he exerted himself. But he decided to accept – a challenge I imagine he couldn't refuse.

His acceptance set off the usual round of discussions, negotiations and meetings, and some not so usual. A member of the real Delta Force came to Tucson to show Lee some of the new weaponry, and they went far out of town to what Lee thought was empty land in the rolling desert. To Lee's great embarrassment, the owners of the land, whose house was totally hidden from view behind a rise, came out to find out what all this machine-gun noise was about. Lee was most apologetic, but the good-natured ranchers took it all in good humor, laughing to friends and neighbours about finding Lee Marvin and some military man shooting up their desert.

Just before filming started, our dear friend Barbara Ford died. Lee and I sat in the Good Shepherd church in Beverly Hills with Nancy and John Bryson, Peter Bogdanovitch, Jimmy Stewart, Dobey and Marilyn Carey, and other old friends of Barbara's and the Fords. After the service and the burial, near Barbara's father John Ford, we went to her nephew Dan Ford's house with John Wayne's daughters, and then on to John and Nancy Bryson's house where we were spending the night. John was writing a book – a photo-journalistic chronicle of his travels with Armand Hammer – and had rented a house, a 'writery', in town to finish it. Here we had a good amount of Russian vodka and caviar (possibly from one of John's trips to Russia with Dr Hammer). It had been a long day and certainly an emotional one, and when we came back from dinner at Spagos, Lee, who was quite in his cups, said to me in an anguished and angry voice, 'Don't you realize I am leaving you? I am going to Israel to make a movie and *you're* not coming with me.'

No, I hadn't; I just thought he was being ill-tempered. Later in the summer we went to Woodstock, where we rented a house for a month or so each year. Lee usually stayed a week or two and then went back to Tucson while I stayed on. He loved the 110-degree summer temperatures in Tucson, which I found hard to take, and Woodstock for him served mainly to revive old memories of his unhappy days with his family. After seeing his brother and sister-in-law (usually accompanied by the obligatory, age-old custom of 'a few drinks'), my parents, David Ballantine and a few other friends of his, Lee would go home.

When I got back to Tucson, he was still adamant that I was not going with him on this movie. I was devastated. My being with him on movie locations, as well as everywhere else, had been our way of life from the day we were married. More importantly, he wouldn't explain why – at least not with what seemed complete honesty. 'I don't want to have to worry about you or anybody.' I hadn't planned to take Trevor and Emily, now eight and seven, because of the violence in Israel at the time. Kerry too was back in college and unable to go. 'That didn't matter,' he said.

I was not only unhappy, but worried about Lee. He was not feeling well. He had bouts of breathing problems, the early stages of a pulmonary disease. He was struggling to quit smoking, but without success. A trip to the Mayo Clinic in Rochester, Minnesota, only served to anger him. He was given this badly-phrased warning (more a cliché) by the doctor: 'If you don't want to become a burden to your family, we recommend that you stop smoking.'

'What?' exploded Lee, who took care of everybody. 'Me a *burden* to my family?'

Charlie Bronson, Jill told me, had been given exactly the same warning. He immediately stopped smoking, began to run five miles a day and turned it around. For Lee, try as he might, the struggle was in vain. I searched for smoking addiction clinics. There really weren't any I could find that just addressed smoking. There were plenty if you were on drugs or alcohol, but Lee wasn't about to tackle drinking and smoking at the same time. He did not want to go to the Pritikin Center because it was in LA. 'Right next to my old haunts,' he said. 'It wouldn't do me any good.'

I couldn't believe that he didn't want me with him at this time, especially when he might need me more than ever: my care, my company, my fending off intrusions. And the two of us would have been alone together for the first time in quite a while. I took it as a rejection: I was puzzled, deeply hurt and depressed – which is what he intended. He said really harsh things: that I was a 'pain in the ass' on location rather than a help. Since most of our life together had been spent on location, this was a real shock, a repudiation of so many years, that sent me agonizing to Norman Lessing, Lee's most intimate friend.

'He doesn't want you to go, and he's making sure that you won't,' was his immediate observation. 'He's just holding himself together... don't you see?... and he can't be *worrying* about you over there.' What's there to worry about? was my feeling. *He* was the one to worry about, I thought.

Lee packed his best formal clothes – his handsome and very expensive suits from *Gorky Park* – to go to make an action movie in the heat and dust of the Israeli desert. Usually he would only take his most casual and comfortable clothes, and if we were lucky, one good jacket. By this time I was angry as well as sad, and wondered why he wanted such an elegant wardrobe and where he was planning to be entertained – quite insensitive to the idea that the person he wanted to impress might be himself.

Lee wavered, but didn't relent. On the way to the airport he said to me, 'Look, honey, it won't be long. I know it. I'll send for you as soon as the time is right.' There was a first-class plane ticket waiting for me at the Cannon office in LA, he told me, and when I needed it I should just call them.

We got to the airport early. He was always a prompt person, but recently he had been making sure he was really early. He didn't want to have to feel hurried physically or mentally. It made him short of breath if he did. At Tucson airport there is a long uphill gradient to the gates, and we walked along slowly, casually. He nodded to people, who called out, 'Hello, Mr Marvin', or 'Hi, Lee'. He was flying from Tucson to Israel's Ben Gurion airport, with a change of planes in Chicago. I had found a diet, 'Overcoming Jet

Lag', which worked very well: we had used it on the last couple of flights to Europe. Lee had been following it for a week before he left for this really long haul, and when he arrived in Israel he was completely without jet lag.

He kissed me good-bye and boarded the plane. I was left with very mixed feelings – caused by him as well as coming from within myself. We had never been apart for this long, and it was by design . . . but I did confidently believe that, having proved his point, so to speak, he would settle in and summon me to come. He didn't.

Several days after he left, the kids came running up from the tennis court to tell me that there was a rattlesnake wrapped around the spokes of Trevor's bicycle. Lee insisted that there should always be a hoe in the big pot by the swimming pool for just such a situation. I grabbed it, ran down the brick stairs outside, managed to unwind the snake, and against the laws of the state of Arizona, killed it with the hoe and a rock. My heart was pounding and I was sweating, but it was done. We were back in the living room when a knock came at the door. I opened it to see two men standing there in three-piece suits, unusual dress for Tucson. They flashed their FBI badges and I invited them in. I immediately told them that I had thought the snake was a danger and so had killed it – forgetting, of course, that it had happened only moments before. They looked at me as though I was crazy and then asked me where Lee was.

'Gone,' I said. 'He's away in Israel.'

They asked me, 'Would he have taken a trip lately?'

It was my turn to wonder if *they* were crazy.

'Yes,' I answered, 'he went to Israel.'

Actors in the old days (the 1940s and 1950s to us) were not particularly fond of the FBI. Too many had been subjected to harassment during the McCarthy period. That flashed through my mind briefly, but those days were over, and it was not something that would have affected Lee anyway.

Although initially very mysterious – asking for flight numbers, dates, the cities he went through – they asked if Lee might have sent a postcard to anyone from an airport en route.

I said, 'Absolutely not, but he might have signed an autograph for someone.'

Which is exactly what he did do. The someone, it turned out, happened to be Edward Lee Howard, an ex-CIA agent who spied for the Soviets – the most damaging double agent in American history – who was that instant defecting to Russia. He had left Tucson on the same plane as Lee, and sat chatting to him between flights in Chicago. It was here that he asked Lee to sign a postcard for his son Lee – the same child he was presumably leaving for ever. He obviously then mailed it to his home address in Santa Fe, New Mexico, where it was snatched out of the mailbox by waiting FBI agents. Here was a man leaving his wife, son and country, fleeing for his very life, stopping to pass the time of day with Lee and getting an autograph. You wonder who sits on high and directs such encounters throughout a person's lifetime. We in the family immediately thought that; to Lee, of course, it wouldn't seem too far-fetched.

Lee recalled the man when we spoke the next night. He remembered asking him how he had managed to get such an early flight after leaving Albuquerque, which is where he said he had come from. He hadn't, he answered casually; he had been in Tucson for a few days for a meeting of accountants – which is what he claimed to be. In fact, he had driven through the night in disguise, a woman's wig on his head and a dummy by his side, after finding his house under surveillance by the FBI. Several agents – FBI or CIA, I don't recall which – were sent to Israel to question Lee about his recollections.

Shortly after the agents came to our house, I saw an article about the defection of Edward Lee Howard. It had made headline news all over the country, although, of course, there was no mention of his meeting with Lee. I clipped the article out and sent it to Lee with a letter. The letter arrived at his hotel with a neat slice out of the top of the envelope, no article, and only my letter. I had sent him a card at about the same time, for our anniversary. He called, quite annoyed at *me*: not only was there no article, as I had said there was, but the card had been rerouted to Ireland and opened. It was clearly marked:

Mr Lee Marvin
Tel Aviv Sheraton
Suite 2017

115 Hayalov St.
Tel Aviv, ISRAEL

'Oh,' I thought, 'they wouldn't really, would they?' and wondered if our phone was tapped as well.

Lee brought both envelopes back with him when he came home. 'There,' he said, plonking them down on the table in front of me, as though I must surely have had something to do with it, just to annoy him.

Time passed, and though we spoke or I wrote often, Lee still did not ask me to come to location. He was very comfortable: the Sheraton Hotel in which he stayed was a vast improvement over the hotel we had been in some years before in Hertzlia. The food too was much improved, he reported. 'I'm behaving myself,' he said – meaning he was not drinking. One night I called and he wasn't in his room, although it was really late. The next day he was angry: 'God dammit! Wouldn't you know the one time I'm out you would call!' He said he had been out with a group of flyers from the 103rd fighter squadron.

The warnings and the whisperings of the other wives came into my mind: having to show up on location to put the kibosh on a rumored affair, and claim back their husbands in the nick of time. A movie star alone, in such intense circumstances, is a great target: for women working on the production, for the fawning public – for anyone, should the movie star choose to be vulnerable. I knew this, of course, but wild horses could not have dragged me there. I canceled a planned trip to the Nile with my dear friend Dulcy (a shame, because later she died tragically) because I would have landed at the airport in Israel and it would have seemed to be a maneuver, a disingenuous way of 'showing up'. There is no way I could have been in Israel, minutes away from his hotel or the set (a good deal of the filming was actually *at* Ben Gurion airport) and not go there. Added to that, I knew I couldn't carry off simply arriving and being casual about it. It was late in the game: cast and crew had developed that protective, loving family club. I knew that, under the circumstances, Lee would be cold, punishing – even if only briefly – that I would be made to feel the fool and would become angrier than perhaps would be healthy for a long marriage. Furthermore, I, who knew him better than anyone else in the world, did not know *why* he didn't want me there. I vacillated between various conjectures:

He *was* physically desperate and didn't want to have to worry about me (which is what, among other things, he had said).

He was physically desperate and didn't want me to see it.

He was sixty-one and wanted to have a fling.

He was punishing me for being so involved with the children (a plausible thought, even though he had urged me to do just that).

He wanted to prove to himself that he didn't depend on me.

I *was* a pain in the ass.

Maybe it was a combination of them all, maybe none of them – who knows?

I took to jogging, then to running. I was certainly busy. The kids had riding lessons, music lessons, doctor's appointments, school things, birthdays. I went to Los Angeles for a party celebrating the publication of John Bryson's book *The World of Armand Hammer*. It was an elegant affair, held in the atrium of the Los Angeles County Museum of Art with several hundred invited guests, including John Huston, Jerry Brown the former Governor, Gregory and Veronique Peck, Cesar Romero and many people from the literary world. John Huston's arrival, quite late, was a happy surprise. Weakened by emphysema, he came in a wheelchair pushed by a nurse carrying an oxygen respirator. He was disappointed to miss Lee, but sent his warm wishes for him on the movie.

Kerry and I went to New York where she was to have surgery, a delicate operation for a thyroid condition. This was the first time something major was happening when Lee wasn't in attendance and we missed his support. He was waiting it out by the telephone in Tel Aviv while she was in the operating room. Perry Lang came and stood in for him, keeping me company in the waiting room for long hours with moral support. Mitch Ryan was in New York, where he was on *All My Children*, and took me to dinner. We went to one of those wonderful French restaurants on Lexington Avenue – down two steps, packed. The hostess recognized him and seated us immediately, glowing, 'Please enjoy your dinner, Mr Ryan.'

After we sat down, Mitch said with a wry smile, 'You work in the theater all your life doing Shakespeare's plays, O'Neill, Greek tragedies, make lots of movies, nobody knows you; you do one television soap opera . . .'

We were staying at the Sherry Netherland Hotel, and in the mornings I donned my jogging sweats and ran in the cold and snowy Central Park – very warily. People were nervous about the mounting violence; they stayed in groups, or looked about themselves constantly. Israel had little on Central Park.

Soon after I got back to Tucson, Lee's ten-week shooting schedule was completed. He said to me, 'I'll get home from the airport myself. *No*, don't meet me,' he commanded.

We were rather like cold card-players, not wanting to tip our emotional hands. He was angry, I was angry. I knew mine was only superficial, because it sat on top of an aching feeling of regret in my chest. I didn't *know* whether his was until it dropped off in frosty shards over several weeks. Then he slowly became *him* again. He sat on a camp chair on the patio in front of his den (which houses his trophy 1232-pound marlin on the wall and my world record 607-pound fish). His feet up on the low wall, he was smacking the occasional flies that came within reach of his mesh fly-swatter.

'I thought of leaving you,' he said as we sat having a drink, 'but I knew I wouldn't be happy.'

'I'd far rather you left than wonder about it,' I retorted. I was so angry I had to walk away. I thought about telling him to go.

To exacerbate these turbulent thoughts, we kept getting overseas telephone calls – and hang-ups (at the time, overseas calls were recognizable because of the bleeps). A woman's voice, accented, asked, 'Lee?' and when I answered, hung up. 'What's that?' I asked, but he said, 'I have no idea, but don't read too much into it,' in a voice of admonition.

Not long after the movie was finished, we went to LA. 'I want you to meet Menachem,' Lee said. We had been invited to a wrap party being given for the cast and production company by Cannon, but Lee declined to go. Instead, we went to the office to meet the head of the company, Menachem Golan. Before starting the film, Lee had heard mutterings about people having money problems with the company, having difficulty in getting their salary payments, but afterwards Lee refuted that totally. 'Menachem,' he said, 'was a total gentleman throughout. I have not one complaint and the money was not only prompt . . . it was better than most.'

Lee introduced me and, after giving a polite greeting, Menachem looked at me and asked, 'How come you don't appreciate your husband?'

I was completely taken aback. 'What?' I stammered, 'I *do* appreciate my husband.'

'No, you don't,' he said, shaking his head. 'Why, why you don't? He's a wonderful actor, a wonderful man.'

I had never met Menachem Golan in my life. I was utterly astonished at his assessment of my personal feelings, and said again, 'But of course I do . . . I certainly do,' my anger beginning to rise. He just shook his head, showing that he didn't believe me in the least.

Lee didn't react one way or the other, and while they talked about the upcoming movie publicity, I sat silently pursing my lips and wondering just what Lee had managed to say about me in the ten weeks he had been with this man – and why.

We went to New York, where Lee did the rounds of the television shows there: 'Good Morning America', 'The Today Show' and the others. Now that I was in contact with all these people from the movie, I was pretty sure a zing would come to me from somewhere – and it did. One of the people in Chuck's entourage felt compelled to tell me, well after the fact, that it's 'no good to leave a man alone on a movie location', shaking her head.

'Thank you, thank you,' I thought to myself, but smiled dumbly. To cap this whole episode, Mrs Golan, a seemingly intelligent woman, also took the opportunity to show displeasure at my apparent disregard for my husband. We were staying in a suite at the Park Lane Hotel, where the Golans kept an apartment. We had dinner with them one evening in the dining room of the hotel. Mrs Golan had very little to say to me, although I tried valiantly to engage her in conversation. Finally she turned to me and said, '*You* should come to Israel some day, it's quite nice.'

'I know,' I said. 'I was there for some months once.'

'You were?' she said, still only glancing my way. 'Well, why didn't you come *this* time?' she asked politely, but with a decided edge.

I let silence fall over the table for a long moment. I looked at Lee, thinking, 'Well, I'll give him the opportunity, let's see what he does.'

He didn't do anything. He looked completely blasé, at ease; she might have been asking me about the weather or something he knew nothing about.

I blushed, I'm sure, but finally answered, 'Well, I couldn't. We have two grandchildren who live with us and I had to take care of them.'

Lee knew I would do it – cover for him.

'What? They *live* with you?' she asked, surprised, and then looked rather thoughtful. Thereafter she warmed up considerably.

So that was my job on this film, I thought, realizing I was important because of my absence: Lee had been 'abandoned'. We got back to our rooms and I called Lee an unprintable name. 'You don't understand,' he hissed emotionally, hoarsely, 'I never thought I would make it out of Israel!'

I *should* have known that. He had been just too adamant about my not going with him for there not to have been some major worry. He didn't want me to see him keeping up a front – which I would have recognized – and he didn't want me telegraphing my concern to anyone in the movie company.

It was February and it was snowing, damp and cold in New York. Most of the television shows were taped early in the morning. We arrived at the 'Good Morning America' studios in the middle of a snowstorm. Lee was really tired, worn out and coughing. Again, he pulled himself together to get through the work. During the day, under the spotlight of publicity and cameras, it was not noticeable, but his face was becoming deeply lined, shadowed below his cheekbones. He would go pale when he coughed. We needed to get home and to the sun. But he had great strength, stamina and will power, and nothing would prevent him from finishing a job. We got through it.

15 Keeping the Faith

Lee was invited to the 58th Academy Awards presentations in March 1986.

'You'll enjoy it,' he said. 'Let's go.'

We left the Beverly Wilshire Hotel in a good mood. There was no heat on: Lee was not nominated for anything or presenting, but there as a movie star, sitting prominently with the nominees and presenters in one of the front rows. Lee wanted to attend, he said, because he felt it was important for the old guard of Hollywood, of which he now was one, to support the other actors, particularly the young ones coming up. 'Of late they haven't been doing that,' was Lee's feeling.

Our limousine pulled up in front of the Dorothy Chandler Pavilion and Lee stepped out, waiting to take my hand. I don't know how any woman can clamber out of the middle seat of a limousine elegantly. Of course, the door is held open for you to enter the limo first, which is all very nice, but then you have either to slide over the seat with your long skirts, bunching them up, or hunch over in a half-crouch a few steps and sit. Getting out, it's all moving over, untangling, and rising – but not so far as to hit your head – and then stepping out as effortlessly as possible.

We walked the gauntlet of roped-off fans and photographers, and then up to the wooden platform where we were greeted by the official Academy greeter, Army Archerd, who used my first name as well, being his usual well-prepared and pleasant self. Once inside the entrance hall of the pavilion, you felt a great sense of energy. More than two thousand people all in the same business – actors, actresses, directors, producers, agents, their families – the whole spectrum was together there and comfortably protected from the fervent fans outside. Spotlights for television cameras splashed over knots of people as someone was singled out for comment; there were actors

396

and others drumming their recent pictures to the privileged press as well as visiting, vying, complimenting each other. It is very exciting. You see people you haven't seen for years and meet others for the first time. There were many familiar faces, including Jon Voight, who was nominated for Best Actor for *Runaway Train,* Jack Nicholson for John Huston's *Prizzi's Honor,* William Hurt for *Kiss of the Spider Woman . . .* and Britisher Kit West, with whom we had spent more than five months on two back-to-back movies, *Avalanche Express* and *The Big Red One.* Kit was nominated for his visual effects for *Young Sherlock Holmes.*

As we were walking toward our seats, Klaus Maria Brandauer and Lee spied one another from a distance. In a moment they had clasped each other in an impromptu and mutually joyous embrace. They had never met before: their *simpatico,* however, was instantaneous. A few words and we were gone. Klaus was nominated for Best Supporting Actor for his role in *Out Of Africa,* in which he was brilliant. We had seen him in *Mephisto,* the German film that won the Academy Award for Best Foreign Film in 1981, and had never forgotten his performance: 'stunning', Lee called it.

I was seated with Donald O'Connor and his wife on my left. He was presenting the music awards along with Gene Kelly and Debbie Reynolds. When he left to present the Oscar, his wife leaned over to me to exchange a word. I told her how much in love with Donald we girls had all been in the 1940s, watching him dance, sing and woo the girl. She, heavier than the slim Donald, confided to me that she broke in his tap shoes for him. She walked around the house in them doing the dishes and dusting and did a little dance herself. I contemplated that mental picture while my mind glided back in time.

Lee would occasionally get up and go out into the hallway for a cigarette. To insure that the television audience never sees an empty seat whenever anyone leaves, a paid stand-in comes to take his or her place. This is all directed and choreographed from the wings; the doorway to the hall was off-camera. The wardrobe for the stand-in is often somewhat startling when seen close up. Although dressy from afar, these were probably costumes that had been used over and over again in the world of the extra.

It was an entertaining night of watching people – and having people watching you. Cher appeared as a presenter in tall black boots, lots of midriff and a high, wild, black feathery Indian-like headdress, to both a burst of applause and a chorus of groans. Lionel Richie sang 'Say You, Say Me', and across the aisle I could see William Hurt mouthing each word of the song for Marlee Matlin sitting with him so she would miss nothing. (The following year Bill would present her with the Oscar for Best Actress for the movie they made together, *Children of a Lesser God*.) Jessica Lange, so very good in *Sweet Dreams* and nominated this year for Best Actress, was with Sam Shepard, who kept glancing back, seeming to study Lee.

Angelica Huston, strikingly beautiful in an emerald-green dress, received the Oscar for Best Supporting Actress in the movie her father directed, *Prizzi's Honor*. Near the end of the program, Sally Field came on to the podium to open the envelope for Best Actor. I had always known in my heart that Bill Hurt would win for *Kiss of the Spider Woman*. He was extraordinary in that role. It was a thrilling moment for me, as though I were somehow personally involved, when Bill's name was announced. He jumped up and hugged Marlee and his director before heading off to the stage, where he gave a brief acceptance speech, recognizing his co-star Raul Julia, and then commented, 'I'm very proud to be an actor.' As he left the stage, he gave a short laugh – much more an exclamation of emotion than of humor.

There were quite a few moving moments for us that evening: hearing *Mask* (the movie that the recently-deceased Barbara Ford had edited for Peter Bogdanovitch) nominated for Best Makeup; the appearance of the ailing John Huston, a man Lee was very fond of, who was nominated for Best Director for *Prizzi's Honor* (which our dear friend John Foreman produced); and seeing the great Japanese director Akira Kurosawa. His film *Ran* had been nominated in four different categories, one of them Best Director.

Before voting for his choices for the awards, Lee and I would make the rounds of all the movie houses and catch up on the nominated films. We had seen *Ran* not long before. Lee's regard for Kurosawa was immense, and his relationship with Toshiro Mifune, who had appeared in so many Kurosawa movies, added a more personal dimension. Just two years before, in March 1984, Lee had spoken at a tribute to Mifune held at the Japan House in New York.

That evening had begun with a reception at the home of Mrs John D. Rockefeller III, and here Lee and Toshiro saw each other for the first time in more than ten years. A few telephone calls and Christmas cards were all there had been in between. It was a good moment. Lee's later speech honoring Toshiro was as emotional a one as I had ever heard him give.

He said, amongst other things:

> I know it sounds trite and old-fashioned, but I still can't help saying what a tremendous honor it is for me to be here to meet my friend Toshiro Mifune and to talk about some of his movies. He and I have only made one picture together, *Hell in the Pacific*, but that single experience was an intense one, and it developed in me an enormous admiration for Toshiro . . . We made that movie together in 1968, on the tiny island of Palau. He plays a Japanese soldier stranded on the island and I play an American soldier in the same situation. We hate each other, love each other, need each other, destroy each other and try to save each other . . . all at the same time . . . So it's an honor, and a great, great personal pleasure for me to be here to welcome my friend to America, to join all of you in honoring this wonderful man, and to show you some of his films.

After the reception, we were taken to the Japan House by limousines that drew up one after the other for us. I, with Lee just behind me, mistook Mick Jagger's long silver limo for ours and began to get in. Noting the quandary this seemed to put the Jagger party in, an amused Francis Ford Coppola called us into his for the short ride over.

The tribute began with a darkened stage. Very slowly the lights came up to reveal a life-sized statue of a Samurai warrior dressed in ancient robes. The arm was cocked and the still hand placed on the hilt ready to draw the sheathed sword. Lights rose, slowly illuminating the otherwise empty stage, and suddenly the statue moved, swiftly drawing out the sword and yelling an explosive warrior cry. It was, of course, Toshiro. The place went wild.

At the Academy Awards presentation that night the Best Picture presenters were John Huston with his now-familiar oxygen tank, Billy Wilder and Akira Kurosawa. It was a really theatrical close.

As we were leaving the auditorium and standing in the salon where hundreds and hundreds of people were talking, posing for pictures or waiting for their cars to drive up, I noticed that Kurosawa and his entourage of Japanese men and women were sitting alone in a corner of the room. The ceremonies over, they were now being completely ignored by the glitterati of the Hollywood film industry, who were walking by happily engrossed in their own auras or urgencies. I mentioned this to Lee, who grabbed my arm and steered me directly to him, bowing as he introduced us. Akira rose and bowed in return. With the aid of interpreters Lee paid his deep respects. Afterwards they spoke of Toshiro Mifune and then we said our good-byes.

'Can you believe that?' Lee said as we left. 'Here is one of the most revered directors alive today and nobody here cares.'

We sped off to the Governor's Ball and dinner with the rest of the Academy members who were either not invited to Swifty Lazar's dinner at Spago's, were spurning Swifty Lazar's dinner at Spago's, or were going late to Swifty Lazar's dinner at Spago's. Most of the others appeared to be relatives or money people who were owed a favour – at least, so it seemed at our table. A young relative of the well-known movie mogul Kirk Kerkorian sat next to Lee. He was clad in a tuxedo and sockless loafers, and whenever he wanted to leave the table he just put his hand on the back of Lee's chair and vaulted over him. Coming back, he merely dropped off the railing behind us into his seat.

It was a ball, however, and Elizabeth Taylor danced, though Ginger Rogers didn't – she was at a table near us and from behind was completely recognizable, with her silver hair in a pageboy and wearing a blue sequin dress. Much more visiting than dancing went on. Bill Hurt came and brought Marlee over. Lee stood up and fondly shook his hand, saying to him, among other personal things, 'Congratulations, you stood up for acting.' Jack Nicholson came over and squatted down, talking to Lee. His arm was in a cast, broken – I think he said – skiing. He seemed unfazed at not getting an Oscar, but very pleased that Angelica had. When I congratulated Angelica, who has a gentle but savvy elegance, she said to me, 'I think your husband is so' – hunting for the right word of praise – 'so *cool*.' Her father, there briefly, had gone off to Spago's pushed by his nurse. Lee was disappointed not to see him this time; sadly, they did not see each other again.

We sat with Ernie and Tov Borgnine at their table for a few minutes before leaving. Also at the table was Max Schell, in his preferred white suit, and his sister Maria. After a while, perhaps forgetting that she was with him, he rose and ambled off toward the exit. She grabbed her things and hurried after him, calling, 'Max, Max, you bastard . . . wait for me!' There's no doubt about it: well done, poorly done, good taste and bad, it's a great celebration.

Lee was asked by Menachem Golan and Cannon Films to repeat his role in *Delta Force* in the newly-planned *Delta Force II*. He had received the script, a revised second draft, in May 1986 and broken it down into scenes – something he did when he was contemplating whether or not to accept a movie. He did not do that film. The last movie Lee made, and it seems profoundly fitting, was for the United States Marine Corps.

It is a training film for young Marine recruits, but it is also an impressive document, poignant and well executed. Entitled *Combat Leadership: The Ultimate Challenge*, it not only extols the virtues of rigorous training, but includes the advice and heartfelt reflections, unscripted and in their own words, of the heroic Marine combat officers from World War One, World War Two, Korea, Vietnam and Grenada. One veteran, Colonel William Lee, had served in Nicaragua in 1934 with the famed general Chesty Puller. Another was Dr E. B. Sledge, whose book *With the Old Breed* Lee had insisted I read: 'If you want to know what war is *really* like, you *have* to read this book.' Dr Sledge himself described it as 'The savage, brutal, exhausting, and dirty business of war.'

In a departure from past training films, the staff of the Marine education center decided to go 'first class', as they said, and contacted Lee.

'I'll do it anywhere, anytime!' was Lee's immediate response. Meyer Mishkin brought up a conflicting engagement. 'Cancel it,' was Lee's reply. 'This is important. I'm doing this one for free.' Meyer brought up the union, SAG. Lee said he'd take minimum scale and endorse his check back to a Marine Corps charity. Which is just what he did.

A Hollywood director, Mike Christy, was brought in as well; he had not only been a Marine himself, but had retired from the Army as an infantry lieutenant colonel after serving two tours of duty in Vietnam. Lee was asked to narrate, to introduce the officers and to film with the troops out in the field. The major filming was shot at Camp Pendleton, California, at the end of April 1986. Lee stayed on the base in a suite. The last time the Marines had put him up at Camp Pendleton was in 1943, preparing him for the invasion of the Marshall Islands, and as he pointed out, he wasn't sleeping in any suite (nor was he sharing a bottle of Myer's rum with the commanding officer after work). He would call me at night, as enthusiastic as I have ever heard him. To be there once more after forty-three years and under such different circumstances was, as can be imagined, very affecting for him. He was a movie star *and* a Marine, and he still found it mind-boggling when a general would salute and call him 'Sir' – but most of all, he had survived. He often said, 'Look, everything after 1945 is just gravy.'

For the shooting of the movie, Lee decided to wear jeans, a dark blue Levi shirt and suspenders. He didn't want to be masquerading in a semi-uniform. In the last scene, however, he stood in front of a table on which a dress blue uniform was lying. Lee touched it, drew the sword slowly out of its sheath, slid it back and smoothed out the trousers, respectfully straightening the accessories. Behind him on a hanger was a uniform shirt blouse with battle ribbons, as Lee would once have worn as well.

We were unable to go to the première of the completed film in Quantico, Virginia, the following summer as Lee was in desperate straits by then. Major General Jonas M. Platt, a combat veteran of World War Two, Korea and Vietnam, was pressed into service at the last minute and spoke in Lee's stead. He talked of the movie, about Lee's involvement and his vast disappointment at not meeting him here.

He mentioned that Lee had praised the new breed as being 'terrific':

He asked me to tell you: that he had great regret at not being here tonight; that he felt it was an honor to work on the film; and that he really liked the finished product because of its basic message – that Marines fight for other Marines. In a recent TV interview, Lee Marvin said this film was the most important he had ever worked on because it contributed to a legacy – and *this* from a man who won an Oscar for *Cat Ballou* . . . He is still very much a Marine and very proud of the Marine Corps. From one World War Two Marine to another, I salute him.

The year before, after the making of *Combat Leadership: The Ultimate Challenge*, Lee had caught flu. Combined with an asthma episode, it led to a series of circumstances that ultimately caused his death . . .

16 End

Lee died on 29 August 1987. He died not from a sudden heart attack, but from a combination of incompetence and arrogance: a doctor who did not recognize a case of peritonitis, and who refused to take the symptoms seriously because they were reported by 'silly, overwrought' women. Added to this was Lee's stoicism when in pain (something our generation was taught to have: tell it calmly, clearly, and understatedly); his stubbornness and his aversion to hospitals; and a cumulative reversal of his past extraordinary good luck. All this was, in the end, coupled with a force that became so overwhelming that I could feel its power, an inexorable force that would not be denied.

A series of events led to this day, starting nearly a year before in October 1986. A neighbour was having work done on the dirt road in front of our house without watering down – against the law in the desert. Each day backhoe tractors threw forth clouds of dust that seeped into our house. It began to bother Lee's breathing.

One night during this time we had dinner with our friends and neighbours Howard and Marlies Terpning. When we came home from dinner Lee took the clip out of his hand gun, a Belgium Browning 9 mm semi-automatic, which he had taken with him – something he often did when we were out at night, even next door or on a drive. His carrying guns didn't worry me. I felt comfortable about it because he was not only expert with guns, but a very controlled person. I knew he wouldn't make any kind of mistake or over-react to anything. He also had an axe under our bed and a hatchet hidden under the seat of his pickup truck. When you are once called upon to protect your life, you're not going to be taken by surprise.

He told me he had not felt well all evening; he felt 'dingy' . . . almost hallucinating. He felt warm. He woke me at about six o'clock to call Rod to come; he couldn't breathe because of an asthma attack, and wanted us to call an ambulance. Most importantly, he wanted me to make sure the ambulance drivers didn't use a siren: he didn't want the neighbours 'disturbed'.

Once in hospital Lee was given oxygen and massive doses of intravenous cortisone – steroids. He was no better all night and sat up, leaning his elbows on the bedside table. The next day, his oxygen was removed by one of the attending doctors. Shortly afterwards I heard Lee's doctor in the hallway whispering hoarsely to him: 'Do you want to be responsible for this man's death?' – a statement which received my close attention. I realized very quickly that hospitals are not places where a patient is watched all the time, and that mistakes can be made. In China it is routine for a member of a patient's family to be with him at all times in hospital – which is what I wound up doing. Here, entire families of Hispanic patients stay night and day in the waiting rooms, little babies on the floor with bottles; the grandparents, parents and other relatives never leave the area. The following day it was discovered that Lee had flu as well: influenza A, the first documented case of the year in Arizona.

Six days later he had 'plateaued', he said, and began walking around. He was a very popular patient. Besides being a movie star, he was self-reliant, straightforward and non-complaining, even under the worst of circumstances. He also had the ability to describe his condition in his own short-cut manner: facial expressions, hand gestures or succinct, if novel, verbal imagery.

He was about to come home when he mentioned some minor stomach pains. I came back to Lee's room in the early afternoon to find a bevy of doctors around his bed. Lee's pain had suddenly become severe, and immediate exploratory surgery was suggested. Although his breathing had markedly improved, this pain had them puzzled. I called his internist Dr Edgar Desser, who had come to Tucson from the New York Hospital and whom Lee had been seeing recently. He was unavailable, away playing violin some-where. I called a surgeon we knew. He was in the middle of a heart bypass operation at his hospital, and would come afterwards. I came back to the room to the urgings of the young doctors asking us to make haste with a decision, and that the surgeon *they* had called was on his way. Before he came, the surgeon was described to me thus: 'Don't be surprised when he comes in – he's, er, quite short.' The surgeon arrived and was indeed short, dramatically so, with quite long arms. The anaesthesiologist was with him. I didn't like the way this was going at all. A small operation Lee had had six months before had *resulted* in an asthma attack. I called the head of the pulmonary department of Cedars Sinai in California, who suggested an ambulance plane bring Lee there. Lee nixed that idea. He was hurried down to Intensive Care, where he had cat scans and all sorts of tests and was hooked up to the very invasive looking Swan-Ganz, a risky and probably unnecessary catheter needle in his neck. I held everyone at bay, much against their wishes, waiting for the surgeon, who finally came in the evening. He felt there was an internal perforation due to the cortisone, and reiterated that to operate should not be the first course of action but rather the last. If we wanted him to take over, we would have to move Lee by ambulance immediately.

One doctor, his voice rising in anger, told me that Lee's death would be on my hands, but I had no control over how I was feeling: I simply knew that if Lee was operated on he would die. Lee left it up to me – but he wouldn't get into the ambulance to go to the other hospital. It was becoming a horror story. Then, quite suddenly, Lee appeared to be improving on his own, everything was beginning to stabilize. It was well into the middle of the night, and with Lee's improvement the hospital surgeon came into the room, so crammed with apparatus of every kind, and said to me, 'Oh Mrs Marvin, you must have prayed to God and he answered you. I know that I did,' and left looking decidedly beatific. Not being very religious, I was rather taken aback by this summation of medical theory.

A day later Lee was moved out of Intensive Care and into a room. It was a cubicle of a room – windowless, narrow, dingy – but the hospital had become so overcrowded that it was all that was available. The room was extraordinarily depressing for Lee, and very much affected his mood. He raised his hand and dropped it down on the bed in discouragement, the first gesture of defeat I had ever seen from him.

By morning, Lee had decided to transfer to Tucson Medical

Center. 'God, what a relief,' he said, 'I can get better here.' We would wait it out; meanwhile, he was to have no food by mouth, only IVs and antibiotics to heal the 'perforated sigmoid diverticulum' caused by the cortisone (an unfortunate side effect of this sometimes wonderful but powerful drug). It became a very long wait indeed. For twenty-eight days thereafter, he had not one spoonful of food.

Time went by as in a dream. It became an almost unimaginable physical trial. I thought before it was over that he was going to die of starvation surrounded by a host of doctors, who were checking his charts daily, and lovely, caring nurses. We became quieter as time ticked away, conserving strength, waiting. One day, in the only clue he ever gave us about his feelings of hunger, he described a grapefruit he was thinking about. He talked more and more eloquently for what seemed many minutes: the sensation of the squirting juices on the roof of his mouth, the flavour, the texture, the color of a ripe and luscious Florida Red River grapefruit. He became more and more caught up in the ecstasy of the memory; words coming faster and faster, humorously, but with undeniable craving. Thanksgiving came and went, and Wendy and Kerry brought me the dinner from home and a drink of Jack Daniels bourbon spirited into the cafeteria. I couldn't believe he could waste away without something drastic happening. I complained bitterly to the doctors. He could not walk or barely even stand. It seemed on closer examination that his chart was in error, that his weight was not reflected properly, even with people seeing him daily. When he was weighed at last – too weak to stand, he had to be raised on a mechanical pulley – the doctors were shocked. Lee, six feet two inches tall, weighed a hundred and twenty-five pounds: appallingly, frighteningly thin.

We could have had a private nurse, but there was no way I would leave Lee. I had to be in the hospital, as much for myself as for him. It wasn't as if someone was just in hospital waiting for an operation or recuperating; the situation was completely unknown and constantly on the verge of an emergency. I was cautioned by a nurse to watch for a change – and when it did come, I was the one to see it. This wonderful nurse then said, 'That's it, surgery . . . and five transfusions.' And so it was. I had gathered four compatible.

I did not think Lee would survive this operation. I summoned his children from California: Chris, Courtenay, Cynthia and Claudia, who came immediately, as did Ralph O'Hara, a neighbor and chum from Malibu. Ralph had lived with Bill Bixby on the beach near our house, helping him remodel the place and standing in for him on his television show, *The Incredible Hulk*. It was evening before the operation was over. I was overwhelmed with a feeling of dread. We all were. It seemed impossible that after all this time and in such a condition, he would be able to pull through. When the three doctors appeared in the doorway, I was so terrified I didn't even hear what they said – telling me it was over and that he was all right. Jane Loew Sharpless, who had come to wait with me, told me calmly, word for word, what they had said: 'I knew you'd be too upset to listen.'

I went into the recovery room and he was awake, drowsy but absolutely fine. I was told by the nurses firmly, adamantly, that I could not be with him at all in Intensive Care that night – and so for the first time in five weeks I went home to sleep. When we went to see Lee the next day, he was a new man. It was absolutely amazing. Within the week he was home. He was back, he had survived, he was eating, gaining weight – and he had stopped smoking! For the first time since he was ten years old he didn't want a cigarette. Twelve inches had been cut out of his colon to repair the perforation and the colon temporarily rediverted to rest and repair for a short time. He said, 'Let me try a rum.' I brought him a drink: his Meyers rum, the one drink he had discovered he was not allergic to. He took one sip and put it down, shaking his head, 'It's not doing it for me, I don't need it,' and never had another drink of alcohol. John and Christel Boorman, deeply concerned, came from Ireland to see him. It was wonderful: no smoking, no drinking, getting strong, breathing so much better. One morning I noticed that his complexion had a tinge of yellow. I called the internist and told him Lee had hepatitis. 'I just saw him,' he said, 'I don't think so.' But he had. The blood bank had supplied a pint which must have given him hepatitis: non-A, non-B type. I asked why they didn't screen for that and was told it was too expensive.

'How expensive?' I asked.

'About $25,' was the answer. Had we but known . . . or been told.

Lee again lost some weight and was very depressed – symptoms, of course, of hepatitis. He occasionally talked of suicide, ominously getting his guns out and cleaning them; calling Marine Corps buddies he hadn't spoken to since the war. His doctor thought it might be depression because of the surgery and suggested it might be time for the next repair. Hearing that, I urged him as well. Lee was not particularly anxious to do it. 'It doesn't really bother me,' but by spring he had decided to go ahead. He was cleared for surgery by the doctor, by all of them.

When he was being wheeled into the operating room he looked at me with a quixotic smile and said, 'Well, on to the next . . .' A slight pause, and he continued, '. . . the next great experience'; calmly and without even a hint of anxiety or regret – more one of curiosity and even expectation. Now this time, although it was simple surgery, *he* was the one who thought he wasn't going to make it.

It was a quick procedure to reconnect the colon. 'It was nothing,' he said, surprised to be alive, and in just a few days he was home, repaired. Again we were elated. But soon his appetite decreased once more. He got a hospital bed and had it put at the foot of our bed. He exercised from the bar overhead, and a friend of Wendy and Fred's brought him a medicine bag with an eagle's feather in it and other sacred things. Kerry brought Lee healing crystals. Our bedroom had French doors which faced the eastern sunrise; every morning, Lee would wake up and call out, 'Oh boy, another beautiful day' – but often by day's end he would be feeling low. 'It's all gone downhill from there,' he would say. He was undoubtedly still ill from the hepatitis. Lee's brother Robert was very sick, in bad shape from drinking, in and out of hospital, and Lee's sister-in-law had just had a massive stroke, hospitalized with a very poor prognosis; the hospital wanted her out of there. Lee wanted me to go to Woodstock to see what I could do. Lee's internist assured me that he was fine, that this was the perfect time for me to go to get a 'rest'. I didn't believe it. The surgeon's trauma doctor was gravely concerned. He wanted Lee to come to the hospital right away. Lee refused. 'No,' he said, he already had an appointment with another doctor and would see him first. Lee was adamant. He dressed for the appointment in a handsome sport jacket and slacks; he wore his panama hat and carried a cane jauntily. When we walked in, the doctor scolded me right away, 'Oh, Mrs Marvin, I thought your husband was *dying* the way you spoke on the phone,' and gave him a clean bill of health. I said to him, as I had to Dr Desser, 'Please don't be fooled by Lee's presence – he's an actor, you're seeing Lee Marvin the actor,' but they pooh-poohed the notion out of hand. But Lee knew how to project the image he wanted to: all strings and cuts and mirrors, as he would say. The moment was gone. Lee didn't go to the hospital. I got nurses around the clock, and Kerry moved home. They were so compatible that Lee liked that anyway. 'Go, go, go,' he urged. I went.

Lee and I spoke every night, and he constantly assured me he was fine, to keep on and get things done there. I didn't know that Lee had jaundice once more; he had sworn Kerry and our dear housekeeper Laura to silence. Lee was extremely strong-willed when he was being adamant about something. Kerry *did* tell me, however, that he had chills and fever. And then he admitted it. He was so concerned about his brother's welfare that he did not want me to worry about him. I called Dr Desser, who thought it was probably flu. Again Rod took Lee to him. He still thought it was flu. I asked Lee if he had pain, and he answered me 'Ehhh,' which I knew meant yes. 'Some,' he said. I demanded that Lee see another specialist, who ordered him to hospital for emergency surgery. I packed up the two children and we raced to the airport. We arrived in Tucson in the hot brilliant August sun and got to the hospital in time to meet the doctors coming out of surgery. The internal stitches had pulled loose, resulting in more perforation. He had had peritonitis for the past ten days, a condition that should never have escaped notice – worse, really, than a ruptured appendix, and for such a long period. Dr Kartchner whipped off his mask and said to me, 'He's OK. He has a constitution that is just unbelievable. I've never seen anything like it. I never want to see him here again.'

He was fine. He had done it again. Over the previous nine or ten months we had lived through the most extraordinary emotional ups and downs, and now all the nurses from his first stay many months before came in to see him and congratulate us. Rod and Kerry, Wendy, Fred and Hideko had all been at his side or sleeping in turns in the waiting rooms, the children playing out in the courtyard. Jess came home from college. We got to know the other people staying all day or night, and swapped information about how each other's family members were doing. There were triumphs and tragedies. We, too, were now like the Hispanic families I had noticed before: our whole family was sleeping in chairs under shawls or sweaters, doing the same thing as these families here. Lee was in a private room and I stayed with him. One evening there was a thunderstorm, and we opened the curtains and the window so that he could see and feel it. Tucson has magnificent summer storms, which he loved. I was very tired that night – there had only been the lounge chair by his bed available for me to sleep in – and I asked how he would feel about my going home for one night. 'Yes, yes, do go,' he said enthusiastically, 'get some rest . . . it doesn't matter, because when you're not here there is a long silver line that stretches from me to you at home.'

Eight days after the operation, I was called aside and told some worrying news. Lee was losing platelets and there was nothing anyone could do about it. By the end of the day he seemed to have got over that, but he was taken to the Intensive Care unit – his blood pressure had dropped. He was again hooked up to monitors. Dr Desser came in, joked his jolly 'Well, you look fine to me,' and laughed. I laughed lightly back, just in response, and Lee shot me a look of reproach. 'Don't laugh with that man,' and that was all he ever said about the doctor. What had happened was a tragedy, not cause for humor, and Lee knew it. I didn't.

As each day came, something else would happen of grave concern: he began to get transfusions, he refused painkillers – 'No, I don't need any dope' – more tubes, more monitors, more lines. John Boorman was so concerned that I had to call him daily. He wondered if he should come from Ireland. I didn't think so. One day something negative would happen, but the next it seemed positive, and I knew always that he could overcome anything. Once when I was talking to John I looked up and saw a man's body, a tall man, covered by a sheet on a gurney just beside me, a tag on his toe. Two attendants were standing by the man chatting and laughing, totally unaffected. I felt a chilling sense of fear, and John said, 'What is it? Is something the matter?' I had paused at the sight. 'Nothing,' I said, not wanting to share the experience.

One day Lee looked at me and said, 'Look, when it gets close to the end, I want you to leave. I don't want you in the room.' 'What are you *talking* about?' I asked, 'the end of *what*?' 'Yes, yes, I mean it,' he said, very seriously and unemotionally. 'I want you to go. Send Rod in or Fred. In fact, go now.'

I was completely taken off guard. I didn't know what to say. I knew what he was thinking, of course: I knew he was saying that he didn't want me there when things got rough for him, he didn't want me to see that – the hero, the gentleman, the protector. Even now. Mostly now. I stood up thinking, 'Well, I'll have to humor him.' He didn't look at me. He just nodded his head; his jaw was set and his face was without emotion. I said, 'OK,' and went out, and a little later Rod went in to him. He told Rod to make sure that the hoe was outside by our swimming pool at home. Mitch Ryan, hearing that Lee was 'ailing', drove down from California. 'I drove all night. I love the dawn coming up over the desert. It reminds me of Lee and of our times on *Monte Walsh*,' Mitch said. He saw Lee and then took me out for dinner, a very welcome meal.

The next day a candida infection was showing up in his blood. I was already aware that the 'wound', the incision, did not look too good. Quite a term, I thought, 'wound' – it sounds suddenly so military. Like a gunshot. Lee's oxygen level was getting low, he was getting 'dingy', light-headed, again. The doctors wanted to put him on a respirator. 'Is there no other way?' I asked, and was firmly told, 'No.' Our daughter Maury, a respiratory therapist, nodded yes. With deep reluctance, I OK'ed it. When it was over, the doctor came out and said, shaking his head, 'I have never seen a man so strong. He fought it. We call it bucking the machine. And he bucked it like no one I've ever seen before.'

All of us wished fervently we hadn't heard that. I went in to see him for the first time since he had told me to leave. I felt he was glad I was there. I hoped he was. He couldn't talk because of the tube, and he looked down at his wrists which were tied down and he was lifting them to show me. I called the nurse and asked her to take them off, but she refused. The 'patient' might pull the ventilating tube out. I assured her Lee wouldn't, I knew he wouldn't – but 'No,' she said, 'orders.' She did loosen them. All I could think about was Lee telling me about *People Need People*, when he was immobilized in a straitjacket in one scene and nearly lost it in panic. I knew he was fiercely frustrated at being rendered helpless. He opened and shut his hands, and his eyes showed anger and disgust. Another nurse came in and brusquely, uncompromisingly tightened the cloth bindings. One would loosen, another tighten. Some nurses would let me stay with him, some would not and I would have to wait outside until their shift was over. They had absolute authority according to hospital procedure. Doctors were coming by, looking grim. One called me out to the hall. 'There's nothing more we can do,' he said. I mentioned that Lee could certainly *hear*. Another doctor came from the University Hospital: 'I hear Lee's not doing too well?' Again we were just outside his open door. I said, 'Yes, he is, he's all right.' 'Oh, no,' he insisted, 'that's not what I hear.' I was appalled that because Lee could not speak, he was being treated as though he were deaf or a child. I felt he was going to turn this around; he always did. It was only a matter of time. I got a tape recorder with earphones and a tape of classical guitarists: he shook his head. He was fighting, concentrating, he wasn't 'drifting'. On the night of the 28th, he seemed to be resting well. For some unknown reason I felt relaxed about leaving and decided to go home for a night's sleep. Rod was staying in the waiting room and he seemed at ease too. I slept surprisingly deeply, even late, and did not get to the hospital until eight in the morning, quite unhurried for once.

Lee seemed the same when I came in, awake and greeting me with his eyes, but there appeared to be a heightened sense of activity. There were so many lines and tubes and transfusions going on, it seemed impossible for anyone to keep track of what they all were. A nurse would come in, rush out then come back with another. Mitch came in to visit. He left, telling Lee and me that he would be back the next day. Dr Rogers came not long after and called me outside. He told me that Lee had experienced some heart-rate changes, some irregular rhythms. He asked whether, if Lee had a heart attack, I wanted them to use extraordinary measures. I was stunned. 'Of course,' I answered. He explained that the shock might restart the heart, there might be brain damage, but it could also kill him. Another wonderful choice, I thought to myself, one that I hadn't been prepared for and knew so little about. Yes, certainly risk it. I would rather have him *there*, and I didn't care in what mental shape. The conversation made me very apprehensive.

I sat with Lee for the rest of the morning, watching his heart monitor and talking to him quietly. Kerry, Abid (who would later become her husband) and Wendy went to the cafeteria, and we were alone. Two nurses were chatting outside at their intensive care station. At a movement from Lee, I looked at him and saw he was flashing his eyes toward the heart monitor above. He was trying to get my attention. 'What is it?' I asked, and he again flashed his eyes toward the monitor. I could see the needle line was jumping up and down. He was telling *me* he was having a heart attack. I ran out to the nurses, who hadn't noticed, and yelled to them. They called code 99, or whatever it is. Everyone came running and pushed me out of the room. I ran down the hall for Kerry and Wendy and then ran back. Two attendants were standing in front of the ICU corridor, and would not even allow me in the corridor, let alone his room. Then Dr Rogers came out and led us all into a nearby room. Rod, Wendy, Fred, Kerry and Abid; the young kids Pammy and John were outside in the courtyard. Lee had died, he said; it was twelve noon. The telephone rang, it was Dr Desser wanting to talk to me. His office was . . . tops . . . ten minutes away. I wouldn't speak to him. But at least that instant feeling of anger allowed me to cry, and I sobbed my thanks to Dr Rogers, who had fought so heroically night and day to stem every disaster that happened. 'This man is not going to die if *I* can help it,' he had said.

Lee was ready, we were told, we could go in. He looked perfect, healthy, sleeping. He was warm. They must be mistaken. A hospital spokesman came in with us. He would cool. The lines in his face would relax, he said, he would look at peace. 'Go away,' was all we could think. His beeper kept going off. 'I'll leave you alone.' 'Yes.' He came back. 'Don't hurry, take your time.' 'Thank you.' He put his head back in: 'We had one family that stayed all day.' His beeper went off and he left to satisfy its call. We stood in the silence, the dreadful, overwhelming silence; palpable, obstinate, uncompromising silence – no deals to be made here. Everyone in his own grief, and communal grief for each other, mingled with a feeling of unreality and disbelief. My children's faces, almost unbearable to see, had the crumpled look of sadness and defeat. Fred stood sobbing at the foot of the bed, his white cowboy hat in his hand, the hat Lee had given him when his son John was born. The curtains suddenly parted and Mitch was standing there. Some inexplicable feeling had made him turn around and come back. 'Oh, no,' he said softly, his voice trailing off.

We donated Lee's corneas. I thought that if someone could see the world through Lee's eyes, they would see something indeed. Someone handed me his things: his medicine bag with the eagle feather, his hat, his blue New Zealand carry-on bag we had bought on a trip to Australia once. We left as a thunderstorm was brewing; dark clouds swirled and rain began to fall. A nice big storm. Wouldn't Lee have loved it?

That night we all huddled together in the house, all of us for the night. Emily lit a candle and the younger children sat in a circle. Emily talked 'to' Lee, then handed the candle to the other children as they spoke. Howard and Marlies came in crying. We had a drink. Lee's Bunn coffee maker, so reliable for twenty years under his care, refused to work and never would again. A scorpion, somehow on the kitchen floor, stung Kerry's toe . . . but without any other effect. 'Are you seeing double?' the woman from poison control asked on the telephone. 'No, but my brother is,' Kerry laughed, in that hysteria that comes out of great grief.

Lee was cremated. Cause of death: septicaemia, peritonitis. He was sixty-three years old. Poor Rod, so deeply grief-stricken himself, had to attend to it with Mitch Ryan, who was a rock for us all. Perry Lang came down from LA. Somehow he put death in perspective: 'If Lee can do it, I guess I can.' Huge bouquets of flowers arrived, and letters and messages from all over the world with words of disbelief and pain. 'We are with you in heart and soul sharing your grief. We have lost our dearest friend and the world has lost a great artist,' the telegram from John and Christel Boorman said. William Hurt sent flowers and a letter poignantly telling of his great sadness and admiration. Yves Montand's message said simply, 'I loved him . . . courage, Madame.'

Keith Carradine wrote about how remarkable a man he felt Lee was, how privileged he felt to have known him and honored to have been his friend. Bobby Carradine and all 'the boys', as Lee fondly called them, from *The Big Red One* sent flowers and wrote –

Bobby DiCicco, Kelly Ward and Mark Hamill. Mark wrote, 'I consider myself a lucky man to have known and loved dear Lee and Pam and Kerry' and that 'his artistry will live forever'.

The members of the Los Angeles City Council stood in tribute and reverence and adjourned their meeting.

Josh and Nedda Logan wrote, 'Oh, what sad and devastating news of dear Lee. We all loved him so.' Ernest Borgnine recalled the good times and the happiness of their friendship, but broke down in tears when speaking about it on television. Charlie Bronson called – did I need anything? Terry Moore and Sharley Wynn called, and David and Diane Bennent invited me to repair in Paris or Switzerland. Bob Filkosky, his best buddy from the 4th Marines, was heartbroken; and Mitch Paige and many more of Lee's Marine friends, directors, stunt men, actors from all over the world: Ian Holm, Rene Kolldehoff, Sigi Rausch, Eddie Lauter, who wrote again and again. Buddy Van Horn, Brian Dennehy and Dennis Potter, who articulated so beautifully what so many others who knew him well commented on when he wrote, 'I quickly came to value the modesty and gentleness of spirit which he also carried with such quiet grace.' Amy Marie George (who acted with Lee in *Death Hunt*, daughter of Chief Dan George) wrote from Canada. A letter from Dr Michael Brewer carried a message from Sir Laurens Van der Post sending his love and sympathy. 'Two old soldiers, with very deep sensibilities,' Michael wrote. A card arrived announcing an enrollment in the Marianist Alliance, and that a mass had been said for Lee by the relatives of Ross Marvin, member of the North Pole Peary Expedition, it said. There was no return address, so I could never thank them. Lee would have loved to have heard that. I thought, 'Oh, I can't wait to tell Lee about this' . . . forgetting for the moment that I couldn't.

The newspapers carried headline reports. John Huston's death the day before was often reported in articles side by side with Lee's. Jane Fonda said, 'He taught me a very important thing, which is that when you're a movie star, you have the responsibility to think of the crew.'[1] Photographer Eddie Adams summed up in a final accolade, 'He was everything I wanted him to be.'[2]

1 *LA Times* staff writers Bob Baker and Patt Morrison 30 August 1987.
2 *Arizona Daily Star*, 13 October 1987, J. C. Martin.

We held a private memorial gathering of family and close friends in our living room, in front of the fireplace of the house that Lee had put so much of himself into. Jim Mahoney came immediately to handle all that needed to be done: the extraordinary outburst in the press and television, and so much more. He was smoothly accomplished at this, but also caring and thoughtful. MaryPat Ware, our much-loved neighbour and friend, brought her grandmother's Belgium lace tablecloth and silver, and took everything off my hands – as she can so beautifully, tirelessly, without being asked.

All Lee's close associates from California came: Lou Goldman, David Kagon and their wives, Barry Felsen, Meyer Mishkin and Lee's business manager Ed Silver (with whom Lee had been so patient and forgiving). His secretary, there as well, drew me aside and daringly, with all my attorneys only rooms away, had me sign bank signature cards giving him access to accounts he shouldn't have had. Such is the nature of some of the people in the big-stakes, monied world of 'the business'.

We sat in a wide circle, the children all standing in the foyer doorway. Mitch Ryan spoke first: 'Rod, Perry Lang and I thought we would begin by reading several of Lee's favorite selections.'

Mitch has a voice somewhat reminiscent of Lee's, not quite so deep nor gravelly, but with a rich timbre and an ease born from his long years in the theater. Someone, I don't remember who, began by reading 'Do Not Go Gentle Into That Good Night' by Dylan Thomas.

I remember very little about myself all day, except for holding tightly on to my breathing as each emotion rose and being aware of twisting a handkerchief fiercely as I listened to their words.

Mitch read parts of 'The Wild Party' by Joseph Moncure March from a book I had given him when he was making *The Iceman Cometh*.

Perry talked of his closeness to Lee, and Lee's great fondness for Australia, then read 'Out Back' by the Australian poet Henry Lawson.

For time means tucker, and tramp you must . . .

A painting by Tim Storrier hanging on the wall of our dining room contains the first stanza of that poem written over the outback sand. It was something we saw daily.

Rod read a portion of a book he had given Lee, *The Seed And The Sower* by Sir Laurens Van der Post. Later it became a film, *Merry Christmas, Mr Lawrence* starring David Bowie. It is a novel based on his own experiences in a Japanese prisoner of war camp during World War Two and speaks of dying and rebirth, evil intertwined with good, and forgiveness.

It had been difficult for Rod to finish but after a moment of quiet, he spoke of Lee in his own words:

Lee had a way of guiding me through huge parts of the world, and a generosity of spirit which took the form of a tap on the shoulder and a wave of his hand toward whatever form the subject took. He would say, 'Look, there it is – the Great Barrier Reef or Africa,' in a way that made me feel a part of it right there and then. Not very many people are as generous with their knowledge and enthusiasm, and I hope we can carry on that giving and sense of wonder.

Mitch told of how their close friendship started:

It began on the movie *Monte Walsh*. I had just started and I went into the bar, the lounge at the Desert Inn where all the cast and crew hung out. I was at one end of the bar and Lee at the other. At the perfect moment Lee, at the top of his voice, spoke; he was obviously talking about me. 'Well,' he growled out, 'He can't shoot a gun . . . He can't wear his chaps . . . He can't even ride a horse. I sure hope to fuck he knows how to act!'

When our laughter had died down, Mitch said everybody in the bar had broken up laughing. It wasn't malicious, it was real cowboy humor – just what the roles demanded. Lee was being Monte and he was Shorty: 'He was just rehearsing, really.'

Jane Loew Sharpless spoke next. She had been raised in a world of movie giants and movie stars. Her maternal grandfather was Adolph Zukor, who pioneered the movie industry in America and founded Paramount Pictures, and her father, Arthur Loew Sr, uncle and grandfather owned the Loews cinema chain and movie companies including MGM. Her brother and our good friend, producer Arthur Loew Jr, was also one of the world's greatest humorists and Film Commission powerhouses. He too was with us, accompanied by his wife Regina. Her feelings toward Lee, Jane said:

> Were that if I were in need of anything, I could rely on him. If I were scared, or in doubt about something, he was like a father-protector figure. But my favorite story was when I moved into my new house.
>
> Lee noticed one day that my garden was being eaten by weeds and took me past a neighbor's house to show me they had taken over the whole yard and were starting up the house. 'Won't you let me come over and take those weeds out?' he asked me, but he couched it in terms almost being a favor to him.
>
> 'Well,' I said, 'of course, just any day you like.' One day I wasn't home and two men came to repair a brick walkway. Here they found Lee Marvin on his hands and knees and digging and pulling out these impossible weeds. They were totally surprised at seeing him; he just nodded and went on working while they kept sneaking glances at him. Apparently it began to rain and Lee rang my doorbell. My housekeeper answered and Lee said to her, 'Would you please tell Mrs Shelton' – which was my name then – 'that I can't finish today but I'll be back.' When I got home she said, 'Your gardener left, but he said he'd be back.' I started to laugh and said, 'Josephine, don't you know who this is? He's one of the biggest film stars of our day!'
>
> Lee was an intellectual, but he didn't flaunt it and I felt complete freedom in walking in and out of your kitchen . . . I never knew where the front door was! It was so warm here, it was like Grand Central Station.

After everyone had spoken, there were silences: not uncomfortable or waiting silences, but moments of quietness, reflection – then someone would pick it up again.

Lou Goldman talked of their long and close friendship, which quickly became more important than the attorney – client relationship, and of how Lee's word alone meant so much. The huge deals or contracts they made together were sealed by a handshake or word.

My sister Gale told a story that she felt typified Lee to her. One winter my father and mother were visiting us in Tucson. My father, such a strong man in the past, was using steel canes and a wheelchair. On the plane coming out he had fallen and had needed Lee's help to get up. This was apparently preying on Lee's mind when they were to fly home. We took them to the airport and as we were saying goodbye Lee suddenly said, 'I'm not going to have them go back alone.' He bought a ticket on the spot and flew with them to LaGuardia Airport in New York. Gale met them, surprised to see Lee, who told her to go get the car and bring it to the front of the airport – where you are not allowed to park, stop or 'stand'. She drove up to find Lee in the middle of the busy street, arms raised, stopping traffic, holding some cars up, waving others on with sure, policeman-like hand signals. And cars were doing as he directed, screeching to a halt, honking, recognizing Lee and yelling, 'Hiya, Lee, how are ya?' He looked just like a soldier or a cop, and the cabbies loved it. He was answering back, 'Hi Buddy, can you do us a favor here?' moving them this way and that, saluting and waving his thanks. He got my parents in the car and the last thing he did was to lean in the window with a roll of bills to 'make sure you have enough for the tolls'. He got right back on the next plane and flew the six or seven hours back home.

Rod's son Morgan was the first of our grandchildren to say something – rather to our surprise, as he was just seven and quite shy. He drew himself up and spoke clearly and seriously about how good Lee was to him and that he would miss him. One by one they spoke: Morgan's younger brother Ian, Wendy's children (John, also seven, and Pamela, five, shyly, sweetly in her little black velvet dress). Trevor, who had lived with us for half of his ten years, came forward: 'Whenever I needed him, he was always there to help me.' Emily, so often by his side during the past few years and still only eight, expressed her feelings of loss with a presence far beyond her years. Claudia said excitedly, 'Yes, yes, and he could fix *anything*. If something broke, my dad could fix it.'

Jess was in college, he said, and his mother called saying Lee was sick:

A few nights later I had a dream about Lee. He was young and strong with black hair and he was talking to me about normal everyday things, but I started to cry in the dream. When the morning came, I knocked on the coach's door and said, 'My grandfather is sick, I have to go.' I can't explain how much I looked up to him. People would say, 'Man, you're so lucky your grandfather is a movie star,' but I just knew him as Lee.

Susan Brown's memory recalled Lee and children. One night when John and Susan Brown were visiting us we were sitting outside by the swimming pool. There was a full moon and we were sitting without lights. Emily, then about five years old, came out and began walking slowly round and round the pool. Lee asked her what she was looking for, and she said, 'I'm looking for the dark.' Lee went into the house and came out with a little red lantern. He lit it and handed it to her saying, 'You go ahead and look, I'll be right here until you find it,' and sat down and watched while she peered here and there.

Dotty Kagon later recalled the feeling of that day:

The great feeling of love and extraordinary warmth that was going around the room. Everyone sat in a circle. There were moments of peace and then bursts of laughter as someone would tell something really funny that everyone else would recognize as familiar. There were little stories, then quiet, a reluctance to give Lee up.

Her own vivid recollections were of him during the trial in California, when we came to their house on Sundays: 'He was so very neat and so much the gentleman, as apt to discuss Irish Sterling Silver, of which he knew a great deal, than anything else.' It occurred to her how vastly different he was from his image: the rough, tough, hard-drinking Lee.

Dr Harry Wilmer, in a voice breaking with emotion, spoke of mountains, humility and experiencing the ocean:

The monstrous brooding endless seas out of which the morning sun is born, and into which the evening sun dies and out of night's darkness is reborn again in the eternity of life.

Jane and I sat with Pam and Lee and watched the ocean at California years ago. Like Lee, I have been drawn to the ocean. And yes, we should also live – sometime – among the great masses of people to experience the wonder of our individuality and the miracle of people like Lee, who rose as a star above the multitude, and at the same time – knowing that the mass of humanity was humble, a real man unimpressed with triumphs.

Lee, we miss you and your great humanity, your humility, your courage and your honesty and your pain. Through violence, mountains, seas, wars, masses of people, you found at last the eternal way of the heart.

We then went to Arlington National Cemetery. Howard Terpning had painted an eagle's feather on the inside of the lid of the urn that holds Lee's ashes. Kerry felt it would be fitting to give Howard the eagle feather Lee had kept by his bed in the hospital before he died – something Howard had not known about. We needed a box to place it in, and I called Tom Bredlow, friend, artist, blacksmith, to ask if he would make one for it. He had a piece of teak, he said, and knowing of Lee's love of that wood and his use of it in our house, he thought it would be right. He made it that same night: a beautiful rectangular box of rich wood, softly polished and warm. When I held it in my hand I was surprised to see a thin thread of silver inlaid down the length of the lid. I asked Tom about the silver, what had made him think of it. 'I don't know why, but just as I finished the box the thought came into my mind to do it.' Well, I thought to myself, here is a piece of that long silver line from Lee to me.

Australia awoke to the news of Lee in newspaper headlines and television broadcasts. Deeply affected herself, Yvonne Wallace did not want Dennis to hear about it from anyone else. He was seventy or so miles out to sea on the Great Barrier Reef with a fishing charter, and so she hired the single-engined seaplane to take her to him.

As she was flying back in the late afternoon, she looked out of the window at the sea far below. Stretching out beneath to the horizon as far as the eye could see, the ocean had turned a brilliant, shimmering gold. Neither she nor the pilot had ever seen anything like it before, and she immediately felt that it was Lee's goodbye to us all.

Index

and *Monte Walsh*, 171
moves to Woodstock (1945), 8, 17
as a pistol enthusiast and marksman, 11
relationship with L, 30–31, 123
in the Second World War, 12, 17, 30
shortens his name, 10, 171
social life, 14
works for Kodak, 12
Marvin, Lee
  Academy Award as best actor (*Cat Bal-
    lou*), 49, 61, 63, 67–8, 80, 176, 184, 209,
    220, 231, 239–40
  affair with Jeanne Moreau, 68, 171–2
  at the American Theater Wing, 41, 42, 43
  appearance, 1, 18, 22, 43, 59, 78, 90
  appearances off Broadway, 43, 49
  and athletics, 19, 91
  attends Academy Awards presentations
    (1986), 396–401
  birth in New York City (19 February
    1924), 14
  'breakthrough' role (Emmy nomination
    for *People Need People*), 44
  and charities, 173
  childhood, 14
  and children, 62–3, 85, 380, 381–3, 392
  and Christmas, 84
  and clothes, 43–4, 87, 155, 203–4, 388,
    409–10
  death (29 August 1987), 404, 414–15
  divorce decree (13 January 1967), 299
  early relationship with P, 21, 22–3, 31–2,
    41–2
  his earnings, 149, 178
  education, 17–20, 21, 41, 134, 369
  and Edward Lee Howard, 390
  and fans, 124
  and his father's death, 15, 116, 117, 118
  film début, 54
  first acting role in public, 31
  first marriage, 48, 55, 62, 189, 190, 202
  and fishing, 15, 17, 20–21, 75, 84, 89,
    111, 114, 115, 132–7, 140–43, 148,
    149, 152, 155, 156, 158–60, 162–5,
    167, 225, 232, 233, 278, 363, 369–70,
    372–4, 386
  funeral, ix–xii, 49
  and 'the glory of man', 145
  goes from Broadway directly to
    Hollywood, 43, 55
  goes to LaJolla to avoid Michelle, 344–7
  and his grandchildren, 380–2
  on Hollywood, 169

honours, 20, 67–8, 184
and hunting, 15, 27
Hurt on, 368–77
illness, 363, 365–6, 378, 379–80, 383,
  384, 386, 387–8, 395, 403, 404–14
and the Institute for the Humanities, 49
and the International Festival of Culture
  and Psychiatry, 47
at Jack Feeley's funeral, 15
leaves Betty, 76, 86, 231
in the Marine Corps *see under* United
  States Marine Corps
marries Pamela, 65, 69–71, 73, 181
meets Michelle, 202, 237
meets Pamela, 1
and Michelle's arrest, 347–8
and motorcycling, 78–9, 131, 382–3
moves to Tucson (1974), 168
moves to Woodstock (1945), 8, 17
paintings, 109
'palimony' trial (1979) *see* 'palimony' trial
as a plumber's assistant, 32–3
and poetry, 132–3
private memorial gathering, 417–22
professionalism, 45, 121–2, 181
and P's abortion, 39
refusal to be typecast, 49
relationship with Boorman, 73–4
relationship with Chris, 86–7
relationship with his brother, 30
relationship with his father, 30–31, 117,
  123
relationship with his mother, 30
relationship with Wilmer, 47
similarities with Jack Feeley, 15, 23, 55
and skiing, 131
and smoking, 363, 380, 387, 397, 408
in summer stock, 41–2, 43, 119, 128, 134
treatment of P while making movies, 127–
  9
and violence, 27, 46–7, 83, 125, 180, 385
visits the Boormans in Ireland, 16
visits his father, 62, 68–9
voice, 24, 43, 63, 179, 417
and 'Wand'rin' Star', 67, 68, 88, 253–4
as a war hero, 1, 22, 90
and weapons, 11–12, 15, 18, 27, 30–31,
  90, 101, 105, 121, 300–301, 404
wounded in Second World War, xi, xii, 1,
  11, 28, 41, 90–91, 96, 97, 98, 100–
  103, 107, 109, 111, 113, 162, 184
personality, 82, 181
  courage, 96, 97